Lecture Notes in Computer Scien

T0238164

Commenced Publication in 1973
Founding and Former Series Editors:
Gerhard Goos, Juris Hartmanis, and Jan van Leeuwen

Editorial Board

Jessica Fridrich (Ed.)

Information Hiding

6th International Workshop, IH 2004
Toronto, Canada, May 23-25, 2004
Revised Selected Papers

 Springer

Volume Editor

Jessica Fridrich
SUNY Binghamton, Department of Electrical and Computer Engineering
Binghamton, NY 13902-6000, USA
E-mail: fridrich@binghamton.edu

Library of Congress Control Number: Applied for

CR Subject Classification (1998): E.3, K.6.5, K.4.1, K.5.1, D.4.6, E.4, C.2, H.4.3, H.3, H.5.1

ISSN 0302-9743
ISBN 3-540-24207-4 Springer Berlin Heidelberg New York

Springer is a part of Springer Science+Business Media

springeronline.com

© Springer-Verlag Berlin Heidelberg 2004
Printed in Germany

Typesetting: Camera-ready by author, data conversion by Boller Mediendesign
Printed on acid-free paper   SPIN: 11371847   06/3142   5 4 3 2 1 0

Preface

It is an honor and great pleasure to write a preface for this postproceedings of the 6th International Workshop on Information Hiding. In the past 10 years, the field of data hiding has been maturing and expanding, gradually establishing its place as an active interdisciplinary research area uniquely combining information theory, cryptology, and signal processing.

This year, the workshop was followed by the Privacy Enhancing Technologies workshop (PET) hosted at the same location. Delegates viewed this connection as fruitful as it gave both communities a convenient opportunity to interact.

We would like to thank all authors who submitted their work for consideration. Out of the 70 submisions received by the program committee, 25 papers were accepted for publication based on their novelty, originality, and scientific merit. We strived to achieve a balanced exposition of papers that would represent many different aspects of information hiding. All papers were divided into eight sessions: digital media watermarking, steganalysis, digital forensics, steganography, software watermarking, security and privacy, anonymity, and data hiding in unusual content. This year, the workshop included a one-hour rump session that offered an opportunity to the delegates to share their work in progress and other brief but interesting contributions.

The program committee consisted of Ross J. Anderson (University of Cambridge, UK), Jan Camenisch (IBM Zurich Research Laboratory, Switzerland), Christian Collberg (University of Arizona, USA), Ingemar J. Cox (University College London, UK), John McHugh (SEI/CERT, USA), Ira S. Moskowitz (Naval Research Laboratory, USA), Job Oostveen (Philips Research, Netherlands), Richard C. Owens (University of Toronto), Fabien A.P. Petitcolas (Microsoft Research, UK), Andreas Pfitzmann (Dresden University of Technology, Germany), Mike Reiter (Carnegie Mellon University, USA), and Jessica Fridrich (SUNY Binghamton, USA).

The following external reviewers participated in the review process: Richard Clayton (University of Cambridge, UK), Farid Ahmed (The Catholic University of America, USA), Dogan Kesdogan (Aachen University of Technology, Germany), Hany Farid (Dartmouth College, USA), Deepa Kundur (Texas A&M University, USA), Slava Voloshinovsky (CUI, University of Geneva, Switzerland), Fernando Perez-Gonzales (University of Vigo, Spain), Nasir Memon (Polytechnic University, USA), Scott Craver (Princeton University, USA), Li Wu Chang (Naval Research Laboratory, USA), Lisa Marvel (University of Delaware, USA), Frederic Deguillaume (CUI, University of Geneva, Switzerland), Andrei Serjantov (University of Cambridge, UK), Rainer Böhme (Dresden University of Technology, Germany), Andreas Westfeld (Dresden University of Technology, Germany), George Danezis (University of Cambridge, UK), Sandra Steinbrecher (Dresden University of Technology, Germany), Phil Sallee (Booz Allen Hamilton, USA), Richard E. Newman (University of Florida, USA), Paul Syverson (Naval Research Laboratory, USA), John McDermott (Naval Research Laboratory, USA), Dagmar Schönfeld (Dresden

University of Technology, Germany), Tim McChesney (Naval Research Laboratory, USA), Karen Spärck Jones (University of Cambridge, UK), Sebastian Clauß (Dresden University of Technology, Germany), Sorina Dumitrescu (McMaster University, Canada), Elke Franz (Dresden University of Technology, Germany), Edward Carter (University of Arizona, USA), Andrew Huntwork (University of Arizona, USA), Saumya Debray (University of Arizona, USA), Kelly Heffner (University of Arizona, USA), Ginger Myles (University of Arizona, USA), Clark Thomborson (University of Auckland, New Zealand), Jasvir Nagra (University of Auckland, New Zealand), Viktor Raskin (Purdue University, USA), Nicholas Hopper (Carnegie Mellon University, USA), Aweke Lemma (Philips Digital Systems Laboratories, The Netherlands), Gerhard Langelaar (Philips Digital Systems Laboratories, The Netherlands), Frans Willems (Technical University of Eindhoven, The Netherlands), Fons Bruekers (Philips Research, The Netherlands), Arno van Leest (Philips Research, The Netherlands), Michiel van der Veen (Philips Research, The Netherlands), and Ton Kalker (Hewlett-Packard, USA).

This year, for the first time this workshop had two program chairs, one for multimedia watermarking and steganography (myself) and the second for anonymous communication, covert channels, and privacy (Mike Reiter). I would like to thank Mike for helping me with the review process and managing the communication with authors.

The general chair Richard C. Owens and his assistant Alison Bambury did a wonderful job organizing the event. Many thanks to them for such a tasteful selection of a comfortable meeting place. The workshop was held at The Radisson located on the Ontario Waterfront. In the evening of the second day, the attendees had an opportunity to relax at a dinner cruise while admiring the Ontario city silhouette lit by fireworks for Victoria Day.

Special thanks belong to Tim Olson from Microsoft Conference Management Services. The submission of papers and reviews as well as notification of authors and reviewers was greatly simplified both for the authors and program committee members.

Finally, I would like to thank The Information and Privacy Commissioner/Ontario, The Centre for Innovation Law Policy, and Bell University Laboratories for their sponsorship of this workshop.

September 2004   Jessica Fridrich
                                                           SUNY Binghamton
                                                           New York, USA

Table of Contents

Session 4 - Steganography
Session Chair: Andreas Westfeld (Dresden University of Technology)

Session 5 - Software Watermarking
Session Chair: John McHugh (SEI/CERT)

Session 6 - Security and Privacy
Session Chair: Ross Anderson (University of Cambridge)

Session 7 - Anonymity
Session Chair: Andreas Pfitzmann (Dresden University of Technology)

Session 8 - Data Hiding in Unusual Content
Session Chair: Christian Collberg (University of Arizona)

An Implementation of, and Attacks on, Zero-Knowledge Watermarking

Scott Craver, Bede Liu, and Wayne Wolf

Department of Electrical Engineering
Princeton University

Abstract. A problem of considerable theoretical interest in digital watermarking is that of asymmetric, or *zero-knowledge* watermarking. In this problem, we wish to embed a watermark in a piece of multimedia and later prove that we have done so, but without revealing information that can be used by an adversary to remove the signal later.

In this paper we develop a watermarking system based on the ambiguity attack method outlined in [14], constructing a vector-based watermarking system applicable to images, audio and video. An example of image watermarking is provided. We also outline some important attacks and thus important design principles for asymmetric watermarking systems.

1 Introduction

A problem of considerable interest in recent years is the *asymmetric watermarking problem:* can we prove that a watermark has been embedded in a piece of multimedia without providing the information that would allow its removal?

Several methods to solve this problem have been proposed, some of which have since been broken, and some of which possess properties we would like to remove, such as the need for a trusted third party. Still other ideas are embryonic, such as the watermarking approach based on ambiguity attacks outlined but not implemented in [14]. An overview of various asymmetric watermarking techniques can be found in [3].

In this paper we develop a watermarking system based on the ambiguity attack method, mechanizing the process of constructing counterfeit watermarks for a blind detector. Real and counterfeit watermarks are then used in a zero-knowledge proof to show that at least one of a set of watermarks is valid. This yields a general algorithm for vector-based watermarking applicable to images, audio and video multimedia.

We also discuss some of the design principles we have encountered in the development of this system. In analyzing zero-knowledge watermarking systems, we find that some are vulnerable to ambiguity attacks, which we continue to stress are a serious problem in asymmetric watermarking systems and not to be ignored. This problem highlights general design philosophies regarding what a watermark is meant to mean, and what we are attempting to prove when passing data through a detector.

J. Fridrich (Ed.): IH 2004, LNCS 3200, pp. 1–12, 2004.

2   The Still Very Serious Problem of Ambiguity Attacks

Ambiguity attacks, once an easily preventable curiosity, become a critical problem in zero-knowledge watermarking, perhaps partially because they are mistakenly regarded as trivial application issues [5,2,6]. However, if one does not carefully design a watermarking scheme to rule out these attacks, they may never be preventable. We provide several examples of such attacks on existing systems.

2.1   The Basic Attack

The basic attack is very simple: find an arbitrary signal that sets off the watermark detector. Then, claim that this signal is a watermark. This is often very easy, and it can be performed by inspection of both the detector structure and the multimedia to be attacked. For example, for a correlator detector, we can construct a counterfeit signal consisting of the multimedia itself, attenuated and perhaps processed to disguise it. This signal will naturally correlate with the original signal.

In symmetric systems, this is prevented by requiring a watermark to be the output of a secure hash $w = h(\text{seed})$. Now, an arbitrary signal can not easily be found for which a seed can be presented; and so the seed is evidence that a watermark was legitimately added, rather than found in place. This is a well known, simple and effective remedy, perhaps enough to relegate this attack to the domain of "implementation issues."

The problem now is that in an asymmetric system, a watermark owner cannot simply produce the seed or the watermark as proof of its authenticity. The parameters of the new problem can disallow the usual remedy, allowing this simple but serious vulnerability to appear.

2.2   An Example

A straightforward example is proposed in [7], in which a wartermark is embedded in data and a randomly selected subset of coefficients is revealed. For security, this subset is immersed in a random vector with each coefficient of a public watermark being either a coefficient of the secret vector or a random value. This signal is detectable as long as the embedding is sufficiently strong.

How do we prevent someone from presenting as a watermark any vector that correlates with the data, or encodes an arbitrary message? Proving that a randomly selected subset, immersed within a random vector, is drawn from a legal watermark is indeed difficult. To be fair, however, the authors do not propose this scheme specifically for proof of ownership applications, in which ambiguity attacks are a problem. In other so-called "digital rights management" applications, these attacks less important.

2.3   Another Example

A watermarking system proposed in [15] outlines a method of secure, blinded correlation. In this system, multimedia data and watermarks are represented as vectors, and detection consists of correlation followed by thresholding—all of which the authors are able to perform in a blinded domain. Given a commitment of an image vector I and a commitment of a watermark vector w, one can compute their dot-product and compare this result to a threshold without revealing w.

Thus, one is able to prove in zero knowledge (and this the authors establish rigorously) that a watermark signal w sets off a detector $D(w, I)$. The authors provide both a blind and non-blind case, although we will focus on the less ambiguous case of blind watermarking.

The simple vulnerability of this protocol, by itself, is that anyone can find a signal w for which $D(w, I) = 1$. The attacker has access to the signal itself and $D(I, I) = 1$ for a correlator detector. Likewise, the attacker can use all sorts of signals derived from I. Under the blinding conditions of the protocol, there is no way of determining if this trivial form of cheating is taking place, so anyone can prove the presense of a watermark in anything.

Knowledge of such a vector w is therefore not valuable information and does not need to be proven by any protocol. By analogy, imagine a zero-knowledge proof that one knows a factor of an integer n. Anyone can pass this test because everybody knows a factor of n. What is valuable is a proof that one knows a *nontrivial* factor or a legally constructed watermark.

Thus, the basic ambiguity attack cannot be prevented by the standard remedy. The authors in [15] propose a trusted third party to prevent ambiguity; images are registered with an authority who performs the watermarking, computes the blinded versions of mark and image, and provides a verifiable certificate to the image owner. Images are not allowed to be registered if they are "similar" to one previously registered. Given a third party of such capabilities, however, do we need asymmetric watermarking at all? The trusted third party can simply perform the detection itself.

2.4   Discussion

The important problem with asymmetric watermarking is not that these attacks are possible; but that *whenever they are possible, they are difficult to prevent*. In our experience analyzing and desigining asymmetric watermarking systems, we find that a successful scheme should be designed from the start with resistance to ambiguity. Only by luck can we expect an ambiguity-related flaw to be patchable in implementation.

We also observe that this class of vulnerabilities highlights an important semantic issue regarding watermarking in general: we are not trying to prove that a watermark signal is *detectable;* we are trying to prove that a signal has been *embedded*. These are very different notions, and ambiguity attacks generally disguise examples of the former as examples of the latter.

This semantic requirement for watermarking can in turn be considered a special case of the *nontriviality* requirement of a zero-knowledge proof: to be useful, it should demonstrate that one possesses *valuable* knowledge, knowledge not available to everybody—or in more concrete terms, there should be people who can not pass the protocol, making the ability to pass the protocol valuable in some way[1]. This nontriviality requirement is not actually part of the definition of a zero-knowledge proof as defined in textbooks on the subject [10,11,8].

3   An Implementation of Public-Key Watermarking Using Ambiguity Attacks

As described in [14], we can use ambiguity attacks constructively, as components in a watermarking system. The idea is simple: if there is no way for an adversary to distinguish a valid watermark from an invalid one, as is commonly the case, we can conceal a real watermark in a collection of false ones using zero-knowledge protocols to demonstrate that at least one is real.

The fake watermarks are components of the original multimedia signal. They are not added, but already reside "within" the multimedia, in the sense that they set off a watermark detector. In a sense, we decompose the multimedia signal into a sum of false watermarks plus residual data; thus removing a large number of false watermarks is the same as removing a significant part of the image or audio clip.

Note that we use zero-knowledge protocols not to show that a watermark is detectable; the detection process has no asymmetric properties. Rather, we focus our zero-knowledge efforts on verification, showing in zero knowledge that at least one of a collection of watermarks is legal.

If we embed M_r watermarks and find M_f counterfeit watermarks, and an attacker can selectively damage K watermarks, the probability of a successful attack is

$$P_{\text{attack}} = \binom{M_f}{K - M_r} / \binom{M_f + M_r}{K}$$

... a value roughly equal to p^{M_r}, where p is the fraction $K/(M_r + M_f)$ of watermarks the attacker can damage. We expect the collection of real watermarks to fall within a power budget, so that increasing M_r is not a matter of adding more power, but dividing that same power among more watermarks. Thus, attack probability drops exponentially with M_r, although we will see a penalty in detector probability unless we make the watermarks longer.

Note that by adding multiple marks rather than one, we avoid the *oracle attack* of removing each watermark one at a time, in M separate challenges, until the protocol cannot succeed. We also note that this attack probability will in practice be small but macroscopic: a probability of 2^{-64}, for instance,

---

[1] Or the dual *efficiency* requirement: a zero-knowledge proof of something everyone knows should take zero steps.

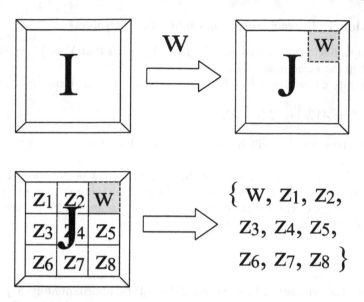

Fig. 1. Basic watermarking using invertibility attacks. Left, the original image I is watermarked with w, then a sufficiently large number of fake watermarks are found by inspection. Then, the set of watermarks is published, without disclosing which watermark is legitimate.

is unrealistic. However, this is the probability of the attacker defeating a legal challenge by the watermark owner, a time-consuming process not amenable to brute-force. If P_{attack} is as large as 1/10000, an attacker need "only" lose 5000 lawsuits before defeating the watermarking system.

3.1 Implentation: The Gaussian Case

Consider first that we have a data signal to watermark which is a vector s of Gaussian random variables, independent and identically distributed $\sim N(0, \sigma_s^2)$. For practical purposes, we construct a signal vector s from an image or audio clip by extracting and processing a collection of features, usually in the frequency domain. Ideally, the extracted features are both well-behaved and significant, in the sense that damaging the features will greatly damage the multimedia.

In any case, we wish to generate M_r real watermark vectors $\{W_k\}$, and also decompose our N-dimensional vector s into into M_f false watermarks $\{Z_k\}$. To accomplish this, we require that a watermark also be a vector of iid Gaussian random variables $\sim N(0, \sigma_w^2)$, $\sigma_w < \sigma_s$.

Since a sum of Gaussian vectors is itself a Gaussian vector, we can easily generate a decomposition of s into $\{Z_k\}$ as follows:

Algorithm 1 *A decomposition of s into false watermarks*

1. *Compute K random watermarks $Y_1 \cdots Y_k$, such that $Y = \sum_i Y_i$ is approximately the same length as s.*
2. *Generate an arbitrary (random) orthonormal matrix A such that $AY = (1 + \lambda)s$.*
3. *Set $Z_i = AY_i$, and $M_f = K$.*

Since these vectors will be very large, of dimension $N \sim 100000$, we need an efficient method of generating and applying an orthonormal transformation. Fortunately, there is indeed a linear-time algorithm for both generating such an A, and computing Ax for a vector x, without constructing huge matrices. This takes advantage of the fact that all coefficients of s and $\sum Y_i$ are nonzero with high probability, facilitating Gaussian elimination.

3.2   Error Probabilities

Note that the number of false watermarks will be approximately $M_f = \sigma_s^2 / \sigma_w^2$, and so our attack probability is wholly dependent upon the chosen watermark strength. If Alice has a power budget σ_A^2, then she can choose a value for σ_w^2 to make M_f large, and then add $M_r = \sigma_A^2 / \sigma_w^2$ watermarks.

Meanwhile, consider the detector false alarm and miss probabilities. For a watermark detected by correlation, we have for the maximum-likelihood detector,

$$p_f = p_m = 1 - \Phi(\frac{\sqrt{(N)}\sigma_w}{2\sigma_s})$$

...where N is the dimensionality of the vectors. This means that a weaker σ_w (and thus a large M) must be compensated by increasing N. For a fixed p_f, N and M are directly proportional.

A note about so-called false-alarm "probabilities": in security applications, false alarms do not occur at random, but are often engineereed. Hence p_f should be intepreted not as a probability, but as an indicator of the feasibility of a brute-force attack. If an attacker randomly generates legal watermarks in hopes of finding one which sets of the detector (an attack which can not be prevented), he will succeed after approximately $1/2p_f$ attempts. This is the attacker's *worst-case* scenario, and so p_f should be far smaller than is needed in signal processing applications. We tentatively choose $p_f = 2^{-56}$, with a plan to choose smaller values in the future.

Of course, if we can choose N as large as we want, we can make all direct attack probabilities as small as we wish, while making added watermarks as weak, and thus imperceptible, as we wish. However, images only contain so much information, and extracting hundreds of thousands of useful feature coefficients can be impractical.

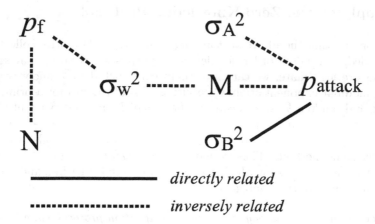

Fig. 2. Watermark parameters. False alarm probability is dictated by both N and watermark power. Meanwhile, mark power determines the number of false watermarks, which along with Alice's and Bob's power budgets, determine the probability of a successful mark removal.

3.3 An Attack

So far we have been considering the case of independent vector coefficients. If in practice we have (and, in practice, we have) vectors of coefficients which are not independent, there is an attack on the above scheme: false watermark vectors will not appear to be white, because the rotation turns each watermark into a significant component of s plus orthogonal noise. The fraction of a false watermark's energy that lies along s will decrease with M, and so statistical effects of s will become harder to detect with larger M. *iid* and can thus be differentiated from false ones.

For this reason, we must ensure the data vectors are well-behaved, likely by whitening the coefficients. There are two caveats which need to be told to the aspiring watermark designer: one, that any whitening process must be robustness-preserving, so that large changes in the whitened data look or sound bad in the original data; and also that the damage inflicted by a watermark in the whitened domain does not inflict too much damage in the original.

The second caveat is that some whitening tricks are insecure; not only should the whitening process whiten false watermarks, but the inverse process should color real watermarks. One whitening trick consists of pseudorandomly scrambling samples, a method which does not truly whiten data but does eliminate detectable correlations to any algorithm without the scrambling key. In this case, descrambling whitened fake watermarks will reveal colored fake watermarks; meanwhile, a descrambled real watermark will still appear white.

4   Applying the Zero-Knowledge Protocol

Upon constructing the above vectors $\{w_k\}$ and $\{z_k\}$, the entire collection can be provided, in random order, for detection purposes. To prove that some watermarks are legitimate, we can have them constructed by a one-way process, namely modular exponentiation. Computing $H = a^h(\mathrm{mod}p)$ for a prime p, generator a and random h, we can convert the bits of H into independent Gaussian random variables using standard methods such as described in [9]. Conversely, we can compute counterfeit bit strings which generate given false watermarks under the same methods. Thus we have integers $\{H_k\} = \{W_k\} \cup \{Z_k\}$, the first set of which are integers for which we know a discrete logarithm, and the second set of which are arbitrary integers.

Protocol 1 *A zero-knowledge watermark verification protocol using invertibility attacks*

1. Alice sends Bob the collection of integers $\{H_k\}$
2. Bob renders these as Gaussian vectors, and verifies they are detectable in a test image I.
3. Alice blinds each H_k with a randomly selected exponent: $B_k = a^{b_k}$., yielding the set $\{H_k B_k\}$.
4. Alice reorders the set $\{H_k B_k\}$ and sends it to Bob.
5. Bob knows a and p, and depending on the outcome of a coin toss challenges Alice to either:
   (a) Reveal all blinding exponents $\{b_k\}$, to verify that each blinded mark is a legally blinded version of a member of the set $\{H_k\}$.
   (b) Select one of the marks $H_k B_k$ (the blinded version of a real watermark, which is therefore of the form $a^{x+b_k}(\mathrm{mod}p-1)$,) and reveal its logarithm.
6. Alice reveals the desired value(s).
7. The blinding factors b_k are discarded. New ones will be constructed for every iteration of this protocol.

This is a straightforward extension of the zero-knowledge proof using discrete logarithm, described in numerous textbooks [10,11,8]   □

5   Results

We applied the above technique to features extracted from DCT and LOT coefficients of monochrome images. Our pre-conditioned data consists of the N frequency coefficients of highest magnitude, ordered spatially. The choice of coefficients must be published to prevent some mismatch attacks.

After comparing full-frame DCTs with block DCTs and LOTs, we decided that a block-based DCT is preferable in terms of the amount of damage inflicted by an attacker. In practice, we hope to find an embedding method with a decently

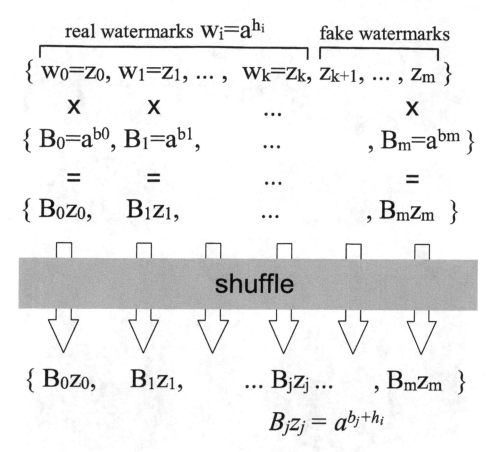

Fig. 3. Blinding of real and false watermarks. Each watermark is multiplied by a blinding factor constructed from a random exponent b_i. Then they are shuffled, and the results passed to Bob. At this point Alice can prove she knows the logarithm of at least one blinded, shuffled value.

high power budget for Alice σ_A, allowing the embedding of multiple marks, with a suitable limit on the attacker's power as well. By using a block-based DCT of size 32, we allow about $p < 1/4$ of the signals to be damaged, while M_f is very small, e.g. $M_f < 8$ for $N = 60000$. This gives an attack probability of 2^{-16}, or about 2^{15} separate challenges.[2]

We also find that N cannot be raised far beyond our chosen values; our algorithm uses about half of the monochrome image's energy for the signal s. Examples are shown in figure 4 and figure 5.

---

[2] Rather than calling this a probability, we could perhaps say that is a measure of difficulty of brute force, in this case expressed in units of inverse-lawsuits.

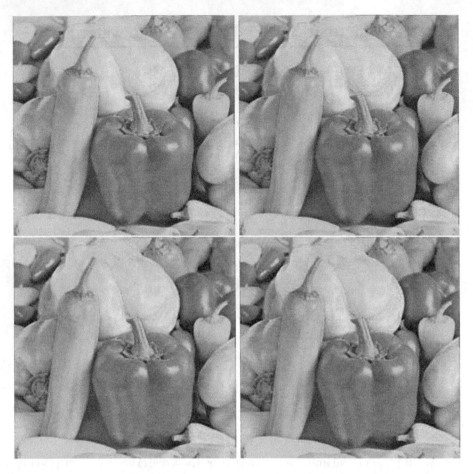

Fig. 4. Watermarked images. Upper left is the original, upper right, an image with one watermark. Below left, an image with four marks, below right, eight marks.

5.1   Applications Beyond Copyright Marking

The above discussion assumed that the purpose of the robust watermark is copyright verification—that is, the embedded watermark is evidence of some kind of ownership, which can be shown without revealing the watermark itself. Other applications may also exist for this watermarking approach.

One possibility is fragile or forensic watermarking, in which the watermark is used to locate alterations to an image. In this case, the real and false watermarks can be used as a sort of certificate of the image's authenticity—similar at least conceptually to a photographic negative. Just as removal of the legitimate watermark is difficult, so too is re-embedding the legitimate watermark after a portion of the image is replaced. This is because the adversary does not know

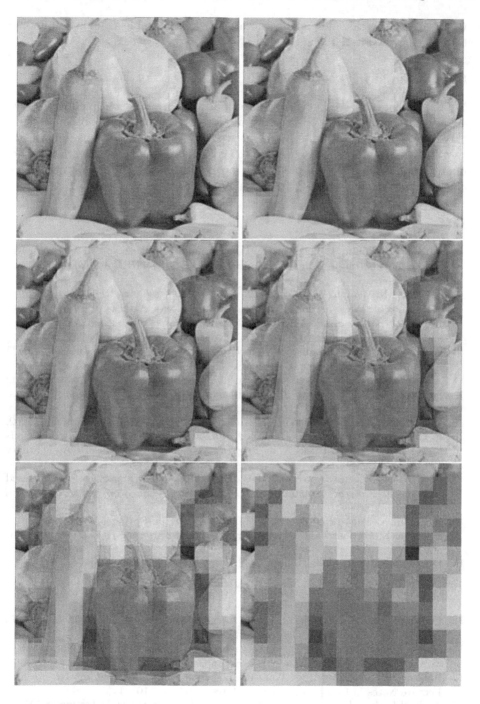

Fig. 5. Attacked images. In the first row, an image with 5 and 10 published watermarks removed. In the second row, 20 and 40 published watermarks are removed. In the third row, 80 and then all 200 published watermarks are removed.

which marks are real, and making all watermarks detectable again is tantamount to replacing the altered image content.

6 Conclusion

We implement one zero-knowledge watermarking technique outlined in [14], developing a general approach to vector-based watermarking. Unlike other systems, this system publishes all watermark data to allow normal detection, and reserves zero-knowledge protocols for watermark verification. Our approach establishes quantitative estimates for brute-forcing probabilities, and outlines a method for constructing false watermarks from random vectors.

References

1. I.J. Cox, J. Kilian, T. Leighton, and T. Shamoon, "Secure spread spectrum watermarking for multimedia," Technical Report 95-10, NEC Research Institute, 1995.
2. S. Craver, N. Memon, B. L. Yeo, and M. M. Yeung, "Resolving Rightful Ownerships With Invisible Watermarking Techniques:, Limitations, Attacks, and Implications" *IEEE Journal on Selected Areas of Communications*, special issue on Copyright and Privacy Protection, April 1998 (IBM Research Report, RC 20755, March 1997.)
3. G. Hachez and J-J. Quisquater, "Which directions for asymmetric watermarking?" *Proceedings of EUSIPCO* (Toulouse, France, September 2002).
4. S. Craver and S. Katzenbeisser, "Security Analysis of Public-Key Watermarking Schemes." in *Proceedings of SPIE, Mathematics of Data/Image Coding, Compression and Encryption IV* v 4475, July 2001. Pp. 172-182.
5. I. Cox, M. Miller, and J. Bloom. *Digital Watermarking.* Morgan Kaufmann, 2002.
6. F. H. Hartung, J. K. Su, and B. Girod, "Spread spectrum watermarking: malicious attacks and counterattacks." in *Proceedings of SPIE* (San Jose, CA, February 1999,) pp. 147–158.
7. F. H. Hartung, and B. Girod, "Fast Public-Key Watermarking of Compressed Video." in *Proceedings of IEEE International Conference on Speech and Signal Processing,* 1997
8. A. Salomaa, *Public-Key Cryptography, 2nd ed.* Berlin: Springer-Verlag, 1996.
9. J. Viega, Z. Girouard and M. Messier, *Secure Programming Cookbook.* O'Reilly, 2003.
10. D. Stinson, *Cryptography: Theory and Practice.* Boca Raton, Florida: CRC Press, 1995.
11. B. Schneier, *Applied Cryptograpy: Protocols, Algorithms, and Source Code in C, 2nd ed.* New York: John Wiley and Sons, 1996.
12. P. Wong, "A Watermark for Image Integrity and Ownership Verification." In *Proceedings of IS&T PIC Conference* (Portland, OR, May.). 1998.
13. M. M. Yeung and F. Mintzer, "An Invisible Watermarking Technique for Image Verification." in *Proceedings of ICIP* (Santa Barbara, CA, Oct.). IEEE press, 1997.
14. S. Craver, "Zero Knowledge Watermarking." in *Information Hiding III,* Springer Lecture Notes in Computer Science v 1768 (2000), pp 101–116.
15. A. Adelsbach and A-R. Sadeghi, "Zero-Knowledge Watermark Detection and Proof of Ownership." in *Information Hiding IV,* Springer Lecture Notes in Computer Science v 2137 (2001), pp 273–288.

On the Possibility of Non-invertible Watermarking Schemes

Qiming Li and Ee-Chien Chang

[1] Temasek Laboratories
National University of Singapore
tslliqm@nus.edu.sg
[2] Department of Computer Science
National University of Singapore
changec@comp.nus.edu.sg

Abstract. Recently, there are active discussions on the possibility of non-invertible watermarking scheme. A non-invertible scheme prevents an attacker from deriving a valid watermark from a cover work. Recent results suggest that it is difficult to design a provably secure non-invertible scheme. In contrast, in this paper, we show that it is possible. We give a scheme based on a cryptographically secure pseudo-random number generator (CSPRNG) and show that it is secure with respect to well-accepted notion of security. We employ the spread spectrum method as the underlying watermarking scheme to embed the watermark. The parameters chosen for the underlying scheme give reasonable robustness, false alarm and distortion. We prove the security by showing that, if there is a successful attacker, then there exists a probabilistic polynomial-time algorithm that can distinguish the uniform distribution from sequences generated by the CSPRNG, and thus contradicts the assumption that the CSPRNG is secure. Furthermore, in our scheme the watermark is statistically independent from the original work, which shows that it is not necessary to enforce a relationship between them to achieve non-invertibility.

1 Introduction

There are many discussions on the uses of watermarking schemes in resolving ownership disputes. An interesting and well-known scenario is the *inversion attacks* studied by Craver et al. [7]. Under this scenario, Alice has the original image I and a secret watermark W_A. She releases the watermarked image $\tilde{I} = I + W_A$ into the public domain. Given $\tilde{I}$ and not knowing W_A, Bob (who is an attacker) wants to find a watermark W_B that is present in both $\tilde{I}$ and I. If such a watermark W_B is found, Bob can create confusion of the ownership by claiming that: (1) $\tilde{I}$ is watermarked by his watermark W_B, and (2) the image $\tilde{I} - W_B$ is the original. If Bob can successfully and efficiently find such W_B, we say that the scheme is *invertible*.

Craver et al. [7] give an attacker when the underlying watermarking scheme is the well-known spread spectrum method. To overcome such attackers, they

J. Fridrich (Ed.): IH 2004, LNCS 3200, pp. 13–24, 2004.
© Springer-Verlag Berlin Heidelberg 2004

propose a protocol that employs a secure hash, and claim that it is non-invertible. Qiao et al. [8, 9] also give watermarking schemes for video and audio which are claimed to be non-invertible. Subsequently, there are a number of works [10, 1, 2] exploiting weaknesses of known non-invertible schemes. Ramkumar et al. [10] give an attack for the scheme by Craver et al. [7], and they also give an improved scheme. On the other hand, [1, 2] give a formal definition of ambiguity attacks and mention that most proposed non-invertible schemes either do not come with a satisfactory proof of security, or the proofs are flawed. They also point out that if the false alarm of the underlying watermarking scheme is high (for e.g. 2^{-10}), then successful ambiguity attacks are possible. However, there is no mention of cases when the false alarm is low. Thus, it is interesting to know whether non-invertibility can be achieved when false alarm is low. Due to the difficulty of obtaining a non-invertible scheme, [2] propose to use a *trusted third party* (TTP) to issue valid watermarks. Although using a TTP is provably secure, there is still a question of whether it can withstand attackers that probe the system. The development of the studies of non-invertibility seems to lead to the conclusion that a stand-alone (in the sense that there is no TTP) non-invertible scheme does not exist. In this paper, in contrast, we argue that with low false alarm, it is possible to have a non-invertible scheme. We support our argument by giving a provably secure protocol that employs a *cryptographically secure pseudo-random number generator* (CSPRNG). The main idea is to show that if the scheme is invertible, then the CSPRNG is not secure, and thus lead to a contradiction.

Our protocol requires a computationally secure one-way function, whose existence is a major open problem in computer science. Nevertheless, it is well accepted that such functions exist. In practice, many cryptographic protocols rely on this unproven assumption.

Actually, we show that our protocol is secure against *ambiguity attacks*, of which inversion attacks are a special case. Given a work $\tilde{I}$, a successful ambiguity attack outputs a watermark W that is embedded in $\tilde{I}$, and a key K that is used to generate W. In a weaker form, the attack is also required to output an original I. In our discussion, we do not require the attacker to do so.

There are two components in our scheme. The first component addresses the issue of robustness, false alarm and distortion. This component is often called the *underlying* watermarking scheme. Due to the theoretical nature of this problem, we adopt the usual assumption that the hosts and noise are Gaussian, and distortion is measured by Euclidean 2-norm. In our protocol, we employ the well-known spread spectrum method as the underlying scheme.

The second component consists of key-management and watermark generation. In our setting, Alice (the owner) has a secret key K_A, and she generates a watermark W_A using a CSPRNG with K_A as the seed. Next, she watermarks the original I using W_A. To prove the ownership, Alice needs to reveal (or show that she knows) K_A and W_A. Interestingly, our scheme does not use the original I to derive the key K_A, nor the watermark W_A. Hence the watermark is statistically independent from the original. This is in contrast to the method given by Craver et al. [7], where Alice computes the hash of the original I, and uses the hash value $h(I)$ to generate the watermark W_A. Hence, to achieve non-invertibility, it is not necessary to enforce a relationship between the watermark and the original work.

We give our main idea of our protocol in Section 2. We further give precise notations and describe the models that we use in Section 3. The details of the non-invertible scheme will be given in Section 4, followed by a proof of security in Section 5. Finally we give some remarks (Section 6) and conclude our paper (Section 7).

2   Main Idea

In our scheme, a watermark W is a sequence of -1 and 1 of length n, i.e. $W \in \{-1, 1\}^n$. We call W a *valid watermark* if it is generated by a CSPRNG using some m-bit seed, where $m < n$. Thus, the number of valid watermarks is not more than 2^m, and not all sequences in $\{-1, 1\}^n$ are valid watermarks.

Suppose we have a probabilistic polynomial-time algorithm B such that given any work $\widetilde{I}$ that is embedded using some valid watermark W, B can successfully find a valid watermark $\widehat{W}$ embedded in $\widetilde{I}$ with probability that is not negligible[3].

Now, we want to use B to construct a polynomial statistical test T that distinguishes a truly random sequence from a sequence generated by the CSPRNG, thus lead to a contradiction.

Given a sequence W, T carried out the following steps:

1. Embed W in I to get $\widetilde{I}$, where I is a randomly chosen work.
2. Ask B for a valid watermark $\widehat{W}$ embedded in $\widetilde{I}$.
3. Declare that W is from the random source if B fails to find such a watermark, and declare that W is generated by the CSPRNG otherwise.

By carefully choosing parameters for the underlying watermarking scheme, the probability that a valid watermark exists in a randomly chosen $\widetilde{I}$ can be exponentially small.

Hence, if W is generated by the truly random source, then it is very unlikely that a valid watermark exists in $\widetilde{I}$, and thus most of the time, B fails and the decision by T is correct. On the other hand, if W is indeed generated from the CSPRNG, the chances that a valid $\widehat{W}$ can be found is not negligible since B is a successful attacker. So, with probability that is not negligible, the decision made by T is correct.

Combining the above 2 cases leads to the conclusion that T can distinguish the two distributions. This contradicts with the assumption that the pseudo random number generator is secure. Therefore, no such B exists, and the scheme is non-invertible as a consequence.

---

[3] W and $\widehat{W}$ can be different.

3   Notations and Models

3.1   Overall Setting

A *work* is a vector $I = (x_1, x_2, \ldots, x_n)$ where each x_i is a real number. A *watermark* W is a sequence in $\{-1, 1\}^n$. A *key* K is a sequence of m binary bits. A watermark generator $f : \{0, 1\}^m \to \{-1, 1\}^n$ maps a key to a watermark. We say that a watermark W is *valid* if and only if w is in the range of f, i.e., it is generated from some key K by f.

The *underlying* watermarking scheme consists of an embedder and a detector. Given an original work I and a watermark W, the embedder computes a watermarked work $\tilde{I}$. Given a work $\tilde{I}$ and a watermark W, the detector declares whether W is embedded in $\tilde{I}$, or not.

Before watermarking an original work I, Alice chooses a secret key K_A and generates a watermark $W_A = f(K_A)$. Alice then embeds W_A into I. To resolve disputes of ownership, Alice has to reveal both the secret key K_A and the watermark W_A. (In zero-knowledge watermarking setting [3, 6], Alice only has to prove that she knows K_A and W_A).

In a successful ambiguity attack, given $\tilde{I}$, Bob (the attacker) manages to find a pair K_B and W_B such that $f(K_B) = W_B$ and W_B is already embedded in $\tilde{I}$. A formal description of ambiguity attacks will be presented in Section 3.3.

It is unreasonable to require a successful attacker to be always able to find the pair K_B and W_B for every work $\tilde{I}$. Thus, we consider an attacker *successful* as long as the probability that he succeeds, on a randomly chosen $\tilde{I}$, is non-negligible (greater than $1/p(n)$ for some positive polynomial $p(\cdot)$). Note that the probability distribution to be used in the definition of a successful attacker is important in the formulation. In Section 3.3 we will give more details on this.

We measure computational efficiency with respect to n, the number of coefficients in a work. Thus, an algorithm that runs in polynomial time with respect to n is considered efficient.

3.2   Statistical Models of Works and Watermarked Works

In this section, we give the statistical models of works. Recall that a work I is expressed as $I = (x_1, x_2, \ldots, x_n)$, where each x_i is a real number. We assume that I is Gaussian. That is, the x_i's are statistically independent and follow zero-mean normal distribution. Thus, to generate a random I, each x_i is to be independently drawn from the normal distribution $\mathcal{N}(0, 1)$. Note that the expected energy $E(\|I\|^2)$ is n.

Although the distribution of the original works is Gaussian, the distribution of the watermarked works is not necessarily Gaussian. Consider the process where an $\tilde{I}_r$ is obtained by embedding a randomly chosen W_r from $\{-1, 1\}^n$ into a randomly chosen original work I. If the embedder simply adds the watermark to the original work, then the distribution of such watermarked work $\tilde{I}_r$ is the convolution of the distribution of the watermarks and that of the original works, which is not necessarily Gaussian. Let us denote the distribution of $\widetilde{I}_r$ as $\mathbf{X}_r$ and call it the distribution of *randomly watermarked works*.

Now, consider the process where a **valid** watermark W_v is uniformly chosen (by uniformly choosing the key for the watermark generator), and then the watermarked work $\widetilde{I}_v$ is obtained by embedding W_v into a randomly chosen original work I. Let us denote the distribution of such $\widetilde{I}_v$ as $\mathbf{X}_v$, and call it the distribution of *valid watermarked works*.

For clarity in notation, we use the symbol I to denote an original work, and add the tilde $\widetilde{I}$ to denote a work drawn from either $\mathbf{X}_r$ or $\mathbf{X}_v$ [4].

3.3   Formulation of Ambiguity Attacks

We follow the formulation of ambiguity attacks given in [2] with slight but important modification.

Let B be a probabilistic polynomial-time algorithm. Given some watermarked work $\widetilde{I}$, we say that B successfully attacks $\widetilde{I}$ if it outputs a pair (W, K) s.t. $\widetilde{I}$ contains the watermark W and $W = f(K)$, or outputs a symbol $\perp$ to correctly declare that such pair does not exist. Let us write $B(\widetilde{I}) = \mathsf{PASS}$ when the attack is successful. We denote $\Pr[B(\widetilde{I}) = \mathsf{PASS}]$ to be the probability that B successfully attacks a particular $\widetilde{I}$. The probability distribution is taken over the coin tosses made by B. Note that for $\widetilde{I}$ there does not exist such a pair (W, K), B has to output $\perp$ and hence is always successful.

We further denote $\widetilde{\mathcal{I}_n}$ to be a work that consists of n coefficients, and that is randomly drawn from the distribution of valid watermarked works $\mathbf{X}_v$. Let $\Pr[B(\widetilde{\mathcal{I}_n}) = \mathsf{PASS}]$ to be the probability that an attack by B is successful. In this case, the probability distribution is taken over the coin tosses made by B, as well as the choices of watermarked $\widetilde{\mathcal{I}_n}$. Then we have the

DEFINITION 1 *Let B be a probabilistic polynomial-time algorithm. We say that B is a successful attacker if, there exists a positive polynomial $p(\cdot)$, s.t. for all positive integer n_0, there exists an integer $n > n_0$, and*

$$\Pr[B(\widetilde{\mathcal{I}_n}) = \mathsf{PASS}] > 1/p(n).$$

In other words, B is a successful attacker if B successfully output a watermark-key pair with probability that is not negligible.

Note that our definition is a slight modification from [2]. The definition in [2] does not take into account cases where there is no valid watermark in a work. Moreover, the distribution of the watermarked work $\widetilde{I}$ is taken over the random choices of the original works. In our formulation, the watermarked work is drawn from $\mathbf{X}_v$, and we differentiate the case where there are some valid watermarks in the given work from the case where there is not any.

---

[4] Clearly these two distributions $\mathbf{X}_r$ and $\mathbf{X}_v$ are different. However, by an argument similar to that in Section 5, it is not difficult to show that these two distributions are computationally indistinguishable.

This modification is important. We cannot simply say that an attacker is successful if $\Pr[B(\widetilde{\mathcal{I}_n}) = \mathsf{PASS}]$ is high. This is because we observe that, it is possible to design a watermarking scheme such that for a randomly chosen work $\tilde{I}$, the probability that it does not contain a valid watermark is very high. In that case, a trivial algorithm that always declares "can not find a valid watermark" is correct with high probability, and thus by definition is a successful attacker. Due to this consideration, we decide to consider $\mathbf{X_v}$ in the definition, and separate the two cases where valid watermarks do or do not exist.

3.4   Cryptographically Secure Pseudo-random Number Generator

Loosely speaking, a *pseudo-random number generator* (PRNG) takes a seed of a certain length as input and outputs a string, which is of a longer length than that of the seed.

A *cryptographically secure pseudo-random number generator* (CSPRNG) is a PRNG whose output string cannot be computationally distinguished from a truly random distribution. Formal definition of the security of CSPRNG is done in terms of polynomial statistical tests [11]. We follow a simplified definition of statistical tests used in [4].

Let $\{0,1\}^n$ be the set of binary strings of length n, and $\{0,1\}^*$ denotes the set of all binary strings of all lengths. Formally, we have the following definitions.

DEFINITION 2 *A PRNG g is a deterministic polynomial-time algorithm g : $\{0,1\}^m \rightarrow \{0,1\}^{q(m)}$, for some positive integer m and positive polynomial $q(m)$.*

DEFINITION 3 *A probabilistic polynomial-time statistical test $\mathcal{T}$ is a probabilistic polynomial-time algorithm that assigns to every input string in $\{0,1\}^*$ a real number in the interval $[0,1]$.*

In other words, $\mathcal{T}$ can be considered as a function $\mathcal{T} : \{0,1\}^* \rightarrow [0,1]$, which terminates in polynomial time, and whose output depends also on the coin tosses during execution. Let r_n be the expected output of $\mathcal{T}$ over all truly random n-bit strings drawn uniformly from $\{0,1\}^n$, and all coin tosses made by $\mathcal{T}$. We have

DEFINITION 4 *A PRNG g passes test $\mathcal{T}$ if, for every positive integer t, and every positive polynomial $q(m)$, there exists a positive integer m_0, such that for all integers $m > m_0$, the expected output of $\mathcal{T}$, given a $q(m)$-bit string generated by g, lies in the interval $(r_{q(m)} - m^{-t}, r_{q(m)} + m^{-t})$, assuming the seed of g is uniformly distributed over $\{0,1\}^m$.*

If a PRNG g does not pass a test $\mathcal{T}$, we say that $\mathcal{T}$ has an *advantage* in distinguishing g from a truly random source. Then we can define CSPRNG as

DEFINITION 5 *A CSPRNG is a PRNG g that passes every probabilistic polynomial-time statistical test $\mathcal{T}$.*

In other words, no test T can have an advantage in distinguishing a CSPRNG g from a truly random source.

In this paper, we employ the CSPRNG due to Blum et al. [4]. A Blum number N is an integer that is the product of two primes, each congruent to 3 (mod 4). Let QR_N be the set of all quadratic residues in $\mathbb{Z}_N^*$. That is, $x \in QR_N$ if and only if there exists an $x_0 \in \mathbb{Z}_N^*$ such that $x_0^2 \equiv x \mod N$. Let $s \in QR_N$ be a seed to the Blum CSPRNG, the i-th bit b_i in the output string is computed as

$$b_i = (s^{2^i} \mod N) \mod 2. \tag{1}$$

In other words, we compute the output string by squaring the current number (starting from the seed) to get the next number, and take the least significant bit as the output.

Following the above notations, we have the

DEFINITION 6 *A Blum PRNG is a function $g : QR_N \to \{0,1\}^{q(m)}$ defined as $g(s) = b_0, b_1, \cdots, b_{q(m)-1}$, where $b_i = (s^{2^i} \mod N) \mod 2$, N is a Blum number of length m, and $q(m)$ is a positive polynomial of m.*

It is proved in [4] that, under the well accepted assumption that integer factorization is hard, this PRNG is secure. That is, it passes every polynomial statistical test T. We shall refer to it as the Blum CSPRNG.

4 A Non-invertible Scheme

Now, we describe the proposed secure protocol. The parameters for the protocol are three constants T, k and m.

In the proof of security, the parameters should be expressed in terms of n. We will choose

$$k = 1/100, \quad T = nk/2 = n/200, \quad m = \sqrt{n}. \tag{2}$$

4.1 Underlying Watermarking Scheme

The underlying watermarking scheme is essentially the spread spectrum method. For completeness and clarity, we describe the embedding and detection processes.

Embedding: Given an original I and a watermark W, the watermarked $\widetilde{I}$ is

$$\widetilde{I} = I + kW,$$

where k is a predefined parameter.

Detection: Given a work $\hat{I}$ and a watermark W, declare that $\hat{I}$ is watermarked if and only if

$$\hat{I} \cdot W \geq T,$$

where $\cdot$ is the vector inner product and T is a predefined parameter.

For simplicity, we omit normalization in the embedding. Thus, the energy $\|\widetilde{I}\|^2$ of a watermarked work is expected to be higher than the original work. Our proof can be modified (but tedious) when normalization is to be included.

4.2   False Alarm, Robustness, and Distortion (Parameters T and k)

The performance of a watermarking scheme is measured by its false alarm, robustness and distortion. Detailed analysis can be found in [5]. Here, we are more concerned with the false alarm.

The false alarm F is the probability that a randomly chosen $\widetilde{I}$ is declared to be watermarked by a random valid watermark W. That is

$$F = \Pr[\widetilde{I} \cdot W > T] \tag{3}$$

where $\widetilde{I}$ is drawn from the distribution of randomly watermarked works $\mathbf{X_r}$, and W is uniformly chosen from $\mathcal{W}$ the set of valid watermarks.

The false alarm F is small. To see that, consider any given $W \in \mathcal{W}$ and $\widetilde{I}$ randomly chosen from distribution $\mathbf{X_r}$, it is not difficult to show that the distribution $(\widetilde{I} \cdot W)$ is a zero-mean normal distribution with standard derivation δ where δ can be analytically derived. If $T = C_0 \delta$ where $C_0 > 0$ is some positive constant, then the probability that a random $\widetilde{I}$ satisfies $(\widetilde{I} \cdot W > T)$ is less than $\exp(-C_0^2/2)$. Using the parameters in (2), $\delta < 2\sqrt{n}$. Since $T = n/200$, it is many times larger than the standard derivation δ.

For each $W_i \in \mathcal{W}$, where $1 \le i \le |\mathcal{W}|$, let F_i be the probability that $\widetilde{I} \cdot W_i > T$ for random $\widetilde{I}$ from $\mathbf{X_r}$. By the argument above, F_i is exponentially small with respect to n. More precisely, given the parameters in (2) and random $\widetilde{I}$ from $\mathbf{X_r}$,

$$F_i = \Pr[\widetilde{I} \cdot W_i > T] = \exp(-d_i n) \tag{4}$$

for some positive constant d_i. Therefore,

$$F = \sum_{i=1}^{|\mathcal{W}|} F_i \Pr[W = W_i] \le \exp(-C_1 n) \tag{5}$$

where C_1 is the maximum d_i in (4), which is a positive constant.

By choosing $k = 1/100$, the distortion introduced during embedding is 1% of the original work. We could also choose k to be a slow decreasing function, for e.g. $k = 1/\sqrt{\log n}$, so that the ratio of the distortion over the energy of the work tends to 0 as n increases. Our proof still holds for this set of parameters.

Similarly, the scheme is very robust. Since the expected inner product of a watermarked image and the watermark is $E[(I + kW) \cdot W] = kn$, a noise of large energy is required to pull the inner product below the threshold $T = kn/2$. In this case, for noise with energy n (i.e. same as the original image), the watermark can still be detected in the corrupted work with high probability.

4.3   Watermark Generation (Parameter m)

A watermark is generated using a CSPRNG $f : \{0,1\}^m \to \{-1,1\}^n$ where $m \le n$. Thus, it takes a small seed of m bits and produces a watermark. Note that this CSPRNG can be easily translated from the Blum CSPRNG by mapping the output 0 to -1, and 1 unchanged. Let $\mathcal{W}$ to be the range of the function f, and it is actually the set of valid watermarks. Clearly, $|\mathcal{W}| \leq 2^m$.

Intuitively, for better security, we should have large m so that given a valid watermark, it is computationally difficult for an attacker to find the key K, such that $f(K) = W$. However, in some applications and our proof, we need the number of valid watermark to be small, so that it is computationally difficult for an attacker to find a valid watermark. On the other hand, if m is too small, an attacker can look for a suitable valid watermark using brute-force search.

In our construction, we choose $m = \sqrt{n}$, thus $|\mathcal{W}| = 2^{\sqrt{n}}$. As a result, it is computationally infeasible to do a brute-force search in the set of valid watermarks. At the same time, consider a randomly watermarked work $\widetilde{\mathcal{I}_n}$ drawn from distribution $\mathbf{X_r}$, which is of length n. With the parameters as in (2), the probability that $\widetilde{\mathcal{I}_n}$ contains any valid watermark $W \in \mathcal{W}$ is very small. Let us denote this probability $V(n)$ as a function of n, that is,

$$V(n) = \Pr[\exists W \in \mathcal{W}, \quad \widetilde{\mathcal{I}_n} \cdot W > T] \tag{6}$$

where $\widetilde{\mathcal{I}_n}$ is drawn from $\mathbf{X_r}$. Recall from Section 4.2 that the probability F_i that a randomly watermarked work can be declared as watermarked by a given valid watermark $W_i \in \mathcal{W}$ is exponentially small with respect to n. In particular, $F_i \leq \exp(-C_1 n)$ for some positive constant C_1 and for all $1 \leq i \leq |\mathcal{W}|$. Therefore,

$$V(n) = 1 - \prod_{i=1}^{|\mathcal{W}|}(1 - F_i) \leq 1 - (1 - \exp(-C_1 n))^{2^m}$$
$$< 2^m \exp(-C_1 n) < \exp(-C_1 n + \sqrt{n}) \tag{7}$$

where C_1 is some positive constant. Note that $V(n)$ is a negligible function of n.

5 Proof of Security

Now, we are ready to prove that the proposed protocol is secure. We assume that the function f is a CSPRNG. Suppose that there is a successful attacker B as defined in DEFINITION 1, we want to extend it to a statistical test $\mathcal{T}$ that has an advantage in distinguishing sequences produced by f from that by a truly random source. Since f is a CSPRNG, this leads to a contradiction, and thus such a B is impossible.

Given an input $W \in \{-1, 1\}^n$, the following steps are carried out by $\mathcal{T}$:

1. Randomly pick an original work I.
2. Compute $\widehat{I} = I + kW$. That is, embed W into I.
3. Pass $\widehat{I}$ to B and obtain an output.
4. If the output of B is a pair $(\widehat{W}, \widehat{K})$, such that $\widehat{W} = f(\widehat{K})$, then $\mathcal{T}$ declares that W is generated by f by outputting a 0. Otherwise B outputs a $\perp$, then $\mathcal{T}$ declares that W comes from a random source by outputting a 1.

We want to calculate the expected output of $\mathcal{T}$ for the following 2 cases. If the difference of the expected outputs of these 2 cases is non-negligible, then by the definitions in Section 3.4, f is not a CSPRNG, thus leads to a contradiction.

Case 1: W is from a random source.   Suppose W is from a random source, then the probability that there exists a valid watermark $\widehat{W} \in \mathcal{W}$ in $\widetilde{I}$ is exactly the probability $V(n)$ in (7), which is negligible with respect to n as we have shown in Section 4.3. Hence, we know that $\mathcal{T}$ will almost always output a 1 to correctly declare that it is from the random source, except in the unlikely event $\mathcal{E}$ where $\widetilde{I}$ happens to contain a valid watermark. Clearly $\mathcal{E}$ happens with negligible probability $V(n)$. We observe that, when $\mathcal{E}$ happens, $\mathcal{T}$ may output a 0 with a probability that is not negligible (since B is a successful attacker). We consider the obvious worst case (best case for the attacker) that, $\mathcal{T}$ always output 0 when $\mathcal{E}$ happens. In this case, the fraction of 0's output by $\mathcal{T}$ is $V(n)$, which is still negligible. Therefore, let $E_1(\mathcal{T})$ be the expected output of $\mathcal{T}$, we have

$$E_1(\mathcal{T}) > 1 - V(n). \tag{8}$$

Case 2: W is from the CSPRNG f.   Suppose W is generated by f, then W is a valid watermark. Since B is a successful attacker, by definition B is able to find a valid watermark $\widehat{W}$ that is already embedded in $\widetilde{I}$ with a probability that is not negligible. More specifically, for any positive integer n_0,

$$\Pr[B(\widetilde{I}) = \mathtt{PASS}] > 1/p(n)$$

for some positive polynomial $p(\cdot)$ and for some $n > n_0$. Hence, the probability that $\mathcal{T}$ decides that W is from the CSPRNG f is more than $1/p(n)$. Hence, let $E_2(\mathcal{T})$ be the expected output of $\mathcal{T}$ in this case, and we have

$$E_2(\mathcal{T}) < \left(1 - \frac{1}{p(n)}\right). \tag{9}$$

Consider the difference between (8) and (9). Since $V(n)$ is negligible but $1/p(n)$ is not, the difference cannot be negligible because the sum of two negligible functions is still negligible. Hence, the difference between $E_1(\mathcal{T})$ and $E_2(\mathcal{T})$ is not negligible. Thus $\mathcal{T}$ has an advantage in distinguishing the truly random source from the the output of f, therefore f by definition is not a CSPRNG, which is a contradiction. As a result, such a successful attacker B does not exist.

6   Remarks and Future Works

Choice of m.   In our construction we require the parameter m to be small. However, it seems that even if it is large, say $m = n/2$, the protocol is still secure. Thus it would be interesting to find an alternative proof that handles large m.

Underlying watermarking scheme.   For simplicity in the proof, we use a simple watermarking scheme, and "discretized" watermark $W \in \{-1, 1\}^n$. The draw back is that the performance of false alarm, robustness and distortion would be far from optimal. Recent results in communication theory offer schemes that can achieve much higher performance. Thus, we can have much lower false alarm, with other requirement fixed. On the other hand, it is also not clear whether we can make these schemes secure against inversion attacks. This is because in these schemes, the watermark is usually derived from the original in an insecure manner. It is interesting to investigate this issue. Furthermore, our proof requires valid watermarks to be "sparsely populated" in $\{-1, 1\}^n$. On the other hand, schemes with high performance usually require the watermarks to be densely populated, so as to reduce the distortion. Therefore, it is interesting to know if our proof can be extended.

Proving ownership.   As mentioned earlier, to prove the ownership of a work $\tilde{I}$, Alice has to show that she knows a pair (K_A, W_A), such that W_A is correctly generated from K_A and is detectable in $\tilde{I}$. However, directly revealing such a pair in the proof might leak out information that leads to successful attacks. One alternative is to use zero-knowledge interactive proofs to prove the relationship between K_A and W_A without revealing the actual values. We note that it is straight forward to apply known zero-knowledge interactive proofs efficiently in our scheme. This is an advantage of our construction over schemes that involves hash functions (such as [7]), which are difficult to prove using known zero-knowledge interactive proofs.

Generation of watermarks.   In Craver et al. [7], Alice computes a secure hash of the original I, and uses the hash value $h(I)$ to generate the watermark W_A, which is then embedded into I. It is commonly believed that we need to generate the watermark from the original in a one-way manner to achieve non-invertibility since the attacker would be forced to break the underlying one-way function.

Interestingly, our scheme does not use the original I to derive the key K_A, nor the watermark W_A. Hence the watermark is statistically independent from the original. Although we can view the hash value $h(I)$ as the secret key K_A in our setting, our results show that it is not necessary to enforce a relationship between the watermark and the original work.

7   Conclusions

Resistance to inversion attacks is an important requirement for a secure digital right management system. Many schemes have been proposed to improve security. On the other hand, there are also attacks proposed to break these schemes. In this paper, we give a provably secure protocol that is resistant to inversion (and ambiguity) attacks. We prove the security using well accepted techniques in cryptography. Specifically, we show that if an inversion attack is possible, then we can computationally distinguish a truly random sequence from a sequence generated from a cryptographically secure pseudo-random number generator. It is interesting to investigate how to bring our proposed protocol into practice.

References

[1] A. Adelsbach, S. Katzenbeisser, and A.-R. Sadeghi. On the insecurity of non-invertible watermarking schemes for dispute resolving. *International Workshop on Digital Watermarking (IWDW)*, pages 374–388, 2003.

[2] A. Adelsbach, S. Katzenbeisser, and H. Veith. Watermarking schemes provably secure against copy and ambiguity attacks. *DRM*, pages 111–119, 2003.

[3] A. Adelsbach and A. Sadeghi. Zero-knowledge watermark detection and proof of ownership. *4th Int. Workshop on Info. Hiding*, LNCS 2137:273–288, 2000.

[4] L. Blum, M. Blum, and M. Shub. A simple secure unpredictable pseudo-random number generator. *SIAM Journal on Computing*, 15:364–383, 1986.

[5] I.J. Cox, M.L. Miller, and J.A. Bloom. *Digital Watermarking*. Morgan Kaufmann, 2002.

[6] S. Craver. Zero knowledge watermark detection. *3rd Intl. Workshop on Information Hiding*, LNCS 1768:101–116, 2000.

[7] S. Craver, N. Memon, B.L. Yeo, and M.M. Yeung. Resolving rightful ownerships with invisible watermarking techniques: Limitations, attacks, and implications. *IEEE Journal on Selected Areas in Communications*, 16(4):573–586, 1998.

[8] L. Qiao and K. Nahrstedt. Non-invertible watermarking methods for MPEG encoded audio. In *Proceedings of the SPIE 3675, Security and Watermarking of Multimedia Contents*, pages 194–202, 1998.

[9] L. Qiao and K. Nahrstedt. Watermarking schemes and protocols for protecting rightful ownerships and customer's rights. *Journal of Visual Communication and Image Representation*, 9(3):194–210, 1998.

[10] M. Ramkumar and A. Akansu. Image watermarks and counterfeit attacks: Some problems and solutions. In *Symposium on Content Security and Data Hiding in Digital Media*, pages 102–112, 1999.

[11] A. Yao. Theory and application of trapdoor functions. *23rd IEEE Symposium on Foundation of Computer Science*, pages 80–91, 1982.

Reversing Global and Local Geometrical Distortions in Image Watermarking

Dariusz Bogumił

Institute of Computer Science, Warsaw University of Technology
ul. Nowowiejska 15/19, 00-665 Warszawa
dbogumil@ii.pw.edu.pl

Abstract. A new method improving watermark robustness against both global and local geometrical distortions is presented in this article. The proposed approach is based on a self-reference concept and exploits special autocorrelation features of a spatial template. The template allows identifying both the transformation parameters and translation coordinates. Distortions are estimated and reversed on a level as global as possible to maximize watermark recovery effectiveness and minimize a time needed for that purpose. Experimental results showed that an inserted watermark could be successfully read even after Stirmark attack.

1 Introduction

In the course of a few last years intensive research has been done in the field of digital watermarking. Many algorithms, methods, techniques and fully functional systems hiding information in images have been elaborated. Several industrial solutions have also been developed. Nevertheless, an important problem concerning most current watermarking methods is their vulnerability to geometrical distortions. Such distortions as translation, scaling, rotation, shearing, projection and random bending do not remove the watermark but desynchronize its detection and make automatic decoding impossible. Although many systems are more or less robust against global affine geometrical transformations, it appears that utilized algorithms are often insecure. Local and nonlinear distortions are even more difficult to resist.

The state of the art methods for detecting watermarks after geometrical distortions can be divided into the following groups:

- methods operating in transformation invariant domain,
- methods using exhaustive search for an *a priori* known template,
- methods exploiting permanent image features,
- methods inserting some easy to find features,
- methods exploiting the self-reference of a template,
- other methods (self similarity, fractals).

The methods operating in transformation invariant domain often exploit the properties of Fourier-Mellin transform (FMT) [1][2]. Other methods, like embedding a circular watermark in Fourier transform domain [3], are to some degree similar to FMT. An important property of the discrete Fourier transform (DFT) is that its magnitude is

J. Fridrich (Ed.): IH 2004, LNCS 3200, pp. 25-37, 2004.
© Springer-Verlag Berlin Heidelberg 2004

invariant to translations in the spatial domain. Spatial shifts affect only the phase representation of an image, thus a watermark inserted into a magnitude spectrum is robust against cropping. If we represent a DFT magnitude spectrum as a log-polar map, both rotation and scaling are converted to a translation that can be estimated by cross-correlation with the template. Similarly, a log-log map converts aspect ratio changes to a translation. However, the effect of more general geometrical transformations cannot be reversed. Another important disadvantage of those methods is their poor robustness against JPEG compression and other non-geometrical attacks, because of the use of magnitude components, which are less robust and have more visual impact than phase components.

A completely different strategy was presented by Hartung et al. [4]. Hartung proposes an exhaustive search for an *a priori* known template. The decoder examines each combination of scaling, translation or rotation for every small block (e.g. 16x16 pixels). The authors suggest that only a small percentage of all search positions have to be tested. However, this approach, although functioning, is in general very time consuming.

Some researchers present methods exploiting permanent image features. Alghoniemy and Tewfik [5] propose to compute two indicators to estimate scaling and rotation parameters. The "Edges Standard Deviation Ratio" gives an estimation of the scaling factor. The rotation angle is approximated by the "Average Edges Angles Difference". These indicators are computed from wavelet maxima locations.

A more sophisticated approach based on image features was proposed by Bas et al. [6]. Firstly, feature points of the image are extracted and a Delaunay tessellation on the set of points is performed. Then the mark is embedded inside each triangle of the tessellation using a classical additive scheme. The detection is done using correlation properties on the different triangles. The presented technique permits automatic resynchronization of the watermark after both local and slight global (rotations, scaling) geometrical transformations. An important advantage of that method is that the orientation of the signature is carried by the content of the image itself. Celik *et al* showed another example of using certain features of the image itself as a watermark's synchronization points [7]. Johnson *et al* proposed a different approach related to the concept of permanent image features [8]. A small set of "salient" image points is saved as an identification mark of the image. The coordinates of those points are used as a key to recover an original size and appearance of geometrically distorted images.

Another group of methods concerning the synchronization problem insert some easy-to-find features to the image. Gruhl and Bender suggested a scheme in which a predefined reference pattern (for example multiple cross shapes) is embedded into a host image using any of the high bit-rate coding techniques (for example by LSB plane manipulation) [9]. Estimation of the geometric transformation of the image is achieved by comparing the original shape, size, and orientation of the reference pattern to that found in the transformed image. The drawback of this scheme is its low robustness towards compression and noise. Kostopoulos, Skodras and Christodoulakis also propose to embed a reference pattern consisting of cross-shaped figures [10]. The method uses a predefined set of attacked cross-shaped patterns in order to approximate a possible attack. However, usability of the proposed scheme is limited to detection of the predefined geometrical attacks only.

The same group includes methods inserting "peaks" in Fourier transform domain. Pereira and Pun propose to embed the template consisted of a random arrangement of peaks in the Fourier domain [11]. Then a point-matching algorithm between the peaks extracted from an image and the reference template points estimates the geometric transformation. Another method based on a calibration signal in the Fourier domain has been patented by Digimarc Corporation [12]. Unfortunately, template peaks can be easily removed by an attacker. In addition, such an operation can improve the quality of the attacked image [13].

The methods exploiting the self-reference of a template have very promising results. Kutter suggested embedding four shifted copies of the same template [14]. Deguillaume et al. propose to insert many neighboring copies of a relatively small template [15]. A similar approach was presented by Honsinger and Rabbani [16] where a watermark itself is copied. Multiple copies of the same pattern produce local peaks in an autocorrelation function spectrum. These peaks undergo the same transformations as the image, so estimating the transform matrix is possible. The self-reference concept is useful to recover from global geometrical distortions, and with some enhancements, it can help in a local distortions case [17]. However, multiple copies of the same small pattern create a possibility of an autocorrelation attack [18].

Other methods exploit fractal properties and self-similarity of the image [19]. First results were promising (robustness to basic geometric transformations), but that concept still needs further research.

Most of the approaches described above assume that geometrical changes introduced into an image have global, affine character. Local or nonlinear distortions cannot be detected with those methods mainly because such distortions do not affect globally transform domains (Fourier, autocorrelation) and the size of modified regions is often smaller then the templates' size. Unfortunately, small nonlinear distortions, which efficiently destroy watermarks, do not result in a sufficient perceptible image quality loss, so the watermarking systems that fail to resist such attacks, cannot be considered robust and secure.

It is noteworthy, that some watermarking algorithms do not need perfect decoder synchronization and can resist some very small geometrical distortions [20][21]. This property can reduce the template search space and enhance the watermark resistance to approximation errors. To achieve such synchronization tolerance, a watermark can be embedded in mid- or low-frequencies, so its autocorrelation is not as narrow as for a high-frequency watermark.

This work presents a method based on the self-reference concept, allowing estimation and recovering from local or nonlinear geometrical transformations. The watermark is decoded after reversing geometrical distortions.

2   Geometrical Distortions

Nonlinear geometrical distortions can be introduced in the printing/scanning process (it especially depends on scanner quality) or with adequate software. The Stirmark benchmarking tool applies some almost unnoticeable geometric distortions: combination of stretching, rotating, cropping, shifting, and bending by small random amounts. Additionally, slight random displacements, both low and high frequency, are applied to each pixel [22].

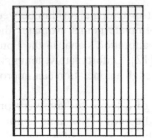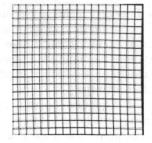

Fig. 1. A regular grid (*left*) and a grid subjected to Stirmark attack – small local distortions are visible (*right*)

The Stirmark attack, although nonlinear on the global level, can be considered as a composition of affine transforms concerning small local regions of the image. The size of those regions is not constant, because the frequency of attack displacements varies randomly. The approach proposed herein is based on that observation.

Geometrical transformations, such as scaling, rotation, shearing or any combination of them, can be represented as an affine transform:

$$\begin{bmatrix} x' \\ y' \end{bmatrix} = A \cdot \begin{bmatrix} x \\ y \end{bmatrix} + T, \quad A = \begin{bmatrix} a & b \\ c & d \end{bmatrix}, \quad T = \begin{bmatrix} t_x \\ t_y \end{bmatrix} \tag{1}$$

The expression (1) maps each point of the original image from Cartesian coordinates (x, y) to new coordinates (x', y') in the transformed image, where a, b, c, d are the components of the transformation matrix A and t_x, t_y are the components of the translation vector T. Equation 1 does not describe all possible image distortions, e.g. perspective or trapezium-like transformations. However, we can use it for local regions of the image to approximate global, generally non-linear distortion.

The estimation of affine transformation parameters is decomposed into two parts. The A matrix components are calculated with the use of a self-referencing template and its autocorrelation. Subsequently the image is transformed to restore the original image position. Then the translation is estimated by calculating the cross-correlation matrix of a distorted watermarked image and a key-dependant, *a priori* known template.

3   Self-referencing Template Embedding

As stated before, the proposed method is based on the self-reference concept. A specially designed template is used to recover from geometrical distortions. Generally, there were two approaches to the self-referencing template design presented in the previous work. Kutter proposed embedding four shifted copies of the same template in the spatial domain [14]. A schematic view of that idea is depicted on Fig. 2. In ideal conditions, the template autocorrelation function has 9 peaks with the strongest one in the center. The four peaks on the axes are two times weaker, and four peaks on the diagonals are four times weaker then the center one. Such autocorrelation function properties enable both identifying parameters of the geometrical transformation (the A matrix) and finding translation of the attacked image (the T vector). Another advantage of the Kutter's approach is its relatively good resistance to autocorrelation attack, because only four copies of the template are embedded into the image. On the other hand the scheme makes it difficult to recover from local or non-linear geometrical distortions. In that case the dx and dy shifts should be small, in order to detect geometrical transformations on local level, but too small shifts can cause unacceptable approximation errors. A different problem is overlapping of the shifted copies, which can – depending on an implementation - increase visible artifacts (when overlapping template pixels) or lower robustness to non-geometrical distortions (when not overlapping pixels, but embedding watermark in very high frequencies).

Another idea assumes inserting into the image multiple adjoining copies of the same pattern (Fig. 3)[15][16]. The corresponding autocorrelation function spectrum has some very useful features. First of all there are many peaks placed in the corners of a regular grid and each peak has the maximum autocorrelation value 1 (in ideal conditions). That fact makes it possible to successfully recover even from local and non-linear geometrical distortions. Unfortunately, the regular template grid cannot be used to identify translation. To obey that drawback another template can be used, or a watermark can be embedded in translation invariant domain. However, the first solution enhances visible artifacts and the second usually reduces watermark robustness against non-geometrical attacks, i.e. JPEG compression.

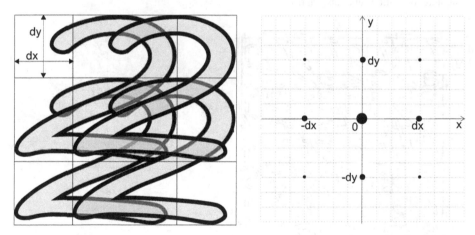

Fig. 2. A schematic view of the "shifted-copies" template design [14] and the corresponding autocorrelation function graph

The template proposed herein consists of two parts, which produce periodical peaks on the axes of the autocorrelation function graph (Fig. 4). Each part forms a narrow rectangle, which is copied along its shorter side. The longer side is as long as possible (lengths wx, wy), taking into account performance constraints and the expected image size. The shorter sides of the rectangles are relatively small (lengths dx and dy). The vertical rectangle is copied horizontally, so the copies form strong peaks on the OX coordinate axis, whereas the horizontal one is copied in the vertical direction, which forms peaks on OY. Additionally, every second copy of the template has a negated value of each pixel. This feature lowers visible artifacts, because it reduces the risk that an observer would notice a regular pattern on the watermarked image. The parts of the template do not overlap, but they have separate locations shown as digits and letters on Fig. 4. They jointly fill the whole image surface.

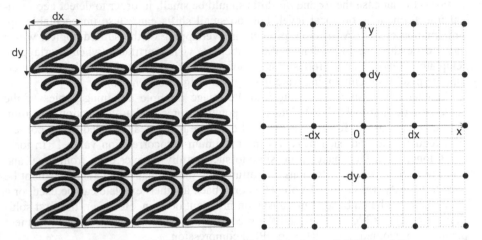

Fig. 3. A schematic view of the "multiple-copies" template design [15][16] and the corresponding autocorrelation function graph

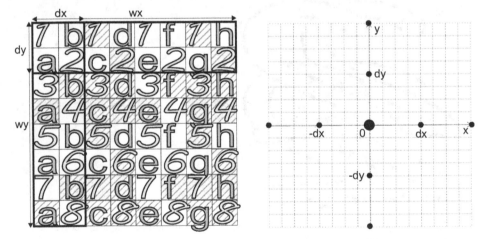

Fig. 4. A schematic view of the proposed template design and the corresponding autocorrelation function graph

The initial template (before copying) is a spread spectrum sequence with zero mean, distributed on all frequencies and taking into account contrast sensitivity of the Human Visual System. It is constructed in discrete cosine transform (DCT) domain in order to achieve better robustness against JPEG compression. The embedding process is defined as adding the template values to image pixels' values in specified color space (i.e. luminance).

The proposed scheme has some advantages comparing to the two described above. In ideal conditions the autocorrelation function is defined as:

$$R(x,y) = \begin{cases} 1, & (x,y) = (0,0) \\ \dfrac{1}{2} \cdot (-1)^{|n|}, & (x,y) = (n \cdot dx, 0) \vee (x,y) = (0, n \cdot dy), n \neq 0 \\ 0, & (x,y) \neq (n \cdot dx, n \cdot dy) \end{cases} \tag{2}$$

where dx and dy are the parameters of the template and n is an integer. Such properties allow the decoder to estimate both the geometrical transformation matrix A and the translation vector T. Regularly repeated autocorrelation peaks are used to determine geometrical distortions with good accuracy (approximation and rounding errors are minimized). Thanks to small dx and dy intervals it is possible to identify transformations on local level. Artifacts caused by a regularly repeated pattern are reduced, which improves a subjective image quality perception.

4 Recovering from Geometrical Deformations

The objective of that operation is to identify geometrical transformations performed on the watermarked image. At the initial stage it is necessary to minimize autocorrelation properties of the given image itself, and leave only the predicted template information. We use the second derivative of the image as the template prediction, using Laplace filters with various kernels (Fig. 5) to approximate the second derivative.

$$\begin{pmatrix} 0 & -1 & 0 \\ -1 & 4 & -1 \\ 0 & -1 & 0 \end{pmatrix} \quad \begin{pmatrix} -1 & 0 & -1 \\ 0 & 4 & 0 \\ -1 & 0 & -1 \end{pmatrix} \quad \begin{pmatrix} 0 & 0 & -1 & 0 & 0 \\ 0 & 0 & -1 & 0 & 0 \\ -1 & -1 & 8 & -1 & -1 \\ 0 & 0 & -1 & 0 & 0 \\ 0 & 0 & -1 & 0 & 0 \end{pmatrix}$$

Fig. 5. Laplace filter kernels used to predict the hidden template

For each template prediction thus obtained, the following procedure is executed. We choose a fragment of the image and compute its autocorrelation function. At first we try to identify geometrical distortions on the global level (i.e. the image was simply scaled), so initially the chosen fragment covers the whole image.

Having computed the autocorrelation function values, all the local extreme peaks are found. Then we choose the two angles for which the sum of autocorrelation peaks is the biggest. Extremes with other angles are filtered out as a noise. For the chosen angles, all the extremes are compared to find the period in the sequence of their distances from the (0, 0) point. That step is carried out with computing for each pair of peaks' distances the equivalent of the greatest common divisor in real numbers domain, defined as:

$$RealGCD(a, b) = max\{d: a \bmod d < \varepsilon \ \& \ b \bmod d < \varepsilon\} \tag{3}$$

where ε is a tolerance. A modified version of Euclidean algorithm is used to calculate the extremes' distances period. The best fitting period for each angle is converted to a point in Cartesian coordinates. As a result of the presented sequence of operations, we obtain the coordinates of two points and a corresponding summary autocorrelation value. The two points represent the original template points *(0, dx)* and *(dy, 0)* after performing geometrical transformation. If the results of the self-referencing template detection for the chosen image block are satisfactory (summary autocorrelation value exceeds a given threshold), we can reverse geometrical distortions. Firstly an inverse transformation matrix is computed according to the formula:

$$A^{-1} = \begin{bmatrix} 0 & d_x \\ d_y & 0 \end{bmatrix} \cdot \begin{bmatrix} x_1 & x_2 \\ y_1 & y_2 \end{bmatrix}^{-1} \tag{4}$$

where d_x, d_y are initial template's shorter side lengths and (x_1, y_1), (x_2, y_2) are the co-ordinates of periodical peaks found before. Then the image block is transformed with A^{-1} matrix to recover its original position. The transformed block is saved to be used in the next step of the algorithm – the translation finding.

In the case of global affine deformations, most of the found extreme peaks are strong, regular and located on two straight lines. In such a situation, we do not need to acquire more information to restore the original image position. However, when distortions are local or nonlinear we do not obtain peaks satisfying the above requirements. If that happens, we divide the image into 5 blocks (each four times smaller than the divided block – see Fig. 6 (left)) and repeat recursively the template detection process for each block. The presented division scheme is a compromise between the accuracy of the sliding correlator and the effectiveness of the algorithm. It is also influenced by partial autocorrelation properties of the template. Thanks to the template properties, autocorrelation peaks should be relatively strong on each decomposition level until the block size is comparable with the initial template size.

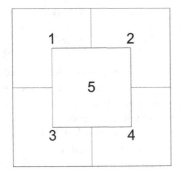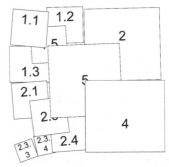

Fig. 6. Template division schema (*left*) and a schematic view of template recovering from some example local distortions (*right*)

In other words, we terminate the recursion either when we find the two extreme peaks fulfilling some requirements (they have to be placed periodically on two straight lines, with the total autocorrelation exceeding a given threshold) or if the block size is too small. The result is a list of transformed image fragments. The effects of the geometrical transformations that were performed on the watermarked image are reversed in the obtained image fragments; however, in general the fragments are not yet placed in the original positions. Some watermarking algorithms assume translation invariance, but usually synchronization of a decoder in respect of translation allows achieving better robustness against non-geometrical distortions (i.e. JPEG compression, filtering, etc.). Such watermarking schemes as spread-spectrum wavelet or DCT watermarking require synchronizing a decoder, so both geometrical distortions and translation effects should be reversed.

5   Restoring the Original Image Placement

As stated before, the self-referencing template can be used to identify translation of the attacked image comparing to the original watermarked image. This is possible, because the function that correlates the predicted template (retrieved from the previous step of the algorithm) with the *a priori* known template produces, in ideal case, an output similar to the autocorrelation of that template (Fig. 4 (right)). The output has a strong central peak and many other peaks (two times weaker) on the two straights parallel to the axes OX and OY, and crossing in the central peak. The coordinates of the main peak follow the translation of the processed image in relation to the watermarked image.

In order to reverse the translation, for each image fragment coming from the previous step of the algorithm, a cross-correlation between the predicted template and the *a priori* known template is computed to find the maximum correlation peak. That peak validity is verified using information from the secondary peaks, which should be present on the straight lines as described above. The coordinates of the resulting peak are used to estimate the translation vector coefficients t_x and t_y. The image fragment is now shifted according to t_x and t_y, to restore its original position. Finally, all the restored image blocks are painted on the destination image. Blocks with higher correlation are painted on top of worse fitting blocks so that the resulting image is as close to the original undistorted image as possible (Fig. 6 (right)).

Blocks that were too heavily distorted are not recovered and sometimes can form "black holes" (Fig. 7). However, watermark information still can be read because of the watermark's itself robustness against non-geometrical artifacts [23].

6   Experimental Results

The performance of the proposed scheme was tested with Stirmark 3.1. The standard test images were watermarked with 72 bits of information, without any error correction. The description of the used watermarking algorithm [23] is not the aim of this article. We will only mention that it is a private, key-dependant, spread-spectrum scheme, optimized for JPEG compression robustness. The watermark is embedded in

Fig. 7. An original watermarked image "lena.jpg" (*left*), an image attacked with Stirmark (*middle*), and a recovered image (*right*) – 64-bit watermark was decoded correctly

DCT domain and its decoding routine does not need the original image (blind algorithm). Beside an "information carrier" part of the watermark, the synchronization template was embedded into the images, according to the algorithm described herein. Throughout the evaluation, the template parameters were set to:

$dx = 32$, dy = 32,   - the shorter side of the template rectangle,
wx = 1024, wy = 1024   - the longer side of the template rectangle.

The PSNR of the watermarked image was kept not less than 38 dB. The detection was done without the presence of the original image. The test case was marked as successful, if at least 64 bits of hidden information were decoded correctly.

The results in **Table 1** show the effectiveness of the proposed scheme. The synchronization template proved its ability to recover from geometrical distortions in almost all cases. Only the cases of 90 degree rotation and 50% scaling were usually not detected correctly. However, that limitation could be easily overcome, at a cost of time efficiency, by performing template search for pre-transformed image versions: rescaled 200%, rotated 90, 180, 270 degrees.

Table 1. Stirmark 3.1 benchmark results

Image modifications class	Average response
Signal enhancement	**1.00**
Gaussian	1.00
Median	1.00
Sharpening	1.00
FMLR	1.00
Compression	**0.94**
JPEG	0.89
GIF	1.00
Scaling	**0.86**
Without JPEG 90	0.89
With JPEG 90	0.83
Cropping	**0.96**
Without JPEG 90	1.00

	With JPEG 90	0.93
Shearing		**1.00**
Rotation		**0.92**
	Auto-crop	0.93
	Without JPEG 90	0.92
	With JPEG 90	0.94
	Auto-scale	0.92
	Without JPEG 90	0.92
	With JPEG 90	0.92
Other geometric trans.		**1.00**
	Col & line removal	1.00
	Flip	1.00
Random Geometric Dist.		**1.00**
Overall Performance		**0.96**

Both the synchronization template and the "information hiding" watermark are resistant to non-geometrical distortions. In the experiment, the watermark (in fact its "information" part) was robust against JPEG compression up to quality factor equal 10. Relative robustness of different watermark parts can be adjusted in the embedding process, with respect that they both influence the image quality.

For all images, it was possible to decode the watermark even after the "Stirmark" attack [22]. The results show that the proposed scheme is applicable and efficient to recover from both global and local or non-linear geometrical distortions. The overall performance at the level of 0.96 is very high.

7 Discussion and Conclusions

The watermarking system is as insecure as its weakest part. Here, although the template is created with a secret key, its autocorrelation could be read without the knowledge of the key. It creates a possibility for an attack, aiming to remove synchronization template from the watermarked image [13]. Especially, an autocorrelation attack is threatening [18]. The proposed scheme to some degree lowers the risk of a successful autocorrelation attack, because the template is constructed from two distinct parts, which correlate independently. The naive implementation of the autocorrelation attack would introduce too big artifacts to accept the results. To provide against more sophisticated attacks, taking into account the specific template design, it is possible to introduce a different, key-dependant method of merging the parts of the template.

Another threat is an attack that introduces some strong peaks into the autocorrelation function of the watermarked image. This could mislead the decoder. The remedy for such an attack is possible but it would heavily influence the computational performance of the detection process – the watermark detector would have to try some combinations of the autocorrelation function peaks other than the strongest ones.

The approach introduces a few novel elements on various stages of template embedding and detection. The template design makes it possible to obtain a high autocorrelation response for different block sizes. This feature is used during detection, which is held on a level as global as it is possible. The same template is used to estimate translation parameters. The use of one template in those two operations allows to achieve better robustness with smaller decrease of image quality at the same time. Experimental results showed that the described approach survives local geometrical attacks, which only a few watermarking systems can resist today.

References

[1] Joseph J.K. O'Ruanaidh, Thierry Pun: Rotation, scale and translation invariant spread spectrum digital image watermarking. In Signal Processing 66 (1998), pp. 303-317.
    http://www1.elsevier.nl/cas/tree/store/sigpro/sub/1998/66/3/1170.pdf
[2] C-Y. Lin, M. Wu, J.A. Bloom, M.L. Miller, I.J Cox, and Y.M. Lui: Rotation, Scale, and Translation Resilient Watermarking for Images, IEEE Transactions on Image Processing, Vol. 10, No. 5, pp. 767-782, May 2001.
    http://citeseer.nj.nec.com/article/lin01rotation.html

[3] H.Guo and N.D.Georganas: Multiresolution Image Watermarking Scheme in the Spectrum Domain. In Proc. Can. Conf. on Elec. And Comp. Eng., Winnipeg, May 2002
http://www.mcrlab.uottawa.ca/papers/Huiping_CCECE2002.pdf

[4] F. Hartung, J.K. Su, B. Girod: Spread Spectrum Watermarking: Malicious Attacks and Counter-Attacks. In Proceedings of SPIE Vol. 3657, Security and Watermarking of Multimedia Contents, San Jose, CA, January, 1999.
http://www.nt.e-technik.uni-erlangen.de/LNT_I/publications/pub_list/pub_files/lnt1999_008
.pdf

[5] M. Alghoniemy and A. H. Tewfik: Geometric distortion correction in image watermarking. In Proc. SPIE, pages 82--89, January 2000.
http://citeseer.nj.nec.com/alghoniemy00geometric.html

[6] P. Bas, J-M Chassery and Benoît Macq: Geometrically Invariant Watermarking Using Feature Points, IEEE Transactions on Image Processing, September 2002
http://www.lis.inpg.fr/scientifique/bas/IEEE.pdf

[7] M.U. Celik, E. S. Saber, G. Sharma, A.M. Tekalp: Analysis of Feature-based Geometry Invariant Watermarking. In Proceedings of SPIE, Security and Watermarking of Multimedia Contents III, San Jose, CA., January 2001, pp. 261-268

[8] Neil F. Johnson, Zoran Duric and Sushil Jajodia: Recovery of Watermarks from Distorted Images. In: Third Information Hiding Workshop, Dresden, Germany, 29 September - 1 October 1999.
http://cs.gmu.edu/~zduric/WebPages/Papers/GMU_JDJ.PDF

[9] W. Bender, D. Gruhl, N. Morimoto, A. Lu: Techniques for data hiding, Proc. SPIE 2420 (1995) 40.
http://www.research.ibm.com/journal/sj/mit/sectiona/bender.pdf

[10] V. Kostopoulos, A.N. Skodras and D. Christodoulakis: Digital Image Watermarking: On the Enhancement of Detector Capabilities, in Proc. Fifth Int. Conf. on Mathematics in Signal Processing, Warwick, Dec 18-20, 2000.
http://www.upatras.gr/ieee/skodras/pubs/ans-c38.pdf

[11] Shelby Pereira, Thierry Pun: Fast Robust Template Matching for Affine Resistant Image Watermarks. University of Geneva.
http://cuiwww.unige.ch/~vision/Publications/postscript/99/PereiraPun_wih99.ps.gz

[12] Digimarc Corporation.
http://www.digimarc.com

[13] S. Voloshynovskiy, A. Herrigel, and Y. B. Rytsar: Watermark template attack. In Ping Wah Wong and Edward J. Delp, editors, EI'2001: Security and Watermarking of Multimedia Content III, SPIE Proceedings, San Jose, California USA, 22–25 January 2001.
http://vision.unige.ch/publications/postscript/2001/HerrigelVoloshynovskiyRytsar_spie2001
.pdf

[14] M. Kutter: Watermarking resisting to translation, rotation and scaling, In Proceedings of SPIE, November 1998.
http://citeseer.nj.nec.com/kutter98watermarking.html

[15] Frédéric Deguillaume, Sviatoslav Voloshynovskiy and Thierry Pun: Method for the Estimation and Recovering from General Affine Transforms in Digital Watermarking Applications, In SPIE Photonics West, Electronic Imaging 2002, Security and Watermarking of Multimedia Contents IV, San Jose, CA, USA, January 20-24 2002
http://vision.unige.ch/publications/postscript/2002/DeguillaumeVoloshynovskiyPun_SPIE2
002.pdf

[16] Chris Honsinger, Majid Rabbani: Data Embedding Using Phase Dispersion. Imaging Science Division, Eastman Kodak Company, Rochester, NY, USA, 2000.
http://www.kodak.pl/US/plugins/acrobat/en/corp/researchDevelopment/dataEmbedding.pdf

[17] Svyatoslav Voloshynovskiy, Frédéric Deguillaume and Thierry Pun: Multibit Digital Watermarking Robust Against Local Nonlinear Geometrical Distortions, In IEEE International Conference on Image Processing, ICIP2001, pp. 999-1002, Thessaloniki, Greece, 2001.
http://vision.unige.ch/publications/postscript/2001/VoloshynovskiyDeguillaumePun_ICIP2001.pdf

[18] Dariusz Bogumił: Removing digital watermarks based on image autocorrelation features (in Polish). TPO 2002, Serock, November 2002.
http://www.ii.pw.edu.pl/~dbogumil

[19] P. Bas, J-M. Chassery and F. Davoine: A Geometrical and Frequential Watermarking Scheme Using Similarities, Proc of SPIE Electronic Imaging, Security and Watermarking of Multimedia Content I, p264-272, 1999, San-Jose, USA

[20] Jin Soo Seo: On the design of watermark pattern in the autocorrelation domain, KAIST Electrical Eng. & Computer Science, 2002.
http://www.samsung.com/AboutSAMSUNG/SocialCommitment/HumantechThesis/downloads/8th/b9.pdf

[21] P. Dong, N. Galatsanos: Geometric Robust Watermarking Through Watermark Pattern Design, In Proceedings of the IEEE International Conference on Image Processing (ICIP-03), Barcelona, Spain, September 2003.
http://www.cs.uoi.gr/~galatsanos/PAPERS/IPL-Conferance_papers/icip03_watermarking.pdf

[22] F.A.P. Petitcolas, R.J. Anderson: Evaluation of copyright marking systems. In IEEE Multimedia Systems (ICMCS'99), pages 574--579, 1999.
http://citeseer.nj.nec.com/petitcolas99evaluation.html

[23] Dariusz Bogumił: Digital watermarks resistant to JPEG compression (in Polish). Master Thesis, Warsaw University of Technology, September 2001.
http://www.ii.pw.edu.pl/~dbogumil

On Achievable Regions of Public Multiple-Access Gaussian Watermarking Systems*

Wei Sun and En-hui Yang**

Department of Electrical and Computer Engineering
University of Waterloo, 200 University Ave. W. , Waterloo
Ontario, Canada,N2L 3G1.
{wsun,ehyang}@bbcr.uwaterloo.ca

Abstract. A public multiple-access digital watermarking system is studied, in which two correlated Gaussian covertexts are watermarked independently and then sent to one authorized receiver via memoryless Gaussian attack channels. Given two distortion level pairs (D_1, D_2) and (D'_1, D'_2) with respect to the average squared error distortion measure, an achievable region is given in single-letter information quantities. An example is also utilized to illustrate the gain of correlated sources over uncorrelated sources.

1   Introduction

In digital watermarking, a watermark is embedded into a host signal (or a covertext) , resulting in a watermarked signal. The watermarked signal can be used for different purposes ranging from copyright protection, data authentication, fingerprinting, to information hiding in some video applications. In all these cases, the watermark should be embedded in such a way that the watermarked signal is robust to certain distortion caused by either standard data processing in a friendly environment or malicious attacks in an unfriendly environment. Typically, the effect of standard data processing/malicious attacks is modelled by statistical attack channels in the information theoretic research of watermarking. Under this framework, a major information theoretic research problem is to determine best trade-offs among the distortion between the host signal and watermarked signal, the distortion between the watermarked signal and attacked

* This work was supported in part by the Natural Sciences and Engineering Research Council of Canada under Grants RGPIN203035-98 and RGPIN203035-02 and under Collaborative Research and Development Grant, by the Communications and Information Technology Ontario, by the Premier's Research Excellence Award, by the Canadian Foundation for Innovation, by the Ontario Distinguished Researcher Award, and by the Canada Research Chairs Program.

** En-hui Yang is also on sabbatical with the Department of Information Engineering, the Chinese University of Hong Kong, Shatin, New Territories, Hong Kong

J. Fridrich (Ed.): IH 2004, LNCS 3200, pp. 38–51, 2004.

watermarked signal, the embedding rate, and the robustness of the watermarked signal.

Previously, the above problem was addressed mainly for the watermarking model in which one covertext is watermarked and then sent to one authorized receiver via public channels. For instance, a few theoretical results about the watermarking capacity and random watermarking coding error exponent of such a watermarking model have been reported in [1,3,8,9,12,13] and references therein.

In some applications, however, two or more correlated covertexts may be watermarked independently and then sent to one authorized receiver. For instance, consider the scenario in which music and video frames are watermarked independently, but they will be transmitted in one bit stream and played by one DVD player. In such a case, there will be two (or more if there are more than two covertexts) separate watermarking encoders—one for each covertext—and one joint watermarking decoder. In analogy to multiple-access communications, we shall call the resulting watermarking model a **multiple-access watermarking model**. The model is called **private** if all covertexts are available to the receiver, and **public** if none of the covertexts is available to the receiver.

In this paper, we study the public multiple-access watermarking system with correlated Gaussian covertexts and give an achievable region in single-letter information quantities for given distortion levels with respect to the square error distortion measure. From the multiple-terminal source coding viewpoint, our result is analogous to that of Slepian and Wolf [11] in the sense that the total embedding rate of separate encoding is the same as that of joint encoding. The case of public multiple-access watermarking model with discrete alphabets will be treated in a campanion[16].

Related to the multiple-access watermarking model we proposed above are fingerprinting [9,14,15] and parallel Gaussian watermarking [9,10]. In fingerprinting [9,14,15], the covertexts to be watermarked are identical for all fingerprints, and there are essentially only one encoder and one decoder; the same encoder is used to generate different fingerprinted copies and the same decoder is used to detect only one member of the coalition each time. In parallel Gaussian watermarking [10] the watermarking encoders are cooperative and the problem of total watermarking capacity is addressed.

2   Model Description and Main Result

As a first step in multiple-access watermarking, we consider the watermarking system shown in Figure 1 with correlated Gaussian covertexts, two separate encoders, and one joint decoder. We shall call such a system a **public multiple-access Gaussian watermarking system**.

In Figure 1, the two users' watermarks M_1 and M_2 are independent random variables uniformly distributed over their respective alphabets $\mathcal{M}_1$ and $\mathcal{M}_2$, and the covertexts (S_1^N, S_2^N) are N independent copies of a jointly Gaussian random vector $(S_1, S_2) \sim N\left(0, \begin{bmatrix} \sigma_{S_1}^2 & \rho\sigma_{S_1}\sigma_{S_2} \\ \rho\sigma_{S_1}\sigma_{S_2} & \sigma_{S_2}^2 \end{bmatrix}\right)$, where ρ is the correla-

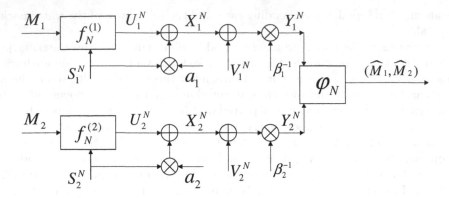

Fig. 1. A public multiple-access Gaussian watermarking system

tion coefficient between S_1 and S_2. Given a watermark m_i and covertext s_i^N, user i generates a codeword $u_i^N = f_N^{(i)}(m_i, s_i^N) \in \mathbb{R}^N$ and then forms a stegotext $x_i^N = u_i^N + a_i s_i^N$, where $a_i > 0$. The attacker obtains a forgery $Y_i^N = \beta_i^{-1}(x_i^N + V_i^N)$ where $\beta_i > 0$ and V_i^N is N independent copies of a Gaussian random variable $V_i \sim N(0, \sigma_{V_i}^2)$. Upon receiving forgeries y_1^N and y_2^N, the single decoder φ_N estimates watermarks $(\hat{m}_1, \hat{m}_2)$. Without ambiguity, let $p(s_1, s_2)$ be the pdf of (S_1, S_2), $p(v_i)$ the pdf of V_i, and $p(s_1^N, s_2^N) = \prod_{j=1}^N p(s_{1j}, s_{2j})$, $p(v_i^N) = \prod_{j=1}^N p(v_{ij})$ if $s_i^N = (s_{i1}, s_{i2}, \ldots, s_{iN})$ and $v_i^N = (v_{i1}, v_{i2}, \ldots, v_{iN})$. Moreover, we assume that the distortion measure d is the square error distortion, that is, $d(x, y) = (x - y)^2$ for $x, y \in \mathbb{R}$, and define for $x^N, y^N \in \mathbb{R}^N$, $d(x^N, y^N) = 1/N \sum_{i=1}^N (x_i - y_i)^2$.

The watermarking model described above is a special multiple-access Gaussian watermarking model. Our motivation to study this special model is twofold. First, in the case of public additive Gaussian watermarking with one sender and one receiver, Moulin et al [9] showed the optimality of such encoders and attack channels. Second, we want to use this special model to demonstrate that indeed, joint decoding can afford gains in the total embedding rate over separate decoding—which is the essence of multiple-access watermarking. Our aim in this paper is to give an achievable region of this special watermarking model to show the gains.

Definition 1. *A **multiple-access watermarking encoder** of length N with rate pair (R_1, R_2) subject to distortion level pair (D_1, D_2) is a quadruple $(\mathcal{M}_1, \mathcal{M}_2, f_N^{(1)}, f_N^{(2)})$ such that $f_N^{(i)}$, $i = 1, 2$, are mappings from $\mathcal{M}_i \times \mathbb{R}^N$ to $\mathbb{R}^N$ satisfying $\mathrm{E}[d(S_i^N, X_i^N)] \leq D_i$, where $X_i^N = f_N^{(i)}(M_i, S_i^N) + a_i S_i^N$, and $(R_1, R_2) = (\frac{1}{N} \log |\mathcal{M}_1|, \frac{1}{N} \log |\mathcal{M}_2|)$. A **watermarking decoder** φ_N of length N is a mapping from $\mathbb{R}^N \times \mathbb{R}^N$ to $\mathcal{M}_1 \times \mathcal{M}_2$ with $(\hat{m}_1, \hat{m}_2) = \varphi_N(y_1^N, y_2^N)$ as an estimate of (m_1, m_2).*

Definition 2. *Given a multiple-access watermarking encoder* $(\mathcal{M}_1, \mathcal{M}_2, f_N^{(1)}, f_N^{(2)})$ *and distortion level pair* (D_1', D_2'), *if* $(\sigma_{V_i}^2, \beta_i)$ *satisfies* $\mathrm{E}[d(Y_i^N, X_i^N)] \leq D_i'$, *then* $(\sigma_{V_i}^2, \beta_i)$ *is called an* **attack channel**. *Denote by* $\mathcal{A}_i(f_N^{(i)}, D_i')$ *the set of all attack channels.*

Definition 3. *The* **error probability of coding** *of an encoder* $(\mathcal{M}_1, \mathcal{M}_2, f_N^{(1)}, f_N^{(2)})$ *and a decoder* φ_N *subject to attack channels* $(\sigma_{V_i}^2, \beta_i) \in \mathcal{A}_i(f_N^{(i)}, D_i')$, $i = 1, 2$ *is defined by* $P_e(f_N^{(1)}, f_N^{(2)}, \varphi_N, \sigma_{V_1}^2, \beta_1, \sigma_{V_2}^2, \beta_2) \triangleq \Pr\{(\hat{M}_1, \hat{M}_2) \neq (M_1, M_2)\}$.

Definition 4. *A rate pair* (R_1, R_2) *is* **achievable** *subject to distortion level pairs* (D_1, D_2) *and* (D_1', D_2') *if for every* $\epsilon > 0$, *there exist a sequence of encoders* $(\mathcal{M}_1, \mathcal{M}_2, f_N^{(1)}, f_N^{(2)})$ *of length* N *with rate pair* $(R_1 - \epsilon, R_2 - \epsilon)$ *subject to distortion level pair* (D_1, D_2) *such that*

$$\sup_{(\sigma_{V_1}^2, \beta_1) \in \mathcal{A}_1(f_N^{(1)}, D_1')} \sup_{(\sigma_{V_2}^2, \beta_2) \in \mathcal{A}_2(f_N^{(2)}, D_2')} \inf_{\varphi_N \in \mathcal{G}_N} P_e(f_N^{(1)}, f_N^{(2)}, \varphi_N, \sigma_{V_1}^2, \beta_1, \sigma_{V_2}^2, \beta_2) \to 0$$

as $N \to \infty$, *where* $\mathcal{G}_N$ *is the set of all decoders with length* N. *The closure of the set of all achievable pairs is defined as the* **capacity region** *subject to the distortion level pairs* (D_1, D_2) *and* (D_1', D_2').

Now we are ready to state the main result of the present paper.

Theorem 1. *Given distortion level pairs* (D_1, D_2) *and* (D_1', D_2') *with respect to the average square error distortion measure, let* $\mathcal{W}_i(D_i)$ *be the set of all memoryless channels* $W_i(u_i | s_i)$ *with input* S_i *and real-value output* U_i *such that* (S_i, U_i) *is jointly Gaussian and* $Ed(S_i, X_i) \leq D_i$, *where* $X_i = U_i + a_i S_i$. *Then the following region is achievable*

$$\bigcup_{i=1,2, W_i \in \mathcal{W}_i(D_i)} C(W_1, W_2),$$

where $C(W_1, W_2)$ *denotes the region of pairs* (R_1, R_2) *such that*

$$\begin{cases} 0 \leq & R_1 & \leq I(U_1; U_2, Y_1, Y_2) - I(U_1; S_1), \\ 0 \leq & R_2 & \leq I(U_2; U_1, Y_1, Y_2) - I(U_2; S_2), \\ 0 \leq & R_1 + R_2 & \leq I(U_1, U_2; Y_1, Y_2) - I(U_1, U_2; S_1, S_2), \end{cases}$$

$\beta_i = \dfrac{\sigma_{X_i}^2}{\sigma_{X_i}^2 - D_i'}$ *and* $\sigma_{V_i}^2 = \beta_i^2 D_i' - (\beta_i - 1)^2 \sigma_{X_i}^2$, $i = 1, 2$.

Discussions and remarks:

- The region is characterized in single-letter information quantities.
- The technique of random bin coding and typical sequence is utilized to prove the achievability.

- From the main result, $R_1 + R_2$ can achieve $\max_{W_i \in \mathcal{W}_i(D_i), i=1,2}[I(U_1, U_2; Y_1, Y_2) - I(U_1, U_2; S_1, S_2)]$, which in formula is similar to the capacity in case of joint encoding [9]. On the other hand, in Slepian and Wolf's model [11] two memoryless correlated sources are encoded separately and decoded jointly, and their surprising result is that the total rate is the same as that of joint encoding of correlated sources. So, from a viewpoint of source coding the result in the paper is analogous to that of [11] about encoding of correlated sources.
- For facilitating watermarking distortion constraints we restrict memoryless channels $W_i(u_i|s_i)$ such that (S_i, U_i) is jointly Gaussian. However, the result still holds for memoryless channels without such restriction if typical sequence is defined in a more elaborate manner.

3 Preliminaries on Typical Sequences

In this section we give the definitions of typical sequence and jointly typical sequence and some of their properties; detailed treatment on typical sequences can be found in [5].

Definition 5. *Let X be a random variable with pdf $p(x)$ and finite differential entropy $H(X)$, and $\epsilon > 0$ be a small number. If $x^N = (x_1, x_2, \ldots, x_N) \in \mathbb{R}^N$ satisfies*

$$\left| -\frac{1}{N} \log p(x_1, x_2, \ldots, x_N) - H(X) \right| \leq \epsilon$$

where $p(x_1, x_2, \ldots, x_N) = \prod_{j=1}^{N} p(x_j)$, then x^N is called ϵ-typical with respect to $p(x)$. Denote by $A_\epsilon^{(N)}(X)$ the set of all such x^N.

Definition 6. *Let (X, Y) be a random vector with joint pdf $p(x, y)$ and marginal pdfs $p(x), p(y)$. For $\epsilon > 0$ and N, define the joint typical set $A_\epsilon^{(N)}(X, Y)$ with respect to $p(x, y)$ as follows:*

$$A_\epsilon^{(N)}(X, Y) = \left\{ (x^N, y^N) \in \mathbb{R}^N \times \mathbb{R}^N : \begin{array}{l} \left| -\frac{1}{N} \log p(x^N) - H(X) \right| \leq \epsilon \\ \left| -\frac{1}{N} \log p(y^N) - H(Y) \right| \leq \epsilon \\ \left| -\frac{1}{N} \log p(x^N, y^N) - H(X, Y) \right| \leq \epsilon \end{array} \right\}$$

if $p(x, y) \neq p(x)p(y)$, and

$$A_\epsilon^{(N)}(X, Y) = \left\{ (x^N, y^N) \in \mathbb{R}^N \times \mathbb{R}^N : \begin{array}{l} \left| -\frac{1}{N} \log p(x^N) - H(X) \right| \leq \epsilon \\ \left| -\frac{1}{N} \log p(y^N) - H(Y) \right| \leq \epsilon \\ \left| \frac{1}{N} \sum_{j=1}^{N} x_j y_j \right| \leq \epsilon \end{array} \right\}$$

if $p(x, y) = p(x)p(y)$ and $E[X]E[Y] = 0$, where $p(x_1, x_2, \ldots, x_N) = \prod_{j=1}^{N} p(x_j)$, $p(y_1, y_2, \ldots, y_N) = \prod_{j=1}^{N} p(y_j)$, and $p(x_1, x_2, \ldots, x_N, y_1, y_2, \ldots, y_N) = \prod_{j=1}^{N} p(x_j, y_j)$. The pair $(x^N, y^N) \in A_\epsilon^{(N)}(X, Y)$ is called jointly ϵ-typical.

Moreover, for any given $y^N \in A_\epsilon^{(N)}(Y)$, let $A_\epsilon^{(N)}(X, y^N)$ denote the set of all $x^N \in A_\epsilon^{(N)}(X)$ such that $(x^N, y^N) \in A_\epsilon^{(N)}(X, Y)$. Similarly, $A_\epsilon^{(N)}(X, Y, Z, ...)$ can be defined to designate the set of all jointly ϵ-typical sequence $(x^N, y^N, z^N, ...)$ with respect to the joint pdf $p(x, y, z, ...)$ of $(X, Y, Z, ...)$.

Lemma 1. *[5] Let (X, Y) be a random vector with joint pdf $p(x, y)$ and $\epsilon > 0$ be a small number. Then for sufficiently large N*

(1) $2^{-N[H(X)+\epsilon]} \le p(x^N) \le 2^{-N[H(X)-\epsilon]}$ *for any* $x^N \in A_\epsilon^{(N)}(X)$;
(2) $\Pr\{X^N \in A_\epsilon^{(N)}(X)\} > 1 - \epsilon$;
(3) $(1 - \epsilon)2^{N[H(X)-\epsilon]} \le \int_{A_\epsilon^{(N)}(X)} \mathrm{d}x^N \le 2^{N[H(X)+\epsilon]}$.
(4) $\Pr\{(X^N, Y^N) \in A_\epsilon^{(N)}(X, Y)\} > 1 - \epsilon$;
(5) $(1 - \epsilon)2^{N[H(X,Y)-\epsilon]} \le \int_{A_\epsilon^{(N)}(X,Y)} \mathrm{d}x^N \mathrm{d}y^N \le 2^{N[H(X,Y)+\epsilon]}$.

Lemma 2. *Let (X, Y) be a random vector with joint pdf $p(x, y)$ and $\epsilon > 0$ be a small number. Then for sufficiently large N,*

a) with probability at least $1 - \epsilon$, $Y^n = y^n$ satisfies

$$\Pr\{(X^N, Y^N) \text{ is jointly } \epsilon^2\text{-typical} | Y^N = y^N\} \ge 1 - \epsilon; \tag{1}$$

b) with probability at least $1 - \sqrt{\epsilon}$, $Y^n = y^n$ satisfies

$$(1 - \sqrt{\epsilon})2^{N[H(X|Y)-2\epsilon]} \le \int_{A_\epsilon^{(N)}(X,y^N)} \mathrm{d}x^N \le 2^{N[H(X|Y)+2\epsilon]}; \tag{2}$$

c) with probability at least $1 - \sqrt{\epsilon}$, $Y^n = y^n$ satisfies

$$(1 - \sqrt{\epsilon})2^{-N[I(X;Y)+3\epsilon]} \le \int_{A_\epsilon^{(N)}(X,y^N)} p(x^N)\mathrm{d}x^N \le 2^{-N[I(X;Y)-3\epsilon]}. \tag{3}$$

The proof of the lemma will be given in the Appendix.

4   The Optimal Attack Channel

For any given watermarking encoders $f_N^{(1)}, f_N^{(2)}$, let $\sigma^2_{f_N^{(i)}} = \frac{1}{N}E(X_i^N)^2$, where $X_i^N = f_N^{(i)}(M_i, S_i^N) + a_i S_i^N$ and $(X_i^N)^2$ denotes the sum of the squared value of components of X_i^N. If $\sigma^2_{f_N^{(i)}} \le D_i'$, $i = 1, 2$, then the attacker can always choose the forgery $Y_i^N = 0$, resulting in a zero embedding rate for encoder $f_N^{(i)}$. So, we assume $\sigma^2_{f_N^{(i)}} > D_i'$, and let

$$A_i^*(f_N^{(i)}, D_i') = \{(\sigma^2_{V_i}, \beta_i) : \beta_i^{-2}\sigma^2_{V_i} + (\beta_i^{-1} - 1)^2\sigma^2_{f_N^{(i)}} = D_i'\}.$$

Then

$$\sup_{(\sigma_{V_i}^2, \beta_i) \in \mathcal{A}_i(f_N^{(i)}, D_i'), i=1,2} \inf_{\varphi_N \in \mathcal{G}_N} P_e(f_N^{(1)}, f_N^{(2)}, \varphi_N, \sigma_{V_1}^2, \beta_1, \sigma_{V_2}^2, \beta_2)$$

$$= \sup_{(\sigma_{V_i}^2, \beta_i) \in \mathcal{A}_i^*(f_N^{(i)}, D_i'), i=1,2} \inf_{\varphi_N \in \mathcal{G}_N} P_e(f_N^{(1)}, f_N^{(2)}, \varphi_N, \sigma_{V_1}^2, \beta_1, \sigma_{V_2}^2, \beta_2).$$

Now, let $\sigma_{V_i}^2 = \beta_i^2 D_i' - (\beta_i - 1)^2 \sigma_{f_N^{(i)}}^2$, and define

$$f(\sigma_1^2, \sigma_2^2) = \sup_{(\sigma_{V_i}^2, \beta_i) \in \mathcal{A}_i^*(f_N^{(i)}, D_i'): \sigma_{V_i}^2 = \sigma_i^2, i=1,2} \inf_{\varphi_N \in \mathcal{G}_N} P_e(f_N^{(1)}, f_N^{(2)}, \varphi_N, \sigma_{V_1}^2, \beta_1, \sigma_{V_2}^2, \beta_2).$$

Then $f(\sigma_1^2, \sigma_2^2)$ is a non-decreasing function of σ_1^2, σ_2^2. So the optimal attack channel must meet a) $\beta_i^{-2} \sigma_{V_i}^2 + (\beta_i^{-1} - 1)^2 \sigma_{f_N^{(i)}}^2 = D_i'$, and b) $\sigma_{V_i}^2$ should be as large as possible. It is easy to see that as a function of β_i, $\sigma_{V_i}^2$ achieves the maximum at $\beta_i = \frac{\sigma_{f_N^{(i)}}^2}{\sigma_{f_N^{(i)}}^2 - D_i'}$. Therefore, in the following, we shall fix the optimal β_i and the corresponding $\sigma_{V_i}^2$ for the given encoders $f_N^{(i)}$, $i = 1, 2$.

5   Proofs

This section is devoted to the proof of our main result, that is, for any channels $W_i(\cdot|\cdot) \in \mathcal{W}_i(D_i)$, $(R_1, R_2) \in C(W_1, W_2)$ is achievable with respect to distortion level pairs (D_1, D_2) and (D_1', D_2'). Let $\epsilon > 0$ be sufficiently small and N large enough.

5.1   Random Coding Scheme

To show the achievability, the following random bin coding argument is employed.

- **Codebook Generation**: For each watermark $m_i \in \mathcal{M}_i = \{1, 2, \ldots, 2^{N(R_i - 3\epsilon)}\}$, $i = 1, 2$, user i generates at random $t_i = 2^{N[I(U_i; S_i) + 2\epsilon]}$ vectors $C_i(m_i) = \{\tilde{u}_i^N(m_i, 1), \ldots, \tilde{u}_i^N(m_i, l_i), \ldots, \tilde{u}_i^N(m_i, t_i)\}$, of which each component is generated independently by a real-valued random variable $\tilde{U}_i$ with the same pdf as U_i, which is derived from W_i. Denote the codebook of user i as $C_i = \{C_i(m_i)\}_{m_i=1}^{2^{N(R_i - 3\epsilon)}}$.
- **Encoding**: For any given watermark m_i and covertext s_i^N, user i chooses the first $\tilde{u}_i^N(m_i, l_i)$ in $C_i(m_i)$ such that $(\tilde{u}_i^N(m_i, l_i), s_i^N)$ is jointly ϵ-typical with respect to the joint pdf of (U_i, S_i) determined by $W_i(\cdot|\cdot)$, and then generates a stegotext $x_i^N = \tilde{u}_i^N(m_i, l_i) + a_i s_i^N$. If no such a $\tilde{u}_i^N(m_i, l_i)$ is found in $C_i(m_i)$, then an encoding error is declared, and let the output be zero.

- **Decoding**: Given y_1^N and y_2^N, the decoder finds $(\tilde{u}_1^N(\hat{m}_1, l_1), \tilde{u}_2^N(\hat{m}_2, l_2)) \in C_1 \times C_2$ such that $(\tilde{u}_1^N(\hat{m}_1, l_1), \tilde{u}_2^N(\hat{m}_2, l_2), y_1^N, y_2^N)$ is jointly ϵ-typical with respect to the joint pdf of (U_1, U_2, Y_1, Y_2), and then decodes the watermarks $(\hat{m}_1, \hat{m}_2)$.
  Note that $X_i = U_i + a_i S_i$, $Y_i = \beta_i^{-1}(X_i + V_i)$ and $V_i \sim N(0, \sigma_{V_i}^2)$ where $\beta_i, \sigma_{V_i}^2$ are specified in the main theorem. So W_i induce a joint pdf of (U_1, U_2, Y_1, Y_2), which is used for decoding.

5.2   Analysis of Error Probability of Coding

For any deterministic codebook $C = (C_1, C_2)$, let $P_e(C_1, C_2)$ be the error probability of coding averaged over all M_i, S_i^N. Since the watermarks are drawn uniformly, without loss of generality, it's assumed $M_1 = m_1$,$M_2 = m_2$, and let

$$P_e(C) = \int_{s_1^N} \int_{s_2^N} p(s_1^N, s_2^N) \Pr\{(\hat{M}_1, \hat{M}_2) \neq (m_1, m_2)|m_1, m_2, s_1^N, s_2^N\} ds_1^N ds_2^N$$

and $P_e = EP_e(C)$ be the error probability averaged over the random codebook $C = (C_1, C_2)$.

- **Encoding Error:** For a codebook $C = (C_1, C_2)$, let $E(C_1, C_2)$ be the event that an encoding error occurs, that is,

$$\bigcup_{i=1,2}\{S_i^N \notin A_\epsilon^{(N)}(S_i)\} \qquad \bigcup_{\substack{i=1,2 \\ s_i^N \in A_\epsilon^{(N)}(S_i)}} \{(\tilde{u}_i^N, s_i^N) \notin A_\epsilon^{(N)}(U_i, S_i) \text{ for all } \tilde{u}_i^N \in C_i(m_i)\}.$$

Then

$$\Pr\{E(C_1, C_2)\} \leq \sum_{i=1,2} \Pr\{S_i^N \notin A_\epsilon^{(N)}(S_i)\}$$

$$+ \sum_{i=1,2} \int_{s_i^N \in A_\epsilon^{(N)}(S_i)} \Pr\{(\tilde{u}_i^N, s_i^N) \notin A_\epsilon^{(N)}(U_i, S_i) \text{ for all } \tilde{u}_i^N \in C_i(m_i)\} d\, s_i^N$$

$$\leq 2\epsilon + \delta(C_1, C_2), \tag{4}$$

where the last inequality follows Lemma 1-(2), and

$$\delta(C_1, C_2) = \sum_{i=1,2} \int_{s_i^N \in A_\epsilon^{(N)}(S_i)} \Pr\{(\tilde{u}_i^N, s_i^N) \notin A_\epsilon^{(N)}(U_i, S_i) \text{ for all } \tilde{u}_i^N \in C_i(m_i)\} d\, s_i^N.$$

In virtue of the inequality $(1 - t)^m \leq \exp(-tm)$, one has

$$E_{C_1, C_2}\delta(C_1, C_2) = \sum_{i=1,2} \int_{s_i^N \in A_\epsilon^{(N)}(S_i)} E_{C_1, C_2} \Pr\{(\tilde{U}_i^N, s_i^N) \notin A_\epsilon^{(N)}(U_i, S_i)$$

$$\text{for all } \tilde{U}_i^N \in C_i(m_i)\} d\, s_i^N$$

$$= \sum_{i=1,2} \int_{s_i^N \in A_\epsilon^{(N)}(S_i)} \left(\Pr\{(\tilde{U}_i^N, s_i^N) \notin A_\epsilon^{(N)}(U_i, S_i)\}\right)^{2^{N[I(U_i; S_i) + 2\epsilon]}} d\, s_i^N$$

$$\overset{(a)}{\leq} \sum_{i=1,2} \int_{s_i^N \in A_\epsilon^{(N)}(S_i)} \left(1 - 2^{-N[I(U_i;S_i)+\epsilon]}\right)^{2^{N[I(U_i;S_i)+2\epsilon]}} d s_i^N$$

$$\leq 2^{-2^{N\epsilon}}$$

for sufficiently large N, where (a) follows Lemma 2-(c). Therefore, by the Markov Inequality,

$$\Pr\{\delta(C_1,C_2) > 2^{-2^{N\epsilon-1}}\} \leq \frac{\mathrm{E}_{C_1,C_2}\delta(C_1,C_2)}{2^{-2^{N\epsilon-1}}} \leq 2^{-2^{N\epsilon-1}}. \tag{5}$$

Combing (4) and (5) yields

$$\Pr\{E(C_1,C_2)\} \leq 3\epsilon \tag{6}$$

with high probability as N goes to infinity.

- **Distortion Constraints:** For a codebook C, let

$$B_C(i) = \{s_i^N \in \mathbb{R}^N : \text{encoding } s_i^N \text{ is successful}\},$$

$$\bar{B}_C(i) = \{s_i^N \in \mathbb{R}^N : \text{encoding } s_i^N \text{ is not successful}\}.$$

Then

$$\begin{aligned}
\mathrm{E}[d(X_i^N, S_i^N)|C] &= \int_{B_C(i)} p(s_i^N) d(x_i^N, s_i^N) ds_i^N + \int_{\bar{B}_C(i)} p(s_i^N)(s_i^N)^2/N ds_i^N \\
&\leq \int_{B_C(i)} p(s_i^N) d(x_i^N, s_i^N) ds_i^N + D_0 \Pr\{\bar{B}_C(i)\} \\
&\leq \int_{B_C(i)} p(s_i^N) d(x_i^N, s_i^N) ds_i^N + 3\epsilon D_0
\end{aligned}$$

by (6), where D_0 is a constant. If $s_i^N \in B_C(i)$, then there exists $\tilde{u}_i^N \in C_i(m_i)$ such that $(s_i^N, \tilde{u}_i^N)$ is jointly ϵ-typical, and it is easy to verify that

$$\left| \frac{1}{N} \sum_j s_{ij}^2 - \sigma_{S_i}^2 \right| < \frac{2\sigma_{S_i}^2}{\log e}\epsilon, \quad \left| \frac{1}{N} \sum_j \tilde{u}_{ij}^2 - \sigma_{U_i}^2 \right| < \frac{2\sigma_{U_i}^2}{\log e}\epsilon.$$

Moreover, $\left| \frac{1}{N} \sum_{j=1}^N s_{ij}\tilde{u}_{ij} \right| < \epsilon$ if S_i and U_i are independent, and $\left| \frac{1}{N} \sum_j s_{ij}\tilde{u}_{ij} \right.$
$\left. -\mathrm{E}(S_i U_i) \right| < \frac{\epsilon(3-\rho_i^2)\sigma_{S_i}\sigma_{U_i}}{\rho_i \log e}$ if S_i and U_i are dependent and $\rho_i \neq 0$.

Since W_i are chosen such that (S_i, U_i) is jointly Gaussian and $Ed(S_i, X_i) < D_i$, we have

$$(a_i - 1)^2\sigma_{S_i}^2 + \sigma_{U_i}^2 + 2(a_i - 1)\mathrm{E}(U_i S_i) < D_i - \delta',$$

where δ' can be as small as possible. Thus, $d(x_i^N, s_i^N) = \frac{1}{N}\sum_{j=1}^N (x_{ij} - s_{ij})^2 < (a_i - 1)^2\sigma_{S_i}^2 + \sigma_{U_i}^2 + 2(a_i - 1)\mathrm{E}(U_i S_i) + \delta < D_i - \delta' + \delta$, where $\delta =$

$\left[(a_i - 1)^2 \frac{2\sigma_{S_i}^2}{\log e} + \frac{2\sigma_{U_i}^2}{\log e} + 2(a_i - 1)\frac{(3-\rho_i^2)\sigma_{S_i}\sigma_{U_i}}{\rho_i \log e}\right]\epsilon$. So, with high probability $E[d(X_i^N, S_i^N)|C] \leq D_i + \delta + 3\epsilon D_0 - \delta'$. Since δ and ϵ can small enough, for any codebook C, with high probability the encoding distortion constraints are met.

- **Decoding Error:** Fix a codebook $C = (C_1, C_2)$. For any $(s_1^N, s_2^N) \in A_\epsilon^{(N)}(S_1, S_2)$. Define the following events:

$$A_1(s_1^N, s_2^N) = \left\{ \text{no } (\tilde{u}_1^N, \tilde{u}_2^N) \in C_1 \times C_2 \text{ such that } (\tilde{u}_1^N, \tilde{u}_2^N, Y_1^N, Y_2^N) \right.$$
$$\left. \in A_\epsilon^{(N)}(U_1, U_2, Y_1, Y_2) \right\},$$

$$A_2(s_1^N, s_2^N) = \left\{ \exists (\tilde{u}_1^N, \tilde{u}_2^N) \in C_1(m_1) \times C_2(\hat{m}_2) \text{ such that } \right.$$
$$\left. (\tilde{u}_1^N, \tilde{u}_2^N, Y_1^N, Y_2^N) \in A_\epsilon^{(N)}(U_1, U_2, Y_1, Y_2) \text{ and } \hat{m}_2 \neq m_2 \right\},$$

$$A_3(s_1^N, s_2^N) = \left\{ \exists (\tilde{u}_1^N, \tilde{u}_2^N) \in C_1(\hat{m}_1) \times C_2(m_2) \text{ such that } \right.$$
$$\left. (\tilde{u}_1^N, \tilde{u}_2^N, Y_1^N, Y_2^N) \in A_\epsilon^{(N)}(U_1, U_2, Y_1, Y_2) \text{ and } \hat{m}_1 \neq m_1 \right\},$$

$$A_4(s_1^N, s_2^N) = \left\{ \exists (\tilde{u}_1^N, \tilde{u}_2^N) \in C_1(\hat{m}_1) \times C_2(\hat{m}_2) \text{ such that } (\tilde{u}_1^N, \tilde{u}_2^N, Y_1^N, Y_2^N) \right.$$
$$\left. \in A_\epsilon^{(N)}(U_1, U_2, Y_1, Y_2) \text{ and } \hat{m}_1 \neq m_1 \text{ and } \hat{m}_2 \neq m_2 \right\}.$$

In the following, we shall analyze the probabilities of events $A_j(s_1^N, s_2^N), j = 1, 2, 3, 4$.

(I). On the one hand, the probability of successful encoding s_i^N and m_i is greater than $1 - \epsilon/2$. On the other hand, if encoding s_i^N and m_i is successful, then there exist codewords $\tilde{u}_1^N, \tilde{u}_2^N$ such that $(\tilde{u}_1^N, \tilde{u}_2^N, s_1^N, s_2^N) \in A_\epsilon^{(N)}(U_1, U_2, S_1, S_2)$. Moreover, as $N \to \infty$,

$$\Pr\{(\tilde{u}_1^N, \tilde{u}_2^N, Y_1^N, Y_2^N) \in A_\epsilon^{(N)}(U_1, U_2, Y_1, Y_2)| \text{ successful encoding}\} \geq 1 - \epsilon/2$$

since the attack channel is memoryless.
Thus, as $N \to \infty$

$$E_{C_1, C_2} \Pr\{A_1(s_1^N, s_2^N)\} \leq 1 - (1 - \epsilon/2)^2 \leq \epsilon. \tag{7}$$

(II).

$$E_{C_1, C_2} \Pr\{A_2(s_1^N, s_2^N)|\overline{A_1(s_1^N, s_2^N)}\}$$

$$\overset{(c)}{\leq} 2^{N[I(U_2;S_2)+R_2-\epsilon]} \int_{(\tilde{u}_1^N, y_1^N, y_2^N) \in A_\epsilon^{(N)}(U_1, Y_1, Y_2)} p(\tilde{u}_1^N, y_1^N, y_2^N) \tag{8}$$

$$\left(\Pr\{(\tilde{U}_2^N, \tilde{u}_1^N, y_1^N, y_2^N) \in A_\epsilon^{(N)}(U_2, U_1, Y_1, Y_2)\} \right) d\tilde{u}_1^N dy_1^N dy_2^N$$

$$\overset{(d)}{\leq} 2^{-N[I(U_2;U_1, Y_1, Y_2)-R_2-I(U_2;S_2)+\epsilon-\epsilon_1]}, \tag{9}$$

where (c) follows from the fact that $\tilde{U}_2^N$ is independent of $\tilde{U}_1^N, Y_1^N, Y_2^N$ since m_2 is transmitted and $\hat{M}_2 \neq m_2$, and $\epsilon_1 \to 0$ as $N \to \infty$, and (d) is derived from Lemma 2-(c). In a symmetrical manner, we have

$$\mathrm{E}_{C_1,C_2}\Pr\{A_3(s_1^N,s_2^N)|\overline{A_1(s_1^N,s_2^N)}\} \le 2^{-N[I(U_1;U_2,Y_1,Y_2)-R_1-I(U_1;S_1)+\epsilon-\epsilon_2]},$$

(10)

where $\epsilon_2 \to 0$ as $N \to \infty$.

(III).

$$\mathrm{E}_{C_1,C_2}\Pr\{A_4(s_1^N,s_2^N)|\overline{A_1(s_1^N,s_2^N)}\} \le \int_{(y_1^N,y_2^N)\in A_\epsilon^{(N)}(Y_1,Y_2)} p(y_1^N,y_2^N)$$

$$\cdot \sum_{\substack{\tilde{U}_1^N \notin C_1(m_1),\tilde{U}_2^N \notin C_2(m_2)\\(\tilde{U}_1^N,\tilde{U}_2^N)\in A_\epsilon^{(N)}(U_1,U_2)}} \Pr\{(\tilde{U}_1^N,\tilde{U}_2^N,y_1^N,y_2^N) \in A_\epsilon^{(N)}(U_1,U_2,Y_1,Y_2)\}$$

$$\le \int_{(y_1^N,y_2^N)\in A_\epsilon^{(N)}(Y_1,Y_2)} p(y_1^N,y_2^N) \sum_{\substack{\tilde{U}_1^N \notin C_1(m_1),\tilde{U}_2^N \notin C_2(m_2)\\(\tilde{U}_1^N,\tilde{U}_2^N)\in A_\epsilon^{(N)}(U_1,U_2)}} 2^{-N[I(U_1,U_2;Y_1,Y_2)-\epsilon_3]}.$$

By noting that the number of pairs $(\tilde{u}_1^N,\tilde{u}_2^N) \in C_1 \times C_2 \bigcap A_\epsilon^{(N)}(U_1,U_2)$ for any fixed C_1 and C_2 is about $2^{N[I(U_1,U_2;S_1,S_2)+R_1+R_2]}$, one has

$$\mathrm{E}_{C_1,C_2}\Pr\{A_4(s_1^N,s_2^N)|\overline{A_1(s_1^N,s_2^N)}\}$$
$$\le 2^{-N[I(U_1,U_2;Y_1,Y_2)-I(U_1,U_2;S_1,S_2)-R_1-R_2-\epsilon_3]},$$

where $\epsilon_3 \to 0$ as $N \to \infty$.

Since

$$0 \le \quad R_1 \quad < I(U_1;U_2,Y_1,Y_2) - I(U_1;S_1),$$
$$0 \le \quad R_2 \quad < I(U_2;U_1,Y_1,Y_2) - I(U_2;S_2),$$
$$0 \le R_1 + R_2 < I(U_1,U_2;Y_1,Y_2) - I(U_1,U_2;S_1,S_1),$$

one has $P_e < 7\epsilon$ as $N \to \infty$. Note the probability P_e depends on the attack channel which is determined by the random code instead of the desired deterministic code. We denote the attack channel $A(W_1,W_2)$, and rewrite P_e as $P_e(W_1,W_2)$. Also the attack channel depending on the encoders $(f_N^{(1)},f_N^{(2)})$ is designed by $A(f_N^{(1)},f_N^{(2)})$ and the corresponding probability is denoted by $P_e(f_N^{(1)},f_N^{(2)})$.

Since the random variable $A(f_N^{(1)},f_N^{(2)})$ converges to $A(W_1,W_2)$ in probability for large enough N, with high probability

$$A(f_N^{(1)},f_N^{(2)})(y_1,y_2|x_1,x_2) < (1+\epsilon)A(W_1,W_2)(y_1,y_2|x_1,x_2).$$

Thus, with high probability $P_e(f_N^{(1)},f_N^{(2)}) < (1+\epsilon)^N \, P_e(W_1,W_2) < 8\epsilon$. The proof is finished.

6　Gains Obtained from the Correlated Sources

In this section, we will give an example to illustrate the gain region obtained by using correlated covertext sources over independent ones.

Let D_1, D_2 be the distortion levels of two users, and $D' = (D'_1, D'_2)$ be the distortion level of the attacker and let $\sigma_i^2 = \sigma_{S_i}^2$. Let $X_i = b_i S_i + Z_i$ for some $b_i > 0$ and $U_i = \alpha_i S_i + Z_i$, where Z_i are Gaussian random variables with mean zero and variance $\sigma_{Z_i}^2 = D_i - (b_i - 1)^2 \sigma_i^2$ and is independent of all other random variables, and let

$$\beta_i = \frac{\sigma_{X_i}^2}{\sigma_{X_i}^2 - D'_i}, \alpha_i = \frac{\sigma_{Z_i}^2}{\sigma_{Z_i}^2 + \beta_i D'_i}.$$

It is easy to verify that the covariance matrix of the random vector (U_1, U_2, Y_1, Y_2) is given by

$$\begin{bmatrix} \sigma_{U_1}^2 & \alpha_1 \alpha_2 \rho \sigma_1 \sigma_2 & \frac{(\alpha_1 b_1 \sigma_1^2 + \sigma_{Z_1}^2)}{\beta_1} & \frac{\alpha_1 b_2 \rho \sigma_1 \sigma_2}{\beta_2} \\ \alpha_1 \alpha_2 \rho \sigma_1 \sigma_2 & \sigma_{U_2}^2 & \frac{\alpha_2 b_1 \rho \sigma_1 \sigma_2}{\beta_1} & \frac{(\alpha_2 b_2 \sigma_2^2 + \sigma_{Z_2}^2)}{\beta_2} \\ \frac{(\alpha_1 b_1 \sigma_1^2 + \sigma_{Z_1}^2)}{\beta_1} & \frac{\alpha_2 b_1 \rho \sigma_1 \sigma_2}{\beta_1} & \sigma_{Y_1}^2 & \frac{b_1 b_2 \rho \sigma_1 \sigma_2}{\beta_1 \beta_2} \\ \frac{\alpha_1 b_2 \rho \sigma_1 \sigma_2}{\beta_2} & \frac{(\alpha_2 b_2 \sigma_2^2 + \sigma_{Z_2}^2)}{\beta_2} & \frac{b_1 b_2 \rho \sigma_1 \sigma_2}{\beta_1 \beta_2} & \sigma_{Y_2}^2 \end{bmatrix},$$

from which all information quantities for calculation of the achievable region can be derived.

Example: Let $\sigma_1 = 10, \sigma_2 = 10, D_1 = 40, D_2 = 40, D'_1 = 10, D'_2 = 10$. If the two users' covertexts are uncorrelated, that is, $\rho = 0$, then capacity of user i is 1.118519599 bits. While if $\rho = 0.5, 0.9$, point $(1.118519608, 1.118519608)$ and $(1.118519642, 1.118519642)$ are achievable respectively. A typical region is shown in Figure 2.

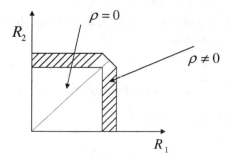

Fig. 2. The gain region

7   Conclusion

In this paper we give in single-letter information quantities an achievable region of a public multiple-access Gaussian watermarking system in which two covertexts are generated by correlated Gaussian sources, and from a viewpoint of source coding our result is analogous to that of Slepian and Wolf in the sense that the total rate of separate encoding is the same as that of joint encoding. Moreover an example is utilized to demonstrate the gain region of correlated covertext sources over uncorrelated ones.

Appendix

Proof of Lemma 2: a) Let B be the event that (X^N, Y^N) are jointly ϵ^2-typical, and B_{y^N} the event that (X^N, y^N) are jointly ϵ^2-typical for $y^N \in A_\epsilon^{(N)}(Y)$. Then by the Markov Inequality

$$\Pr\{Y^N = y^N : \Pr\{B_{Y^N} | Y^N = y^N\} \geq 1 - \epsilon\}$$
$$= 1 - \Pr\{Y^N = y^N : \Pr\{B_{Y^N}^c | Y^N = y^N\} \geq \epsilon\}$$
$$\geq 1 - \frac{\mathrm{E}[\Pr\{B_{Y^N}^c | Y^N\}]}{\epsilon} = 1 - \frac{\Pr\{B^c\}}{\epsilon} \geq 1 - \epsilon,$$

where A^c denotes the complementary event of A.

b) For any $y^N \in A_\epsilon^{(N)}(Y)$, it is easy to verify that in view of Lemma 1, we have

$$2^{-N(H(X,Y)+\epsilon)} \int_{x^N \in A_\epsilon^{(N)}(X,y^N)} dx^N \leq \int_{x^N \in A_\epsilon^{(N)}(X,y^N)} p(x^N, y^N) dx^N$$
$$\leq p(y^N) \leq 2^{-N(H(Y)-\epsilon)}$$

which implies the

$$\int_{x^N \in A_\epsilon^{(N)}(X,y^N)} dx^N \leq 2^{N[H(X|Y)+2\epsilon]}$$

On the other hand, it follows from a) that with probability at least $1 - \sqrt{\epsilon}$, $Y^n = y^N \in A_\epsilon^{(N)}(Y)$ satisfies

$$\Pr\{A_\epsilon^{(N)}(X,y^N) | Y^N = y^N\} \geq 1 - \sqrt{\epsilon} \tag{11}$$

In view of Lemma 1 again, we have for any $y^N \in A_\epsilon^{(N)}(Y)$ satisfying (11),

$$2^{-N(H(Y)+\epsilon)}(1 - \sqrt{\epsilon}) \leq \int_{x^N \in A_\epsilon^{(N)}(X,y^N)} p(x^N, y^N) dx^N$$
$$\leq 2^{-N(H(X,Y)-\epsilon)} \int_{x^N \in A_\epsilon^{(N)}(X,y^N)} dx^N$$

which, together with (11), implies (2). This completes the proof of b).

c) For $y^N \in A_\epsilon^{(N)}(Y)$ satisfying (2), it follows from Lemma 1 that

$$(1 - \sqrt{\epsilon})2^{-N[I(X;Y)+3\epsilon]} = (1 - \sqrt{\epsilon})2^{N[H(X|Y)-2\epsilon]} \cdot 2^{-N[H(X)+\epsilon]}$$
$$\leq \int_{A_\epsilon^{(N)}(X,y^N)} p(x^N) dx^N \leq 2^{-N[H(X)-\epsilon]} \cdot 2^{N[H(X|Y)+2\epsilon]}$$
$$= 2^{-N[I(X;Y)-3\epsilon]}.$$

$\square$

References

1. R. J. Barron, B. Chen and G. W. Wornell, The duality between information embedding and source coding with side information and some applications, *IEEE Trans. Inform. Theory*, vol. 49, pp. 1159-1180, May 2003.
2. B. Chen and G. W. Wornell, Quantization index modulation: A class of provably good methods for digital watermarking and information embedding, *IEEE Trans. Inform. Theory*, vol. 47, pp. 1423-1443, May 2001.
3. A. S. Cohen and Amos Lapidoth, The Gaussian Watermarking Game, *IEEE Trans. Inform. Theory*, vol. 48, pp. 1639-1667, June 2002.
4. M. H. M. Costa, Writing on dirty paper, *IEEE Trans. Inform. Theory*, vol. 29, pp. 439-441, May 1983.
5. T. M. Cover and J. A. Thomas, *Elements of Information Theory*, New York: John Wiley & Sons, 1991.
6. I. Cox, M. Miller and J. Bloom, *Digital Watermarking*, Elsevier Science: Morgan Kaufmann Publishers, 2001.
7. S. I. Gel'fand and M. S. Pinsker, Coding for channel with random parameters, *Probl. Contr. Inform. Theory*, Vol. 9, no. 1, pp. 19–31, 1980.
8. N. Merhav, On Random Coding Error Exponents of Watermarking Systems, *IEEE Trans. Inform. Theory*, Vol. 46, pp. 420–430, March 2000.
9. P. Moulin and J. A. O'Sullivan, Information-theoretic analysis of information hiding, *IEEE Trans. Inform. Theory*, vol. 49, pp. 563–593, March 2003.
10. P. Moulin and M. K. Mihcak, The Parallel-Gaussian Watermarking Game, *IEEE Trans. Inform. Theory*, vol.50, pp. 272 - 289, Feb. 2004.
11. D. Slepian and J. K. Wolf, Noiseless coding of correlated information sources, *IEEE Trans. Inform. Theory*, Vol. 19, pp. 471–480, July 1973.
12. A. Somekh-Baruch and N. Merhav, On the Error Exponent and Capacity Games of Private Watermarking Systems, *IEEE Trans. Inform. Theory*, vol. 49, pp. 537-562, March 2003.
13. A. Somekh-Baruch and N. Merhav, On the Capacity Game of Public Watermarking Systems,*IEEE Trans. Inform. Theory*, vol. 50, pp. 511 - 524. March 2004.
14. A. Somekh-Baruch and N. Merhav, On the capacity game of private fingerprinting systems under collusion attacks, available at http://www-ee.technion.ac.il/∼merhav/.
15. J. K. Su, J. J. Eggers and B. Girod, Capacity of Digital Watermarks Subjected to an Optimal Collusion Attack, European Signal Processing Conference (EUSIPCO 2000), Tampere, Finland, September 2000.
16. W. Sun and E. H. Yang, On the Capacity Regions of Public Multiple-Access Digital Watermarking Systems, in preparation.

Fixed-Distortion Orthogonal Dirty Paper Coding for Perceptual Still Image Watermarking

Andrea Abrardo and Mauro Barni

Department of Information Engineering, University of Siena
Via Roma 56, 53100 Siena, ITALY
{abrardo barni}@dii.unisi.it

Abstract. A new informed image watermarking technique is proposed incorporating perceptual factors into dirty paper coding. Due to the equi-energetic nature of the adopted codewords and to the use of a correlation-based decoder, invariance to constant value-metric scaling (gain attack) is automatically achieved. By exploiting the simple structure of orthogonal and Gold codes, an optimal informed embedding technique is developed, permitting to maximize the watermark robustness while keeping the embedding distortion constant. The maximum admissible distortion level is computed on a block by block basis, by using Watson's model of the Human Visual System (HVS). The performance of the watermarking algorithm are improved by concatenating dirty paper coding with a turbo coding (decoding) step. The validity of the assumptions underlying the theoretical analysis is evaluated by means of numerical simulations. Experimental results confirm the effectiveness of the proposed approach.

1 Introduction

Several digital watermarking methods trying to put into practice the hints stemming from the information-theoretic analysis of the watermarking game have been proposed. The main merit of these schemes, globally termed as informed watermarking algorithms, is that they permit to completely reject the interference between the cover signal and the watermark, thus leading to systems in which, in the absence of attacks, a zero error probability is obtained.

Random binning coding (or dirty paper coding) lies at the hearth of the informed watermarking approach [1]. To be specific, let us introduce an auxiliary source of randomness U, let B indicate the set with all the possible to-be-hidden messages, and let 2^{nR} be the number of messages contained in it. Finally, let C be the source emitting the cover feature sequence. The embedder first generates a codebook $\mathcal{U}$ consisting of 2^{nR_t} entries (call them **u**'s) which are randomly generated so to span uniformly the set of typical sequences of $\mathcal{U}$ (for a tutorial introduction to typical sequences see [2, 3]). Then $\mathcal{U}$ is randomly (and uniformly) split into 2^{nR} bins (sub-codebooks) each containing $2^{n(R_t-R)}$ codewords. It is then possible to associate each message $\mathbf{b} \in B$ to a bin of $\mathcal{U}$. In order to transmit a message **b**, the embedder looks at the host feature sequence **c** that is going to host the message, then an entry in the bin indexed by **b** is looked for which is jointly typical with **c**. Next it maps the cover features **c** into a marked feature sequence $\mathbf{c}_w$ which is jointly typical with **u** and **c** . At the other side, the decoder

J. Fridrich (Ed.): IH 2004, LNCS 3200, pp. 52–66, 2004.
© Springer-Verlag Berlin Heidelberg 2004

receives a sequence **r**. In order to estimate the transmitted message, the decoder looks for a unique sequence **u*** in $\mathcal{U}$ which is jointly typical with **r** and outputs the message corresponding to the bin **u*** belongs to. The decoder declares an error if more than one, or no such typical sequence exists. If R is lower than the watermarking capacity then it is possible to choose R_t so that the error probability averaged over al possible codes $\mathcal{U}$ tends to 0 as the length n of the transmitted sequence tends to infinity. The major problem with the random binning approach is that when n increases the dimension of the codebook becomes unmanageable, thus calling for the construction of structured codebooks allowing for an efficient search.

The most popular solution to put the random binning approach into practice is through the use of lattice based codebooks [4, 5, 6, 7]. The major weakness of the lattice approach, is that these schemes are vulnerable against constant value-metric scaling of the host features, a very common operation which consists in multiplying the host feature sequence by a constant factor g which is unknown to the decoder.

To overcome this problem, Miller et al. [8, 9] proposed to use equi-energetic codebooks and a correlation-based decoder, so that invariance to the presence of the constant gain g is automatically achieved. Their system relies on a dirty paper Trellis in which several paths are associated to the same message.

Of course equi-energetic codes do a much worse job in uniformly covering the host feature space, hence it is necessary to devise a particular embedding strategy which permits to move the host features sequence into a point within the decoding region associated to the to-be-transmitted message. This can be done either by fixing the watermark robustness and trying to minimize the embedding distortion, or by fixing the embedding distortion while maximizing the watermark robustness. In [8, 9], a sub-optimum, fixed-robustness, embedding strategy is proposed. In [10], the simple structure of orthogonal, and pseudo-orthogonal, codes is exploited to derive an optimum fixed-robustness embedding algorithm leading to performance which are superior to those obtained by Miller et al. with the further advantage of a reduced computational burden.

A difficulty with the fixed-robustness approach, is that the robustness constraint does not allow to take perceptual factors into account. As a matter of fact, in order to diminish the visibility[1] of the watermark, it is desirable that some features are marked less heavily than others, leading to a constraint on the maximum allowable distortion. In this paper, we extend the analysis contained in [10], to develop a fixed-distortion embedding algorithm for still image watermarking. Then we will use such an algorithm to incorporate perceptually driven considerations within the embedding step. Watermark embedding is performed in the block-DCT domain, since the Human Visual System (HVS) behavior is better modelled by working in the frequency domain. More specifically, we rely on the popular Watson's model [11, 12] measuring the maximum allowable distortion a block-DCT coefficient can sustain before the modification becomes visible. Watson's measure is used to constrain the maximum allowable embedding distortion on a block-by block basis.

Experiments and simulations were carried out to validate both the effectiveness of the proposed embedding strategy and to estimate the overall performance of the new watermarking system in terms of invisibility and robustness. In particular, the experi-

---

[1] We focus on still image watermarking.

ments demonstrated an excellent robustness against attacks involving scaling of the host features and a moderate robustness against more classical attacks such as noise addition and JPEG compression. Watermark invisibility was satisfactorily reached as well.

This paper is organized as follows. In section 2 the basic ideas behind dirty paper coding by means of orthogonal codes are reviewed. In section 3 the optimal algorithm for fixed-distortion embedding is derived, and the extension to quasi-orthogonal dirty paper coding presented. Section 4 explains how perceptual factors are incorporated within the fixed-distortion embedding scheme. The adoption of multistage (turbo) decoding to improve the overall performance of the system is described in section 5. Simulation and experimental results are presented in section 6. Finally, in section 7 some conclusions are drawn and directions for future research highlighted.

2   Orthogonal Dirty Paper Coding

In this section we briefly review the basic ideas of orthogonal dirty paper coding. For a more detailed analysis readers are referred to [10].

Let $\mathbf{c}$ represent the cover feature vector of length $n = 2^w$ and $\mathbf{U}$ a real $n \times n$ unitary matrix such as $\mathbf{U}^T\mathbf{U} = \mathbf{I}_n$ [2]. Each column of $\mathbf{U}$, say it $\mathbf{u}_i$, $i = 0, \ldots, n-1$, represents one out of n available codewords that can be associated to the information blocks to be embedded within $\mathbf{c}$. It is then assumed that a block of k bits is transmitted every side information block of length n and that each k-bit block is associated with one codeword which will be referred to as the carrier codeword. Note that, since the number of available codewords is n, a clear limit exists for k, i.e., $k \leq \log_2(n)$, or, equivalently, $k \leq w$.

Let now consider a partition of $\mathcal{U}$ into 2^k disjoint subsets Q_l, $l = 0, \ldots, 2^k-1$, such that $\bigcup_{Q_l} = \mathcal{U}$. Assume that a one-to-one predefined mapping $p = \beta(l)$ exists between each possible k-bit information sequences $\mathbf{b}_l$, $l = 0, \ldots, 2^k - 1$ and the subsets Q_p, $p = 0, \ldots, 2^k - 1$. This means that each k-bit information sequence can be associated to one out of 2^{w-k} carrier codewords $\mathbf{u}_i$. Of course we must define a strategy to solve the above ambiguity, i.e. we must define how the carrier codeword is chosen among all the codewords in the same bin. Let us start by considering that this strategy has already been defined, and let us indicate the chosen carrier codeword by $\mathbf{u}_m$. We will go back to the choice of $\mathbf{u}_m$ at the end of this section.

We now consider the case in which an AWGN attack is present. In this scenario, denoting by $\mathbf{c}_w$ the transmitted n-dimensional column vector, the received n-dimensional column vector $\mathbf{r}$ can be expressed as:

$$\mathbf{r} = \mathbf{c}_w + \mathbf{n}, \tag{1}$$

$\mathbf{n}$ being an additive white Gaussian noise vector with variance σ_n^2, i.e., $\mathbf{n} \sim N(0, \sigma_n)$.

Upon receiving a sequence $\mathbf{r}$, the decoder performs the estimation of the $\hat{i}$-th carrier sequence by evaluating:

$$\hat{i} = \arg \max_{i=0,\ldots,n-1} \left(\mathbf{r}^T\mathbf{u}_i\right) \tag{2}$$

---

[2] The set with the n columns of $\mathbf{U}$ gives the codebook $\mathcal{U}$

where T stands for transpose operation. The estimated transmitted sequence $\mathbf{b}_{\hat{l}}$ corresponds to the sequence associated to the bin $\mathbf{u}_{\hat{i}}$ belongs to. Note that the decoding rule outlined above, together with the equi-energetic nature of the carrier codewords, ensures that the watermark is robust against multiplication by a scale factor g.

2.1   Constant Robustness Embedding

In order to derive the optimum fixed-robustness embedding strategy, a parameter measuring the robustness of the watermark is needed. To this aim, we propose to use the maximum pairwise error probability between the transmitted codewords and all the codewords of $\mathcal{U}$ belonging to a bin Q_j with $j \neq l$, where by l we indicated the index associated to the transmitted information sequence. Even if such a probability does not coincide with the true error probability of the system, it can be shown [13] that if the attack noise is not too strong, the maximum pairwise error probability is a good approximation of the true error probability[3].

With the above observations in mind, and by denoting with $P_e(m, q)$ the pairwise (error) probability that the receiver decodes the sequence $\mathbf{u}_q$ instead of the carrier sequence $\mathbf{u}_m$, we have:

$$P_e(m, q) = \text{Prob} \left\{ \mathbf{c}_w{}^T (\mathbf{u}_m - \mathbf{u}_q) + \mathbf{z} < 0 \right\} \tag{3}$$

where $\mathbf{z} \sim N\left(0, \sigma_n \sqrt{|\mathbf{u}_m - \mathbf{u}_q|}\right)$. By exploiting the well known approximation [13]:

$$P_e(m, q) \cong \frac{1}{2} \exp \left\{ \left[-\frac{\mathbf{c}_w{}^T (\mathbf{u}_m - \mathbf{u}_q)}{\sqrt{2}\sigma_n \sqrt{|\mathbf{u}_m - \mathbf{u}_q|}} \right]^2 \right\}, \tag{4}$$

and by proceeding as in [10], the fixed robustness embedding problem can be formulated as follows: evaluate the transmitted n-dimensional column vector $\mathbf{c}_w$ that minimizes the distortion $\Delta = (\mathbf{c}_w - \mathbf{c})^T (\mathbf{c}_w - \mathbf{c})$, subject to the linear constraint:

$$\mathbf{c}_w{}^T \mathbf{u}_m - \mathbf{c}_w{}^T \mathbf{u}_q \geq S \ , \ \ \forall q | \mathbf{u}_q \notin Q_l, \tag{5}$$

with:

$$S = 2\sqrt{P_c \times \left(10^{-\frac{\text{DNR}}{10}}\right) \times \log\left(\frac{1}{2P_e^*}\right)}, \tag{6}$$

where is is assumed that the attacker uses the maximum noise power allowed to him, P_e^* indicates the target error probability, $P_c = E[\|\mathbf{c}\|^2]$, and where DNR indicates the Data to Noise Ratio defined as

$$\text{DNR} = 10\log_{10}\left(\frac{P_c}{\sigma_n^2}\right). \tag{7}$$

---

[3] On the other hand, when the attack noise gets high, the system performance deteriorates rapidly, hence making the above analysis useless.

Since the columns of the unitary matrix $\mathbf{U}$ represent an orthonormal basis for $\mathbb{R}^n$, it is possible to express the error vector $\mathbf{e} = \mathbf{c}_w - \mathbf{c}$ as a linear combination of $\mathbf{u}_i$'s, i.e.,

$$\mathbf{e} = \mathbf{U}\mathbf{a}, \tag{8}$$

where $\mathbf{a} = (a_0, a_1, \ldots, a_{n-1})^T$ is the column vector with the weights of the linear combination. Given the above, it is straightforward to observe that $\Delta = \|\mathbf{a}\|^2 = \sum_{h=0}^{n-1} a_h^2$ and $\mathbf{a}^T \mathbf{U}^T \mathbf{u}_i = a_i$. Accordingly, our problem is equivalent to find the vector $\mathbf{a}$ such that:

$$\mathbf{a} = \underset{a_h}{\arg\min} \left(\sum_{h=0}^{n-1} a_h^2 \right)$$
$$subject\ to: \tag{9}$$
$$a_m - a_q + \mathbf{c}^T \mathbf{u}_m - \mathbf{c}^T \mathbf{u}_q \geq S\ ,\ \ q | \mathbf{u}_q \notin Q_l$$

or:

$$\mathbf{a} = \underset{a_m,\, a_q}{\arg\min} \left(a_m^2 + \sum_{q | \mathbf{u}_q \notin Q_l} a_q^2 \right)$$
$$subject\ to: \tag{10}$$
$$a_q \leq a_m - S + \chi_{q,m}\ ,\ \ q | \mathbf{u}_q \notin Q_l$$

where $\chi_{q,m} = \mathbf{c}^T \mathbf{u}_m - \mathbf{c}^T \mathbf{u}_q$. The constraint in (10) can be reformulated as:

$$a_q = \min\left(0, a_m - S + \chi_{q,m}\right) \tag{11}$$

Indeed, if $a_m - S + \chi_{q,m}$ is greater than or equal to zero, the value of a_q which minimizes the error Δ while fulfilling the constraint is $a_q = 0$. Conversely, if $a_m - S + \chi_{q,m}$ is lower than zero the minimum is obtained at the edge, i.e., for $a_q = a_m - S + \chi_{q,m}$. Accordingly, the minimization problem can be expressed as:

$$\mathbf{a} = \underset{a_m}{\arg\min} \left(a_m^2 + \sum_{q \in C_l} a_q^2 \right)$$
$$a_q = \min\left(0, a_m - S + \chi_{q,m}\right) q | \mathbf{u}_q \notin Q_l \tag{12}$$

Note that the problem is now formulated as a mono dimensional minimization problem in the unknown a_m. Such a minimum can be easily computed by means of a numeric approach (e.g., see [14]).

Having defined the optimum embedding rule, we now go back to the choice of $\mathbf{u}_m$. By recalling that the decoder takes its decision by maximizing the correlation between $\mathbf{r}$ and all the codewords in $\mathcal{U}$, we decided to choose the carrier codeword which maximizes the correlation with $\mathbf{c}$, i.e.

$$\mathbf{u}_m = \underset{\mathbf{u}_s \in Q_l}{\arg\max} \mathbf{c}^T \mathbf{u}_s\ . \tag{13}$$

3   Fixed Distortion Embedding

We now want to re-formulate the embedding problem by fixing the distortion Δ and maxime the watermark robustness, i.e. minimize the maximum pairwise error probability. To do so, we can rely on the analysis reported in the previous section, however it is necessary that a closed form expression for Δ is obtained. Let us start by denoting with $\tilde{\chi}_{q,m}$ the reordered set of $\chi_{q,m}$, so that $\tilde{\chi}_{0,m} \leq \tilde{\chi}_{1,m}, \ldots, \leq \tilde{\chi}_{d-1,m}$, where d is the dimension of $\chi_{q,m}$, i.e., $d = n - 2^{w-k}$. Of course, the unknown term a_m will satisfy one of the following mutually exclusive conditions:

$$
\begin{array}{ll}
\text{(I)} & S - a_m < \tilde{\chi}_{0,m} \\
\text{(II)} \; \tilde{\chi}_{0,m} \leq S - a_m < \tilde{\chi}_{d-1,m} \\
\text{(III)} & S - a_m \geq \tilde{\chi}_{d-1,m}
\end{array}
\tag{14}
$$

Let us first assume that condition (I) holds. In this case, since $\tilde{\chi}_{0,m} \leq \tilde{\chi}_{q,m}$, it is also verified $a_m - S + \tilde{\chi}_{q,m} \geq 0$, that is, directly from (12), $a_q = 0$. Besides, since in this case the minimization function is $\Delta_m = a_m^2$ and since for hypothesis $a_m > S - \tilde{\chi}_{0,m}$, we have

$$
a_m^{(0)} = \max\left(0, S - \tilde{\chi}_{0,m}\right),
\tag{15}
$$

and

$$
\Delta_m^{(0)} = \left[\max\left(0, S - \tilde{\chi}_{0,m}\right)\right]^2,
\tag{16}
$$

where the apex 0 means that a_m and Δ_m are evaluated by assuming $S - a_m < \tilde{\chi}_{0,m}$.
If case (II) holds, it is of course possible to find an index f, for which:

$$
\tilde{\chi}_{f,m} \leq S - a_m < \tilde{\chi}_{f+1,m}.
\tag{17}
$$

Hence, $a_m - S + \tilde{\chi}_{q,m} > 0$, for $q > f$, and $a_m - S + \tilde{\chi}_{q,m} \leq 0$, for $q \leq f$. We thus obtain directly from (12) $a_q = 0$, for $q > f$, and $a_q = a_m - S + \tilde{\chi}_{q,m}$, for $q \leq f$. The distortion becomes:

$$
\Delta_m = a_m^2 + \sum_{q=0}^{f} \left(a_m - S + \tilde{\chi}_{q,m}\right)^2.
\tag{18}
$$

Since in this case Δ_m is a quadratic form of a_m, the computation of the minimum distortion subject to (17), say it $\Delta_m^{(f)}$, is straightforward. Indeed, since the derivative of (18) is zero for

$$
a_m = \hat{a}_m = \frac{S(f+1)}{f+2} - \frac{\displaystyle\sum_{q=0}^{f} \tilde{\chi}_{q,m}}{f+2},
\tag{19}
$$

the value of a_m which gives the minimum, call it $a_m^{(f)}$, is:

$$
a_m^{(f)} = \begin{cases}
\hat{a}_m, & \text{for } S - \tilde{\chi}_{f+1,m} \leq \hat{a}_m < S - \tilde{\chi}_{f,m} \\
S - \tilde{\chi}_{f+1,m}, & \text{for } \hat{a}_m < S - \tilde{\chi}_{f+1,m} \\
S - \tilde{\chi}_{f,m}, & \text{for } \hat{a}_m \geq S - \tilde{\chi}_{f,m}.
\end{cases}
\tag{20}
$$

Note that for high values of f, equation (19) can be rewritten as:

$$a_m^{(f)} \cong S - \frac{\sum\limits_{q=0}^{f} \tilde{\chi}_{q,m}}{f+1} \geq S - \tilde{\chi}_{f,m}. \tag{21}$$

We will assume in the following that (21) holds for each f. By considering (21) and (20), we obtain:

$$a_m^{(f)} = S - \tilde{\chi}_{f,m},$$
$$\Delta_m^{(f)} = (S - \tilde{\chi}_{f,m})^2 + \sum_{q=0}^{f} (\tilde{\chi}_{q,m} - \tilde{\chi}_{f,m})^2. \tag{22}$$

Finally, by means of similar considerations, we have for case (III):

$$a_m^{(d-1)} = S - \tilde{\chi}_{d-1,m},$$
$$\Delta_m^{(d-1)} = (S - \tilde{\chi}_{d-1,m})^2 + \sum_{q=0}^{d-1} (\tilde{\chi}_{q,m} - \tilde{\chi}_{d-1,m})^2. \tag{23}$$

According to the above considerations, the distortion minimization problem can be expressed as:

$$h_m = \operatorname*{arg\,min}_{h=0,\ldots,d-1} \Delta_m^{(h)}$$
$$a_m = a_m^{(h_m)} \tag{24}$$
$$\Delta_m = \Delta_m^{(h_m)}.$$

Note that (24) allows to evaluate the minimum distortion for a given robustness S and a given m. Such an estimation can be performed by computing all the d possible values of the error Δ_m and selecting the minimum.

The above procedure can be easily managed so that the inverse problem, that is to evaluate the maximum robustness S for a given error Δ, is addressed. Firstly, observe from (22) that a given error Δ can be achieved only if

$$\sum_{q=0}^{f} (\tilde{\chi}_{q,m} - \tilde{\chi}_{f,m})^2 < \Delta \tag{25}$$

Accordingly, the search must be restricted to the set of values f which satisfy (25), say $\{0, 1, \ldots, d' - 1\}$, with $d' \leq d$. Now, for a given Δ, it is possible to derive from (23) and (22) the robustness parameter $S_m^{(h)}$, with $h \in \{0, 1, \ldots, d' - 1\}$, as:

$$S_m^{(h)} = \tilde{\chi}_{h,m} + \sqrt{\Delta - \sum_{q=0}^{h} (\tilde{\chi}_{q,m} - \tilde{\chi}_{h,m})^2}, \tag{26}$$

Accordingly, the maximum robustness problem can be expressed as:

$$p_m = \operatorname*{arg\,max}_{p=0,\ldots,d'-1} S_m^{(p)}$$
$$a_m = a_m^{(p_m)}, \tag{27}$$

Note that both (27) and (24) can be evaluated by means of an exhaustive procedure over all d possible values of $\Delta_m^{(h)}$ and $S_m^{(h)}$, respectively.

3.1   Quasi-Orthogonal Dirty Paper Coding

As in [10], to further improve the performance of the proposed system we replace the orthogonal codes with quasi-orthogonal sequences, so to increase the number of available codewords for a given sequence length n. Specifically, we use Gold sequences of length n since their cross-correlation properties ensure that different sequences are almost orthogonal among them [13]. Accordingly, the matrix $\mathbf{U}$ is now a rectangular $n \times h$ matrix with column vectors $\mathbf{u}_i$, $i = 1, \ldots, h$, representing a set of h Gold sequences with length n. Gold sequences have been widely studied in the technical literature, particularly for spread spectrum applications, for their autocorrelation and cross-correlation functions that are reminiscent of the properties of white noise. Specifically, in the following we will assume that $\mathbf{u}_i$ are normalized Gold sequences [15] with $u_i(l) = \pm \frac{1}{\sqrt{n}}$, $\forall i, l$. Note that all Gold sequences have the same norm, thus ensuring that the decoder performance are invariant with respect to multiplication by a gain factor g. In this case, for a given length $n = 2^w - 1$, the number of possible Gold sequences that are characterized by good periodic cross-correlation properties is $n + 2$. Since each cyclic shift of any Gold sequence is still characterized by the same properties, the overall number of Gold sequences that can be considered for information embedding is $h = n(n + 2)$. Note that, as required to write (8), Gold sequences are a frame for $\mathbb{R}^n$, hence ensuring that every element of $\mathbb{R}^n$ can be expressed as a linear combination of the $\mathbf{u}_i$'s.

Let us now consider the distortion introduced by watermark embedding, we have:

$$d = \left| \sum_{i=1}^{h} a_i \mathbf{u}_i \right|^2 = \sum_{i=1}^{h} a_i^2 + \sum_{i \neq j} a_i a_j \mathbf{u}_i^T \mathbf{u}_j. \tag{28}$$

We can argue that, due to the particular properties of Gold sequences, the first term of the above equation is predominant with respect to the second one, even if the second term is not exactly equal to zero due to the non perfect orthogonality of Gold sequences. Such an assumption will be validated through numerical simulations in section 6. By relying on the above observations, the fixed distortion constraint can still be replaced by a constraint on $\sum_{i=1}^{m} a_i^2$.

4   Perceptual Dirty Paper Coding

The analysis carried out in the previous section gives the possibility of fixing the embedding distortion. This turns out to be a very useful feature if we want to give to the embedding systems a perceptually-flavored behavior. More specifically, we consider the watermarking of still images in the block-DCT domain. The host image is first partitioned into non-overlapping 8×8 blocks, that then are DCT-transformed. For each DCT block a set of intermediate frequency coefficients is extracted to form the host feature vector. In our implementation we considered 12 DCT coefficients for each block, more specifically after zig-zag scanning the DCT block we skip the first 3 coefficients and select the next 12 ones.

At this point we need a system to measure the maximum amount of distortion that can be tolerated by each coefficient before the watermark becomes visible. Though many algorithms are available to this aim, we decided to adopt the approach proposed by Watson in [11] for its simplicity.

At a general level Watson's visual model consists of three main parts: a sensitivity function giving the visibility of a visual stimulus as a function of frequency; two masking components, taking into account the capacity of the host image to mask the stimulus; and a pooling function to consider how visual stimuli at different frequencies combine together to form the final visual appearance of the composite stimulus.

The sensitivity function is given as a table specifying for each DCT position the smallest magnitude (Just Noticeable Difference - JND) of the corresponding DCT coefficient that is visible in the absence of any masking components. Let us denote the, so to say, threshold values contained in the sensitivity table by $t(i,j)$, where the indexes i and j indicate the position of the DCT coefficient within the 8×8 block. The exact values of the sensitivity table depends on a number of parameters, including viewing conditions, environment lightness, etc. Here we used the values given in [12]. To take into account luminance masking, Watson suggests to modify the threshold values as:

$$t_l(i,j,k) = t(i,j)\left(\frac{C(0,0,k)}{C_{0,0}}\right)^{0.649}, \tag{29}$$

where $C(0,0,k)$ is the DCT coefficient of the k-th block and $C_{0,0}$ is the average value of all the DCT coefficients of the image. Note that the modified thresholds vary from block to block due to the presence of the $C(0,0,k)$ term. Finally, the modified thresholds $t_l(i,j,k)$ are adjusted to take into account iso-frequency contrast masking, leading to a final masked threshold (or slack) given by:

$$s(i,j,k) = \max\{t_l(i,j,k); \|C(i,j,k)\|^{0.7}t_l(i,j,k)^{0.3}\}. \tag{30}$$

Of course a different $s(i,j,k)$ is obtained for each coefficient, however in our case we need to specify the same distortion, for all the n coefficients bearing the same bit. For this reason the embedder considers an average distortion computed as:

$$\Delta_{max,av}^2 = \frac{\sum s(i,j,k)^2}{n}, \tag{31}$$

where the sum is extended to all the n coefficients hosting the same bit. Note that since typically n is larger than 12, the sum spans several DCT blocks. For instance, for $n = 32$, the sum spans three blocks[4].

At this point the fixed distortion embedding algorithm described in the previous section is applied to embed the bit of the information message into the host features. Note that a different distortion constraint is applied to DCT blocks hosting different bits, hence each bit will be characterized by a different robustness.

5   Multistage Decoding

As we pointed out at the end of the previous section, bit hosted by different DCT blocks are characterized by different levels of robustness. As an extreme case, for some blocks

---

[4] We neglect border effects for simplicity.

the admissible distortion may be so low that the embedding algorithm fails to enter the correct decoding region. In other words, in certain regions the interference of the host image can not be rejected completely, leading to a non-null error probability even in the absence of attacks. In order to improve the robustness of the watermark, an additional channel coding step prior to orthogonal (or Gold) dirty paper coding is introduced. More specifically a turbo coding (decoding) step is performed prior to watermark embedding. To this aim, let us observe that the detection strategy (2) generates hard estimates of the bits $\mathbf{b}_l = (b_{l,0}, \ldots, b_{l,k-1})$. On the other hand, when dealing with multistage decoding it is preferable that the inner decoder produces soft estimates to be delivered to the outer decoder [13]. In order to provide the outer decoder with a soft estimate of the hidden bit, we follow the same approach described in [10]. Let the sets $I_{1,s}$ and $I_{0,s}$ be defined as:

$$I_{1,s} = \{l : b_{l,s} = 1\},$$
$$I_{0,s} = \{l : b_{l,s} = 0\}, \tag{32}$$

that is $I_{1,s}$ ($I_{0,s}$) represents the set of 2^{k-1} sequences $\mathbf{b}_l$ for which the s-th bit is 1 (0). Then we use the following soft estimate of the s-th bit:

$$v_s = P_{1,s} - P_{0,s} = \max_{\mathbf{u}_i \in Q_l, l \in I_{1,s}} \left(\mathbf{r}^T \mathbf{u}_i\right) - \max_{\mathbf{u}_i \in Q_l, l \in I_{0,s}} \left(\mathbf{r}^T \mathbf{u}_i\right). \tag{33}$$

The sign of (33) determines the hard estimate of the s-th bit and its absolute value represents the soft output information that can be used by the outer decoder.

It is worth pointing out that the above soft decoding strategy can be applied to any kind of binary outer coder's structure. In this paper, the outer code is the $R_c = 1/2$ binary punctured parallel concatenated turbo coder presented in [16] which allows to achieve error correction performance that are very close to the theoretical Shannon limit.

We conclude this section by highlighting the necessity of scrambling the to-be-hidden bits after the turbo encoder, prior to embedding. This is because due to the coherence of natural still images, the DCT blocks characterized by a very low admissible distortion are likely to be contiguous, hence resulting in the introduction of bursty errors. The scrambler avoids this problem by transforming bursty errors into isolated errors. Of course, de-scrambling is applied at the decoder prior to turbo decoding.

6 Simulations and Experimental Results

The validity of the above analysis and the performance of the watermarking scheme deriving from it, have been tested by means of both numerical simulations and experimental tests. Simulations aimed at validating the fixed distortion embedding strategy derived theoretically. This is a necessary step when we use Gold sequences instead of orthogonal codewords, since the analysis we carried out relies on the assumption that the second term in equation (28) is negligible with respect to the first one. In figure 1 the histogram of the actual embedding distortion d (measured in terms of of DWR) when a target DWR of 15dB was asked is shown. The histogram was built by applying the

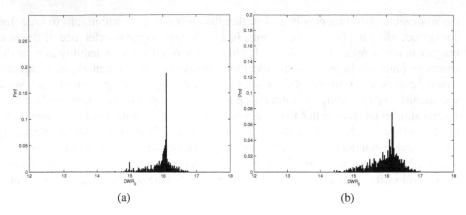

Fig. 1. Histogram of the actual DWR when a target DWR of 15dB is asked, for Gold sequences of length 32 (a) and 64 (b).

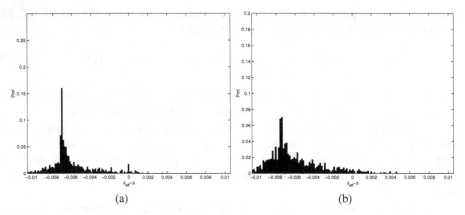

Fig. 2. Histogram of the second term in equation (28) when a target DWR of 15dB is asked, for Gold sequences of length 31 (a) and 63 (b). The histograms should be compared with the value of $\sum_i a_i^2$, that, for DWR = 15dB, is approximately equal to 0.0316 (we let $P_c = 1$).

embedding algorithm to several cover sequences. As it can be seen the actual DWR is slightly higher than the target one. In figure 2 the histogram of the second term in equation (28) is plotted (linear scale). As it can be verified the error we made by neglecting this term is negligible. As a matter of fact with DWR = 15dB, and since in our simulations we let $P_c = 1$, we have that $\sum_i a_i^2 = 10^{-1.5} \approx 0.0316$ which is much higher than the values reported in figure 2. In addition in most of the cases this term turns out to be negative, hence ensuring that the actual distortion is lower than the target one.

In order to estimate the overall performance of the system, a selection of the results we obtained on real images is now described. For sake of brevity we describe only the performance of the algorithm based on Gold sequences. Similar results (actually, slightly worse) were obtained for the orthogonal case, which, on the other hand, ensured a much faster embedding phase.

6.1 Watermark Invisibility

We fist checked whether the proposed fixed distortion strategy actually ensures the invisibility of the watermark. To do so, we built a database of 40 1024 × 1024 images, and embedded the watermark in all of them by letting $n = 32$ and $k = 1, 2$, thus obtaining an overall rate of 1/64 and 1/32 respectively. We visually inspected all the marked images and the watermark resulted to be invisible in all the cases: the observer could individuate the watermark only by comparing two magnified versions of the original and watermarked images on a high resolution monitor. No visual artifact was perceived by looking at the images in normal conditions or by looking at the images after printing by means of a high quality printer.

For all the images we measured the DWR (data to watermark ratio) both by considering only the watermarked DCT coefficients and globally, i.e. by exploiting the fact the not all the DCT coefficients are marked. The results we obtained are reported in table 1. In the same table, the Watson distance [12] between the watermarked and the original images is also given.

Table 1. Objective measures of the distortion introduced by the watermark. The results have been obtained by averaging those obtained on a test database consisting of 40 1024 × images. By DWR$_{all}$, DWR$_{sel}$ and D$_{wats}$, the DWR computed on the overall image, the host DCT coefficients and the Watson distance are meant respectively.

Rate	DWR$_{all}$(db)	DWR$_{sel}$ (db)	D$_{Wats}$ (db)
$n = 32, k = 2$	37.46	13.24	17.43
$n = 32, k = 1$	37.52	13.12	17.49

6.2 Watermark Robustness

With regard to robustness, given the fixed distortion embedding strategy we adopted, we first had to evaluate whether host signal rejection was actually achieved or not (the admitted distortion could not be enough to ensure that the right decoding region is entered). Hence we tried to detect the watermark on the marked images in the absence of attacks. We repeated this test on all the images of the database and no errors were found. Then we considered a number of attacks involving scaling (not necessarily uniform) of the host features. In particular we considered histogram stretching, histogram equalization and sharpening. In all the cases the watermark was successfully recovered with no errors in all the images of the database. To give an idea of the robustness of our system against this kind of attacks, two examples of images attacked by means of histogram equalization are shown in figure 3. As it can be seen the attack strength may be very high, and amplitude scaling of DCT coefficients highly non-uniform, nevertheless the watermark is correctly retrieved.

As a second test we considered robustness against white noise addition. More specifically the watermarked image was impaired by spatially adding a white Gaussian noise, with increasing variance. The results we obtained demonstrate only a moderate robustness against this kind of attack. For example, when the variance of noise is set to 10, the bit error probability was equal to $1.1 \cdot 10^{-1}$ ($k = 1$). Note that adding a white Gaussian noise with variance 10 results in a visible, yet slight, degradation of the marked image. It has to be noted, though, that such an attack results in an average WNR - computed only on the host features - approximately equal to -2 db, and that for negative WNR values, a high robustness can only be achieved for lower rates (or by relaxing the invisibility constraint).

Fig. 3. Robustness against histogram equalization. Despite the great difference between the marked (left) and the marked and attacked (right) images, no decoding error was found.

Similar considerations hold when robustness against JPEG compression is considered. The results we obtained in this case are summarized in table 2.

Table 2. Robustness against JPEG compression. The bit error probability averaged over all the images of the database is given as a function of the JPEG quality factor (Q).

Rate	$Q = 90$	$Q = 80$	$Q = 70$
$n = 32, k = 2$	0	$1.2 \cdot 10^{-2}$	0.34
$n = 32, k = 1$	0	$3 \cdot 10^{-3}$	$1.2 \cdot 10^{-1}$

7 Conclusions

By relying on the simple structure of orthogonal and Gold sequences, we have presented a new dirty paper coding watermarking scheme. The main merit of the proposed scheme is the use of an optimum embedding strategy, which permits to maximize the robustness of the watermark for a fixed distortion. Another advantage of the new scheme is that due to the equi-energetic nature of the codewords and to the adoption of a correlation-based decoder, robustness against value-metric scaling is automatically achieved, thus achieving a very good robustness against common image processing tools such as image enhancement and histogram manipulation. We have also shown how the performance of the system are improved by concatenating the dirty paper code with an outer turbo code. To this aim, we had to introduce a new soft dirty paper decoding scheme which allows the iterative multistage decoding of the concatenated codes. The validity of the proposed techniques has been assessed through experimental results which demonstrated an excellent behaviour from the point of view of watermark invisibility and robustness against attacks involving scaling of the host features.

Several directions for future work remain open, including the usage of more powerful spherical codes [17, 18, 19] instead of the simple orthogonal codes used here and the adoption of more sophisticated HVS models to improve watermark invisibility.

References

[1] Eggers, J.J., Girod, B.: Informed Watermarking. Kluwer Academic Publishers (2002)
[2] El Gamal, A., Cover, T.M.: Multiple user information theory. Proceedings of the IEEE **68** (1980) 1466–1485
[3] Cover, T.M., Thomas, J.A.: Elements of Information Theory. Wiley, New York (1991)
[4] Chen, B., Wornell, G.: Quantization index modulation: a class of provably good methods for digital watermarking and information embedding. IEEE Trans. on Information Theory **47** (2001) 1423–1443
[5] Eggers, J.J., Bäuml, R., Tzschoppe, R., Girod, B.: Scalar Costa scheme for information embedding. IEEE Trans. on Signal Processing **4** (2003)
[6] Perez-Gonzalez, F., Balado, F., Hernandez, J.R.: Performance analysis of existing and new methods for data hiding with known-host information in additive channels. IEEE Trans. on Signal Processing **51** (2003) 960–980

 [7] Chou, J., Ramchandran, K.: Robust turbo-based data hiding for image and video sources. In: Proc. 9th IEEE Int. Conf. on Image Processing, ICIP'02. Volume 2., Rochester, NY, USA (2002) 133–136

 [8] M. L. Miller, G. J. Doerr, I.J.C.: Dirty-paper trellis codes for watermarking. In: Proc. 9th IEEE Int. Conf. on Image Processing, ICIP'02. Volume II., Rochester, NY (2002) 129–132

 [9] Miller, M.L., Doerr, G.J., Cox, I.J.: Applying informed coding and embedding to design a robust, high capacity, watermark. IEEE Trans. on Image Processing **13** (2004) 792–807

[10] Abrardo, A., Barni, M.: Orthogonal dirty paper coding for informed watermarking. In Wong, P.W., Delp, E.J., eds.: Security, Steganography, and Watermarking of Multimedia Contents VI, Proc. SPIE Vol. 5306, San Jose, CA, USA (2004)

[11] Watson, A.B.: DCT quantization matrices visually optimized for individual images. In Allebach, J.P., Rogowitz, B.E., eds.: Human Vision, Visual Processing, and Digital Display, Proc. SPIE vol. 1913, San Jose, CA (1993) 202–216

[12] Cox, I.J., Miller, M.L., Bloom, J.A.: Digital Watermarking. Morgan Kaufmann (2001)

[13] Proakis, J.G.: Digital Communications, 2nd Edition. McGraw-Hill, New York (1989)

[14] Forsythe, G.E., Malcolm, M.A., Moler, C.B.: Computer Methods for Mathematical Computations. Prentice Hall (1976)

[15] Gold, R.: Optimal binary sequences for spread spectrum multiplexing. IEEE Trans. on Information Theory **13** (1967) 619–621

[16] Berrou, C., Glavieux, A., Thitimajshima, P.: Near shannon limit error-correcting coding and decoding: Turbo-codes. In: Proceedings of ICC, IEEE International Conference on Communications, Geneva, Switzerland (1993) 1064–1070

[17] Conway, J.H., Sloane, N.J.A.: Sphere Packings, Lattices, and Groups. Springer-Verlag, New York (1988)

[18] Hamkins, J., Zeger, K.: Asymptotically dense spherical codes - part I: wrapped spherical codes. IEEE Trans. on Information Theory **43** (1997) 1774–1785

[19] Hamkins, J., Zeger, K.: Asymptotically dense spherical codes - part II: laminated spherical codes. IEEE Trans. on Information Theory **43** (1997) 1786–1798

Feature-Based Steganalysis for JPEG Images and Its Implications for Future Design of Steganographic Schemes

Jessica Fridrich

Dept. of Electrical Engineering, SUNY Binghamton, Binghamton, NY
13902-6000, USA
fridrich@binghamton.edu
http://www.ws.binghamton.edu/fridrich

Abstract. In this paper, we introduce a new feature-based steganalytic method for JPEG images and use it as a benchmark for comparing JPEG steganographic algorithms and evaluating their embedding mechanisms. The detection method is a linear classifier trained on feature vectors corresponding to cover and stego images. In contrast to previous blind approaches, the features are calculated as an L_1 norm of the difference between a specific macroscopic functional calculated from the stego image and the same functional obtained from a decompressed, cropped, and recompressed stego image. The functionals are built from marginal and joint statistics of DCT coefficients. Because the features are calculated directly from DCT coefficients, conclusions can be drawn about the impact of embedding modifications on detectability. Three different steganographic paradigms are tested and compared. Experimental results reveal new facts about current steganographic methods for JPEGs and new design principles for more secure JPEG steganography.

1 Introduction

Steganography is the art of invisible communication. Its purpose is to hide the very presence of communication by embedding messages into innocuous-looking cover objects. Each steganographic communication system consists of an embedding algorithm and an extraction algorithm. To accommodate a secret message in a digital image, the original cover image is slightly modified by the embedding algorithm. As a result, the stego image is obtained.

Steganalysis is the art of discovering hidden data in cover objects. As in cryptanalysis, it is assumed that the steganographic method is publicly known with the exception of a secret key. Steganography is considered secure if the stego-images do not contain any detectable artifacts due to message embedding. In other words, the set of stego-images should have the same statistical properties as the set of cover-images. If there exists an algorithm that can guess whether or not a given image contains a secret message with a success rate better than random guessing, the steganographic

J. Fridrich (Ed.): IH 2004, LNCS 3200, pp. 67–81, 2004.

system is considered broken. For a more exact treatment of the concept of steganographic security, the reader is referred to [1,2].

1.1 Steganalytic Methods

Several trends have recently appeared in steganalysis. One of the first general steganalytic methods was the "chi-square attack" by Westfeld [3]. The original version of this attack could detect sequentially embedded messages and was later generalized to randomly scattered messages [4,5]. Because this approach is based solely on the first order statistics and is applicable only to idempotent embedding operations, such as LSB (Least Significant Bit) flipping, its applicability to modern steganographic schemes, that are aware of the Cachin criterion [2], is rather limited.

Another major stream in steganalysis is based on the concept of a distinguishing statistic [6]. In this approach, the steganalyst first carefully inspects the embedding algorithm and then identifies a quantity (the distinguishing statistics) that changes predictably with the length of the embedded message, yet one that can be calibrated for cover images. For JPEG images, this calibration is done by decompressing the stego image, cropping by a few pixels in each direction, and recompressing using the same quantization table. The distinguishing statistic calculated from this image is used as an estimate for the same quantity from the cover image. Using this calibration, highly accurate and reliable estimation of the embedded message length can be constructed for many schemes [6]. The detection philosophy is not limited to any specific type of the embedding operation and works for randomly scattered messages as well. One disadvantage of this approach is that the detection needs to be customized to each embedding paradigm and the design of proper distinguishing statistics cannot be easily automatized.

The third direction in steganalysis is formed by blind classifiers. Pioneered by Memon and Farid [7,15], a blind detector learns what a typical, unmodified image looks like in a multi-dimensional feature space. A classifier is then trained to learn the differences between cover and stego image features. The 72 features proposed by Farid are calculated in the wavelet decomposition of the stego image as the first four moments of coefficients and the log error between the coefficients and their globally optimal linear prediction from neighboring wavelet modes. This methodology combined with a powerful Support Vector Machine classifier gives very impressive results for most current steganographic schemes. Farid demonstrated a very reliable detection for J-Steg, both versions of OutGuess, and for F5 (color images only). The biggest advantage of blind detectors is their potential ability to detect any embedding scheme and even to classify embedding techniques by their position in the feature space. Among the disadvantages is that the methodology will always likely be less accurate than targeted approaches and it may not be possible to accurately estimate the secret message length, which is an important piece of information for the steganalyst.

Introducing blind detectors prompted further research in steganography. Based on the previous work of Eggers [8], Tzschoppe [9] constructed a JPEG steganographic scheme (HPDM) that is undetectable using Farid's scheme. However, the same scheme is easily detectable [10] using a single scalar feature – the calibrated spatial blockiness [6]. This suggests that it should be possible to construct a very powerful feature-based detector (blind on the class of JPEG images) if we used *calibrated* features computed directly in the *DCT domain* rather than from a somewhat arbitrary wavelet decomposition. This is the approach taken in this paper.

1.2   Proposed Research

We combine the concept of calibration with the feature-based classification to devise a blind detector specific to JPEG images. By calculating the features directly in the JPEG domain rather than in the wavelet domain, it appears that the detection can be made more sensitive to a wider type of embedding algorithms because the calibration process (for details, see Sec. 2) increases the features' sensitivity to the embedding modifications while suppressing image-to-image variations. Another advantage of calculating the features in the DCT domain is that it enables more straightforward interpretation of the influence of individual features on detection as well as easier formulation of design principles leading to more secure steganography.

The proposed detection can also be viewed as a new approach to the definition of steganographic security. According to Cachin, a steganographic scheme is considered secure if the Kullback-Leibler distance between the distribution of stego and cover images is zero (or small for ε-security). Farid's blind detection is essentially a reflection of this principle. Farid first determines the statistical model for natural images in the feature space and then calculates the distance between a specific image and the statistical model. This "distance" is then used to determine whether the image is a stego image. In our approach, we change the security model and use the stego image as a *side-information* to recover some statistics of the cover image. Instead of measuring the distance between the image and a statistical model, we measure the distance between certain parameters of the stego image and the same parameters related to the original image that we succeeded to capture by calibration.

The paper is organized as follows. In the next section, we explain how the features are calculated and why. In Section 3, we give the details of the detection scheme and discuss the experimental results for OutGuess [11], F5 [13], and Model Based Steganography [12,14]. Implications for future design of steganographic schemes are discussed in Section 4. The paper is summarized in Section 5.

2   Calibrated Features

Two types of features will be used in our analysis – first order features and second order features. Also, some features will be constructed in the DCT domain, while others in the spatial domain. In the whole paper, scalar quantities will be represented with a non-bold italic font, while vectors and matrices will always be in bold italics. The L_1 norm is defined for a vector (or matrix) as a sum of absolute values of all vector (or matrix) elements.

All features are constructed in the following manner. A vector functional F is applied to the stego JPEG image J_1. This functional could be the global DCT coefficient histogram, a co-occurrence matrix, spatial blockiness, etc. The stego image J_1 is decompressed to the spatial domain, cropped by 4 pixels in each direction, and recompressed with the same quantization table as J_1 to obtain J_2. The same vector functional $\boldsymbol{F}$ is then applied to J_2. The final feature f is obtained as an L_1 norm of the difference

$$f = \left\| \boldsymbol{F}(J_1) - \boldsymbol{F}(J_2) \right\|_{L_1}. \tag{1}$$

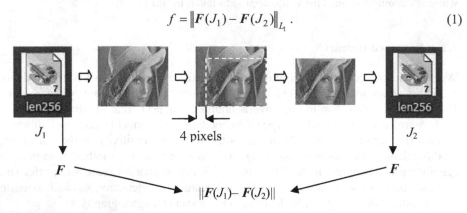

The logic behind this choice for features is the following. The cropping and recompression should produce a "calibrated" image with most macroscopic features similar to the original cover image. This is because the cropped stego image is perceptually similar to the cover image and thus its DCT coefficients should have approximately the same statistical properties as the cover image. The cropping by 4 pixels is important because the 8×8 grid of recompression "does not see" the previous JPEG compression and thus the obtained DCT coefficients are not influenced by previous quantization (and embedding) in the DCT domain. One can think of the cropped /recompressed image as an approximation to the cover image or as a side-information. The use of the calibrated image as a side-information has proven very useful for design of very accurate targeted steganalytic methods in the past [6].

2.1 First Order Features

The simplest first order statistic of DCT coefficients is their histogram. Suppose the stego JPEG file is represented with a DCT coefficient array $d_k(i, j)$ and the quantization matrix $Q(i, j)$, $i, j = 1,...,8$, $k = 1, ..., B$. The symbol $d_k(i, j)$ denotes the (i, j)-th quantized DCT coefficient in the k-th block (there are total of B blocks). The global histogram of all $64k$ DCT coefficients will be denoted as H_r, where $r = L, ..., R$, $L = \min_{k,i,j} d_k(i, j)$ and $R = \max_{k,i,j} d_k(i, j)$.

There are steganographic programs that preserve $\boldsymbol{H}$ [8,10,11]. However, the schemes in [8,9,11] only preserve the global histogram and not necessarily histograms of individual DCT modes. Thus, we add individual histograms for low frequency DCT modes to our set of functionals. For a fixed DCT mode (i, j), let h_r^{ij}, $r = L, ..., R$, denote the individual histogram of values $d_k(i, j)$, $k = 1, ..., B$. We only use histograms of low frequency DCT coefficients because histograms of coefficients from medium and higher frequencies are usually statistically unimportant due to the small number of non-zero coefficients.

To provide additional first order macroscopic statistics to our set of functionals, we have decided to include "dual histograms". For a fixed coefficient value d, the dual histogram is an 8×8 matrix g_{ij}^d

$$g_{ij}^d = \sum_{k=1}^{B} \delta(d, d_k(i, j)),$$ (2)

where $\delta(u, v) = 1$ if $u = v$ and 0 otherwise. In words, g_{ij}^d is the number of how many times the value d occurs as the (i, j)-th DCT coefficient over all B blocks in the JPEG image. The dual histogram captures how a given coefficient value d is distributed among different DCT modes. Obviously, if a steganographic method preserves all individual histograms, it also preserves all dual histograms and vice versa.

2.2 Second Order Features

If the corresponding DCT coefficients from different blocks were independent, then any embedding scheme that preserves the first order statistics – the histogram – would be undetectable by Cachin's definition of steganographic security [2]. However, because natural images can exhibit higher-order correlations over distances larger than 8 pixels, individual DCT modes from neighboring blocks are not independent. Thus, it makes sense to use features that capture inter-block dependencies because they will likely be violated by most steganographic algorithms.

Let I_r and I_c denote the vectors of block indices while scanning the image "by rows" and "by columns", respectively. The first functional capturing inter-block dependency is the "variation" V defined as

$$V = \frac{\sum_{i,j=1}^{8} \sum_{k=1}^{|I_r|-1} |d_{I_r(k)}(i,j) - d_{I_r(k+1)}(i,j)| + \sum_{i,j=1}^{8} \sum_{k=1}^{|I_c|-1} |d_{I_c(k)}(i,j) - d_{I_c(k+1)}(i,j)|}{|I_r| + |I_c|}.$$ (3)

Most steganographic techniques in some sense add entropy to the array of quantized DCT coefficients and thus are more likely to increase the variation V than decrease.

Embedding changes are also likely to increase the discontinuities along the 8×8 block boundaries. In fact, this property has proved very useful in steganalysis in the past [6,10,12]. Thus, we include two blockiness measures B_α, $\alpha = 1, 2$, to our set of functionals. The blockiness is calculated from the decompressed JPEG image and thus represents an "integral measure" of inter-block dependency over all DCT modes over the whole image:

$$B_\alpha = \frac{\sum_{i=1}^{\lfloor (M-1)/8 \rfloor} \sum_{j=1}^{N} |x_{8i,j} - x_{8i+1,j}|^\alpha + \sum_{j=1}^{\lfloor (N-1)/8 \rfloor} \sum_{i=1}^{M} |x_{i,8j} - x_{i,8j+1}|^\alpha}{N \lfloor (M-1)/8 \rfloor + M \lfloor (N-1)/8 \rfloor}.$$ (4)

In the expression above, M and N are image dimensions and x_{ij} are grayscale values of the decompressed JPEG image.

The final three functionals are calculated from the co-occurrence matrix of neighboring DCT coefficients. Recalling the notation, $L \leq d_k(i, j) \leq R$, the co-occurrence matrix C is a square $D \times D$ matrix, $D = R - L + 1$, defined as follows

$$C_{st} = \frac{\sum_{k=1}^{|I_r|-1} \sum_{i,j=1}^{8} \delta\big(s, d_{I_r(k)}(i,j)\big)\delta\big(t, d_{I_r(k+1)}(i,j)\big) + \sum_{k=1}^{|I_c|-1} \sum_{i,j=1}^{8} \delta\big(s, d_{I_c(k)}(i,j)\big)\delta\big(t, d_{I_c(k+1)}(i,j)\big)}{|I_r| + |I_c|}$$

(5)

The co-occurrence matrix describes the probability distribution of pairs of neighboring DCT coefficients. It usually has a sharp peak at $(0,0)$ and then quickly falls off. Let $C(J_1)$ and $C(J_2)$ be the co-occurrence matrices for the JPEG image J_1 and its calibrated version J_2, respectively. Due to the approximate symmetry of C_{st} around $(s, t) = (0, 0)$, the differences $C_{st}(J_1) - C_{st}(J_2)$ for $(s, t) \in \{(0,1), (1,0), (-1,0), (0,-1)\}$ are strongly positively correlated. The same is true for the group $(s, t) \in \{(1,1), (-1,1), (1,-1), (-1,-1)\}$. For practically all steganographic schemes, the embedding changes to DCT coefficients are essentially perturbations by some small value. Thus, the co-occurrence matrix for the embedded image can be obtained as a convolution $C*P(q)$, where P is the probability distribution of the embedding distortion, which depends on the relative message length q. This means that the values of the co-occurrence matrix $C*P(q)$ will be more "spread out". To quantify this spreading, we took the following three quantities as our *features*:

$$N_{00} = C_{0,0}(J_1) - C_{0,0}(J_2) \tag{6}$$
$$N_{01} = C_{0,1}(J_1) - C_{0,1}(J_2) + C_{1,0}(J_1) - C_{1,0}(J_2) + C_{-1,0}(J_1) - C_{-1,0}(J_2) + C_{0,-1}(J_1) - C_{0,-1}(J_2)$$
$$N_{11} = C_{1,1}(J_1) - C_{1,1}(J_2) + C_{1,-1}(J_1) - C_{1,-1}(J_2) + C_{-1,1}(J_1) - C_{-1,1}(J_2) + C_{-1,-1}(J_1) - C_{-1,-1}(J_2).$$

The final set of 23 functionals (the last three are directly features) used in this paper is summarized in Table 1.

3 Steganalytic Classifier

We used the Greenspun image database (www.greenspun.com) consisting of 1814 images of size approximately 780×540. All images were converted to grayscale, the black border frame was cropped away, and the images were compressed using an 80% quality JPEG. We selected the F5 algorithm [13], OutGuess 0.2 [11], and the recently developed Model based Steganography without (MB1) and with (MB2) deblocking [12,14] as three examples of different steganographic paradigms for JPEG images.

Each steganographic technique was analyzed separately. For a fixed relative message length expressed in terms of bits per non-zero DCT coefficient of the cover image, we created a training database of embedded images. The Fisher Linear Discriminant classifier was trained on 1314 cover and 1314 stego images. The generalized eigenvector obtained from this training was then used to calculate the ROC curve for the remaining 500 cover and 500 stego images. The detection performance was evaluated using detection reliability ρ defined below.

Table 1. All 23 distinguishing functionals

Functional/feature name	Functional F
Global histogram	$H / \| H \|_{L_1}$
Individual histograms for 5 DCT modes	$\dfrac{h^{21}}{\| h^{21} \|_{L_1}}, \dfrac{h^{31}}{\| h^{31} \|_{L_1}}, \dfrac{h^{12}}{\| h^{12} \|_{L_1}}, \dfrac{h^{22}}{\| h^{22} \|_{L_1}}, \dfrac{h^{13}}{\| h^{13} \|_{L_1}}$
Dual histograms for 11 DCT values ($-5, \ldots, 5$)	$\dfrac{g^{-5}}{\| g^{-5} \|_{L_1}}, \dfrac{g^{-4}}{\| g^{-4} \|_{L_1}}, \ldots, \dfrac{g^{4}}{\| g^{4} \|_{L_1}}, \dfrac{g^{5}}{\| g^{5} \|_{L_1}}$
Variation	V
L_1 and L_2 blockiness	B_1, B_2
Co-occurrences	N_{00}, N_{01}, N_{11} (features, not functionals)

The reason why we used in our tests message lengths proportional to the number of non-zero DCT coefficients in each image was to create stego image databases for which the detection is approximately of the same level of difficulty. In our experience, it is easier to detect a 10000-bit message in a smaller JPEG file than in a larger JPEG file. The testing was done for the following relative embedding rates expressed in bpc (Bits Per non-zero DCT Coefficient), bpc = 0, 0.05, 0.1, 0.2, 0.4, 0.6, 0.8. If, for a given image, the bpc rate was larger than the maximal bpc rate bpc_{max} determined by the image capacity, we took bpc_{max} as the embedding rate. The only exception to this rule was the MB2 method, where we took $0.95 \times bpc_{max}$ as the maximal rate because, for the maximal embedding rate, the deblocking algorithm in MB2 frequently failed to embed the whole message. Fig. 1 shows the capacity for all three methods expressed in bits per non-zero DCT coefficient.

The detection results were evaluated using 'detection reliability' ρ defined as

$$\rho = 2A-1, \tag{7}$$

where A is the area under the Receiver Operating Characteristic (ROC) curve, also called an accuracy. We scaled the accuracy in order to obtain $\rho = 1$ for a perfect detection and $\rho = 0$ when the ROC coincides with the diagonal line (reliability of detection is 0). The detection reliability for all three methods is shown in Table 2.

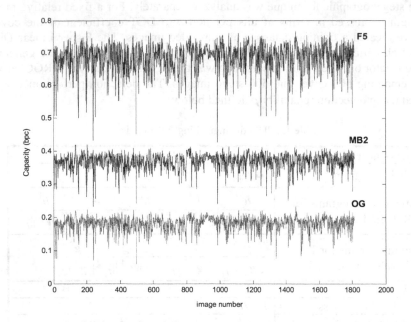

Fig. 1. Capacity for the tested techniques expressed in bits per non-zero DCT coefficient. The capacity for MB1 is double that of MB2. The F5 and MB1 algorithms provide the highest capacity

Table 2. Detection reliability ρ for F5 with matrix embedding $(1, k, 2^k - 1)$, F5 with turned off matrix embedding $(1,1,1)$, OutGuess 0.2 (OG), Model based Steganography without and with deblocking (MB1 and MB2, respectively) for different embedding rates (U = unachievable rate)

bpc	F5	F5_111	OG	MB1	MB2
0.05	0.2410	0.6451	0.8789	0.2197	0.1631
0.1	0.5386	0.9224	0.9929	0.4146	0.3097
0.2	0.9557	0.9958	0.9991	0.7035	0.5703
0.4	0.9998	0.9999	U	0.9375	0.8243
0.6	1.0000	1.0000	U	0.9834	U
0.8	1.0000	1.0000	U	0.9916	U

One can clearly see that the OutGuess algorithm is the most detectable. Also, it provides the smallest capacity. The detection reliability is relatively high even for embedding rates as small as 0.05 bpc and the method becomes highly detectable for messages above 0.1 bpc. To guarantee a fair comparison, we have tested F5 both with and without matrix embedding because some programs could be easily adapted to incorporate it (e.g., OutGuess). Turning off the matrix embedding, the F5 algorithm still performs better than OutGuess. The matrix embedding significantly decreases the detectability for short messages. This is understandable because it improves the embedding efficiency (number of bits embedded per change). Because OutGuess needs to reserve a relatively large portion of coefficients for the correction step, its embedding efficiency is lower compared to F5. This seems to have a bigger impact on the detectability than the fact that OutGuess preserves the global histogram of DCT coefficients.

Table 3. Detection reliability for individual features for all three embedding algorithms for *fully* embedded images (for fully embedded images, F5 with matrix embedding and without matrix embedding coincide)

Functional/feature	Method			
	F5	OutGuess 0.2	MB1	MB2
Global histogram	0.9936	0.8110	0.1224	0.0359
Indiv. histogram for (2,1)	0.9343	0.6625	0.6166	0.3775
Indiv. histogram for (3,1)	0.9940	0.7521	0.1018	0.0606
Indiv. histogram for (1,2)	0.8719	0.6353	0.4686	0.3828
Indiv. histogram for (2,2)	0.9827	0.7879	0.5782	0.3499
Indiv. histogram for (1,3)	0.9879	0.7718	0.0080	0.0095
Dual histogram for −5	0.1294	0.0853	0.1350	0.1582
Dual histogram for −4	0.1800	0.2727	0.0338	0.0448
Dual histogram for −3	0.2188	0.4239	0.6675	0.3239
Dual histogram for −2	0.2939	0.9921	0.2724	0.0733
Dual histogram for −1	0.4824	0.9653	0.7977	0.4952
Dual histogram for 0	0.9935	0.6160	0.2697	0.0859
Dual histogram for 1	0.5101	0.4068	0.6782	0.3336
Dual histogram for 2	0.2740	0.8437	−0.0058	0.0311
Dual histogram for 3	0.1990	0.7060	0.0904	0.1208
Dual histogram for 4	0.1421	0.1933	0.0169	0.0100
Dual histogram for 5	0.1315	0.1055	0.4097	0.2540
Variation	0.7891	0.5576	0.7239	0.2337
L_1 blockiness	0.9908	0.1677	0.5749	0.2737
L_2 blockiness	0.9411	0.1064	0.2485	0.2253
Co-occurrence N_{00}	0.9997	0.4180	0.8818	0.6088
Co-occurrence N_{01}	0.9487	0.9780	0.8433	0.5569
Co-occurrence N_{11}	0.9954	0.9282	0.7873	0.4957

Both MB1 and MB2 methods clearly have the best performance of all three tested algorithms. MB1 preserves not only the global histogram, but all marginal statistics (histograms) for each individual DCT mode. It is quite remarkable that this can be achieved with an embedding efficiency slightly over 2 bits per change (compared to 1.5 bits per change for F5 and roughly 1 for OutGuess 0.2). This is likely because MB1 does not avoid any other coefficients than 0 and its embedding mechanism is guaranteed to embed the maximal number of bits given the fact that marginal statistics of all coefficients must be preserved. The MB2 algorithm has the same embedding mechanism as MB1 but reserves one half of the capacity for modifications that bring the blockiness of the stego image to its original value. As a result, MB2 is less detectable than MB1 at the expense of a two times smaller embedding capacity. Both methods perform better than F5 with matrix embedding and are significantly better than F5 without matrix embedding. Even for messages close to 100% capacity, the detection of MB2 is not very reliable. An ROC with $\rho = 0.82$ does not allow reliable detection with a small false positive rate (c.f., Fig. 2). Never the less, in the strict formulation of steganographic security, whenever the embedded images can be distinguished from cover images with a better algorithm than random guessing, the steganography is detectable. Thus, we conclude that the Model based Steganography is detectable using our feature-based approach on our test database.

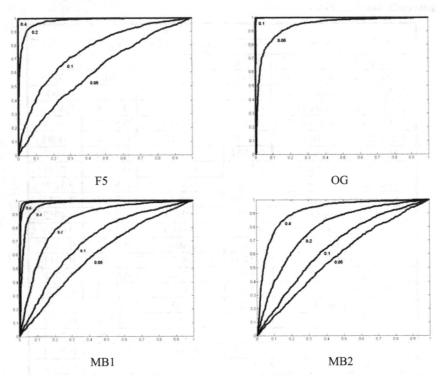

Fig. 2. ROC curves for embedding capacities and methods from Table 2.

For each steganographic method, we also measured the influence of each individual feature f as its detection reliability $\rho(f)$ obtained from the ROC curve calculated from the single feature f and no other features. We acknowledge that the collection of individual reliabilities $\rho(f)$ does not have to necessarily capture the performance of the whole detection algorithm in the 23 dimensional space. This is because it is possible that none of the individual features themselves has any distinguishing power, yet the collection of all features achieves a perfect detection. Never the less, we use $\rho(f)$ as an indication of how much each feature contributes to the detection.

In Table 2, we show the influence of each feature for each steganographic method for the maximal bpc rate. In the next section, we interpret the results and draw conclusions concerning the existing and future design principles of steganographic schemes for JPEG images.

We note that in our tests, we did not include double compressed images. It is likely that such images would worsen our detection results. In agreement with the conclusion reached in [6], the double compression needs to be first estimated and then corrected for during the feature calibration. Although we have not tested this, we believe that the feature-based blind steganalysis would work in this case as well.

4 Implications for Steganography

The F5 algorithm uses a non-idempotent embedding operation (subtracting 1) to prevent the attacks based on the chi-square attack and its generalizations [3–5]. It also makes sure that the global stego image histogram is free of any obvious artifacts and looks "natural". In fact, it has been argued by its authors [13] that the stego image looks as if the cover image was originally compressed with a lower JPEG quality factor. However, the F5 predictably modifies the first order statistics and this is why the first six functionals are so influential (see Table 2). It is also not surprising that the dual histogram for 0 has a big influence because of the shrinkage. Note that the second-order statistics significantly contribute to the detection as well. Most features with the exception of dual histograms have high influence on detection.

OutGuess 0.2 was specifically designed to preserve the *global* coefficient histogram. However, OutGuess does not have to necessarily preserve the *individual* histograms or the dual histograms, which is reflected by a relatively large influence for these functionals in Table 2. The most influential functional is the dual histogram for the values -1 and -2. This is again, understandable, considering the embedding mechanism of OutGuess. The values -1 and -2 determine the maximum correctable capacity of the method and thus form the most changed pair of values during the embedding (and the correction step). Although the coefficient counts are preserved, their positions in the JPEG file are highly disturbed, which is why we see a very high influence of features based on dual histograms for values -1 and -2. Another reason why OutGuess is more detectable than F5 is its low embedding efficiency of 1 bit per change compared to 1.5 for F5.

Considering the large influence of the dual histogram, it seems feasible that one could design a targeted steganalytic scheme of the type described in [6] by using the dual histograms for values -1 and -2 as the *distinguishing statistic*. This is an example how the blind analysis may, in turn, give us direct ideas how to estimate the length of the embedded message.

What is somewhat surprising is that the global histogram also has quite a large influence on detection, despite the fact that it is preserved by OutGuess. We will revisit this peculiar finding when we discuss the results for Model Based Steganography below. Another seemingly surprising fact is that although L_1 blockiness proved very useful in designing successful attacks against OutGuess [6], its influence in the proposed detection scheme is relatively small (0.16). This fact is perhaps less surprising if we realize that the distinguishing statistic in [6] was the *increase* of blockiness after full re-embedding rather than the blockiness itself, which appears to be rather volatile.

Looking at the results in Table 1 and 2, there is no doubt that the Model Based Steganography [12,14] is by far the most secure method out of the three tested paradigms. MB1 and MB2 preserve not only the global histogram but also *all* histograms of individual DCT coefficients. Thus, all dual histograms are also preserved. Moreover, MB2 also preserves one second-order functional – the L_1 blockiness. Thus, we conclude that the more statistical measures an embedding method preserves, the more difficult it is to detect it. Consequently, our analysis indicates that it is possible to increase the security of JPEG steganographic schemes by identifying a set of key macroscopic statistical features that should be preserved by the embedding. It is most likely not necessary to preserve all 23 features to substantially decrease the detectability because many of the features are not independent.

One of the most surprising facts revealed by the experiments is that even features based on functionals that are preserved by the embedding may have substantial influence. One might intuitively expect that such features would have very small influence. However, as shown in the next paragraph, preserving a specific *functional* does not automatically mean that the *calibrated feature* will be preserved. Let us take a closer look at the L_1 blockiness as an example.

Preserving the blockiness along the original 8×8 grid (solid lines) does not mean that the blockiness along the shifted grid will also be preserved (see Fig. 2). This is because the embedding and deblocking changes are likely to introduce distortion into the middle of the blocks and thus disturb the blockiness *feature*, which is the difference between the blockiness along the solid and dashed lines. Consequently, it is not surprising that features constructed from functionals that are preserved still have some residual (and not necessarily small) influence in our feature-based detection. This is seen in Table 2 for both OutGuess 0.2 and the Model Based Steganography. Therefore, the designers of future steganographic schemes for JPEG images should consider adding *calibrated* statistics into the set of quantities that should be preserved during embedding.

We further point out that the features derived from the co-occurrence matrix are very influential for all three schemes. For the Model based Steganography, these features are, in fact, the most influential. The MB2 method is currently the only JPEG steganographic method that takes into account inter-block dependencies between DCT coefficients by preserving the blockiness, which is an "integral" measure of these dependencies. Not surprisingly, the scalar blockiness feature does not capture all higher-order statistics of DCT coefficients. Thus, it seems that the next generation of steganographic methods for JPEG images should preserve both the marginal statistics of DCT coefficients and the probability distribution of coefficient pairs from neighboring blocks (the co-occurrence matrix). Eventually, if the stego algorithm preserved all possible statistics of the cover image, the embedding would be presumably undetectable. Although this goal will likely never be achieved, as the embedding algorithm preserves more "orthogonal or independent" statistics, its detectability will quickly decrease. We firmly believe that incorporating a model for the co-occurrence matrices and preserving it would probably lead to significantly less detectable schemes. The Model based Steganography [14] seems to be an appropriate guiding principle to achieve this goal. However, the embedding operation should not be idempotent, otherwise targeted attacks based on re-embedding (c.f., the attack on OutGuess [6]) could likely be mounted.

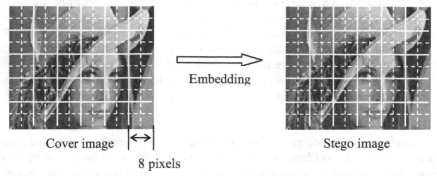

Cover image $\longleftrightarrow$ Stego image

8 pixels

Fig. 2. Blockiness is preserved along the solid lines but not necessarily along the dashed lines

5 Summary and Future Research

In this paper, we developed a new blind feature-based steganalytic method for JPEG images. Each feature is calculated as the L_1 norm of the difference between a specific functional of the stego image and its cropped/recompressed version. This "calibration" can be interpreted as using the stego image as side information to approximately recover some parameters of the cover image. As a result, the calibration decreases image-to-image variations and thus enables more accurate detection.

The features were calculated directly in the DCT domain as first and higher order statistics of DCT coefficients. This enables easier explanation of the impact of embedding modifications on detection as well as direct interpretation of the detection results and easy formulation of design principles for future steganographic methods.

We have applied the detection to several current steganographic schemes some of which are aware of the Cachin criterion [2]. The experimental results were carefully evaluated and interpreted. Conclusions concerning current and future steganographic schemes for JPEGs were also drawn. In particular, we concluded that

1. Secure steganographic schemes must preserve as many statistics of DCT coefficients as possible. It is not enough to preserve the marginal statistics, e.g., the histograms. DCT coefficients exhibit block-to-block dependencies that must be preserved as well.

2. A scheme that preserves more statistics is likely to be more secure than a scheme that preserves fewer statistics. Surprisingly, preserving more statistics may not necessarily lead to small capacity, as shown by Model Based Steganography. This is also because many statistical features one can identify in an image are likely to be dependent.

3. Even though a scheme may preserve a specific statistic $\zeta(X)$ of the cover JPEG image X, the calibrated statistic $\zeta(\text{Compress}(\text{Crop}(X)))$ calculated from the cropped/recompressed image may not necessarily be preserved, thus opening the door for attacks. Future steganographic schemes should add calibrated statistics to their set of preserved statistics.

4.   For all tested schemes, one of the most influential features of the proposed detection was the co-occurrence matrix of DCT coefficients (5), which is the probability distribution of coefficient pairs from neighboring blocks. We hypothesize that a scheme that preserves marginal statistics of DCT coefficients and the co-occurrence matrix (which captures block-to-block dependencies) is likely to exhibit improved resistance to attacks. For this purpose, we propose the Model Based Steganography paradigm [12,14] expanded by the model for joint probability distribution of neighboring DCT coefficients.

Although the calibration process is very intuitive, we currently do not have a quantitative understanding of how much information about the cover image can be obtained from the stego image by calibration. For example, for images that contain periodic spatial structures with a period that is an integer multiple of 8, the calibration process may give misleading results (c.f., the spatial resonance phenomenon [6]). In this case, it may be more beneficial to replace the cropping by other operations that will also break the block structure of JPEG images, such as slight rotation, scaling, or random warping. Further investigation of this issue will be part of our future research.

In the future, we also plan to replace the Fisher Linear Discriminant with more sophisticated classifiers, such as Support Vector Machines, to further improve the detection reliability of the proposed steganalytic algorithm. We also plan to develop a multiple-class classifier capable of recognizing stego images produced by different embedding algorithms (steganographic program identification).

Acknowledgements

The work on this paper was supported by the Air Force Research Laboratory, Air Force Material Command, USAF, under research grant number F30602-02-2-0093. The U.S. Government is authorized to reproduce and distribute reprints for Governmental purposes notwithstanding any copyright notation there on. The views and conclusions contained herein are those of the authors and should not be interpreted as necessarily representing the official policies, either expressed or implied, of Air Force Research Laboratory, or the U. S. Government. Special thanks belong to Phil Sallee for many useful discussions during preparation of this paper and for providing the code for Model Based Steganography.

References

1. Anderson, R. J. and Petitcolas, F.A.P.: On the Limits of Steganography. IEEE Journal of Selected Areas in Communications. Special Issue on Copyright and Privacy Protection, vol. 16(4) (1998) 474–481
2. Cachin, C.: An Information-Theoretic Model for Steganography. In: Aucsmith, D. (ed.): Information Hiding. 2nd International Workshop. Lecture Notes in Computer Science, Vol. 1525, Springer-Verlag, Berlin Heidelberg New York (1998) pp. 306–318

3. Westfeld, A. and Pfitzmann, A.: Attacks on Steganographic Systems. In: Pfitzmann A. (eds.): 3rd International Workshop. Lecture Notes in Computer Science, Vol.1768. Springer-Verlag, Berlin Heidelberg New York (2000) 61–75
4. Westfeld, A.: Detecting Low Embedding Rates. In: Petitcolas, F.A.P. (ed.): Information Hiding. 5th International Workshop. Lecture Notes in Computer Science, Vol. 2578. Springer-Verlag, Berlin Heidelberg New York (2002) 324–339
5. Provos, N. and Honeyman, P.: Detecting Steganographic Content on the Internet. CITI Technical Report 01-11 (2001)
6. Fridrich, J., Goljan, M., Hogea, D., and Soukal, D.: Quantitative Steganalysis: Estimating Secret Message Length. ACM Multimedia Systems Journal. Special issue on Multimedia Security, Vol. 9(3) (2003) 288–302
7. Farid H. and Siwei, L.: Detecting Hidden Messages Using Higher-Order Statistics and Support Vector Machines. In: Petitcolas, F.A.P. (ed.): Information Hiding. 5th International Workshop. Lecture Notes in Computer Science, Vol. 2578. Springer-Verlag, Berlin Heidelberg New York (2002) 340–354
8. Eggers, J., Bäuml, R., and Girod, B.: A Communications Approach to Steganography. In Proc. EI SPIE Electronic Imaging SPIE Vol. 4675 (2002) 26–49
9. Tzschoppe, R., Bäuml, R., Huber, J.B., and Kaup, A.: Steganographic System based on Higher-Order Statistics. Proc. EI SPIE Electronic Imaging. Santa Clara (2003) 156–166
10. Tzschoppe, R.: Personal communication. February (2003)
11. Provos, N.: Defending Against Statistical Steganalysis. 10th USENIX Security Symposium. Washington, DC (2001)
12. Sallee, P.: Model Based Steganography. International Workshop on Digital Watermarking. Seoul, October (2003) 174–188
13. Westfeld, A.: High Capacity Despite Better Steganalysis (F5–A Steganographic Algorithm). In: Moskowitz, I.S. (eds.): Information Hiding. 4th International Workshop. Lecture Notes in Computer Science, Vol.2137. Springer-Verlag, Berlin Heidelberg New York (2001) 289–302
14. Sallee, P.: Model-based methods for steganography and steganalysis. Submitted to International Journal of Image and Graphics. Special issue on Image Data Hiding (2004)
15. I. Avcibas, N. Memon, and B. Sankur, "Steganalysis using Image Quality Metrics", SPIE Security and Watermarking of Multimedia Contents II, Electronic Imaging, San Jose, CA, Jan. 2001.

Exploiting Preserved Statistics for Steganalysis

Rainer Böhme and Andreas Westfeld

Technische Universität Dresden
Institute for System Architecture
01062 Dresden, Germany
{rainer.boehme,westfeld}@inf.tu-dresden.de

Abstract. We introduce a steganalytic method which takes advantage of statistics that were preserved to prevent the chi-square attack. We show that preserving statistics by skipping certain groups of pixels—apart from reducing the maximum payload—does not diminish the ability to recognise steganographic modifications. The effect is quite reverse: The new detection method works more reliably than the chi-square attack, if the same message was embedded by overwriting least significant bits and straddled over the whole image.

1 Introduction

Steganography means "covered writing." Steganographic programs are capable of embedding a message into innocuous looking carrier media. Carrier media can be digitised images sent as E-mail attachments or found in eBay offers. The carrier medium is slightly modified by the embedding function so that an attacker should not perceive such changes. Steganography is one way to communicate confidentially: non-involved persons do not notice whether the secret message exists or not.

If cryptography is used to communicate secretly, a third party may still notice when an encrypted message is sent. However, she cannot read its content. In some countries, such as China, there are legal restrictions for the usage of cryptography [11]. People that are not allowed to encrypt their E-mail may fall back to steganography and embed their secrets in images to transfer them unnoticeable to the receiver.

Beside the topmost goal of changing the carrier medium as inconspicuously as possible, steganographic algorithms try to implement other helpful properties, such as a large payload and an error-free readability of the embedded content after transmission over a distorted channel (e. g., in a radio contact). It is obvious that these are conflicting goals. For example, steganographic changes are less recognisable if payloads keep small.

Apparently, it is hard to satisfy the theoretical security conditions [2,10,16] in practical implementations. Hence, new algorithms are proven to be secure against known attacks and obvious derivations. It is for this reason, that steganalysis, the art of detecting steganographic changes, is so successful in forms and manners [9,15]. Steganalytic attacks aim to detect the use of steganography.

J. Fridrich (Ed.): IH 2004, LNCS 3200, pp. 82–96, 2004.

There is a recurrent alternation of improved embedding methods and success-ful attacks breaking these. Following this tradition, we analyse a steganographic algorithm that was presented by Franz at the last workshop [3]. She constructed this algorithm to overcome histogram attacks. Her new algorithm is based on an embedding function that overwrites the least significant bits (LSB) of a car-rier. The pure application of this method is detectable by visual and statistical chi-square attacks [15]. So, Franz restricts the embedding function to selected pixels to keep the histogram (first order statistics) together with the image struc-ture (second order statistics). These measures secure the algorithm against the aforementioned attacks.[1]

This paper is structured as follows: In the next section we describe the embed-ding algorithm proposed in [3], which was designed to preserve statistical prop-erties (PSP) of the carrier image. This algorithm basically extends the method of overwriting the least significant bits (LSB) to prevent chi-square attacks pre-sented in [15]. Then, in Sect. 3, we outline an attacking strategy which exploits the preserved statistics. As the embedding algorithm keeps some relevant distri-butions in the co-occurrence matrix, an attacker can reproduce the classification criteria applied while embedding. A comparison between the resulting two sets of usable and unusable pixels reveals typical embedding artefacts of the PSP method, which is therefore detectable. Our experimental results (see Sect. 4) in-dicate that the proposed attack detects PSP steganography even more reliably than the chi-square attack does on simple LSB embedded data of comparable capacity. In Sect. 5, we describe possible countermeasures and discuss their im-pact on capacity and security. A final conclusion for future improvements of steganographic algorithms is given in Sect. 6.

2   "Preserving Statistical Properties" Algorithm

The "Preserving Statistical Properties" (PSP) algorithm is an extension to the widely used method of overwriting the least significant bits (LSB) in digitised me-dia data. Both algorithms, LSB as well as PSP, embed steganographic messages into the spatial domain representation of uncompressed or losslessly compressed image data. Given a $X \times Y$ sized greyscale image $B = \{0, \ldots, N-1\}^{X,Y}$ with N possible shades, let

$$S_k = \{(x, y) | b_{x,y} = k\}, \ 0 \leq x < X, \ 0 \leq y < Y, \ 0 \leq k < N$$

be the set of pixels in B with shade k. Obviously the shades S_k are disjoint with each other. Both algorithms assume that the shades $S_{0,\ldots,N-1}$ can be grouped into $\frac{N}{2^l}$ groups G of 2^l shades ($l = 1, 2, \ldots$), so that a replacement with any member of the same group is imperceptible. Let $\mathcal{G}$ be the set of all groups G in a given image. The information which shade $b_{x,y}$ of the visually indistinguish-able group members actually occurs at a certain position (x, y) can be used for

---

[1] As recent analyses showed vulnerable cases against the RS attack [7], Franz addresses the problem that the new method does not consider all higher order statistics [5].

steganographic messages. Grouping shades that differ only in the least significant bit, is the most common way to fulfil this assumption. This leads to $|\mathcal{G}| = N/2$ groups

$$G_k = S_{2k} \cup S_{2k+1}, \ 0 \leq k < |\mathcal{G}|,$$

and a maximum steganographic capacity of one bit per pixel. The imperceptibility assumption is plausible for the least significant bit, because adjacent shades differ minimum in brightness and are at most exposed to quantisation noise. Further generalisations, e. g., colour components of true colour images or indices in sorted palette entries, are extraneous to the following considerations and we therefore forgo a detailed discussion.

The presented LSB method is known to be vulnerable against the chi-square attack presented in [15]. Overwriting the least significant bits according to a uniform distributed message equalises the individual within-group distributions. These pair wise adjustments can be reliably detected by a chi-square goodness-of-fit test between the empirical distributions of $|S_{2k}|$, and $|S_{2k+1}|$, respectively, against the expected distribution for a maximum embedded message

$$\frac{|S_{2k}| + |S_{2k+1}|}{2} = \frac{|G_k|}{2}, \ 0 \leq k < |\mathcal{G}|.$$

The PSP algorithm was designed to resist the chi-square attack and introduces two countermeasures, such as classification of groups and skewness corrected embedding. Both measures are adaptive, i. e., they depend on the content of the carrier image, and both reduce the maximum length of the hidden message.

In this paper, we use the term *classification* of groups to describe a preselection process, which distinguishes groups $\mathcal{G}^+ \subset \mathcal{G}$ that are safe for LSB embedding from $\mathcal{G}^- = \mathcal{G} \backslash \mathcal{G}^+$, that are not. The chi-square attack is successful against LSB embedding, because even heavily unequal distributions of group members are equalised during embedding. Typical skewness between group members results from plain surfaces as well as from saturated areas in the carrier image. To preserve these characteristics, within-group dependency tests are run on co-occurrence matrices C for each group G_k. Only those groups $G_k \in \mathcal{G}^+$ that fail the dependency tests are classified as "safe groups" and thus are used for embedding.

A co-occurrence matrix is a transition histogram between adjacent pixels for a defined relation in the spatial domain. It contains the frequency of a certain shade depending on the shade of a defined neighbour. As described in [3], we calculate

$$c_{i,j} = |\{(i,j)|b_{x,y} = i \ \wedge \ b_{x+\Delta x, y+\Delta y} = j\}|,$$

$$0 \leq i,j < N, \ 0 \leq x < X, \ 0 \leq y < Y$$

for each of the following relations $(\Delta x, \Delta y) \in \{(1,0), (-1,1), (0,1), (1,1)\}$ and test the within-group dependency with four fourfold contingency tables (cf. Table 1). The relevant entries for the dependency calculations are marked boldface in the following co-occurrence matrix

Table 1. Contingency table for classification of group G_k

(x, y)	$(x + \Delta x, y + \Delta y)$		
	$\in S_{2k}$	$\in S_{2k+1}$	$\sum$
$\in S_{2k}$	$c_{2k,2k}$	$c_{2k,2k+1}$	c'_{2k}
$\in S_{2k+1}$	$c_{2k+1,2k}$	$c_{2k+1,2k+1}$	c'_{2k+1}
$\sum$	c''_{2k}	c''_{2k+1}	n

$$C = \begin{pmatrix}
c_{0,0} & c_{1,0} & c_{2,0} & c_{3,0} & \cdots & c_{2k,0} & c_{2k+1,0} & \cdots & c_{254,0} & c_{255,0} \\
c_{0,1} & c_{1,1} & c_{2,1} & c_{3,1} & \cdots & c_{2k,1} & c_{2k+1,1} & \cdots & c_{254,1} & c_{255,1} \\
c_{0,2} & c_{1,2} & \mathbf{c_{2,2}} & \mathbf{c_{3,2}} & \cdots & c_{2k,2} & c_{2k+1,2} & \cdots & c_{254,2} & c_{255,2} \\
c_{0,3} & c_{1,3} & \mathbf{c_{2,3}} & \mathbf{c_{3,3}} & \cdots & c_{2k,3} & c_{2k+1,3} & \cdots & c_{254,3} & c_{255,3} \\
\vdots & \vdots & \vdots & \vdots & \ddots & \vdots & \vdots & \ddots & \vdots & \vdots \\
c_{0,2k} & c_{1,2k} & c_{2,2k} & c_{3,2k} & \cdots & \mathbf{c_{2k,2k}} & \mathbf{c_{2k+1,2k}} & \cdots & c_{254,2k} & c_{255,2k} \\
c_{0,2k+1} & c_{1,2k+1} & c_{2,2k+1} & c_{3,2k+1} & \cdots & \mathbf{c_{2k,2k+1}} & \mathbf{c_{2k+1,2k+1}} & \cdots & c_{254,2k+1} & c_{255,2k+1} \\
\vdots & \vdots & \vdots & \vdots & \ddots & \vdots & \vdots & \ddots & \vdots & \vdots \\
c_{0,254} & c_{1,254} & c_{2,254} & c_{3,254} & \cdots & c_{2k,254} & c_{2k+1,254} & \cdots & \mathbf{c_{254,254}} & \mathbf{c_{255,254}} \\
c_{0,255} & c_{1,255} & c_{2,255} & c_{3,255} & \cdots & c_{2k,255} & c_{2k+1,255} & \cdots & \mathbf{c_{254,255}} & \mathbf{c_{255,255}}
\end{pmatrix}$$

The test statistics χ^2 is calculated according to the following equation

$$\chi^2 = \frac{n(c_{2k,2k}c_{2k+1,2k+1} - c_{2k,2k+1}c_{2k+1,2k})^2}{c'_{2k} \; c'_{2k+1} \; c''_{2k} \; c''_{2k+1}}.$$

We assume independency for values less than $\chi^2 < 3.84$, corresponding to a significance level of $p_\alpha > 0.05$. If one of the four tests rejects the null hypothesis, the whole group is classified as unsafe and excluded from embedding.[4]

For example, 40 shades (15 %) of our example image shown in Fig. 1 were excluded. They cover 29.9 % of the surface and are marked white in Fig. 2. Further examinations with our test database indicate an average share of 43 % of the shades classified as unsafe causing an average loss of 30 % of usable pixels.

As a second modification, the PSP algorithm overwrites the least significant bits with exactly the same distribution as found in the carrier to avoid changes in the first order statistics. This systematic change is the Achilles' heel of LSB embedding and enables successful chi-square attacks with simple histogram analyses. In contrast, PSP makes effort to adopt the message distribution to the prior proportion by adding additional bits of required value and subsequently permuting the message [3]. This second modification limits the capacity of group G_k to $2 \cdot \min(|S_{2k}|, |S_{2k+1}|)$ on average. Assuming a perfectly matching code, the upper bound for the capacity of group G_k can be described with the entropy relation [14]

Fig. 1. Example greyscale image

Fig. 2. Steganographically useable pixels in the example image

$$H_k = -|S_{2k}| \log_2 \frac{|S_{2k}|}{|G_k|} - |S_{2k+1}| \log_2 \frac{|S_{2k+1}|}{|G_k|}.$$

However, the method employed by Franz does not achieve this limit. Using an arithmetic decoding operation, as proposed in [13], offers a more elegant way to preserve first order statistics—but not the exact frequencies—while embedding message bits.

Both measures together, group classification and adaptive message distribution[2], make PSP embedding secure against chi-square attacks (cf. Sect. 4).

Figure 3 contrasts LSB embedding with PSP embedding on a typical gradient part taken from an example image. The white zigzag lines separate shades belonging to different groups. For demonstration purpose, we assume that the shades S_4 and S_5 are excluded from embedding in the PSP case. Also, on the bottom line, the combined co-occurrence matrices are given for the four applied relations

$$(\Delta x, \Delta y) \in \left\{ \begin{array}{ll} (1,0) & (-1,1) \\ (0,1) & (1,1) \end{array} \right\}, \qquad \boxed{\begin{array}{ll} \rightarrow & \swarrow \\ \downarrow & \searrow \end{array}}$$

where *combined* means that the respective elements of the four resulting co-occurrence matrices are printed in each cell.

As the histograms in the middle indicate, the PSP method is not vulnerable to pair wise levelling of shade frequencies: The first order statistics from the carrier histogram are successfully preserved.

3 A Detection Strategy for PSP Steganography

A closer look at the co-occurrence matrices reveals that both embedding schemes leave noticeable traits outside the framed within-group contingency tables. According to the PSP algorithm, groups with high within-group dependencies in the co-occurrence matrix are excluded to prevent a complete erasure of those typical dependencies from the image. In fact, interdependencies in the co-occurrence matrix do not only occur inside the frames. Nevertheless, these within-group dependencies are the only information taken into account for the classification decision.

The PSP scheme does not prevent an attacker from evaluating the between-group dependencies. In addition, the preservation of the first order statistics enables the attacker to re-evaluate the classification decisions and separate used from excluded groups. Strong differences in the higher order statistics between the two classes are a reliable indicator for PSP type steganography.

To construct our attack we need some assumptions about the characteristics of image data. So we state that adjacent pixels correlate strongly, i.e., with high probability they differ only minor in brightness. The majority of dissimilar neighbours of pixels in S_k is expected to be a subset of $S_{k-1} \cup S_{k+1}$. For example, in our test database we found almost 60 % of dissimilar adjacent pixels differing

---

[2] Meanwhile Franz calls these measures *CCM* and *Histo*, respectively [5].

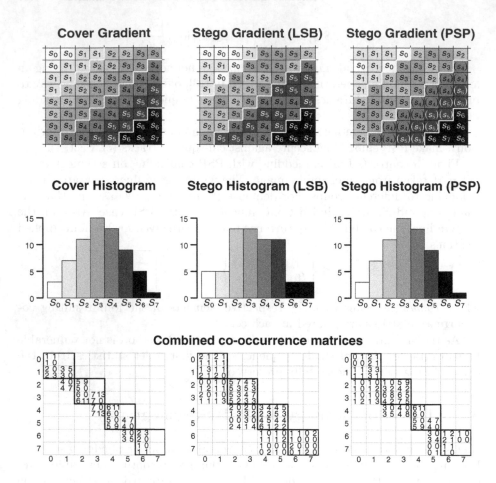

Fig. 3. Comparison of LSB and PSP embedding

by only ±1 in brightness. Hence, any pixel in $S_{<2k}$, darker than the shades in uniformly distributed G_k, is with higher probability neighbour of the darker pixels in $S_{2k} \in G_k$ than the brighter ones in $S_{2k+1} \in G_k$, and vice versa. Still under the assumption that $|S_{2k}| = |S_{2k+1}|$, we assert

$$P(b_{x,y} = a | b_{x',y'} = 2k+1) < P(b_{x,y} = a | b_{x',y'} = 2k) \qquad \text{for } a \leq 2k,$$
$$P(b_{x,y} = a | b_{x',y'} = 2k+1) > P(b_{x,y} = a | b_{x',y'} = 2k) \qquad \text{else,}$$

with $x' = x + \Delta x$, $y' = y + \Delta y$, and $1 \leq \sqrt{\Delta x^2 + \Delta y^2} < 2$. This relation leads to a typical structure in the co-occurrence matrix C. Table 2 shows the two relevant columns for a group G_k and the expected individual proportions between the corresponding frequencies.

Table 2. Structure of G_k columns before embedding

(x', y')	(x, y)		
	$\in S_{2k}$		$\in S_{2k+1}$
$\in S_0$	$c_{2k,0}$	$>$	$c_{2k+1,0}$
$\in S_1$	$c_{2k,1}$	$>$	$c_{2k+1,1}$
$\vdots$	$\vdots$	$>$	$\vdots$
$\in S_{2k-1}$	$c_{2k,2k-1}$	$>$	$c_{2k+1,2k-1}$
$\in S_{2k}$	$c_{2k,2k}$	$>$	$c_{2k+1,2k}$
$\in S_{2k+1}$	$c_{2k,2k+1}$	$<$	$c_{2k+1,2k+1}$
$\in S_{2k+2}$	$c_{2k,2k+2}$	$<$	$c_{2k+1,2k+2}$
$\vdots$	$\vdots$	$<$	$\vdots$
$\in S_{N-2}$	$c_{2k,N-2}$	$<$	$c_{2k+1,N-2}$
$\in S_{N-1}$	$c_{2k,N-1}$	$<$	$c_{2k+1,N-1}$
$\sum$	$|S_{2k}|$	$=$	$|S_{2k+1}|$

As PSP embedding preserves the distribution within the groups and does not mind the neighbourhood relations, it is indistinguishable from a random permutation within each group. Given that $G_k \in \mathcal{G}^+$, it is usable for embedding. The random permutation of the shades within G_k equalises the frequencies for S_{2k} and S_{2k+1} in relation to all other shades in the co-occurrence matrix. The post-embedding structure of the G_k columns in C is shown in Table 3.

Table 3. Structure of G_k columns after PSP embedding

(x', y')	(x, y)		
	$\in S_{2k}$		$\in S_{2k+1}$
$\in S_0$	$c_{2k,0}$	$=$	$c_{2k+1,0}$
$\in S_1$	$c_{2k,1}$	$=$	$c_{2k+1,1}$
$\vdots$	$\vdots$	$=$	$\vdots$
$\in S_{2k-1}$	$c_{2k,2k-1}$	$=$	$c_{2k+1,2k-1}$
$\in S_{2k}$	$c_{2k,2k}$	$=$	$c_{2k+1,2k}$
$\in S_{2k+1}$	$c_{2k,2k+1}$	$=$	$c_{2k+1,2k+1}$
$\in S_{2k+2}$	$c_{2k,2k+2}$	$=$	$c_{2k+1,2k+2}$
$\vdots$	$\vdots$	$=$	$\vdots$
$\in S_{N-2}$	$c_{2k,N-2}$	$=$	$c_{2k+1,N-2}$
$\in S_{N-1}$	$c_{2k,N-1}$	$=$	$c_{2k+1,N-1}$
$\sum$	$|S_{2k}|$	$=$	$|S_{2k+1}|$

We can distinguish the pre- and post-embedding structures shown in Tables 2 and 3 with a contingency test. For this purpose, we interpret a pair of columns

Table 4. G_k columns after embedding with imbalanced frequencies of S_{2k} and S_{2k+1}

(x',y')	(x,y)			(x',y')	(x,y)		
	$\in S_{2k}$		$\in S_{2k+1}$		$\in S_{2k}$		$\in S_{2k+1}$
$\in S_0$	$c_{2k,0}$	$<$	$c_{2k+1,0}$	$\in S_0$	$c_{2k,0}$	$>$	$c_{2k+1,0}$
$\in S_1$	$c_{2k,1}$	$<$	$c_{2k+1,1}$	$\in S_1$	$c_{2k,1}$	$>$	$c_{2k+1,1}$
$\vdots$	$\vdots$	$<$	$\vdots$	$\vdots$	$\vdots$	$>$	$\vdots$
$\in S_{2k-1}$	$c_{2k,2k-1}$	$<$	$c_{2k+1,2k-1}$	$\in S_{2k-1}$	$c_{2k,2k-1}$	$>$	$c_{2k+1,2k-1}$
$\in S_{2k}$	$c_{2k,2k}$	$<$	$c_{2k+1,2k}$	$\in S_{2k}$	$c_{2k,2k}$	$>$	$c_{2k+1,2k}$
$\in S_{2k+1}$	$c_{2k,2k+1}$	$<$	$c_{2k+1,2k+1}$	$\in S_{2k+1}$	$c_{2k,2k+1}$	$>$	$c_{2k+1,2k+1}$
$\in S_{2k+2}$	$c_{2k,2k+2}$	$<$	$c_{2k+1,2k+2}$	$\in S_{2k+2}$	$c_{2k,2k+2}$	$>$	$c_{2k+1,2k+2}$
$\vdots$	$\vdots$	$<$	$\vdots$	$\vdots$	$\vdots$	$>$	$\vdots$
$\in S_{N-2}$	$c_{2k,N-2}$	$<$	$c_{2k+1,N-2}$	$\in S_{N-2}$	$c_{2k,N-2}$	$>$	$c_{2k+1,N-2}$
$\in S_{N-1}$	$c_{2k,N-1}$	$<$	$c_{2k+1,N-1}$	$\in S_{N-1}$	$c_{2k,N-1}$	$>$	$c_{2k+1,N-1}$
$\sum$	$|S_{2k}|$	$<$	$|S_{2k+1}|$	$\sum$	$|S_{2k}|$	$>$	$|S_{2k+1}|$

from C as a contingency table and perform a chi-square test for dependency. The former structure is supposed to show a noticeable dependency, the latter not. We further refer to this procedure as *between-group dependency test*.

Even if we drop the assumption that the membership is uniformly distributed between S_{2k} and S_{2k+1} within G_k, we still expect dependencies in the carrier image, modulated by the proportion $S_{2k} : S_{2k+1}$:

$$|S_{2k}| \cdot c_{a,2k+1} < |S_{2k+1}| \cdot c_{a,2k} \qquad \text{for } a < 2k,$$
$$|S_{2k}| \cdot c_{a,2k+1} > |S_{2k+1}| \cdot c_{a,2k} \qquad \text{else.}$$

As the PSP scheme uses adaptive skewness correction, the imbalanced situation is quite probable. Nevertheless, there are still different directions of the inequality relations between adjacent columns of the co-occurrence matrix, which are equally aligned in the groups "permuted" after the PSP embedding operation (cf. Table 4). These alignments are also recognised as independently distributed events by the contingency test. Hence, the skewness correction does not weaken our ability to distinguish between permuted and original groups.

Certain practical obstacles impede using these analyses to guide a precise attack on PSP embedding. At first, the columns of the co-occurrence matrix hold a lot of low frequency entries that bias the outcome of the chi-square between-group dependency test. Secondly, we have to take into account that the above mentioned interrelations apply to all of the four co-occurrence matrices representing the four relations. We tackle these problems by first summing up the four matrices and then erasing rows with row sums less than a minimum count q. All images, whether with or without a PSP embedded message, contain a certain amount of groups that pass the between-group dependency test. Only the test results of the actually usable groups in $\mathcal{G}^+$ contain valuable information for an attacker about the application of PSP steganography. Therefore, the attacker has to gain knowledge, which groups belong to $\mathcal{G}^+$. Fortunately, this is not difficult, because the PSP scheme preserves the relevant statistics so that the receiver is able to recalculate the initial classification of groups as shown in Sect. 2.

The final step of the proposed attack is an inference from a set of between-group dependency tests to the existence of steganographic content. Since the tests are not accurate for all groups, we cannot expect independency for all members of $\mathcal{G}^+$. Therefore we allow a certain number of tests below a threshold t to pass the between-group dependency test on a $p_\alpha < 0.01$ significance level. It seems sensible to choose q dependent on the number of pixels $X \cdot Y$ and the threshold t on the number of groups $|\mathcal{G}|$. These refinements are subject to further research.

In brief, the attack procedure can be summarised in four steps:

1. Classify all groups according to the embedding scheme,
2. calculate and sum co-occurrence matrices for four relations,
3. test between-group dependencies in column pairs for all usable groups,
4. count positive tests and compare with threshold value.

Our experimental results described in the following section provide a proof of concept for the proposed attack.

4   Experimental Results

To evaluate the practical capabilities of the proposed attack we assembled a test database T_0 of 100 greyscale images sized $X \times Y = 284 \times 213$ pixels ($N = 256$ shades). The images were randomly drawn from a large number of high resolution photographs from a digital camera. An $8 : 1$ size reduction ensures that possible compression artefacts of the initial JPEG encoding are effectively removed [6]. The small images were stored as losslessly compressed PNG files and analysed with the R software for statistical computing [8,12].

To compare the LSB and PSP embedding schemes, we prepared three test sets:

1. T_1: LSB embedding of uniformly distributed random bits using 100 % of the capacity (i.e., 1 bit per pixel),
2. T_2: PSP embedding of uniformly distributed random bits using 100 % of the capacity (between 0.1 and 1.0 bits per pixel, depending on the image, mean $\mu = 0.77$),
3. T_3: LSB embedding of uniformly distributed random bits using the respective maximum capacity of T_2.

The images of all test sets ($T_0, \ldots, T_3$) were exposed to the chi-square attack with a threshold criteria of $p_\alpha < 0.01$, as well as to the proposed PSP attack

Table 5. Summary of experimental attacks

Attack	Test set, algorithm	Results	
		FALSE	TRUE
Chi-square attack			
	T_0: Plain carrier	92	8
	T_1: LSB (full capacity)	0	100
	T_2: PSP (max capacity)	92	8
	T_3: LSB (limited PSP cap.)	22	78
Proposed attack			
	T_0: Plain carrier	94	6
	T_2: PSP (max capacity)	0	100

Test data: 100 greyscale images sized 284 × 213 pixel, $N = 256$

with a maximum number of passed tests of $t = 8$, and a minimum row sum of co-occurrence cells $q = 10$. The results are presented in Table 5.

As expected, the chi-square attack reliably identified all LSB steganograms with full capacity usage. However, we noted that eight percent of the tests of pristine material led to a false positive. The same attack applied to the PSP embedded images was comparably ineffective. The preservation of first order statistics successfully prevents chi-square attacks.

Even if invisible to the chi-square attack, all PSP steganograms can be detected with the proposed attack, although the absolute message length is only a fractional amount of the LSB capacity. In fact, four images with less than 20 % of the respective LSB capacity are reliably detected. Regarding the number of false positives, the discriminatory power of the PSP attack seems to exceed the chi-square attack, even though the numbers are too small to provide strong evidence. The tests on T_3 reveal that passing on full capacity and accepting a reduced message length with the well known LSB algorithm is comparatively safer than using the more sophisticated PSP scheme.

To evaluate the stability over different utilisations of capacity between the two embedding schemes with their respective attacks, we gradually reduced the message lengths embedded with the PSP method. In addition, precisely the same amount of bits embedded with PSP was also LSB embedded in the respective images to build a comparison group. As the results in Table 6 indicate, the proposed PSP attack provides higher detection rates for high capacity utilisations.

5   Discussion of Countermeasures

The proposed attack basically exploits the removal of inter-dependencies between adjacent pixels belonging to different groups. A rather naïve approach to tackle

Table 6. Attack reliability against capacity usage

		Attacks	
Capacity usage	Embedding density	chi-square	proposed
% of max. PSP capacity	av. msg. bits per pixel	# of hits out of 100	# of hits out of 100
100 %	0.77	78	100
75 %	0.58	62	88
50 %	0.39	45	38
25 %	0.20	35	14

Test data: 100 greyscale images sized 284×213 pixel, $N = 256$

this problem could be the exclusion of all pixels with neighbours of other groups. So the set of usable pixels will be reduced to those pixels completely surrounded by neighbours of their own group G_k,

$$G'_k = \{(x,y)|(x + \Delta x, y + \Delta y) \in G_k, \ \forall \Delta x, \Delta y \in \{-1,0,1\}\}.$$

This modification obviously withstands the proposed attack because the between-group interdependencies are kept untouched. However, only a tiny set of pixels meets this strict condition. For example, our test image contains only 15 usable pixels depicted black in Fig. 4. The comparably larger count of grey pixels in Fig. 4 are also surrounded by the same group but were classified as unsafe according to the PSP classification. Because of the vanishing capacity it is hard to say whether an adapted attack regarding the more distant neighbours $(2 \leq \sqrt{\Delta x^2 + \Delta y^2} < 3)$ fails because of the low sample size or is generally impossible. Experiments with larger samples of images with higher resolution are subject to further research.

Regarding this low residual capacity, the LSB algorithm may be a comparably safe alternative. In addition, the security can be further increased by implementing the advices from [15], e. g., to replace LSB overwriting by a more suitable operation such as incrementing or decrementing.

Adaptive embedding, i. e., regarding the carrier structures, is a promising principle for steganography but also opens new pitfalls because the receiver has to recover the structural information to extract the message. For example, the PSP method implements its adaptive mechanism on a group wise classification that can be reproduced both by the receiver but also by an attacker. On the one hand, it is important that the receiver is able to recover all necessary information to extract the message. On the other hand, any information about which pixels are actually usable, gives also an advantage to the attacker: By contrasting the two groups in relevant statistics, she can reveal systematic characteristics that are typical for the embedding scheme but rarely observable in pristine carrier data. We will briefly outline two measures to avoid these problems. At first, the "meta-information approach" aims to hide the classification information by encrypting and embedding it into the safest parts of a carrier.

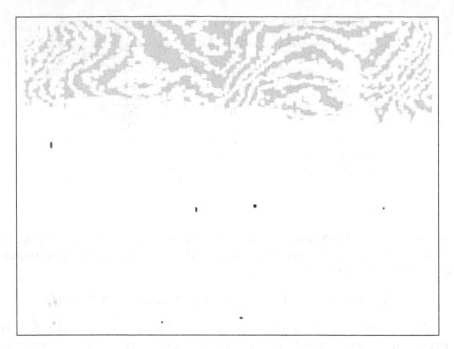

Fig. 4. Pixels surrounded by the same group in our test image. Black pixels belong to safe groups in $\mathcal{G}^+$, grey to unsafe

So, the receiver decodes the meta-information before using it to extract the payload message. Second, the "selection channel approach" [1] completely avoids the share of meta-information concerning the usable positions. Parity encoding ensures that the receiver is always able to extract the message without knowledge about the actually altered bits. Both approaches unfortunately reduce the maximum message length.

6   Conclusion

The presented attack against a steganographic algorithm that preserves some relevant statistics puts into question, whether a rather fussy preservation helps to increase security and therefore should be included in future embedding algorithms. This does not imply that the preservation of statistics is generally a bad idea, but the way it is achieved—i.e., skipping certain "dangerous" groups while modifying others—makes the discussed scheme vulnerable to the proposed attack.

In addition, the exact preservation of statistics that are used for the classification decision enables an attacker to reproduce this decision. This practice causes the sender to give up her superiority of information.

Since first and higher order statistics do heavily vary between different pictures, and given an attacker who has no possibility to guess or estimate these parameters of the carrier, a moderate change of them does not necessarily weaken security. It may be wise, to refocus further development of steganographic methods from compulsive preservation of parameters to the avoidance of typical—and hence conspicuous—patterns and artefacts. For instance, the promising model-based approach for steganography [13] already employs some of these ideas, even though an adversary can still reproduce the distribution model.

Nevertheless, we suppose that adaptive embedding is a promising practice but classification criteria need to be carefully selected. Using or avoiding shades globally may be problematic in two senses. At first, it raises the danger of misclassifications. For example, a bright shade covering large parts of the sky in our example image also occurs in the lower part. The dependencies in the sky cause a global exclusion of the whole group, even if it could be used for data hiding in the lower part. Vice versa, a shade that is independent at the overwhelming majority of occurrences may be classified as usable even if some occurrences in a "dangerous" context give an attacker strong evidence for steganographic modifications. The second problem of global classification concerns large numbers. The statistical tests of an attacker tend to become the more reliable the more observations she has. Given the situation that a defined message could be transferred either in one large or in several tiny images, we face the following obscurity. With global criteria, the probability of detection increases with the amount of data per pass, i. e., one large image is more dangerous than several tiny images. Therefore, we suggest to research local adaptive mechanisms to reduce numbers and keep detection rates low and independent from the actual image size.

As final conclusion we state that a sophisticated selection of positions for embedding is not necessarily inferior to random selection.

Acknowledgement

The work on this paper was supported by the Air Force Office of Scientific Research under the research grant number FA8655-03-1-3A46. The U. S. Government is authorised to reproduce and distribute reprints for Governmental purposes notwithstanding any copyright notation there on. The views and conclusions contained herein are those of the authors and should not be interpreted as necessarily representing the official policies, either expressed or implied, of the Air Force Office of Scientific Research, or the U. S. Government.

References

1. Anderson, R. J., Petitcolas, F. A. P.: On the Limits of Steganography. IEEE Journal on Selected Areas in Communications **16** (1998) 474–481
2. Cachin, C.: An Information-Theoretic Model for Steganography. In: Aucsmith, D. (ed.): Information Hiding. Second International Workshop, LNCS 1525, Springer-Verlag, Berlin Heidelberg (1998) 306–318
3. Franz, E.: Steganography Preserving Statistical Properties. In: Petitcolas, F. A. P. (ed.): Information Hiding. 5th International Workshop, LNCS 2578, Springer-Verlag, Berlin Heidelberg (2003) 278–294

4. Franz, E.: personal communication (2003, Dec)
5. Franz, E., Pandit, V., Schneidewind, A.: Realization of Steganographic Algorithms and Discussion of Possible Problems. Unpublished working paper, Technische Universität Dresden (2004)
6. Fridrich, J., Goljan, M., Du, R.: Steganalysis Based on JPEG Compatibility. In: Tescher A. G., Vasudev B., Bove V. M., Jr. (eds.): Proceedings of SPIE, Multimedia Systems and Applications IV, Vol. 4518, Denver, CO, (2001) 275–280
7. Fridrich, J., Goljan, M., Du, R.: Reliable Detection of LSB Based Image Steganography. Proceedings of the ACM Workshop on Multimedia and Security (2001) 27–30
8. Ihaka, R., Gentlemen, R.: R—A Language for Data Analysis and Graphics. Journal of Computational Graphics and Statistics **5** (1996) 299–314
9. Johnson, N. F., Jajodia, S.: Steganalysis of Images Created Using Current Steganography Software. In: Aucsmith D. (ed.): Information Hiding. Second International Workshop, LNCS 1525, Springer-Verlag, Berlin Heidelberg (1998) 273–289
10. Katzenbeisser, S., Petitcolas, F. A. P.: On Defining Security in Steganographic Systems. Proceeding of SPIE, Security and Watermarking of Multimedia Contents IV, Vol. 4675. San Jose, California (2002) 50–56
11. Koops, B.-J.: Crypto Law Survey. Version 21.0, http://rechten.kub.nl/koops/cryptolaw/ (2002, Oct)
12. R Language for Statistical Computing, http://www.r-project.org
13. Sallee, P.: Model-Based Steganography. In: T. Kalker et al. (eds.): International Workshop on Digital Watermarking, LNCS 2939, Springer-Verlag, Berlin Heidelberg (2004) 154–167
14. Shannon, C. E.: A Mathematical Theory of Communication. Bell System Technical Journal **27** (1948) 379–423 623–656
15. Westfeld, A., Pfitzmann, A.: Attacks on Steganographic Systems. In: Pfitzmann, A. (ed.): Information Hiding. Third International Workshop, LNCS 1768, Springer-Verlag, Berlin Heidelberg (2000) 61–76
16. Zöllner, J., Federrath, H., Klimant, H., Pfitzmann, A., Piotraschke, R., Westfeld, A., Wicke, G., Wolf, G.: Modeling the Security of Steganographic Systems. In: Aucsmith D. (ed.): Information Hiding. Second International Workshop, LNCS 1525, Springer-Verlag, Berlin Heidelberg (1998) 344–354

Improved Detection of LSB Steganography in Grayscale Images

Andrew D. Ker

Oxford University Computing Laboratory, Parks Road, Oxford OX1 3QD, England
adk@comlab.ox.ac.uk

Abstract. We consider methods for answering reliably the question of whether an image contains hidden data; the focus is on grayscale bitmap images and simple LSB steganography. Using a distributed computation network and a library of over 30,000 images we have been carefully evaluating the reliability of various steganalysis methods. The results suggest a number of improvements to the standard techiques, with particular benefits gained by not attempting to estimate the hidden message length. Extensive experimentation shows that the improved methods allow reliable detection of LSB steganography with between 2 and 6 times smaller embedded messages.

1 Introduction

Steganography aims to transmit information invisibly, embedded as imperceptible alterations to cover data; steganalysis aims to unmask the presence of such hidden data. Although by no means the most secure method of embedding data in images, LSB steganography tools are now extremely widespread. It is well known that embedding near-to-maximum size messages in images using the LSB technique is quite reliably detectable by statistical analysis [1,2] but that spreading fewer embedded bits around the cover image makes the steganalyst's task much more difficult [3].

In this paper we present improved steganalysis methods, based on the most reliable detectors of thinly-spread LSB steganography presently known [4,5,6], focussing on the case when grayscale bitmaps are used as cover images. They arise as a result of observations from a distributed steganalysis project, undertaken in response to a general call at the 2002 Information Hiding Workshop for thorough evaluation of the reliability of steganalysis techniques. The project uses a network of computers to provide speedy computation of steganalysis statistics over large image libraries, making it easy to see where improvements can arise. An outline of the project, and the first results, can be found in [7].

The aims of this paper are a) to suggest improved steganalysis statistics for LSB steganography, b) to use large image libraries to give experimental evidence of the improvement, and c) to examine closely the upper limits on bit rate which keep LSB steganography undetectable. We do not give theoretical analysis of the improved statistics and in no way claim that they are necessarily optimal; our intention is simply to advance the state of the art.

J. Fridrich (Ed.): IH 2004, LNCS 3200, pp. 97–115, 2004.

1.1 Scope

We take on the role of an "information security officer", a hypothetical Warden whose job it is to scrutinise electronic communication. We want to answer the *simple classification question* – whether a given image has hidden data or not – and our work is currently focussed solely on the reliability of steganalysis methods to answer this question. Each steganalysis method will be statistic (a function of the input image) designed to discriminate between the two cases. Thus we are looking for a hypothesis test, where the null hypothesis is that no data is hidden, and the alternative hypothesis is that data is hidden[1]. We have to presuppose a fixed method of embedding data and a fixed length of hidden message, so that both null and alternative hypotheses are *simple* (not depending on an unknown parameter). Then it becomes possible to simulate the distributions taken by steganalysis statistics in both cases.

A good steganalysis statistic would give higher values in the case of hidden data and lower values otherwise; the Warden's only sensible strategy is to reject the null hypothesis (make a positive diagnosis of steganography) when the statistic exceeds a certain threshold. But in practice the distributions (histograms) of the statistic in the case of null and alternative hypotheses will overlap so there is no threshold which will make the detector work perfectly. Varying the detection threshold plays off the likelihood of false positive results against missed detections (false negative results), and it is the graph of these two probabilities, the Receiver Operating Characteristic (ROC) curve, which fully describes the reliability of a particular statistic against a particular hidden message length.[2]

A key assumption in this paper is that false positive results are considered more serious than missed detections. If most images which come under the scrutiny of the information security officer are innocent it is important that false positives do not swamp true detections. So for the rest of this work we will assume that the Warden requires a detector with a fairly low false positive rate (in the region of 1-10%) and also that the steganographer acts repeatedly, so that even a missed detection rate of 50% is acceptable because eventually they would be caught. We recognise that the numbers involved are fairly arbitrary but it is necessary to start somewhere.

For now we are *not* interested in more advanced analysis of suspect images such as estimates of hidden message length [4,8,5], except in as much as they function as discriminating statistics for the simple classification problem. Such *threshold-free* statistics are popular, but the lack of a detection threshold is illusory because an information security officer would have to know whether

---

[1] Some other authors have reversed the designation of null and alternative hypothesis, but our exposition fits better with the accepted norms of statistics.

[2] Pierre Moulin has pointed out that randomized detectors are optimal, and in the case when the ROC curve is concave can improve performance up to its convex closure. But to exploit this does require a genuinely simple alternative hypothesis and this is not likely to be the case in practice – the Warden does not have advance warning of the amount of hidden data to expect. So for now we ignore this issue, although the reader may wish mentally to take the convex closure of the ROC curves displayed.

to interpret a particular estimated message length as significantly higher than zero or not. A more precise measure of the certainty of a positive diagnosis is the *p-value* of an observation, which can be computed for any type of statistic. Furthermore, we asked in [7] whether statistics designed to estimate the hidden message length were suboptimal for the simple classification problem and we will show here that the answer is yes.

1.2   LSB Steganography

Here we consider simple Least Significant Bit (LSB) steganography, long-known to steganographers, in which the hidden message is converted to a stream of bits which replace the LSBs of pixel values in the cover image. When the hidden message contains less bits than the cover image has pixels, we assume that the modifications are spread randomly around the cover image according to a secret key shared with the intended recipient of the stego image. This sort of steganography is only suitable for images stored in bitmap form or losslessly compressed. One should clearly distinguish this method (perhaps best called *LSB replacement*) from an alternative described in [9], where the cover pixel values are randomly incremented or decremented so that the least significant bits match the hidden message (this should perhaps be called *LSB matching*). In the latter case the message is still conveyed using the LSBs of the pixel values of the image, but the simple alteration to the embedding algorithm makes it much harder to detect. None of the methods discussed here will detect this alternative form of steganography, and indeed it is a much more difficult task to do so: a detector for LSB matching in full colour bitmaps is described in [2] but it is ineffective for grayscale covers; another detector which works for full colour images is described in [10] but it is only reliable for very large embedded messages and barely effective for grayscale covers.

LSB replacement is by no means the best – or even a sensible – steganographic method. However we consider it extremely worthy of study because of its widespread use. A large majority of freely available steganography software makes use of LSB replacement, but there is a more important reason: it can be performed without any special tools at all. Imagine, for example, a steganographer trying to send secrets out of a corporation. If the corporation takes information security seriously then the very presence of any steganographic software on an employee's computer is certain to be noticed and is *prima facie* evidence of wrongdoing, regardless of the undetectability of the actual messages. But a canny steganographer can simply go to a UNIX-style commandline and type

```
perl -n0777e '$_=unpack"b*",$_;split/(\s+)/,<STDIN>,5;
              @_[8]=~s{.}{$&&v254|chop()&v1}ge;print@_'
              <input.pgm >output.pgm secrettextfile
```

to embed a message (backwards) in the LSBs of the pixels in a PGM image (the PGM format is common and there are widely installed commandline tools to convert from JPEG, BMP or other formats, and then back to BMP if necessary for transmission). This 80 character Perl code is short enough to memorise, and fairly small modifications can be made to spread the embedding around the cover image. The more sophisticated methods of embedding cannot easily be performed without special software[3]. This is why, for now, we focus on LSB replacement.

1.3   Pairs, RS, and Couples Steganalysis

We summarise the methods for the detection of LSB steganography on which our later work builds. Nothing in this section is new and details are omitted; the reader is referred to the original papers for a proper explanation of how each statistic works. We re-present the detection statistics of [4,5,6] in a way which emphasises their fundamental similarities. Firstly, all are "threshold-free" statistics which aim to estimate the length of a hidden message, and we assume that the method is used to answer the simple classification problem by accepting the null hypothesis if the estimated length is less than a certain threshold. Pairs Analysis was designed with paletted images in mind, but there is no theoretical reason why it should not work for grayscale images; RS was designed with colour images in mind, although it works by treating each colour component separately and as such is really a grayscale method.

In each case two measurements are made: in this work we will write $Q(p)$ and $Q'(p)$ for random variables which are the two measurements when $2p$ is the amount of embedded data[4]. In each of [4,5,6] either theoretical calculation or experimental evidence shows that the expectations of $Q(p)$ and $Q'(p)$ are (precisely or a close approximation to) a quadratic in p. For a given image with an unknown amount of embedded data (possibly zero) we can observe $Q(p)$ and $Q'(p)$, and also $Q(1-p)$ and $Q'(1-p)$ by flipping all LSBs. In each case it is also possible to obtain $Q(0.5)$ and $Q'(0.5)$, either by theoretically derived calculation or by randomizing the LSB plane of the image. Finally, in each of the cases of Pairs, RS and Couples we make the assumption that $Q(0) = Q'(0)$ – an assumed property of natural images – and the correctness of this assumption is the major factor in the accuracy of the final estimate. The law of large numbers means that the values of the random variables $Q(p)$ and $Q'(p)$ will be close to their expectations; there is now sufficient information to solve for the parameter p ([6] includes detailed calculations). The measurements Q and Q' differ for the three methods, although they are not dissimilar.

In Pairs Analysis [5], due to Fridrich *et al*, first *colour cuts* are formed by scanning through and selecting only pixels which fall into each pair of values (0,1), (2,3), and so on. The colour cuts are concatenated to form a single stream,

---

[3] The exception is LSB matching, which can be done using code not much larger than that above. There is an urgent need for a improved detectors for LSB matching, especially when the embedded message is not of full length or for grayscale covers.

[4] p is the proportion of pixels with flipped LSBs, which is the expected proportion when $2p$ pixels are used for steganography because about half of the pixels would have carried the correct LSB already.

a re-ordering of the pixels of the original image. The measure Q is the *relative homogeneity* of the LSBs of this stream, the proportion of adjacent pixels with the same LSB. The measure Q' is calculated in the same way except that the pairs of values used to form the colour cuts are the dual pairs (255,0), (1,2), (3,4), etc.

Also due to Fridrich *et al.* is the method of RS [4], also called *dual statistics*. Here the image is sectioned into groups of pixels; the size of the group is variable but in [4] it is either a four-by-one horizontal rectangle, or a two-by-two square. A "mask" is applied to each block – the mask specifies that certain pixels in it should have their LSBs flipped. Each group is classified as *regular, singular,* or neither, depending on whether the noise within the pixel group (as measured by the mean absolute value of the differences between adjacent pixels) is increased, decreased, or unchanged after this flipping; we denote the proportion of regular and singular groups as R and S. The classification is repeated using the dual form of flipping $1 \leftrightarrow 2, 3 \leftrightarrow 4, \ldots, 255 \leftrightarrow 0$; call the proportion of regular and singular groups under the dual flipping R' and S'. The two measurements finally used by RS steganalysis are $Q = R - S$ and $Q' = R' - S'$; under the additional assumption that *both* $R = R'$ and $S = S'$ for natural images it becomes possible to derive $Q(0.5)$ and $Q'(0.5)$ theoretically rather than resort to experimentation.

The third detection method we consider here is due to Dumitrescu *et al*; it was presented in [6] where it was called *Sample Pairs Analysis*. The same technique was discovered independently (but not published) by this author and termed *Couples Analysis*. For this paper we use the latter name, partly out of familiarity and partly because "Sample Pairs" could easily be confused with "Pairs". It is conceptually the simplest method of the three under consideration, and also has the most complete theoretical analysis. We will later show that it is also marginally the most accurate. Consider the set of all horizontally and vertically adjacent pairs of pixels in the image. Let E_k be the proportion of pairs of pixels which a) differ in value by k and b) of which the lower of the two values is even. O_k is the same but with the lower of the two values odd. Suitable measurements are $Q_i = E_{2i+1}$ and $Q'_i = O_{2i+1}$; in [6] it is shown that Q_i and Q'_i (for each i) satisfy the properties listed above of Q and Q'; after some analysis the authors suggest using $Q = \sum_i Q_i$ and $Q' = \sum_i Q'_i$. It is also possible to compute $Q(0.5)$ and $Q'(0.5)$ exactly, without randomizing the LSB plane.

2   Experimental Programme

Experimental results come from our distributed steganalysis project (see [7] for some details). In order to evaluate the performance of a particular steganalysis algorithm against a particular method of steganography we need to approximate the distributions of the discriminating statistic in the two cases of absence and presence of hidden data. We do so using a number of large sets of sample images. We also need to repeat with varying amounts of hidden data to establish the level at which steganography becomes detectable. So for each steganography algorithm under consideration, and each steganalysis method being tested, with a number of message sizes, we compute the discriminating statistic before and after embedding a random message.

Because the number of combinations of steganalysis algorithms (each with a large number of variations), message sizes, and thousands of images to test with the possibility of subjecting them to pre-embedding JPEG compression, is so large we will need millions of computations. This is distributed to network of machines, with the results stored in a relational database. At the time of writing there had been up to 50 machines used at once in the network, and the results database contained over 13 million rows. Results are then extracted, analysed to produce ROC curves for each set of parameters (steganography method, amount of hidden data, steganalysis statistic, image set, etc.) and graphed.

2.1   Sample Results

Figure 1 shows some of the results from the database. The chart displayed shows the ROC curves for a small set of 1200 uncompressed images, when 10% LSB steganography (i.e. 0.1 bits per pixel) is used and the images are tested with the standard RS statistic of [4]. The experiment has been repeated with the cover images first resampled down to a number of different sizes, and it is instructive to see what a difference this makes to the reliability of the RS statistic.

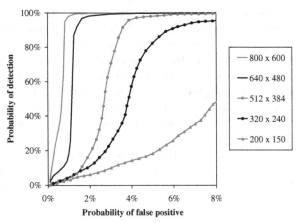

Fig. 1. ROC curves for a set of 1200 uncompressed images, originally 1024×768 but resampled down to a variety of smaller sizes. In each case 10% steganography has been used, and tested against the standard RS statistic of [4]

Compare the curves for the two sets resizes to 640×480 and 320×240. It turns out (ROC curve not displayed) that the performance of the RS statistic in the 640×480 images when 0.1 bits per pixel steganography is embedded is approximately the same as for the 320×240 images when 0.17 bits per pixel LSB steganography is used. This is not contrary to the instinctively obvious fact that larger images can carry larger messages securely, but it does indicate that the increase is not proportional.

Figure 1 also illustrates the general shape of ROC curves, which tend to fall dramatically when the false positive rate goes below a certain level. Thus it is not often useful to fix a particular false-positive rate and compare different statistics' reliability rates at this point. A more reasonable one-dimensional measure of performance, and one we quote on occasion, is the level of false positives when the threshold is set for 50% reliability. We find that this often serves as a fair summary of the performance. At the end we will focus on an even more particular case, determining the minimum embedding rate for which 50% reliability is achieved with a 5% false positive rate.

When choosing which ROC curves to show we will focus on "interesting" cases – we will choose a steganography embedding rate so that the performance is neither too near perfect (in which case any differences are as likely due to chance as anything else) or too poor (because results of that nature are not interesting). We will also scale the x-axis (false positive rate) so that the graph shows only areas of interest (in particular we will not show false positive rates of more than 10%). The y-axis will always run over reliability rates of 0% to 100%.

2.2 Image Sets Used for Testing

In [7] we gave two important examples which warn of some of the difficulties in evaluating steganalysis algorithms. Firstly, we found that cover images which have been JPEG compressed can lead to vastly different reliability of detection, even after the JPEG images were substantially reduced in size in an attempt to "wash out" the compression artifacts. Secondly we found that different resampling methods used to resize sets of images also resulted in different performance when steganalysis methods were tested against them. This makes it clear that there is no such thing as a universally "representative" set of natural images for the purposes of testing steganalysis.

We address this issue in part by obtaining a number of large sets of images and using each set separately, to be sure of covering all image types and also to expose any differences in performance with the eventual aim of explaining them. So in subsequent testing we will use:

Image Set A: 2200 simulated uncompressed images, all 512×512. The "simulation" of uncompressed images is performed by taking very large and mildly compressed JPEG files and reducing (in view of the warnings of [7] we have used a mixture of resampling algorithms). These images are "high-quality" in the sense that out-of-focus and incorrectly exposed images have been removed. Since they are uncompressed we will also repeat experiments by pre-compressing them, to measure how much the statistics' reliability depends on this factor.

Image Set B: 5000 JPEG images, all sized 900×600. Each is compressed at JPEG quality factor 75. These came from a royalty-free image library purchased by the author. The photographs are of quite good quality in terms of exposure and focus, but they appear to have been scanned in from 35mm film and some show granularity. Some have a small black border.

Image Set C: 10000 JPEG images, sizes varying between 890×560 and 1050×691. The JPEG compression levels vary from approximately quality factor 50 to 75. These images came from another royalty-free image library, but the quality of pictures is not as good as Set B; some images are blurred or incorrectly exposed.

Image Set D: 7500 JPEG images of very variable quality. They were obtained from an open image library which the public may contribute to. Accordingly the images' provenance cannot be verified, but they clearly come from a very wide range of sources. The quality is extremely variable – there are a few blurred, grainy and distorted pictures included. Most of the images are sized between 800×600 and 1024×768. The JPEG compression levels are fairly evenly distributed between approximately quality factors 50 and 90.

It will be seen that Image Set A is "difficult" for the steganalyst, in that the statistics' reliability is worse over this set than the others (and this seems the general case for uncompressed images). Set C is the "easiest". Set D is expected to be difficult because of its heterogeneity. Our image library contains other sets but in the interests of space we do not report results for them.

One may ask why we test the spatial-domain LSB steganography method against images which have been stored in JPEG format, especially given the technique of *JPEG compatability analysis* [11]. One reason is that we have found it extremely hard to obtain large sets of images which can be guaranteed never to have undergone compression or other distortions. Furthermore the fact is that most natural images are stored in JPEG format and, just as we are examining LSB steganography for its ease of use and prevalence, we want to test against all likely types of cover image. The casual steganographer may well only have access to JPEG compressed images. Finally, we believe that JPEG compatability analysis can be avoided if simple global operations such as very mild blurring or change of contrast are applied to the JPEG images before LSB embedding.

3   Improved Detection Methods and Experimental Evidence

In the main body of this paper we will suggest a number of improved detectors for LSB steganography. In each case we outline a steganalysis method and give some experimental evidence (in the form of ROC curves) of improved reliability. However it is impossible to display the ROC curves of every combination of image set, embedding rate, variation of detection statistic, and so on; we select a representative sample for display and will also comment on the extent to which the improvements hold in general. We begin with a recap of the improvements suggested in [7]; all subsequent results are new research. A table summarising the performance of all the statistics over all Image Sets can be found in Sect. 4.

3.1   Improved Pairs & Better RS Masks

RS Steganalysis depends on the particular choice of "mask", which determines how pixels are grouped and which are flipped during the noise measurements.

In the presentation of [4] the authors mention two masks – the horizontal row $[0, 1, 1, 0]$ and the square $[1, 0;\ 0, 1]$ – without commenting on why they were chosen. In [7] we investigated a number of other masks and found that a performance improvement could be obtained using the square $[0, 0, 0;\ 0, 1, 0;\ 0, 0, 0]$ instead. (The noise measurement used in the RS calculation is extended to two-dimensional masks by summing differences between both all horizontal and all vertical pixel pairs.)

Pairs Analysis was substantially improved by excluding some pixels from the homogeneity measurement, namely those pixels which were not adjacent in the original image. This amounts to splitting the colour cuts into small subsequences of originally adjacent pixels and measuring the homogeneity within those subsequences. The rest of the algorithm is identical to the standard Pairs method (repeating for the alternative pairs of values and solving the same quadratic equation to find an estimate of hidden message length).

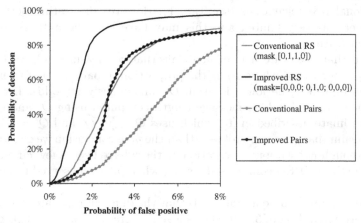

Fig. 2. ROC curves showing the reliability gained by using the suggested RS "mask" and the Improved Pairs measure. The curves are generated from the 15000 images in Image Sets B and C combined; the hidden message length is 3%

Figure 2 shows the effects of these improvements on the ROC curves in one instance. 15000 JPEG images had 3% steganography embedded: here the false positive rate needed to achieve 50% reliability has reduced from 2.7% to 1.2% when the RS mask is switched from the standard $[0, 1, 1, 0]$ to the improved $[0, 0, 0;\ 0, 1, 0;\ 0, 0, 0]$, and the modification to Pairs Analysis has reduced it from 5.3% to 2.7%. Similar improvements are observed across all Image Sets and with all message sizes. In [7] we gave ROC curves showing that in some circumstances the improved Pairs statistic becomes more reliable than the RS method (this is particularly noticeable in the case of uncompressed images, as will be seen in Table 1).

One other minor improvement we mention here, which is not reported in [7], is a simplification of the RS statistic. Recall that the RS message-length estimate is computed from two measures $Q = R - S$ and $Q' = R' - S'$, where R and R' represent the number of *regular* pixel groups under LSB flipping and dual flipping according to the mask, and S and S' the *singular* groups. It is easy to see that the results of [4] show that the measures R and R' alone suffice to estimate the hidden message length, using the assumption that $R = R'$ for natural images, so long as one is prepared to determine $R(0.5)$ by randomizing the LSB plane of the image under consideration. The same applies to S and S'. We have found that just using R and R' to estimate the hidden message length is actually *more* reliable than the full RS method (this does not apply to S and S', which alone make a very poor detector). This is a surprising result but the improvement is not very substantial and we do not display ROC curves to illustrate it; Table 1 illustrates the incremental advantage sufficiently.

3.2 Improving Couples Analysis

As described in [6] Couples Analysis is in fact marginally more reliable than conventional RS steganalysis (see Tab. 1). However the testing performed for that paper was very limited and this may have lead the authors to miss an important feature.

Recall that there are a number of alternative measures, $Q_i = E_{2i+1}$ and $Q'_i = O_{2i+1}$ for $i \geq 0$ (where E_k is the proportion of pairs of pixels which differ by k and of which the lower is even, O_k analogously for odd). Let us write $\hat{p}_i$ for the estimated hidden message length computed using Q_i and Q'_i, and $\hat{p}$ for the estimate described in [6], which uses $Q = \sum_i Q_i$ and $Q' = \sum_i Q'_i$. The authors claim that $\hat{p}$ is "more robust" than the $\hat{p}_i$, a conclusion we generally agree with (although not without reservation as there have been a few circumstances, involving mildly JPEG compressed covers, when $\hat{p}_1$ was observed to be superior to $\hat{p}$).

However a much more useful fact is that the different estimators $\hat{p}_i$ are generally uncorrelated. Figure 3, left, shows a scattergram of $\hat{p}_0$ against $\hat{p}_1$ generated by the images in Set B (with no embedded data); there is no visible relationship, and the Pearson correlation coefficient is only -0.0365. Image Sets C and D have similar results; the uncompressed Image Set A gives a higher correlation coefficient of 0.1743 but this is still quite a weak relationship. The power of these uncorrelated statistics is that it is much less likely that an image with no hidden data would show up as a false positive for *both* statistics. So we could set thresholds for $\hat{p}_0$ and $\hat{p}_1$ and give a positive diagnosis of steganography only if both are exceeded. Furthermore, one need not stop at using two statistics. We also found fairly weak correlation between the other $\hat{p}_i$ statistics, although the correlation does rise with i, and the reliability falls. After some experimentation we determined that taking the three values $\hat{p}_0$, $\hat{p}_1$, and $\hat{p}_2$, and setting the same threshold for each gave the best overall performance. This amounts to using $\min(\hat{p}_0, \hat{p}_1, \hat{p}_2)$ as the discriminating statistic[5].

---

[5] We do not claim that this combination of the $\hat{p}_i$ is necessarily optimal, merely that it is the best we could find; an interesting direction for further research is to find the best ways to combine *all* of the various detection statistics in the optimal way.

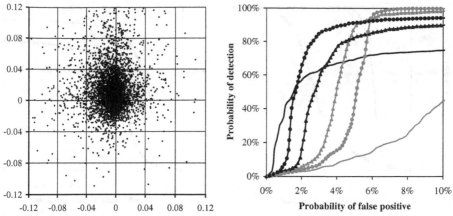

Fig. 3. Left, A scattergram plotting the message-length estimates $\hat{p}_0$ (x-axis) against $\hat{p}_1$ (y-axis). No correlation is evident. Right, ROC curves showing how the reliability of the conventional Couples statistic $\hat{p}$ varies as the covers are pre-compressed (*shaded lines*), and the improvements gained by using $\min(\hat{p}_0, \hat{p}_1, \hat{p}_2)$ instead (*black lines*). The covers used are the 2200 uncompressed images in Set A (*unmarked lines*), and the experiment is repeated with the covers pre-compressed using JPEG quality factors of 90 (*lines marked with triangles*) and 50 (*lines marked with circles*). 3% steganography has been used

Figure 3, right, shows the results. The ROC curves are all generated from Image Set A, with the experiment repeated with the covers first JPEG compressed using quality factors of 90 and 50. In the case of uncompressed covers the false positive rate needed to achieve 50% reliability has reduced from 10.7% to 1.5% (a dramatic improvement indeed!). For the mildly JPEG compressed covers it has reduced from 4% to 2.7%, and for the quite heavily compressed quality factor 50 images it has reduced from 5.1% to 1.7%. It is curious that the relative performance of the Couples statistic, as JPEG compression of the covers varies, is exactly reversed by the improved method. Other observations suggest that mildly compressed covers have particular properties which destroy the accuracy of the estimate $\hat{p}_1$ (but do not affect $\hat{p}_0$ or $\hat{p}_2$ nearly as seriously); further research is called for to see if this can be mitigated.

This modified method of Couples Analysis is now substantially more reliable than any of the conventional steganalysis statistics (see Tab. 1) in answering the simple classification question. However the discrimination statistic $\min(\hat{p}_0, \hat{p}_1, \hat{p}_2)$ is no longer an unbiased estimate of the hidden message length (it will underestimate).

3.3   Dropping the Message Length Estimate

In [7] we asked whether the use of a statistic designed to estimate the hidden message length could be improved upon, given that we only want to answer the

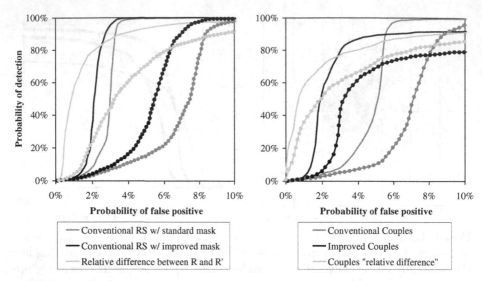

Fig. 4. Left, the effect of switching to the relative difference statistic in RS steganalysis – the ROC curve shown is generated from the 7500 images in Set D and compares the conventional RS statistic (with mask $[0, 1, 1, 0]$), the version with the improved mask $[0, 0, 0; \ 0, 1, 0; \ 0, 0, 0]$, and using the relative difference between R and R' (computed with the mask $[0, 1, 1, 0]$). The experiment is repeated with both 5% (*marked lines*) and 10% (*unmarked lines*) steganography. Right, a similar comparison between conventional Couples Analysis, the improved Couples analysis using $\min(\hat{p}_0, \hat{p}_1, \hat{p}_2)$, and finally using $(Q_0 - Q_0')/(Q_0 + Q_0')$, with both 3% (*marked lines*) and 5% (*unmarked lines*) steganography. The second diagram was generated from the combined 15000 images in Sets B and C

simple question of whether data is hidden or not. We have just seen a statistic which does the latter better at the expense of the former.

Let us return to the most important assumptions which underlie Pairs, RS, and Couples – that $Q(0) = Q'(0)$ in natural images. A simple and obvious statistic to consider is therefore $Q - Q'$, which should be near zero in natural images and (one can show in each of the cases of Pairs, RS and Couples) generally moves away from zero as data is hidden. Unfortunately the magnitudes of Q and Q' can differ appreciably between images, usually depending on how noisy the image under consideration is; therefore a more robust measure is the relative difference $(Q - Q')/(Q + Q')$. One can compute Q and Q' according to any of the methods of Pairs, RS, or Couples. In the case of RS we have found it better to ignore the S and S' components and use the relative difference between R and R' instead.

These statistics are no longer any use for determining the hidden message length. On the other hand we might hope that, uncluttered by the additional observations and quadratic equation needed to do so, they are a reasonable way to answer the simple classification question.

Figure 4, left, shows the result of switching to the relative difference statistic in the case of both RS and Couples (there is some improvement in doing the same with Pairs, but the results are not so good and we do not show them here). We display the ROC curves for the conventional RS statistic, the version with the better mask, and the relative difference statistic[6]. These curves were generated using Image Set D but similar results are seen across all image sets. We have displayed ROC curves for both 5% and 10% embedded message rates to demonstrate that improvement is evident across a range of embedding levels. At the 5% embedding level the false positive rate at which 50% reliability is achieved has fallen from 7.5% (standard mask) and 5.5% (improved mask) to 3.2% with the relative difference statistic.

The right-hand chart in Fig. 4 shows the improvement as we move from the conventional Couples statistic, to the minimum-of-3 statistics described in the previous section, to the relative difference statistic. In this case we have used the relative difference between Q_0 and Q'_0 – we investigated a number of other statistics based on relative differences between combinations of Q_i's but found that Q_0 and Q'_0 was almost always the outstandingly most reliable. The level of improvement is similar to that observed for RS.

3.4   To Overlap or Not to Overlap

Each of the methods of Pairs, RS and Couples involve performing some calculation on pixel groups. For RS the groups are shaped as the mask and the calculation is to see whether noise is increased or reduced after LSB flipping and dual flipping. For Pairs and Couples the groups are simply pairs of pixels adjacent in the image and/or the colour cuts and the calculation is to measure homogeneity (whether the two pixels are equal) or classifying the pair of pixels in one of E_k or O_k by measuring their difference. We ask whether the groups should be disjoint or overlap. Since Pairs measures homogeneity is it clear that the groups of pairs must overlap so that every pair of adjacent pixels is considered. The authors of [6] clearly intended the groups in Couples to overlap ("all pairs of two spatially adjacent samples"). It is not clear whether the RS groups used in [4] were intended to overlap.

We firmly expected that using overlapping groups (in any of the methods of Pairs, RS or Couples) would give at best an insignificant improvement over not doing so, since it parallels a result of [7] in which using the same pixels twice was demonstrated to confer no particular advantage. Indeed this is exactly what we found in the case of the statistics which give estimates of the hidden message length. Most surprisingly, the story was quite different for the relative difference statistics: in these cases there was frequently quite a good improvement when using *non-overlapping* groups.

Figure 5 shows some of the advantages of using non-overlapping groups. The ROC curves displayed are for the relative difference between the measures R and

---

[6] using the standard mask $[0, 1, 1, 0]$; we have observed that the other masks no longer give improved reliability when the relative difference statistic is used and indeed many are much worse.

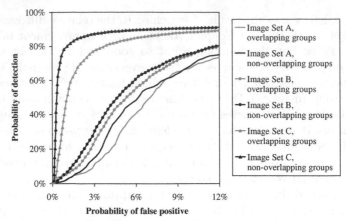

Fig. 5. ROC curves showing the benefits of non-overlapping groups. The two statistics shown are both computed as the relative difference between R and R' (the proportions of regular groups, under the mask $[0,1,1,0]$), but one statistic uses overlapping groups and the other disjoint groups. 2% steganography was used. The experiment is repeated for three sets of images: Image Set A precompressed using JPEG quality factor 90, and Image Sets B and C

R' (computed using the mask $[0,1,1,0]$) with overlapping and non-overlapping groups of pixels, with 2% steganography. Since the mask is 4 pixels long the latter has only 1/4 as many groups, but (for a reason as yet unexplained) gives better reliability. The improvement shown for Image Set A (the graph shown is from the case when the images are precompressed using JPEG quality factor 90) and Set B is significant but not dramatic. For Image Set C it is more pronounced. Generally, improved reliability is seen with any length of hidden message and with both the RS- and Couples-based relative difference statistics, although the extent of the improvement varies. In uncompressed covers there is little improvement.

3.5   Reducing Outliers by Segmenting

The final improvement we suggest is still work-in-progress. Our aim is to mitigate the sometimes alarming outliers in the null distributions, natural images which have a large *bias* (estimated hidden message length when there is no hidden message). We have observed that very large bias sometimes occurs in certain textures in an image when the rest of the image is quite normal – the overall bias comes out too high due to the influence of this abnormal texture. This differs from the situation when LSB steganography is present, where one expects to see a higher message-length estimate in all parts, assuming that the LSB flipping has been spread randomly over the whole image.

We have tried segmenting images according to their texture content and computing the discrimination statistics for each segment, then discarding outliers by taking the median (or a similar centrally weighted measure) of the values for each segment. The picture on the top left of Fig. 6 is a good example. Under the standard RS statistic this image (one of Set A) has a bias of 0.0651, by no means the most extreme outlier in the data sets but still a substantial error. We segment the image according to content and compute the bias for each segment; the results are displayed in the picture on the top right of Fig. 6. The median of the biases for each segment is 0.0052, a much smaller error.

To perform the segmentation we chose the method of [12], partly because it avoids oversegmentation in highly detailed images without human intervention, and partly because an implementation is available for download. As can be seen from the pictures in Fig. 6 its choice of segments is sometimes rather surprising, but it does seem to separate different textures quite well. We make no claim that this segmenting method is in any way optimal for steganalysis purposes (indeed one might hope to perform segmentation according to the steganalysis statistics themselves); the results here are intended as a springboard for further research into the issue.

Segmentation is not particularly fast so we restricted our attention to adding segmentation to the best-performing statistics found so far (non-overlapping relative difference between R and R' or Q_0 and Q_0'). We adjusted the segmentation parameters so that most images were segmented into 6-12 segments and found that lower false positive rates were given by taking roughly the 30th percentile out of the statistics computed for individual segments (this biases the results low, trading worse reliability at high false positives for better reliability at low false positives – precisely the sort of trade we want to make).

The graph in Fig. 6 shows the benefits of using segmentation, comparing the relative difference between the non-overlapping versions of R and R' statistic with and without segmentation. 3% steganography was embedded in Image Sets B, C and D. The improvement in the case of Set C is particularly good, with the false positive rate needed to achieve 50% reliability dropping from 0.26% to less than 0.08%. When segmentation was added to the Couples Q_0 and Q_0' relative difference statistic there was also an improvement, but not as much (ROC curves not shown). We hope to improve more on these results after further investigation.

4 Summary of Results and Conclusions

We conclude with a summary of the improvements made by these new detection statistics. It is necessary to simplify, so we have used a definition of "reliable" detection as meaning 5% false positives and at most 50% missed detections (we recognise that these figures are arbitrary but they are in keeping with the philosophy that false positives are more severe than false negatives – such a detector would be reasonably useful for an Information Security Officer who would only make a definite diagnosis of steganography after seeing a number of positive results coming from the same person). We measured the lowest level of steganography for which such reliability is attained by each statistic, repeating for each Image Set, and also subjected the covers of Image Set A to JPEG compression at mild (quality factor 90), moderate (75) and strong (50) levels so

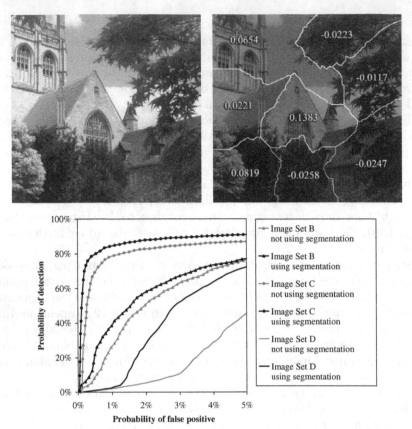

Fig. 6. Above, the results of segmentation. Below, ROC curves showing the benefits; the statistic used is the non-overlapping version of the relative difference between R and R', as computed using the mask $[0, 1, 1, 0]$. The segmenting statistic takes the 30th percentile of the estimates for each segment. 3% steganography was embedded

as to examine this factor. Table 1 contains the results, starting with conventional methods, then listing the improved versions of Pairs and RS suggested in [7] and then displaying the statistics suggested in this paper. The segmenting statistic was not tested against Image Set A because initial results showed no likelihood of improvement.

The table shows, amongst other things, that relative difference statistics (computed using non-overlapping groups) are much better than the alternatives, and that segmenting images is a promising direction for further work. The exception is for the only set of uncompressed images, when the improved version of Couples Analysis performs the best (and note that none of the optimal statistics is capable of estimating the hidden message length). For each Image Set the best-performing statistic will reliably detect LSB steganography at between 2 and 6 times lower rates than the conventional methods, and there is a

Table 1. Final results. The table shows the lowest bit rate (in bits per pixel) of LSB steganography which can be "reliably" detected by the various methods and for each image set. Here we take reliable detection to mean 50% or higher probability of detection when the false positive rate is 5%. Entries in the table higher than 0.04 are accurate to 0.005; entries between 0.01 and 0.04 are accurate to 0.002, and entries below 0.01 are accurate to 0.001

Statistic	Image Set A w/compression				Image Set B	Image Set C	Image Set D
	None	q.f. 90	q.f. 75	q.f. 50			
Conventional Pairs	0.100	0.085	0.060	0.060	0.040	0.018	0.070
Conventional RS	0.110	0.045	0.050	0.055	0.028	0.016	0.070
Conventional Couples	0.090	0.040	0.050	0.050	0.030	0.014	0.065
RS with optimal mask	0.100	0.038	0.045	0.050	0.022	0.012	0.055
Improved Pairs	0.080	0.050	0.030	0.028	0.030	0.012	0.050
RS R only	0.105	0.040	0.040	0.050	0.026	0.014	0.060
Improved Couples	**0.032**	0.030	0.020	0.018	0.020	0.038	0.036
Relative difference of R, R'	0.065	0.026	0.022	0.022	0.022	0.012	0.036
*Relative difference of R, R'	0.065	**0.022**	0.018	0.020	0.020	0.006	0.032
Couples Q_1 relative difference	0.085	0.030	0.016	0.012	0.028	0.009	0.034
*Couples Q_1 relative difference	0.085	0.028	**0.012**	**0.008**	0.024	0.006	0.028
*Relative difference of R, R' with segmenting					**0.014**	**0.005**	**0.020**

* *indicates alternative versions using non-overlapping groups*

suggestion that the best improvements come from the most highly compressed images. Since some improvement has been observed across all Image Sets we can be confident that the new statistics are genuinely and significantly more reliable.

Also important to note is the vast difference in reliability as the statistics are tested across the different Image Sets. One should therefore view the improved bit rates as relative to the conventional ones. We have already commented that image size makes a difference to steganalysis reliability, but it is clear that JPEG compression does too and there may be other factors as yet uncovered. Thus it is impossible to say that there is a definitive "safe" bit rate, below which steganography cannot be detected. It would appear, though, that a steganographer who chooses their covers carefully can still transmit quite a lot of hidden data (and this paper excludes any discussion of adaptive techniques for choosing where to embed, let alone methods other than LSB). This also suggests an interesting line of future research, where suspect images are classified in some way so that the best statistic for that particular type of image can be used. The issue is so complex that a learning machine may be necessary.

In conclusion, we have suggested a number of improved methods for deciding whether a grayscale bitmap contains LSB steganography or not. Thanks to the distributed steganalysis project we are able to give extensive experimental evidence of the extent of the improvement. This depends entirely on the particular weight one gives to false positive or negative results, but we have shown that when the aim is to reduce false positives (and when a fairly arbitrary definition of "reliable" is made) the new statistics allow reliable detection of between 2 and 6 times less embedded data than the previously best methods. In most cases, however, we have not tried to give a theoretical explanation of why the improvement occurs – our new methods are heuristic and there is no claim of optimality. We hope that the results presented here will stimulate research to this end.

Acknowledgements

The author is a Royal Society University Research Fellow. Some of the work presented here was done while a Junior Research Fellow at University College, Oxford with additional funding from DSTL. The author is grateful to Sue Haines and Rob Thompson at DSTL for conversations and suggestions.

References

1. Westfeld, A., Pfitzmann, A.: Attacks on steganographic systems. In: Proc. Information Hiding Workshop. Volume 1768 of Springer LNCS. (1999) 61–76
2. Westfeld, A.: Detecting low embedding rates. In: Proc. Information Hiding Workshop. Volume 2578 of Springer LNCS. (2002) 324–339
3. Chandramouli, R., Memon, N.: Analysis of LSB based image steganography. In: Proc. IEEE International Conference on Image Processing. (2001) 1019–1022
4. Fridrich, J., Goljan, M., Du, R.: Reliable detection of LSB steganography in color and grayscale images. Proc. ACM Workshop on Multimedia and Security (2001) 27–30
5. Fridrich, J., Goljan, M., Soukal, D.: Higher-order statistical steganalysis of palette images. In Delp III, E.J., Wong, P.W., eds.: Security and Watermarking of Multimedia Contents V. Volume 5020 of Proc. SPIE. (2003) 178–190
6. Dumitrescu, S., Wu, X., Wang, Z.: Detection of LSB steganography via sample pair analysis. In: Proc. Information Hiding Workshop. Volume 2578 of Springer LNCS. (2002) 355–372
7. Ker, A.: Quantitive evaluation of Pairs and RS steganalysis. In Delp III, E.J., Wong, P.W., eds.: Security, Steganography, and Watermarking of Multimedia Contents VI. Volume 5306 of Proc. SPIE. (2004) 83–97
8. Fridrich, J., Goljan, M.: Practical steganalysis of digital images – state of the art. In Delp III, E.J., Wong, P.W., eds.: Security and Watermarking of Multimedia Contents IV. Volume 4675 of Proc. SPIE. (2002) 1–13
9. Sharp, T.: An implementation of key-based digital signal steganography. In: Proc. Information Hiding Workshop. Volume 2137 of Springer LNCS. (2001) 13–26
10. Harmsen, J., Pearlman, W.: Higher-order statistical steganalysis of palette images. In Delp III, E.J., Wong, P.W., eds.: Security and Watermarking of Multimedia Contents V. Volume 5020 of Proc. SPIE. (2003) 131–142

11. Fridrich, J., Goljan, M., Du, R.: Steganalysis based on JPEG compatability. In Tescher, A.G., Vasudev, B., Bove, Jr, V.M., eds.: Multimedia Systems and Applications IV. Volume 4518 of Proc. SPIE. (2002) 275–280
12. Felzenszwalb, P.F., Huttenlocher, D.P.: Image segmentation using local variation. In: Proc. IEEE Computer Society Conference on Computer Vision and Pattern Recognition. (1998) 98–104

An Improved Sample Pairs Method for Detection of LSB Embedding*

Peizhong Lu[1], Xiangyang Luo[2], Qingyang Tang[1], Li Shen[2]

[1] Department of Computer Science and Engineering, Fudan University,
Shanghai 200433, China.
pzlu@fudan.edu.cn
[2] Institute of Information Engineering, Information and Engineering University,
Zhengzhou 450002, China.
sun_spring@citiz.net

Abstract. This paper presents a fast algorithm to detect the least significant bit (LSB) steganography. Our approach is inspired by the work of Dumitrescu et al. [1] who detected LSB steganography via sample pair analysis. Our new algorithm combines with the statistical measures developed in [1] and a new least square estimation. The motivation comes from the high accuracy and robustness of the least square method used in parameter estimation. Plentiful experimental results show that our novel method has much lower false alarm rate of 5% than that of 13.79% in [1]. Meanwhile, the estimating precision of our algorithm is about 9% higher than that of the algorithm [1] if the embedding ratio is less than 10%, and the speed of our algorithm is also about 15% faster than the algorithm [1]. Some theoretical derivations are also included.

1 Introduction

As a new art of covert communication, the main purpose of steganography is to convey messages secretly by concealing the very existence of messages under digital media files, such as images, audio, or video files. Similar to cryptanalysis, steganalysis attempts to defeat the goal of steganography. A popular digital steganography technique is so-called least significant bit (LSB) embedding. Because LSB steganography has many advantages such as conceal capability is excellent, capacity of message embedded into image is large, and its realization is easily, it may be used widely in the Internet. So, reliable detection of LSB steganography of images is a valuable topic to study.

Recently, there are a lot of methods for detection of LSB steganography. It is impossible for us to provide an exhaustive review. The algorithms discussed here are examples that are representative of the literatures. Fridrich et. al.[2] developed a steganographic method for detection of LSB embedding in 24-bit color images (the Raw Quick Pairs-RQP method). The RQP method is based on analyzing close pairs of colors created by LSB embedding. It works reasonably well as long as the number of

---

* This work was supported by National Natural Science Foundation of China (10171017, 90204013), Special Funds of Authors of Excellent Doctoral Dissertation in China (200084), and Shanghai Science and Technology Funds (035115019).

J. Fridrich (Ed.): IH 2004, LNCS 3200, pp. 116-127, 2004.

unique colors in the cover image is less than 30% of the number of pixels. Stefan Katzenbeisser[3][4] proposed a steganalysis method based on Laplace transform. The embedding process can be treated as adding noise to images. The Laplace filtering causes obviously differences between the histograms of the covert images and those of the original images. Thus one can make a decision via keenness. This method is simple. It, however, needs training and its decision precision is low.

Fridrich et. al.[5] also presented a powerful RS method (regular and singular groups method) for detection of LSB embedding that utilizes sensitive dual statistics derived from spatial correlations in images. This method counts the numbers of the regular group and the singular one respectively, describes the RS chart, and constructs a quadratic equation. The length of message embedded in image is then estimated by solving the equation. This approach is suitable for color and gray-scale images.

The literature [6] introduced a steganalytic method for detection of LSB embedding via different histograms of image. If the embedding ratio is bigger (more than 40%), the result is more accurate than that of the RS method. The speed of this method is fast and the detection result is better than RS method for uncompressed images. However, if the embedding ratio is less than 40%, the performance is not as good as that of RS method.

S. Dumitrescu et. al.[1] detected the LSB steganography via sample pair analysis (SPA). When the embedding ratio is more than 3%, this method can estimate the embedding ratio with relatively high precision. The average error of estimates is 0.023. The false alarm rate is 13.79%. Dumitrscu also proved some key observations on which the RS method based. SPA method can be realized easily, and its speed is fast, so it can be able to analysis the large number of images.

Being enlightened by SPA method, we improved on it by adding a least square estimation. We propose a novel steganalysis algorithm via finite-state machine and least square method, which we call the algorithm LSM shortly. Simulations show that it has the following advantages: Detection is available under more relaxed conditions, the false alarm rate can be played down from 13.79% to 5%, the estimating precision is about 9% higher than that of SPA method if the embedding ratio is lower than 10%, and the speed of detection is about 15% faster than that of SPA method.

This paper is structured as follows. In Section 2, we will introduce the principle of SPA method as the base of our new method. In Section 3, we describe the principle of LSM method. Section 4 presents the detailed detection steps of the new approach. Then, in Section 5, we present our experimental results.

2   Principle of SPA Method

The principle of SPA method is based on finite-state machine theory. Assuming that the digital signal is represented by the succession of samples $s_1, s_2, \cdots, s_N$, a sample pair means a two-tuple $(s_i, s_j), 1 \leq i, j \leq N$. Let P be a multiset of two tuples (u, v), where u and v are the values of two samples. Denote by D_n the submultiset of P that consists of sample pairs of the form $(u, u+n)$ or $(u+n, u)$, where n is a fixed integer, $0 \leq n \leq 2^b - 1$. For each integer m, $0 \leq m \leq 2^{b-1} - 1$, denote by C_m the submultiset of P that consists of the sample pairs whose values differ by m in the first ($b-1$) bits (i.e., by right shifting one bit and then measuring the difference).

Let $X_{2m+1} = D_{2m+1} \cap C_{m+1}$, $Y_{2m+1} = D_{2m+1} \cap C_m$, $0 \le m \le 2^{b-1}-2$, and $X_{2^b-1} = \varnothing$, $Y_{2^b-1} = D_{2^b-1}$. For natural images, the literature [1] presented the hypotheses:

$$E\{|X_{2m+1}|\} = E\{|Y_{2m+1}|\}. \tag{1}$$

The multiset C_m, $0 \le m \le 2^{b-1}-1$, is partitioned into four trace submultisets $X_{2m-1}, X_{2m}, Y_{2m}, Y_{2m+1}$. Clearly C_m is closed, but its four trace submultisets are not but convert reciprocally under the LSB embedding operations. This phenomenon can be described with the finite-state machine (see Fig. 1).

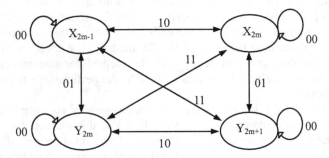

Fig. 1. Finite-state machine whose states are trace multisets of $C_m, m \ge 1$.

The transitions within C_0 are illustrated in Fig.2.

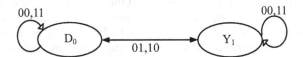

Fig. 2. Finite-state machine associated with C_0.

For each modification pattern $\pi \in \{00,10,01,11\}$ and any $A \subseteq P$, denote by $\rho(\pi, A)$ the probability that the sample pairs of A are modified with pattern π as a result of the embedding. Let p be the length of the embedded message in bits divided by the total number of samples in an image. Then

    i) $\rho(00, P) = (1-p/2)^2$;

    ii) $\rho(01, P) = \rho(10, P) = p/2(1-p/2)$;   (2)

    iii) $\rho(11, P) = (p/2)^2$.

Let X_n, Y_n, C_n, D_n be the multisets of the original (clean) signal, and X_n', Y_n', C_n', D_n' the multisets of the signal tampered by LSB embedding. According to the transitions within the finite-state machines in the Fig.1 and 2, Sorina Dumitrscu et al. derived the following quadratic equations for estimating p if LSB steganography is done via random embedding:

$$|X'_{2m-1}|(1-p)^2 = \frac{p^2}{4}|C_m| - \frac{p}{2}(|D'_{2m}|+2|X'_{2m-1}|) + |X'_{2m-1}|, \tag{3}$$

and

$$|Y'_{2m+1}|(1-p)^2 = \frac{p^2}{4}|C_m| - \frac{p}{2}(|D'_{2m}|+2|Y'_{2m+1}|) + |Y'_{2m+1}|, \tag{4}$$

where $1 \le m \le 2^{b-1}-2$. Using $m+1$ instead m of (3), we can get

$$|X'_{2m+1}|(1-p)^2 = \frac{p^2}{4}|C_{m+1}| - \frac{p}{2}(|D'_{2m+2}|+2|X'_{2m+1}|) + |X'_{2m+1}|. \tag{5}$$

From (4) and (5) together with the hypotheses (1), one finally obtains the following quadratic equation to estimate the value of p:

$$\frac{(|C_m|-|C_{m+1}|)p^2}{4} - \frac{(|D'_{2m}|-|D'_{2m+2}|+2|Y'_{2m+1}|-2|X'_{2m+1}|)p}{2}$$
$$+|Y'_{2m+1}|-|X'_{2m+1}|=0, \qquad m \ge 1. \tag{6}$$

Similarly, if $m=0$, we have

$$\frac{(2|C_0|-|C_1|)p^2}{4} - \frac{(2|D'_0|-|D'_2|+2|Y'_1|-2|X'_1|)p}{2}$$
$$+|Y'_1|-|X'_1|=0, \qquad m=0. \tag{7}$$

The smaller root of quadratic equation (6) [or (7)] is the estimated value of p.

Considering the estimating precision, the literature [1] used the hypotheses

$$E\left\{ \left| \bigcup_{m=i}^{j} X_{2m+1} \right| \right\} = E\left\{ \left| \bigcup_{m=i}^{j} Y_{2m+1} \right| \right\} \tag{8}$$

instead (1), derived the more robust quadratic equations to estimate the value of p:

$$\frac{(|C_i|-|C_{j+1}|)p^2}{4} - \frac{(|D'_{2i}|-|D'_{2j+2}|+2\sum_{m=i}^{j}(|Y'_{2m+1}|-|X'_{2m+1}|))p}{2}$$
$$+\sum_{m=i}^{j}(|Y'_{2m+1}|-|X'_{2m+1}|)=0, \qquad i \ge 1, \tag{9}$$

and

$$\frac{(2|C_0|-|C_{j+1}|)p^2}{4} - \frac{(2|D_0|-|D_{2j+2}|+2\sum_{m=0}^{j}(|Y'_{2m+1}|-|X'_{2m+1}|))p}{2}$$
$$+\sum_{m=0}^{j}(|Y'_{2m+1}|-|X'_{2m+1}|)=0, \qquad i=0. \tag{10}$$

The literature [1] gave the experiential values of i, j and the decision threshold. When $p > 3\%$, $i = 0, j = 30$ and the threshold is 0.018, the estimate value by solving the equations is relatively precise, and the average error is 0.023.

3   Principle of LSM Method

The precision of SPA is based on the hypotheses (1) or (8). Once the hypotheses do not hold, the quadratic equations above will not hold. Hence, when the embedding ratio is small, the errors of those hypotheses will lead the decision error. Thus when there are not embedded messages in images, the false alarm rate is high. In fact, the false alarm rate presented by the literature [1] is 13.79%. Table 1 tabulates the false alarm rates when $p = 0$ and the missing rates when $p > 0$ in [1].

Table 1. Probability of wrong decision with the decision threshold set at 0.018.

Embedding ratio	0%	3%	5%	10%	15%	20%
Error probability	0.1379	0.1103	0	0	0	0

In this section, we will give further analysis for trace submultisets X_{2m-1}, X_{2m}, Y_{2m}, Y_{2m+1}, and present a new algorithm to estimate the embedded rate precisely when the embedded rate is low.

Actually, $E\{|X_{2m+1}|\}$ is not absolutely equal to $E\{|Y_{2m+1}|\}$, and neither is $E\left\{\left|\bigcup_{m=i}^{j} X_{2m+1}\right|\right\}$ equal to $E\left\{\left|\bigcup_{m=i}^{j} Y_{2m+1}\right|\right\}$. Let $\varepsilon_m = |Y_{2m+1}| - |X_{2m+1}|$ ($0 \le m \le 2^{b-1}-2$), where the difference ε_m is small for natural signals. Subtracting (5) from (4) yields

$$\frac{(|C_m|-|C_{m+1}|)p^2}{4} - \frac{(|D'_{2m}|-|D'_{2m+2}|+2|Y'_{2m+1}|-2|X'_{2m+1}|)p}{2}$$
$$+|Y'_{2m+1}|-|X'_{2m+1}| = \varepsilon_m(1-p)^2, \qquad m \ge 1. \tag{11}$$

Similarly, we have

$$\frac{(2|C_0|-|C_1|)p^2}{4} - \frac{(2|D'_0|-|D'_2|+2|Y'_1|-2|X'_1|)p}{2}$$
$$+|Y'_1|-|X'_1| = \varepsilon_0(1-p)^2, \qquad m=0. \tag{12}$$

Note that m can take any of different $2^{b-1}-1$ values, thus we can construct different $2^{b-1}-1$ equations.

Considering the perfect accuracy and robustness of least square method for parameters estimate, we use least square method to estimate the embedding ratio for the different $2^{b-1}-1$ equations. The procedure of our estimation is as follows.

Let

$$A_m = \frac{|C_m|-|C_{m+1}|}{4},$$

$$B_m = -\frac{(|D'_{2m}|-|D'_{2m+2}|+2|Y'_{2m+1}|-2|X'_{2m+1}|)}{2},$$

$$E_m = |Y'_{2m+1}|-|X'_{2m+1}|,$$

then the left of equation (11) is changed into $A_m p^2 + B_m p + E_m$. Let

$$S(i,j,p) = \sum_{m=i}^{j}(A_m p^2 + B_m p + E_m)^2, \tag{13}$$

where, $0 \le i < j \le 2^{b-1}-2$. After differentiating for (13), we have the following equation:

$$2\sum_{m=i}^{j} A^2{}_m p^3 + 3\sum_{m=i}^{j} A_m B_m p^2 + \sum_{m=i}^{j}(2A_m E_m + B^2{}_m)p + \sum_{m=i}^{j} B_m E_m = 0. \tag{14}$$

By solving equation (14), we can find a p such that the $S(i,j,p)$ is minimal.

Usually, this equation has three real roots. To determine which root is the estimated value of p among these three roots, we should consider the second order derivative of (13), namely

$$6\sum_{m=i}^{j} A^2{}_m p^2 + 6\sum_{m=i}^{j} A_m B_m p + \sum_{m=i}^{j} (2A_m E_m + B^2{}_m). \tag{15}$$

If the root p of (14) such that (15) is larger than 0, and $(1-p)^2$ is relative small, then, by (11) and (13), $S(i,j,p) = (1-p)^4 \sum_{m=i}^{j} \varepsilon_m{}^2$ is the least value at p. Thus the p is the value we want to estimate.

In conclusion, the improved algorithm estimates the length of embedding message by solving a third order equation. The new LSM algorithm need a hypothesis that $\| Y_{2m+1} | - | X_{2m+1} \|(1-p)^2$ is small for each m. The conditions of our hypothesis are more relax than that in [1]. It is precision and robust enough for our LSM algorithm to take $i = 0$ and $j = 5$.

4 The LSM Algorithm

We now describe our detection algorithm.

Input: A set BMP images for detecting.

Output: The embedding ratio p for each image I in G, and a decision whether or not I contains hiding messages.

Step1. Prepare the cardinalities of the trace multisets.

For $0 \le m \le 5$ and a given image I in G, we compute the following constants.

$|C_m|$: The number of those pairs whose values differs by m after right shifting one bit.

$|C_{m+1}|$: The numbers of those pairs whose values differ by $m+1$ after right shifting one bit.

$|D'_{2m}|$: The numbers of those pairs whose values differ by $2m$.

$|D'_{2m+2}|$: The numbers of those pairs whose values differ by $2m+2$.

$|X'_{2m+1}|$: The numbers of those pairs whose values differ by $2m+1$ and in which the even component is larger.

$|Y'_{2m+1}|$: The numbers of those pairs whose values differ by $2m+1$ and in which the odd component is larger.

Step 2. Establish the cubic equation.

For each m, $0 \le m \le 5$, we calculate

$$A_m = \frac{|C_m| - |C_{m+1}|}{4},$$

$$B_m = -\frac{(|D'_{2m}| - |D'_{2m+2}| + 2|Y'_{2m+1}| - 2|X'_{2m+1}|)}{2},$$

$$E_m = |Y'_{2m+1}| - |X'_{2m+1}|,$$

and get the following cubic equation:

$$2\sum_{m=0}^{5}A^2{}_m p^3 + 3\sum_{m=0}^{5}A_m B_m p^2 + \sum_{m=0}^{5}(2A_m E_m + B^2{}_m)p + \sum_{m=0}^{5}B_m E_m = 0 \qquad (16)$$

Step 3. Find the appropriate root.

Solve the cubic equation (16) and get the real roots p_1, p_2, p_3. Find $p \in \{p_1, p_2, p_3\}$ such that

$$6\sum_{m=i}^{j}A^2{}_m p^2 + 6\sum_{m=i}^{j}A_m B_m p + \sum_{m=i}^{j}(2A_m E_m + B^2{}_m) > 0 . \qquad (17)$$

If p, q satisfy (17) we chose the p such that $\dfrac{S(i,j,p)}{(1-p)^4} \le \dfrac{S(i,j,q)}{(1-q)^4}$. Then the p is the

embedding ratio of hidden messages in the image I.

Step 4. Make a decision.

If $p > 0.018$ then I is a stego-image, otherwise I is a nature image.

5   Experimental Results

5.1   Validity and Reliability Test

The new LSB steganalytic algorithm is implemented on a PC with P3 933 MHz CPU and 128M-memory. Firstly, we selected 4 standard test images (see Fig.3) with 512×512 pixels for being tested by our algorithm. We created a series of steg-images by embedding secret messages into the four images using random LSB replacement method with embedding ratios 0,3%,5%,10%,20%,...,100%. Then we estimated the embedding ratio from those steg-images using RS method, SPA method and our LSM method, respectively. Table 2 lists the estimated results which indicate that our new algorithm is more effective and reliable than RS method and SPA method.

(a) lena   (b) peppers   (d) milkdrop   (e) lake

Fig. 3. 4 standard test images.

5.2   Correct Rate Test

To compare the correct rate of our algorithm with RS method and SPA method, we did the same experiments for test image database with 150 images of both JPG and BMP types, including a wide range of natural images. Some of these are standard images (Such as barb, balloon, bird, couple, girl, goldhill, etc.), and some images are captured using digital camera or scanner, and the others are nonstandard images. We selected 0.03 as the threshold of RS method, and 0.018 as the thresholds for SPA method and LSM method. The correct rates of experimental results are shown in the Table 3.

Table 2. Test results of 4 standard images (in percent).

	Lena			peppers			milkdrop			lake		
	RS	SPA	LSM	RS	SPA	LSM	RS	SPA	LSM	RS	SPA	LSM
0	1.43	0.49	0.19	1.48	0.65	0.26	1.89	1.26	0.76	1.20	0.82	0.48
3	4.63	3.51	2.81	4.40	3.61	3.34	1.55	1.81	2.19	1.81	2.02	2.39
5	6.35	5.37	4.72	6.55	5.56	5.09	3.40	3.54	4.17	3.93	3.81	4.12
10	11.91	10.77	10.20	11.66	10.71	10.56	8.71	9.08	9.45	8.93	9.05	9.26
20	22.19	21.23	20.40	22.90	21.05	20.83	18.91	19.21	19.54	21.55	20.63	20.14
30	32.22	31.27	30.57	32.70	31.03	30.07	29.42	28.42	29.51	30.28	29.81	30.58
40	41.48	40.69	40.26	41.90	40.46	40.20	39.37	39.40	39.52	42.34	40.86	40.46
50	51.36	50.48	49.99	52.98	50.77	50.50	50.56	51.15	50.20	53.23	50.93	50.07
60	61.23	60.56	60.18	59.81	60.40	60.00	58.55	58.26	58.01	58.68	61.24	60.04
70	70.48	70.31	70.21	72.07	70.62	70.33	72.44	70.89	70.87	72.26	70.85	69.63
80	79.89	78.77	79.05	79.67	78.65	79.04	80.61	78.36	78.88	80.16	78.89	78.84
90	91.07	89.07	89.99	91.08	90.70	90.19	90.85	90.43	89.69	89.27	89.21	88.81
100	96.60	97.72	98.95	96.95	97.80	99.16	100	99.20	98.78	99.21	99.10	100

Table 3. Correct rates of judgments (in percent).

	standard images (50)			images of ours (50)			others images (50)		
	RS	SPA	LSM	RS	SPA	LSM	RS	SPA	LSM
0	90	84	96	94	88	94	76	80	96
3	68	94	94	82	87	100	78	88	98
5	84	94	100	100	99	100	96	100	100
10	96	98	100	100	100	100	98	100	100
15	98	100	100	100	100	100	100	100	100
20	98	100	100	100	100	100	100	100	100
30	100	100	100	100	100	100	100	100	100
40	100	100	100	100	100	100	100	100	100
50	100	100	100	100	100	100	100	100	100
60	100	100	100	100	100	100	100	100	100
70	100	100	100	100	100	100	100	100	100
80	100	100	100	100	100	100	100	100	100
90	100	100	100	100	100	100	100	100	100
100	100	100	100	100	100	100	100	100	100

Compared to RS method and SPA algorithm, our method can greatly decrease the false alarm rate, which is about 5% now. Meanwhile, the missing rate is decreased. From Table 3, we can also find that when the embedding ratio is 3% the estimation accuracy is average 12.67% higher than that of the SPA method, and when the embedding ratio is 5% the estimation accuracy is average 6.59% higher than that of the SPA method. If the embedding ratio is more than 10%, three methods' missing ratios are all about 0.

5.3 Absolute Average Error Analysis

Fig.4, Fig.5 and Fig.6 describe the absolute average error of the three types of test image sets respectively.

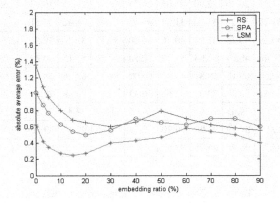

Fig. 4. Result of standard images.

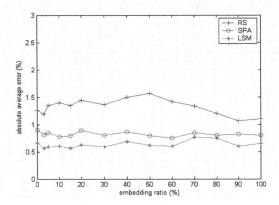

Fig. 5. Result of images of ours.

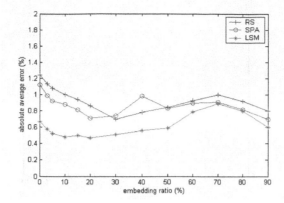

Fig. 6. Result of nonstandard images.

5.4 Standard Deviation Analysis

Fig.7, Fig.8 and Fig.9 describe the absolute average error of the three types of test image sets respectively.

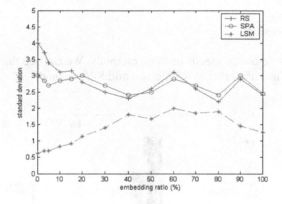

Fig. 7. Result of standard images.

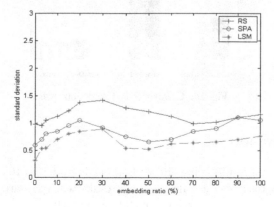

Fig. 8. Result of images of ours.

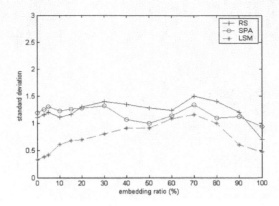

Fig. 9. Result of nonstandard images.

From Fig.4 to Fig.9, we can obtain that the absolute average error and the standard deviation of LSM analysis method are smaller than these of RS method and SPA method.

5.5 Speed of Detection

Fig.10 compares detection speeds of three methods. We can see that the speed of our new method is faster than that of RS method and SPA method.

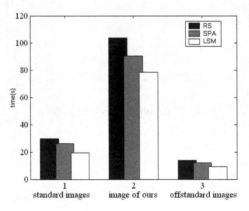

Fig. 10. Comparison of detection speed.

5.6 Range of Parameter m

Table 4 gives the test results using our method (m is from 0 to 10). From Table 4 we know that our approach can get almost same results when m varies from 0 to 10 or from 0 to 5. So we choose m varying from 0 to 5 in practice.

Table 4. Test results for different range of m .

Test result embedding Ratio		50 standard images			50 image of ours			50 nonstandard images		
		Correct Rate	Mean (%)	Test Time(s)	Correct Rate	Mean (%)	Test Time(s)	Correct Rate	Mean (%)	Test Time(s)
0%	$m=5$	96%	0.617	20.64	94%	0.663	84.90	96%	0.666	10.58
	$m=10$	96%	0.596	40.80	96%	0.673	172.43	96%	0.673	20.67
3%	$m=5$	94%	3.118	23.06	100%	3.571	76.33	98%	3.384	9.12
	$m=10$	94%	3.144	48.64	100%	3.528	164.85	98%	3.381	19.30

6 Conclusions

In this paper, we improve the detection of LSB steganography via sample pair analysis proposed by Sorina Dumitrescu [1] by least square method. Our novel method has following advantages: the more relax premise condition, the lower false alarm rate, the more accurate estimation of embedding ratio and the faster detection speed.

References

1. Sorina Dumitrescu, Xiaolin Wu, and Zhe Wang, "Detection of LSB Steganography via Sample Pair Analysis", IEEE Transactions on Signal Processing, VOL.51, NO.7, July 2003
2. J. Fridrich, R.Du, and L. Meng, "Steganalysis of LSB Encoding in Color Images," Proceedings IEEE International Conference on Multimedia and Expo, July 30-Auguest 2,2000, New York City, NY.
3. Stefan Katzenbeisser, "Breaking PGMStealth Using Laplace Filters", access from http://stud3.tuwien. ac.at/~e9625414/
4. R. C.Gonzalez, P. Wintz, "Digital Image Processing", Addison-Wesley Publishing Company, Inc., 1997
5. J. Fridrich, M. Goljan, "Practical Steganalysis of Digital Images - State of the Art", http://www.ssie.Binghamton.edu/fridrich.
6. Tao Zhang, Xijian Ping, "Reliable Detection of LSB Steganography Based on the Difference Image Histogram", ICASSP 2003, Vol. I, pp.545-548.

Statistical Tools for Digital Forensics

Alin C. Popescu and Hany Farid *

Department of Computer Science at Dartmouth College

Abstract. A digitally altered photograph, often leaving no visual clues of having been tampered with, can be indistinguishable from an authentic photograph. As a result, photographs no longer hold the unique stature as a definitive recording of events. We describe several statistical techniques for detecting traces of digital tampering in the absence of any digital watermark or signature. In particular, we quantify statistical correlations that result from specific forms of digital tampering, and devise detection schemes to reveal these correlations.

1 Introduction

The advent of low-cost and high-resolution digital cameras, and sophisticated photo-editing software, has made it remarkably easy to manipulate and alter digital images. In addition, digital forgeries, often leaving no visual clues of having been tampered with, can be indistinguishable from authentic photographs. And while the technology to manipulate digital media is developing at breakneck speeds, the technology to contend with its ramifications is lagging behind.

Digital watermarking has been proposed as a means by which an image can be authenticated (see, for example, [12, 3] for general surveys). Within this broad area, several authentication schemes have been proposed: embedded signatures [10, 24, 25, 18, 2], erasable fragile watermarks [11, 9], semi-fragile watermarks [16, 23, 28, 15], robust tell-tale watermarks [27, 14, 28], and self-embedding watermarks [8]. All of these approaches work by either inserting at the time of recording an imperceptible digital code (a watermark) into the image, or extracting at the time of recording a digital code (a signature) from the image and re-inserting it into the image. With the assumption that tampering will alter a watermark, an image can be authenticated by verifying that the extracted watermark is the same as that which was inserted. The major drawback of this approach is that a watermark must be inserted at precisely the time of recording, which would limit this approach to specially equipped digital cameras. This method also relies on the assumption that the watermark cannot be easily removed and reinserted — it is not yet clear whether this is a reasonable assumption (e.g., [4]).

---

* 6211 Sudikoff Lab, Dartmouth College, Hanover NH 03755 USA (email: **farid@cs.dartmouth.edu**; tel/fax: 603.646.2761/603.646.1672). This work was supported by an Alfred P. Sloan Fellowship, an NSF CAREER Award (IIS-99-83806), a Department of Justice Grant (2000-DT-CS-K001), and an NSF Infrastructure Grant (EIA-98-02068).

J. Fridrich (Ed.): IH 2004, LNCS 3200, pp. 128–147, 2004.

In contrast to these approaches, we describe a class of statistical techniques for detecting traces of digital tampering in the absence of any watermark or signature. These approaches work on the assumption that although digital forgeries may leave no visual clues of having been tampered with, they may, nevertheless, alter the underlying statistics of an image. Consider, for example, the creation of a digital forgery that shows a pair of famous movie stars, rumored to have a romantic relationship, walking hand-in-hand. Such a photograph could be created by splicing together individual images of each movie star and overlaying the digitally created composite onto a sunset beach. In order to create a convincing match, it is often necessary to (1) re-size, rotate, or stretch portions of the images; (2) apply luminance non-linearities (e.g., gamma correction) to portions of the image in order to adjust for brightness differences; (3) add small amounts of noise to conceal evidence of tampering; and (4) re-save the final image (typically with lossy compression such as JPEG). Although these manipulations are often imperceptible to the human eye, they may introduce specific correlations into the image, which when detected can be used as evidence of digital tampering. In this paper, we quantify statistical correlations that result from each of these specific forms of digital tampering, and devise detection schemes to reveal the correlations. The effectiveness of these techniques is shown on a number of simple synthetic examples and on perceptually credible forgeries.

2   Re-sampling

Consider the scenario in which a digital forgery is created by splicing together two, or more, individual images. In order to create a convincing match, it is often necessary to re-size, rotate, or stretch the images, or portions of them. These manipulations require re-sampling an image onto a new sampling lattice using some form of interpolation. Although, the re-sampling of an image is often imperceptible, specific correlations are introduced in the re-sampled image. When detected, these correlations represent evidence of tampering. We describe the form of these correlations, and propose an algorithm for detecting them in any portion of an image.

For purposes of exposition we will first describe how and where re-sampling introduces correlations in 1-D signals, and how to detect these correlations. The relatively straight-forward generalization to 2-D images is then presented.

2.1   Re-sampling Signals

Consider a 1-D discretely-sampled signal $x[t]$ with m samples. The number of samples in this signal can be increased or decreased by a factor p/q to n samples in three steps [21]:

1. up-sample: create a new signal $x_u[t]$ with pm samples, where $x_u[pt] = x[t]$, $t = 1, 2, ..., m$, and $x_u[t] = 0$ otherwise.
2. interpolate: convolve $x_u[t]$ with a low-pass filter: $x_i[t] = x_u[t] \star h[t]$.

3. down-sample: create a new signal $x_d[t]$ with n samples, where $x_d[t] = x_i[qt]$, $t = 1, 2, ..., n$. Denote the re-sampled signal as $y[t] \equiv x_d[t]$.

Different types of re-sampling algorithms (e.g., linear, cubic) differ in the form of the interpolation filter $h[t]$ in step 2. Since all three steps in the re-sampling of a signal are linear, this process can be described with a single linear equation. Denoting the original and re-sampled signals in vector form, x and y, respectively, re-sampling takes the form: $y = A_{p/q}x$, where the $n \times m$ matrix $A_{p/q}$ embodies the entire re-sampling process. For example, the matrices for up-sampling by a factor of 4/3 and 2/1 using linear interpolation have the form:

$$A_{4/3} = \begin{bmatrix} 1 & 0 & 0 & 0 \\ 0.25 & 0.75 & 0 & 0 \\ 0 & 0.50 & 0.50 & 0 \\ 0 & 0 & 0.75 & 0.25 \\ 0 & 0 & 0 & 1 \\ & & & & \ddots \end{bmatrix}, \quad A_{2/1} = \begin{bmatrix} 1 & 0 & 0 \\ 0.5 & 0.5 & 0 \\ 0 & 1 & 0 \\ 0 & 0.5 & 0.5 \\ 0 & 0 & 1 \\ & & & \ddots \end{bmatrix}. \quad (1)$$

Depending on the re-sampling rate, the re-sampling process will introduce correlations of varying degrees between neighboring samples. For example, consider the up-sampling of a signal by a factor of two using linear interpolation. Here, the odd samples of the re-sampled signal y take on the values of the original signal x, i.e., $y_{2i-1} = x_i$, $i = 1, \ldots, m$. The even samples, on the other hand, are the average of adjacent neighbors of the original signal: $y_{2i} = 0.5x_i + 0.5x_{i+1}$, where $i = 1, \ldots, m - 1$. Note that since each sample of the original signal can be found in the re-sampled signal, i.e., $x_i = y_{2i-1}$ and $x_{i+1} = y_{2i+1}$, the above relationship can be expressed in terms of the re-sampled samples only: $y_{2i} = 0.5y_{2i-1} + 0.5y_{2i+1}$. That is, across the entire re-sampled signal, each even sample is precisely the same linear combination of its adjacent two neighbors. In this simple case, at least, a re-sampled signal could be detected (in the absence of noise) by noticing that every other sample is perfectly correlated to its neighbors. To be useful in a general forensic setting we need, at a minimum, for these types of correlations to be present regardless of the re-sampling rate.

Consider now re-sampling a signal by an arbitrary amount p/q. In this case we first ask, when is the ith sample of a re-sampled signal equal to a linear combination of its $2N$ neighbors, that is:

$$y_i \overset{?}{=} \sum_{k=-N}^{N} \alpha_k y_{i+k}, \quad (2)$$

where α_k are scalar weights (and $\alpha_0 = 0$). Re-ordering terms, and re-writing the above constraint in terms of the re-sampling matrix yields:

$$y_i - \sum_{k=-N}^{N} \alpha_k y_{i+k} = 0 \Rightarrow (a_i \cdot x) - \sum_{k=-N}^{N} \alpha_k (a_{i+k} \cdot x) = 0 \Rightarrow \left(a_i - \sum_{k=-N}^{N} \alpha_k a_{i+k} \right) \cdot x = 0,$$

$$(3)$$

where $\boldsymbol{a}_i$ is the ith row of the re-sampling matrix $A_{p/q}$, and $\boldsymbol{x}$ is the original signal. We see now that the ith sample of a re-sampled signal is equal to a linear combination of its neighbors when the ith row of the re-sampling matrix, $\boldsymbol{a}_i$, is equal to a linear combination of its neighboring rows, $\sum_{k=-N}^{N} \alpha_k \boldsymbol{a}_{i+k}$. For example, in the case of up-sampling by a factor of two ($A_{2/1}$ in Equation (1)), the even rows are a linear combination of the two adjacent odd rows. Note also that if the ith sample is a linear combination of its neighbors then the $(i - kp)^{th}$ sample (k an integer) will be the same combination of its neighbors, that is, the correlations are periodic. It is, of course, possible for the constraint of Equation (3) to be satisfied when the difference on the left-hand side of the equation is orthogonal to the original signal $\boldsymbol{x}$. While this may occur on occasion, these correlations are unlikely to be periodic.

2.2 Detecting Re-sampling

Given a signal that has been re-sampled by a known amount and interpolation method, it is possible to find a set of periodic samples that are correlated in the same way to their neighbors. For example, consider the re-sampling matrix, $A_{4/3}$, of Equation (1). Here, based on the periodicity of the re-sampling matrix, we see that, for example, the 3rd, 7th, 11th, etc. samples of the re-sampled signal will have the same correlations to their neighbors. The specific form of the correlations can be determined by finding the neighborhood size, N, and the set of weights, $\boldsymbol{\alpha}$, that satisfy: $\boldsymbol{a}_i = \sum_{k=-N}^{N} \alpha_k \boldsymbol{a}_{i+k}$, Equation (3), where $\boldsymbol{a}_i$ is the ith row of the re-sampling matrix and $i = 3, 7, 11$, etc. If, on the other-hand, we know the specific form of the correlations, $\boldsymbol{\alpha}$, then it is straight-forward to determine which samples satisfy $y_i = \sum_{k=-N}^{N} \alpha_k y_{i+k}$, Equation (3).

In practice, of course, neither the re-sampling amount nor the specific form of the correlations are typically known. In order to determine if a signal has been re-sampled, we employ the expectation/maximization algorithm (EM) [5] to simultaneously estimate a set of periodic samples that are correlated to their neighbors, and the specific form of these correlations. We begin by assuming that each sample belongs to one of two models. The first model, M_1, corresponds to those samples that are correlated to their neighbors, and the second model, M_2, corresponds to those samples that are not (i.e., an outlier model). The EM algorithm is a two-step iterative algorithm: (1) in the E-step the probability that each sample belongs to each model is estimated; and (2) in the M-step the specific form of the correlations between samples is estimated. More specifically, in the E-step, the probability of each sample, y_i, belonging to model M_1 is given by Bayes' rule:

$$\Pr\{y_i \in M_1 \mid y_i\} = \frac{\Pr\{y_i \mid y_i \in M_1\}\Pr\{y_i \in M_1\}}{\Pr\{y_i \mid y_i \in M_1\}\Pr\{y_i \in M_1\} + \Pr\{y_i \mid y_i \in M_2\}\Pr\{y_i \in M_2\}}, (4)$$

where equal priors are assumed, i.e., $\Pr\{y_i \in M_1\} = \Pr\{y_i \in M_1\} = 1/2$. We also assume that:

$$\Pr\{y_i \mid y_i \in M_1\} = \frac{1}{\sigma\sqrt{2\pi}} \exp\left[\frac{-\left(y_i - \sum_{k=-N}^{N} \alpha_k y_{i+k}\right)^2}{2\sigma^2}\right], \tag{5}$$

and that $\Pr\{y_i \mid y_i \in M_2\}$ is uniformly distributed over the range of possible values of the signal $\boldsymbol{y}$. The variance, σ, of the above Gaussian distribution is estimated in the M-step. Note that the E-step requires an estimate of $\boldsymbol{\alpha}$, which on the first iteration is chosen randomly. In the M-step, a new estimate of $\boldsymbol{\alpha}$ is computed using weighted least-squares, that is, minimizing the following quadratic error function:

$$E(\boldsymbol{\alpha}) = \sum_i w(i) \left(y_i - \sum_{k=-N}^{N} \alpha_k y_{i+k}\right)^2, \tag{6}$$

where the weights $w(i) \equiv \Pr\{y_i \in M_1 \mid y_i\}$, Equation (4), and $\alpha_0 = 0$. This error function is minimized by computing the gradient with respect to $\boldsymbol{\alpha}$, setting the result equal to zero, and solving for $\boldsymbol{\alpha}$, yielding:

$$\boldsymbol{\alpha} = (Y^T W Y)^{-1} Y^T W \boldsymbol{y}, \tag{7}$$

where the ith row of the matrix Y is given by: $\left[y_i \cdots y_{N+i-1} \; y_{N+i+1} \cdots y_{2N+i}\right]$, and W is a diagonal weighting matrix with $w(i)$ along the diagonal. The E-step and M-step are iteratively executed until a stable estimate of $\boldsymbol{\alpha}$ is achieved.

Shown in Fig. 1 are the results of running EM on an original and re-sampled (by a factor of 4/3) signal. Shown on the top is the original signal where each sample is annotated with its probability of being correlated to its neighbors (the first and last two samples are not annotated due to border effects — a neighborhood size of five ($N = 2$) was used in this example). Similarly, shown on the bottom is the re-sampled signal and the corresponding probabilities. In the latter case, the periodic pattern is obvious, where only every 4th sample has probability 1, as would be expected by an up-sampling by a factor of 4/3, Equation (1). As expected, no periodic pattern is present in the original signal.

The periodic pattern introduced by re-sampling depends, of course, on the re-sampling rate. As a result, it is possible to not only uncover traces of re-sampling, but also to estimate the amount of re-sampling. It is not possible, however, to uniquely determine the specific amount of re-sampling as there are re-sampling parameters that yield similar periodic patterns. [1] There is also a range of re-sampling rates that will not introduce periodic correlations. For example, consider down-sampling by a factor of two (for simplicity, consider the case where there is no interpolation, i.e., $y_i = x_{2i}$). In this case, the rows of the re-sampling matrix are orthogonal to one another, and as a result no row can be written as a linear combination of its neighboring rows. In general, the detectability of any re-sampling can be estimated by generating the re-sampling matrix and determining if neighboring rows are linearly dependent.

---

[1] In general, two re-sampling rates p_1/q_1 and p_2/q_2 will generate similar periodic patterns if either $\{p_1/q_1\} = \{p_2/q_2\}$, or $\{p_1/q_1\} = 1 - \{p_2/q_2\}$, where $\{\cdot\}$ denotes the fractional part of a number.

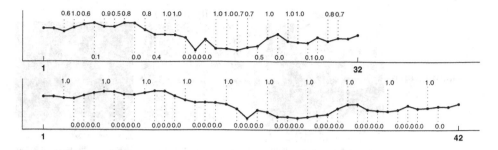

Fig. 1. A signal with 32 samples (top) and this signal re-sampled by a factor of 4/3 (bottom). Each sample is annotated with its probability of being correlated to its neighbors. Note that for the up-sampled signal these probabilities are periodic, while for the original signal they are not.

2.3   Re-sampling Images

In the previous sections we showed that for 1-D signals re-sampling introduces periodic correlations and that these correlations can be detected using the EM algorithm. The extension to 2-D images is relatively straight-forward. As with 1-D signals, the up-sampling or down-sampling of an image is still linear and involves the same three steps: up-sampling, interpolation, and down-sampling — these steps are simply carried out on a 2-D lattice. Again, as with 1-D signals, the re-sampling of an image introduces periodic correlations. Consider, for example, the simple case of up-sampling by a factor of two using linear interpolation. In the re-sampled image, the pixels in odd rows and even columns will be the average of their two closest horizontal neighbors, while the pixels in even rows and odd columns will be the average of their two closest vertical neighbors. That is, the correlations are, as with the 1-D signals, periodic. And in the same way that EM was used to uncover periodic correlations in 1-D signals, the same approach can be used with 2-D images.

2.4   Results

For the results presented here, we built a database of 200 grayscale images in TIFF format. These images were 512×512 pixels in size. Each of these images were cropped from a smaller set of twenty-five 1200×1600 images taken with a Nikon Coolpix 950 camera (the camera was set to capture and store in uncompressed TIFF format). Using bi-cubic interpolation these images were up-sampled, down-sampled, rotated, or affine transformed by varying amounts. Although we will present results for grayscale images, the generalization to color images is straight-forward — each color channel would be independently subjected to the same analysis as that described below.

For the original and re-sampled images, the EM algorithm described in Section 2.2 was used to estimate probability maps that embody the correlation

image　　　probability map (p)　　　$|\mathcal{F}(p)|$

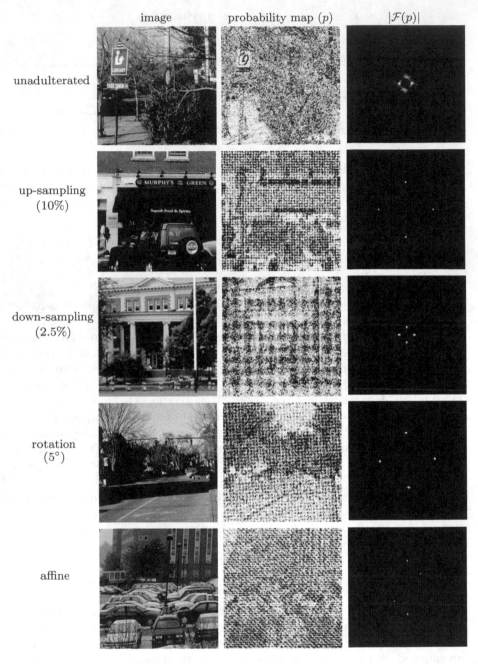

Fig. 2. Shown in the top row is an unadulterated image, and shown below are images re-sampled with different parameters. Shown in the middle column are the estimated probability maps that embody the spatial correlations in the image. The magnitude of the Fourier transforms of these maps are shown in the right-most column. Note that only the re-sampled images yield periodic maps.

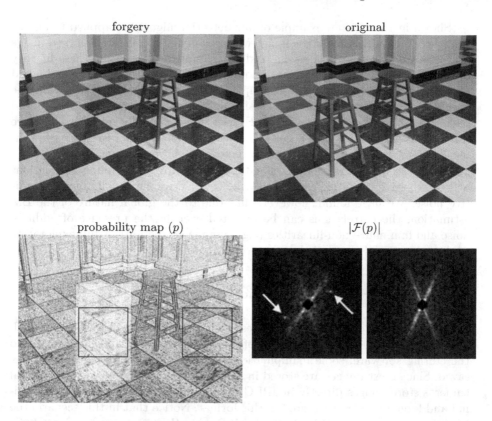

Fig. 3. Shown along the top row is a forgery and the original image. The forgery consists of removing a stool and splicing in a new floor taken from another image (not shown here) of the same room. Shown below is the estimated probability map (p) of the forgery, and the magnitude of the Fourier transform of a region in the new floor (left) and on the original floor (right). The periodic pattern (spikes in $|\mathcal{F}(p)|$) in the new floor suggest that this region was re-sampled.

between each pixel and its neighbors. The neighborhood size was fixed throughout to be 5×5. Shown in Fig. 2 are several examples of the periodic patterns that emerged due to re-sampling. In the top row of the figure are (from left to right) the original unadulterated image, the estimated probability map and the magnitude of the central portion of the Fourier transform of this map (for display purposes, each Fourier transform was independently auto-scaled to fill the full intensity range and high-pass filtered to remove the lowest frequencies). Shown below this row are images uniformly re-sampled (using bi-cubic interpolation) with different parameters. For the re-sampled images, note the periodic nature of their probability maps and the corresponding localized peaks in their Fourier transforms.

Shown in Fig. 3 is an example of our detection algorithm applied to an image where only a portion of the image was re-sampled. That is, the forged image contains a region that was re-sampled (up-sampled, rotated, and non-linearly distorted). Shown are the original photograph, the forgery, and the estimated probability map. Note that the re-sampled region is clearly detected - while the periodic pattern is not particularly visible in the spatial domain at the reduced scale, the well localized peaks in the Fourier domain clearly reveal its presence (for display purposes, the Fourier transform was auto-scaled to fill the full intensity range and high-pass filtered to remove the lowest frequencies).

It may seem, at first glance, that the detection of re-sampling correlations will be sensitive to simple counter-attacks — for example, small amounts additive noise. We have found, however, that due to the global nature of the EM estimation, the correlations can be detected even in the presence of additive noise and luminance non-linearities (e.g., gamma correction). A full exploration of the robustness is beyond the scope of this paper.

3   Double JPEG Compression

Tampering with a digital image requires the use of a photo-editing software such as Adobe PhotoShop. In the making of digital forgeries an image is loaded into the editing software, some manipulations are performed, and the image is re-saved. Since most images are stored in JPEG format (e.g., a majority of digital cameras store images directly in JPEG format), it is likely that both the original and forged images are stored in this format. Notice that in this scenario the forged image is double JPEG compressed. Double JPEG compression introduces specific artifacts not present in singly compressed images (this observation has also been noted in [17]). Note that evidence of double JPEG compression, however, does not necessarily prove malicious tampering. For example, it is possible for a user to simply re-save a high quality JPEG image with a lower quality. The authenticity of a double JPEG compressed image should, however, be called into question. We start by giving a short description of the JPEG compression algorithm and then quantify the artifacts introduced by double compression.

3.1   JPEG Compression

JPEG is a standardized image compression procedure proposed by a committee with the same name JPEG (Joint Photographic Experts Committee). To be generally applicable, the JPEG standard [1] specified two compression schemes: a lossless predictive scheme and a lossy scheme based on the Discrete Cosine Transform (DCT). The most popular lossy compression technique is known as the baseline method and encompasses a subset of the DCT-based modes of operation. The encoding of an image involves three basic steps [26]:

1. Discrete Cosine Transform (DCT): An image is divided into 8×8 blocks in raster scan order (left to right, top to bottom), shifted from unsigned

to signed integers (e.g., from $[0, 255]$ to $[-128, 127]$), and each block's DCT computed.

2. Quantization: The DCT coefficients obtained in the previous step are uniformly quantized, i.e., divided by a quantization step and rounded off to the nearest integer. Since quantization is a non-invertible operation this step represents the main source of information loss.

3. Entropy Encoding: This step involves lossless entropy compression that transforms the quantized DCT coefficients into a stream of compressed data. The most frequently used procedure is Huffman coding, although arithmetic coding is also supported.

The decoding of a compressed data stream involves the inverse of the previous three steps, taken in reverse order: entropy decoding, de-quantization, and inverse DCT.

3.2   Double Quantization

Consider the example of a generic discrete 1-D signal $x[t]$. Quantization is a point-wise operation that is described by a one-parameter family of functions: [2]

$$q_a(u) = \left\lfloor \frac{u}{a} \right\rfloor, \tag{8}$$

where a is the quantization step (a strictly positive integer), and u denotes a value in the range of $x[t]$. De-quantization brings the quantized values back to their original range: $q_a^{-1}(u) = au$. Note that the function $q_a(u)$ is not invertible, and that de-quantization is not the inverse function of quantization. Double quantization is a point-wise operation described by a two-parameter family of functions:

$$q_{ab}(u) = \left\lfloor \left\lfloor \frac{u}{b} \right\rfloor \frac{b}{a} \right\rfloor, \tag{9}$$

where a and b are the quantization steps (strictly positive integers). Notice that double quantization can be represented as a sequence of three steps: quantization with step b, followed by de-quantization with step b, followed by quantization with step a.

Consider an example where the samples of $x[t]$ are normally distributed in the range $[0, 127]$. To illustrate the nature of the double quantization artifacts, we quantize the signal $x[t]$ in four different ways, and show the resulting histograms, Fig. 4. Shown along the top row of this figure are the histograms of the same signal quantized with steps 2 and 3. Shown in the bottom row are the histograms of the same signal double quantized with steps 3 followed by 2, and 2 followed by 3. When the step size decreases (bottom left) some bins in the histogram

---

[2] For the purpose of illustration and in order to make the analysis easier we will use the floor function in the quantization function. Similar results can be shown if integer rounding is used instead.

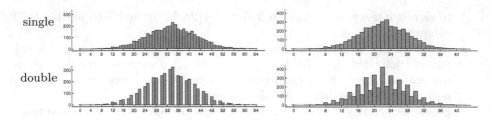

Fig. 4. Shown along the top row are histograms of single quantized signals with steps 2 (left) and 3 (right). Shown in the bottom row are histograms of double quantized signals with steps 3 followed by 2 (left), and 2 followed by 3 (right). Note the periodic artifacts in the histograms of double quantized signals.

are empty. This is not surprising since the first quantization places the samples of the original signal into 42 bins, while the second quantization re-distributes them into 64 bins. When the step size increases (bottom right) some bins contain more samples than their neighboring bins. This also is to be expected since the even bins receive samples from four original histogram bins, while the odd bins receive samples from only two. In both cases of double quantization, note the periodicity of the artifacts introduced into the histograms.

To better understand why the double quantization of a signal introduces periodic artifacts, we will analyze the dependence between the histograms of single and double quantized signals. Consider first the case of a single quantized signal denoted by $x_a[t] = q_a(x[t])$, and denote the histograms of the original and quantized signals by $H(u)$ and $H_a(v)$. Since $q_a(\cdot)$ is a many-to-one function, several values from the range of $x[t]$ will map onto the same value in the range of $x_a[t]$, i.e., several bins from H contribute to a bin in H_a. For example, let v denote a value in the range of $x_a[t]$, then the values in the range of $x[t]$ that map to it are in the range $[av, av + (a-1)]$. Therefore, the relationship between $H(u)$ and $H_a(v)$ is given by: $H_a(v) = \sum_{k=0}^{a-1} H(av + k)$. Note that there are exactly a bins in the original histogram that contribute to each bin in the histogram of the quantized signal. Consider next the case of a double quantized signal denoted by $x_{ab}[t] = q_{ab}(x[t])$, and let its histogram be denoted by $H_{ab}(v)$. In contrast to the single quantization case, the number of bins of H that contribute to a bin of H_{ab} will depend on the double quantized bin value. Let v be a value in the range of $x_{ab}[t]$. Denote u_{min} and u_{max} as the smallest and largest values of u in the range of $x[t]$ that map to v, that is, they satisfy the following:

$$\left\lfloor \left\lfloor \frac{u}{b} \right\rfloor \frac{b}{a} \right\rfloor = v. \tag{10}$$

Using the following property of the floor function:

$$\lfloor z \rfloor = m \quad \Rightarrow \quad m \le z < m + 1, \tag{11}$$

where z is an arbitrary real number and m an integer, Equation (10) implies:

$$v \le \left\lfloor \frac{u}{b} \right\rfloor \frac{b}{a} < v + 1 \quad \Leftrightarrow \quad \frac{a}{b} v \le \left\lfloor \frac{u}{b} \right\rfloor < \frac{a}{b}(v+1). \tag{12}$$

Since $\lfloor u/b \rfloor$ is an integer , Equation (12) can be rewritten using the ceiling function to include only integers:

$$\left\lceil \frac{a}{b} v \right\rceil \le \left\lfloor \frac{u}{b} \right\rfloor \le \left\lceil \frac{a}{b}(v+1) \right\rceil - 1. \tag{13}$$

From Equation (13) it can be seen that u_{min} must satisfy:

$$\left\lfloor \frac{u_{min}}{b} \right\rfloor = \left\lceil \frac{a}{b} v \right\rceil \quad \Rightarrow \quad u_{min} = \left\lceil \frac{a}{b} v \right\rceil b, \tag{14}$$

while u_{max} must satisfy:

$$\left\lfloor \frac{u_{max}}{b} \right\rfloor = \left\lceil \frac{a}{b}(v+1) \right\rceil - 1 \; \Rightarrow \; u_{max} = \left(\left\lceil \frac{a}{b}(v+1) \right\rceil - 1 \right) b + (b-1) = \left\lceil \frac{a}{b}(v+1) \right\rceil b - 1. \tag{15}$$

Since double quantization is a monotonically increasing function, it follows that all the values between u_{min} and u_{max} will map to v through double quantization. The relationship between the original and double quantized histogram then takes the form:

$$H_{ab}(v) = \sum_{u=u_{min}}^{u_{max}} H(u). \tag{16}$$

Note that the number of original histogram bins, $n(v)$, contributing to bin v in the double quantized histogram depends on v, and from Equations (14) and (15), can be expressed as:

$$n(v) = u_{max} - u_{min} + 1 \quad = \quad b \left(\left\lceil \frac{a}{b}(v+1) \right\rceil - \left\lceil \frac{a}{b} v \right\rceil \right). \tag{17}$$

Note that $n(v)$ is a periodic function with period b, i.e., $n(v) = n(v+b)$. This periodicity is the reason periodic artifacts appear in histograms of double quantized signals.

From Equation (17), the double quantization artifacts shown in Fig. 4 can now be explained. Consider first the case of double quantization using steps $b = 3$ followed by $a = 2$, (bottom-left panel in Fig. 4). The number of original histogram bins contributing to double quantized histogram bins of the form $(3k + 2)$ (k integer) is given by:

$$n(3k+2) = 3 \left(\left\lceil \frac{2}{3}(3k+3) \right\rceil - \left\lceil \frac{2}{3}(3k+2) \right\rceil \right) = 3 \left(2k+2 - 2k - \left\lceil \frac{4}{3} \right\rceil \right) = 0. \tag{18}$$

This is consistent with the observation that every $(3k + 2)^{nd}$ (k integer) bin of the double quantized histogram is empty. In the second example of double quantization in Fig. 4, $b = 2$ and $a = 3$, it can be shown that $n(2k) = 4$ and $n(2k + 1) = 2$ (k integer). Again, this is consistent with the periodic artifacts shown in the bottom-right panel of Fig. 4.

There are cases when the histogram of a double quantized signal does not contain periodic artifacts. For example, if in Equation (17) a/b is an integer then $n(v) = a$. Note that the same result is obtained if the signal were single quantized with step a. In this case, single and double quantization of a signal yields the same histogram, therefore it is impossible to distinguish between the two. Notice also in Equation (16) that the histogram of the double quantized signal, H_{ab}, depends on the values of the histogram of the original signal H. It is conceivable that histograms of original signals may contain naturally occuring artifacts that could mask those introduced by double quantization. While this may happen on occasion, such artifacts do not occur often.

3.3   Results

Given an image in JPEG format, our task is to detect if the image has been double compressed. To this end, the histograms of the DCT coefficients are computed. If these histograms contain periodic patterns, then the image is very likely to have been double compressed. Shown in Fig. 5 are the DCT coefficients and their histograms for an image that has been single JPEG compressed with qualities 75 (Fig. 5(a)) and 85 (Fig. 5(c)), and double JPEG compressed with qualities 85 followed by 75 (Fig. 5(b)), and 75 followed by 85 (Fig. 5(d)). The DCT coefficients are shown as images (auto-scaled to fill the full intensity range) where each pixel corresponds to a 8×8 block of the JPEG compressed image, and its intensity represents the coefficient value. These coefficients correspond to DCT frequencies $(1, 1)$ (the DC component) and $(2, 2)$. Note the presence of periodic artifacts in the histograms of the DCT coefficients of the double compressed images (Fig. 5(b) and 5(d)). Note also that these types of artifacts are not present in single compressed images (Fig. 5(a) and 5(c)). These periodic artifacts are particularly visible in the Fourier domain as strong peaks in the mid and high frequencies, Fig. 5(e).

The periodic patterns introduced by double JPEG compression depend on the quality parameters. As a result, it is possible to detect not only if an image has been double compressed, but also the compression qualities that have been used. The second parameter can be found from the quantization table stored in the JPEG file. The first parameter can be inferred from the location of the frequency peaks in the Fourier transforms of the DCT coefficient histograms.

4   Luminance Non-linearities

In order to enhance the perceptual quality of digital images, imaging devices often introduce some form of luminance non-linearity. The parameters of this non-linearity are usually dynamically chosen and depend on the camera and scene dynamics — these parameters are, however, typically held constant within

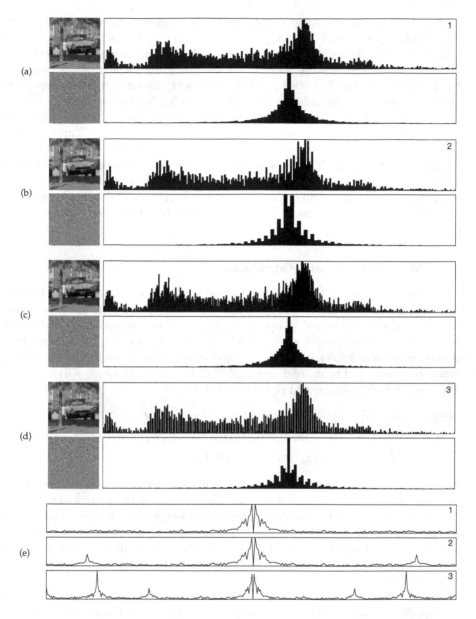

Fig. 5. Shown in the top four panels are DCT coefficients for two frequencies ((1, 1) and (2, 2)), and their histograms for single and double compressed JPEG images: (a) single JPEG compression with quality 75, (b) double JPEG compression with quality 85 followed by 75, (c) single JPEG compression with quality 85, (d) double JPEG compression with quality 75 followed by 85. Shown in panel (e) are the Fourier transforms of three zero-meaned histograms. Note the periodic artifacts introduced by double quantization (panels 2, 3) reflected by the high frequency peaks in the Fourier transforms.

an image. The presence of several distinct non-linearities in an image is a sign of possible tampering. For example, imagine a scenario where two images are spliced together. If the images were taken with different cameras or in different lightning conditions, then it is likely that different non-linearities are present in the composite image. It is also possible that local non-linearities are applied in the composite image in order to create a convincing luminance match.

We have previously proposed a technique to estimate parametric models of geometric and luminance non-linearities from digital images [6, 7]. This technique exploits the fact that a non-linear transformation introduces specific correlations in the Fourier domain. These correlations can be detected and estimated using tools from polyspectral analysis. This same technique can be employed to detect if an image contains multiple non-linearities. We describe below how luminance non-linearities introduce specific correlations, and how these correlations can be estimated.

4.1   Non-linearities and Correlations

Pointwise non-linear transformations introduce specific correlations in the frequency domain. To understand the form of these correlations, consider a one-dimensional discrete signal composed of a sum of two sinusoids with different phases and amplitudes: $x[t] = a_1 \cos(\omega_1 t + \phi_1) + a_2 \cos(\omega_2 t + \phi_2)$. Consider also a generic non-linear function $g(\cdot)$ and its Taylor series expansion where the various scalar constants and terms of degree higher than two are ignored: $g(u) \approx u + u.^2$. The non-linearly transformed signal takes the form:

$$g(x[t]) = -0.5(a_1^2 + a_2^2) + a_1 \cos(\omega_1 t + \phi_1) + a_2 \cos(\omega_2 t + \phi_2) +$$
$$0.5a_1^2 \cos(2\omega_1 t + 2\phi_1) + 0.5a_2^2 \cos(2\omega_2 t + 2\phi_2) + a_1 a_2 \cos((\omega_1 + \omega_2)t +$$
$$(\phi_1 + \phi_2)) + a_1 a_2 \cos((\omega_1 - \omega_2)t + (\phi_1 - \phi_2)). \tag{19}$$

Note that the non-linear transform introduced several new harmonics at frequencies $2\omega_1$, $2\omega_2$, $\omega_1 + \omega_2$, and $\omega_1 - \omega_2$. Note also that the phases of these new harmonics are correlated to the phases of the original ones. For example, the phase of harmonic $(\omega_1 + \omega_2)$ is equal to the sum of the phases of ω_1 and ω_2, and the phase of harmonic $2\omega_1$ is the double of the phase of harmonic ω_1. These type of correlations generalize to any type of underlying signal and pointwise non-linearity.

These phase correlations can be detected and estimated using tools from polyspectral analysis. Let $X(\omega)$ denote the Fourier transform of $x[t]$: $X(\omega) = \sum_{t=-\infty}^{\infty} x[t]e^{-it\omega}$. The power spectrum is a commonly employed tool to estimate second order correlations: $P(\omega) = \mathcal{E}\{X(\omega)X^*(\omega)\}$, where $\mathcal{E}\{\cdot\}$ is the expected value operator, and $*$ denotes the complex conjugate. However the power spectrum is blind to higher-order correlations of the kind introduced by pointwise non-linearities. These correlations can be detected and estimated using higher-order spectra (see [20] for a thorough review). For example, the bispectrum can be employed to estimate third-order correlations: $B(\omega_1, \omega_2) = \mathcal{E}\{X(\omega_1)X(\omega_2)X^*(\omega_1 + \omega_2)\}$.

It can be seen intuitively that the bispectrum reveals correlations between harmonically related frequencies, such as $[\omega_1, \omega_1, 2\omega_1]$, $[\omega_2, \omega_2, 2\omega_2]$, $[\omega_1, \omega_2, \omega_1 + \omega_2]$, and $[\omega_1, \omega_2, \omega_1 - \omega_2]$. Under the assumption that the signal is ergodic, the bispectrum can be estimated as follows: divide $x[t]$ into N (possibly overlapping) segments, compute the Fourier transform of each segment k: $X_k(\omega)$, compute an average estimate of the bispectrum using the Fourier transform of individual segments $\hat{B}(\omega_1, \omega_2) = 1/N \sum_{k=1}^{N} X_k(\omega_1) X_k(\omega_2) X_k^*(\omega_1 + \omega_2)$. The bispectrum has the undesired property that its value at bi-frequency (ω_1, ω_2) depends on $P(\omega_1)$, $P(\omega_2)$, and $P(\omega_1 + \omega_2)$. For analysis purposes, it is useful to work with normalized quantities. To this end, we employ the bicoherence [13] (a normalized bispectrum), defined as:

$$b(\omega_1, \omega_2) = \frac{|B(\omega_1, \omega_2)|}{(\mathcal{E}\{|X(\omega_1)X(\omega_2)|^2\}\mathcal{E}\{|X(\omega_1 + \omega_2)|^2\})^{1/2}}. \tag{20}$$

Note that the bicoherence is a real valued quantity, unlike the bispectrum. It is fairly straightforward to show using the Schwartz inequality [3] that the bicoherence is guaranteed to take values in $[0, 1]$. Just like the bispectrum, the bicoherence can be estimated as:

$$\hat{b}(\omega_1, \omega_2) = \frac{\frac{1}{K}|\sum_k X_k(\omega_1)X_k(\omega_2)X_k^*(\omega_1 + \omega_2)|}{\left(\left(\frac{1}{K}\sum_k |X_k(\omega_1)X_k(\omega_2)|^2\right)\left(\frac{1}{K}\sum_k |X_k(\omega_1 + \omega_2)|^2\right)\right)^{1/2}}. \tag{21}$$

This estimator will be used to measure third-order correlations.

4.2   Detecting Multiple Non-linearities

For simplicity, we assume that pointwise luminance non-linearities can be modeled with a one parameter family of functions of the form: $g(u) = u^\gamma$, where u denotes the intensity of a pixel normalized in the interval $[0, 1]$. We have previously shown that higher order correlations introduced by a non-linear transformation are proportional to the value of the parameter γ [6]. The following technique is used to blindly estimating the value of γ:

1. sample a range of inverse gamma values $1/\gamma$,
2. for each $1/\gamma$ in the selected range, apply the inverse function $g^{-1}(u) = u^{1/\gamma}$ to the signal, and compute the mean bicoherence $\sum_{\omega_1, \omega_2 = -\pi}^{\pi} \hat{b}(\omega_1, \omega_2)$.
3. select the inverse value $1/\gamma$ that minimizes the mean bicoherence.

Blindly estimating the value of γ from a gamma corrected image requires computing the bicoherence of a 2-D signal, a four-dimensional quantity. In order to avoid computational and memory requirements, the analysis will be restricted to horizontal and vertical scan lines of an image. This is reasonable since luminance non-linearities are usually pointwise transformations, and the type of

---

[3] Given two vectors x and y, the Schwartz inequality states: $\|x\|\|y\| \geq |x \cdot y|$, where $\|\cdot\|$ denotes vector norm, and $\cdot$ denotes scalar product.

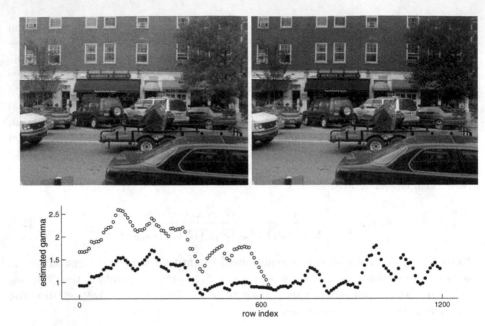

Fig. 6. Top panel: a natural image (left), and the same image whose top portion was gamma corrected with $\gamma = 1.8$ (right). The images are 1200×1600 pixels in size. Bottom panel: Estimated gamma values from horizontal scan lines, where the black dots correspond to estimates from the unadulterated image, and the white dots correspond to estimates from the image whose upper half has been gamma corrected. Each data point corresponds to a running average over 60 scan lines.

correlations introduced in 1-D are similar to those in 2-D. The technique to estimate γ from an image is based on the one used for 1-D signals, as described above.

Shown in the top portion of Fig. 6 is a natural image (1200×1600 pixels in size) and the same image whose upper half has been gamma corrected with $\gamma = 1.8$. The bottom portion shows the estimated gamma values from horizontal scan lines of the unadulterated image (black dots) and the gamma corrected image (white dots). Notice that the values of the gamma estimates from scan lines that span the upper half of the tampered image are generally inconsistent with the lower half.

5   Signal to Noise Ratio

Digital images have an inherent amount of noise introduced either by the imaging process or digital compression. The amount of noise is typically uniform across the entire image. If two images with different noise levels are spliced together, or if small amounts of noise are locally added to conceal traces of tampering, then variations in the signal to noise ratio (SNR) across the image can be used as evidence of tampering. Measuring the SNR is non-trivial in the absence of the original signal. Several *blind* SNR estimators have, however, been proposed [22]. We first describe one such estimator, M_2M_4 [19], and then show its effectiveness in locally measuring noise variance (so as to be invariant to the underlying signal strength, we analyze the noise variance instead of the ratio of signal to noise variances).

We begin by assuming an additive noise model: $y[t] = x[t] + w[t]$, where $x[t]$ is the uncorrupted signal with variance S and $w[t]$ is the noise with variance N. Denote the second and forth moments of the corrupted signal as $M_2 = \mathcal{E}\left\{y^2[t]\right\}$ and $M_4 = \mathcal{E}\left\{y^4[t]\right\}$, where $\mathcal{E}\left\{\cdot\right\}$ is the expected value operator. Assuming that the signal and noise are independent and zero-mean, it can be shown [22] that:

$$M_2 = S + N \qquad \text{and} \qquad M_4 = k_x S^2 + 6SN + k_w N^2, \qquad (22)$$

where $k_x = \mathcal{E}\left\{x^4[t]\right\}/(\mathcal{E}\left\{x^2[t]\right\})^2$ and $k_w = \mathcal{E}\left\{w^4[t]\right\}/(\mathcal{E}\left\{w^2[t]\right\})^2$ are the kurtoses of the original signal and noise. Solving Equation (22) for S and N yields:

$$S = \frac{M_2(k_w - 3) \pm \sqrt{(9 - k_x k_w)M_2^2 + M_4(k_x + k_w - 6)}}{k_x + k_y - 6} \quad \text{and} \quad N = M_2 - S. \, (23)$$

Note that this estimator assumes a known kurtosis for the original signal and the noise, k_x and k_w. In general these quantities may not be known. In the results presented below, we assume that they are known. In the future, the kurtosis of the original signal can be estimated from a region of an image that is believed to be authentic, and the kurtosis of the noise can be estimated by, for example, assuming Gaussian noise ($k_w = 3$), or modeling the noise statistics of JPEG compression.

Shown in the top row of Fig. 7 is an original image, and this image with additive white Gaussian noise with SNRs of 30dB (N=0.08 $\times$ 10^{-3}) and 10dB (N=7.62 $\times$ 10^{-3}) added locally to only the car. Shown in the bottom row of this figure are the estimated noise variances from overlapping (by 32 pixels) 64 $\times$ 64 blocks. The average estimated noise variances, for the blocks overlapping the car, are 0.25 $\times$ 10^{-3} and 7.20 $\times$ 10^{-3}. Notice that the estimator is easily able to detect different noise levels in the image.

6   Discussion

We have described a set of statistical tools for detecting traces of digital tampering in the absence of any digital watermark or signature. We have quantified the nature of statistical correlations that result from specific forms of digital tampering, and have devised detection schemes to reveal these correlations. We are currently developing other tools that, in the same spirit of those presented here, reveal statistical correlations that result from a variety of different manipulations that are typically necessary to create a convincing digital forgery. We

Fig. 7. Shown on the top row is an original image and this image with noise added locally to the car. Shown on the bottom row are the locally estimated noise variances (on the same log scale).

are also analyzing the sensitivity and robustness to counter-attack of each of the schemes outlined in this paper.

There is little doubt that counter-measures will be developed to foil each of the detection schemes outlined in this paper. Our hope, however, is that as more authentication tools are developed it will become increasingly more difficult to create convincing digital forgeries. In addition, as the suite of detection tools expands we believe that it will become increasingly harder to simultaneously foil each of the detection schemes.

References

[1] Digital compression and coding of continuous-tone still images, Part 1: Requirements and guidelines. ISO/IEC JTC1 Draft International Standard 10918-1, 1991.

[2] S. Bhattacharjee and M. Kutter. Compression-tolerant image authentication. In *IEEE International Conference on Image Processing*, 1998.

[3] I.J. Cox, M.L. Miller, and J.A. Bloom. *Digital Watermarking*. Morgan Kaufmann Publishers, 2002.

[4] S.A. Craver, M. Wu, B. Liu, A. Stubblefield, B. Swartzlander, and D.S. Wallach. Reading between the lines: Lessons from the SDMI challenge. In *10th USENIX Security Symposium*, 2001.

[5] A.P. Dempster, N.M. Laird, and D.B. Rubin. Maximum lilelihood from incomplete data via the EM algorithm. *Journal of the Royal Statistical Society*, 99(1):1–38, 1977.

[6] H. Farid. Blind inverse gamma correction. *IEEE Transactions on Image Processing*, 10(10):1428–1433, 2001.

[7] H. Farid and A.C. Popescu. Blind removal of lens distortions. *Journal of the Optical Society of America*, 18(9):2072–2078, 2001.

[8] J. Fridrich and M. Goljan. Images with self-correcting capabilities. In *IEEE International Conference on Image Processing*, 1999.

[9] J. Fridrich, M. Goljan, and M. Du. Invertible authentication. In *SPIE, Security and Watermarking of Multimedia Contents*, 2001.

[10] G.L. Friedman. The trustworthy camera: Restoring credibility to the photographic image. *IEEE Transactions on Consumer Electronics*, 39(4):905–910, 1993.

[11] C.W. Honsinger, P.Jones, M.Rabbani, and J.C. Stoffel. Lossless recovery of an original image containing embedded data. U.S. Patent Application, Docket No. 77102/E-D, 1999.

[12] S. Katzenbeisser and F.A.P. Petitcolas. *Information Techniques for Steganography and Digital Watermarking*. Artec House, 2000.

[13] Y.C. Kim and E.J. Powers. Digital bispectral analysis and its applications to nonlinear wave interactions. *IEEE Transactions of Plasma Science*, PS 7(2), 1979.

[14] D. Kundur and D. Hatzinakos. Digital watermarking for tell-tale tamper proofing and authentication. *Proceedings of the IEEE*, 87(7):1167–1180, 1999.

[15] C.-Y. Lin and S.-F. Chang. A robust image authentication algorithm surviving JPEG lossy compression. In *SPIE Storage and Retrieval of Image/Video Databases*, 1998.

[16] E.T. Lin, C.I Podilchuk, and E.J. Delp. Detection of image alterations using semi-fragile watermarks. In *SPIE International Conference on Security and Watermarking of Multimedia Contents II*, 2000.

[17] J. Lukas and J. Fridrich. Estimation of primary quantization matrix in double compressed JPEG images. In *Digital Forensic Research Workshop*, Cleveland, Ohio, August 2003.

[18] B.M. Macq and J.-J. Quisquater. Cryptology for digital TV broadcasting. *Proceedings of the IEEE*, 83(6):944–957, 1995.

[19] R. Matzner. An SNR estimation algorithm for complex baseband signals using higher order statistics. *Facta Universitatis (Nis)*, 6(1):41–52, 1993.

[20] J.M. Mendel. Tutorial on higher-order statistics (spectra) in signal processing and system theory: Theoretical results and some applications. *Proceedings of the IEEE*, 79(3):278–305, 1991.

[21] A. V. Oppenheim and R. W. Schafer. *Discrete-Time Signal Processing*. Prentice Hall, 1989.

[22] D.R. Pauluzzi and N.C. Beaulieu. A comparison of SNR estimation techniques for the AWGN channel. *IEEE Transactions on Communications*, 48(10):1681–1691, 2000.

[23] C. Rey and J.-L. Dugelay. Blind detection of malicious alterations on still images using robust watermarks. In *IEE Seminar: Secure Images and Image Authentication*, 2000.

[24] M. Schneider and S.-F. Chang. A robust content-based digital signature for image authentication. In *IEEE International Conference on Image Processing*, 1996.

[25] D. Storck. A new approach to integrity of digital images. In *IFIP Conference on Mobile Communication*, pages 309–316, 1996.

[26] G.K. Wallace. The JPEG still picture compression standard. *IEEE Transactions on Consumer Electronics*, 34(4):30–44, 1991.

[27] M. Yeung and F. Mintzer. An invisible watermarking technique for image verification. In *IEEE International Conference on Image Processing*, 1997.

[28] G.-J. Yu, C.-S. Lu, H.-Y.M. Liao, and J.-P. Sheu. Mean quantization blind watermarking for image authentication. In *IEEE International Conference on Image Processing*, 2000.

Relative Generic Computational Forensic Techniques

Jennifer L. Wong and Miodrag Potkonjak

University of California, Los Angeles

Abstract. Computational forensic engineering is the process of identification of the tool or algorithm that was used to produce a particular output or solution by examining the structural properties of the output. We introduce a new Relative Generic Forensic Engineering (RGFE) technique that has several advantages over the previously proposed approaches. The new RGFE technique not only performs more accurate identification of the tool used but also provides the identification with a level of confidence. Additionally, we introduce a generic formulation (integer linear programming formulation) which enables rapid application of the RGFE approach to a variety of problems that can be formulated as 0-1 integer linear programs.

The key innovations of the RGFE technique include the development of a simulated annealing-based (SA) CART classification technique and a generic property formulation technique that facilitates property reuse. We introduce instance properties which enable an enhanced classification of problem instances leading to a higher accuracy of algorithm identification. Finally, the single most important innovation, property calibration, interprets the value for a given algorithm for a given property relative to the values for other algorithms. We demonstrated the effectiveness of the RGFE technique on the boolean satisfiability (SAT) and graph coloring (GC) problems.

1 Introduction

Software and hardware piracy resulted in a loss of over \$59 billion globally between 1995 and 2000, and continues to induce an average of \$12 billion each year in the United States alone. Intellectual Property Protection techniques (IPP), such as watermarking and fingerprinting, have been proposed as solutions. These techniques have shown significant potential. However, they introduce additional overhead on each application of the tool and IP, and they cannot be applied to tools which already exist. Computational forensic techniques removes these limitations. At the point of suspected algorithm or tool infringement, forensic engineering can be applied to show that the tool was used to produce the suspected output. The overhead of the technique is only applied once, off-line. Additionally, the technique can be applied to any existing design or software tool. The underlying approach is to examine the structural properties of the output of different tools for a specific problem and use statistical analysis to identify the tool which was used to create a particular output (infringed).

J. Fridrich (Ed.): IH 2004, LNCS 3200, pp. 148–163, 2004.

Not only does forensic engineering have application for IPP, but it is important to note that it has a number of other applications, which in many situations have even higher economical impact. For instance, forensic engineering can be used for optimization algorithm development, as a basis for developing or improving other IPP techniques, for the development of more powerful benchmarking tools, for enabling security, and facilitating runtime prediction. More specifically, computational forensic engineering can be used to perform optimization algorithm tuning, algorithm development, and analysis of algorithm scaling.

RGFE can be applied to an arbitrary problem which can be formulated as a 0-1 linear programming problem. In this generic formulation, properties of the problem are extracted and used to analyze the structure of both instances of the problem and the output or solutions of a representative set of tools. Using the information gathered, the RGFE technique builds and verifies a Classification and Regression Tree (CART) model to represent the classification of the observed tools. Once built, the CART model can be used to identify the tool used to generate a particular instance output. This RGFE approach consists of three phases: Property Collection, Modeling, and Validation. The key enabling factors in the property collection phase are the ability to extract properties of a given problem systematically and to conduct calibration of these properties to reflect the differences between solutions generated by the tools. We briefly outline the key novelties of the RGFE technique.

- **Generic Forensic Engineering.** We introduce a generic flow for the RGFE technique that allows it to be applied to a variety of optimization problems with minimal retargeting.
- **Generic Property Formulation.** A systematic way to develop instance and solution properties for different problems allows the generic RGFE technique to be applied to a variety of optimization problems. The generic property formulation is applied to a problem which has been formulated in terms of an objective function and constraints. Special emphasis is placed on the widely used 0-1 ILP formulation.
- **Instance Properties.** Problem instances have varying complexity which is often dependent upon particular structural aspects of the instance. Additionally, different algorithms perform differently depending on the complexity or structure of the problem instance it is presented with. We introduce instance properties which provide a measure for comparing instances and therefore facilitate more accurate analysis and classification of the algorithms.
- **Calibration.** Calibration is performed on both instance and solution properties in order to place the data into the proper perspective. For instance properties, calibration provides a way to scale and classify the instances, while the solution properties for each algorithm are calibrated per instance to place the data into the proper perspective to differentiate the algorithms.
- **One-out-of-any Algorithms.** The technique must be able to classify algorithms not only in terms of the algorithms which have been previously analyzed but also as an unknown algorithm.
- **CART model.** We have developed a new CART model for classification. The key novelty is that the new CART model does not only partition the

solution space so that classification can be conducted but also maximizes the volume of space that indicates solutions that are created by none of the observed algorithms. The CART model is created using a SA algorithm.

2   Preliminaries

In this section, we briefly summarize research in the areas which are most directly related: intellectual property protection, forensic analysis, and statistical methods. Additionally, we discuss the relationship between the computation forensic engineering technique and the proposed RGFE approach. Finally, we briefly discuss the generic formulation, the boolean satisfiability problem, algorithms, and the generic formulation for the SAT problem.

Due to the rapidly increasing reuse of intellectual property (IP) such as IC cores and software libraries, intellectual property protection (IPP) has become a mandatory step in the modern design process. Recently, a variety of IPP techniques, such as watermarking, obfuscation, and reverse engineering, have attracted a great deal of attention [1].

We use non-parametric statistical techniques for classification because they can be applied to data which has arbitrary distributions and without any assumptions on the densities of the data [2]. The Classification and Regression Trees (CART) model is a tree-building non-parametric technique widely used for the generation of decision rules for classification. The SA optimization technique originates from statistical mechanics and is often used to generate approximate solutions to very large combinatorial problems [3]. Bootstrapping is a classification validation technique that assesses the statistical accuracy of a model. In the case of nonparametric techniques, bootstrapping is used to provide standard errors and confidence intervals [2].

The Computational Forensic Engineering (CFE) [4] technique identifies an algorithm/tool, which has been used to generate a particular previously unclassified output, from a known set of algorithms/tools. This technique is composed of four phases: feature and statistics collection, feature extraction, algorithm clustering, and validation.

In the feature and statistics collection phase, solution properties of the problem are identified, quantified, analyzed for relevance and selected. Furthermore, preprocessing of the problem instances is done by pertubating the instances - removing any dependencies the algorithms have on the instance format. In the next phase, each of the pertubated instances are processed by each of the algorithms and the solution properties are extracted. The algorithm clustering phase then clusters the solution properties in n-dimensional space, where n is the number of properties. The n-dimensional space is then partitioned into subspaces for each algorithm. The final step validates the accuracy of the partitioned space.

This approach performed well on both the graph coloring and boolean satisfiability problem. However, that was the case only under a number of limiting assumptions. The computational forensic engineering technique performed algorithm classification on one-out-of-k known algorithms, and was tested on a variety of different instances. However many of these instances had similar instance structures. This forensic engineering technique is problem specific and is not easily generalizable to other problems. Lastly, the CFE technique performed analysis of the techniques in the form of blackboxes.

The RGFE technique eliminates several major limitations of the CFE technique. The technique performs one-out-of-any classification instead on one-out-of-k. In this case, output of an algorithm that was never previously analyzed can be classified as unknown. The key enabler for the effectiveness of the Relative Generic Forensic technique is the calibration of problem instances. By identifying, analyzing, and classifying instances by their properties, the quality of the RFGE classification is expanded to another dimension enabling more statistically sound classification. Additionally, we present a generic formulation and generic property formulation that enables the application of this technique to numerous optimization problems.

The boolean satisfiability (SAT) problem has a variety of applications in many areas such as artificial intelligence, VLSI design and CAD, operations research, and combinatorial optimization [5]. Probably the most well-known applications of SAT in CAD are Automatic Test Pattern Generation [6]. Other applications include logic verification, timing analysis, delay fault testing, FPGA routing, and combinational equivalence checking [5]. Formally, the boolean satisfiability problem can be defined in the following way.

Problem: *Boolean Satisfiability*
Instance: *A set U of variables and a collection C of clauses over U.*
Question: *Is there a satisfying truth assignment for C?*

Many different techniques have been developed for solving the boolean satisfiability problem. Techniques such as backtrack search [7], local search [8], continuous formulation and recursive learning [9] are among the most popular. Additionally, several public domain software packages are available such as GRASP [9], GSAT [10] and Sato [7].

3   Forensic Engineering Flow

In this section, we introduce the RGFE technique. The technique operates on a problem instance in the generic formulation, ILP. Our implementation is restricted to instances that are formulated as 0-1 ILP. The technique consists of two stages: analysis and evaluation. In the analysis stage, the goal is to classify the behavior of algorithms for a specific problem specified using the 0-1 ILP format with a high confidence. The flow of the analysis stage is presented graphically in Figure 1 and using a pseudo code format in Figure 2.

The analysis stage of the RGFE technique, shown in Figure 1, is composed of three phases: property collection, model building, and validation phases. The property collection phase defines, extracts, and calibrates instance and solution properties for the given optimization problem. In the modeling phase, the rele-

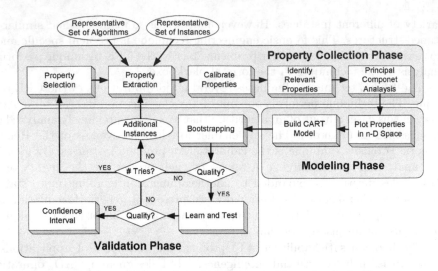

Fig. 1. Overall flow of the RGFE technique: Analysis Stage.

vant properties are used to develop a CART classification scheme. The last phase tests and validates the quality of the CART model.

In this phase, the main steps are property selection and property calibration. We begin by selecting generic instance properties that will assist in classifying the characteristics of the given problem. The solution properties are selected to characterize the decisions or the optimization mechanisms used by an algorithm on a particular type of instance. Once a set of properties have been selected for the targeted optimization problem, we proceed to extract each of the properties from our representative sets of instances and algorithms.

In the final steps, relevant properties are identified. Relevant properties are properties which aid in distinguishing the algorithms from each other. If a property yields the same value for all (or a great percentage of) instances or all algorithms, then it is not useful in the classification process, and is excluded from further consideration. Lastly, principal component analysis is performed in order to eliminate the set of properties which provide similar information as other sets of properties. All of the steps in the property collection phase are encapsulated in Figure 2, lines 1, 2, and 9-14.

In the modeling phase, the calibrated properties are used to model the behavior of each of the algorithms. This is accomplished by representing each solution from each of the available algorithms as a point in n-dimensional space. Each dimension represents either a solution or an instance property. The number of dimensions, n, is the total number of properties. Once the space is populated with the extracted data, we apply a generalized CART approach (see Section 6). The validation stage is an iterative process which uses the statistical techniques, bootstrapping and learn-and-test, to validate and improve the quality of the CART model.

| **Input:** | Representative Set of Instances, I_i, |
| | Representative Set of Algorithm, A_j. |

Algorithm:
1. P_k^S = Define Solution Properties;
2. P_l^I = Define Instance Properties;
3. while $(L_T <$ threshold && $< U_T)\{$
4.   if(exceed U_T)
5.   Add instances to I_i and restart;
6.   while $(E <$ threshold && $< U_T)\{$
7.   if(exceed U_T)
8.   Add instances to I_i and restart;
9. Sol_{ij} = Run each instance, I_i, on every algorithm, A_j;
10. $V_{I,A,P}$ = Extract Properties P from I and Sol;
11.   Calibrate Properties($V_{I,A,P}$);
12. R_p^S = Identify Relevant Solution Properties (P_k^S);
13. R_q^I = Identify Relevant Instance Properties (P_l^I);
14.   Principal Component Analysis($V_{I,A,R}$);
15.   N = Build n-Dimensional Space (R, I, $V_{I,A,R}$);
16.   M = Use Sim. Anneal. to develop CART model (N);
17.   E = Evaluate CART using Bootstrapping(M);
    }
18. L_T = Evaluate CART using Learn and Test (M);
  }
19. C = Build Confidence Interval (M);

Fig. 2. Pseudo-code for the RGFE technique.

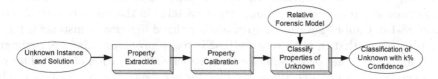

Fig. 3. Flow of the Evaluation Stage.

The overall RGFE goal is to be able to correctly classify the output of an unknown algorithm. Once the Analysis stage has completed, this goal of classification is done in the evaluation stage. The evaluation process, shown in Figure 3, begins with property extraction of both instance properties and solution properties from the unknown instance and algorithm output. The properties that are extracted are the set of properties that we used to build the final CART model in the analysis stage. Next, the properties are properly calibrated according to the selected calibration scheme for each property. The calibrated properties of the unknown instance and solution are then evaluated by the CART model. The algorithm that the CART model classifies the output into is the algorithm which produced the solution with the confidence level of the algorithm in the model, which was found at the end of the analysis stage.

Note that the analysis stage of the approach must only be performed once for a set of observed algorithms. However, once the analysis stage is done, the evaluation stage can be applied repeatedly. Only when new algorithms are observed must the analysis process be repeated. In order to correctly classify the new observed algorithm(s), the properties must be recalibrated to take into account the new algorithm(s). In some cases, it may be necessary to define new properties and to process additional instances on each of the observed algorithms in order to achieve a high confidence level.

4   Calibration

Calibration is the mapping of raw data values to values which contain the maximum amount of information to facilitate a particular task, which in this case is algorithm classification. We introduce calibration using an example. Consider two different SAT instances, par8-2-c and par8-1-c, solved using the GRASP and Walksat SAT algorithms. We evaluate the instances and solutions with the solution property of non-important variables.Non-important variables are variables that may switch their assignment in such a way that the correctness of the obtained solution is preserved. For par8-2-c the property values were 0.529 for GRASP and 0.706 for WalkSAT, and for par8-1-c, 0.391 and 0.594 respectfully.

Without calibration, by considering only these two instances, we would associate a range of 0.39 to 0.59 to the GRASP solutions and of 0.53 to 0.71 to the Walksat solutions. These two ranges overlap and therefore classification is difficult. The reason is obvious; the two instances have different structure. There is intrinsically many more non-important variable in the instance par8-2-c than in par8-1-c. Calibration can compensate for this difference in instances. For example, we see that in both cases, GRASP has a property value approximately 20% lower than that of Walksat for this property. Calibration of the values with respect to the other algorithms enables proper capturing of the relationships between the algorithms, which is not visible from the raw values.

We have developed two calibration schemes. The first calibration approach is a rank-ordered scheme. For each property value on a particular instance, we rank each of the algorithms. Using these rankings, a collaborative ranking for the property is built by examining the rankings of each of the algorithms on all instances. Additional consideration must be made on how to resolve any ties in ranking, and how to combine rankings for individual instances. One can use either average ranking, median ranking, or some other function of ranking on the individual instances. In our experimentations we used modal ranking - where the ranking of each algorithm is defined as the rank that was detected on the largest number of instances.

Rank-order calibration schemes are simple to implement and are robust against data outliers. However, rank order schemes eliminate the information about the relationship between numerical values for a given property of the algorithms. Additionally, the property after rank order calibration does not provide a mechanism for stating an unpopulated region. Unpopulated regions are necessary for the RGFE technique to classify output from an algorithm which has not be observed or studied in the model. Rank-based property calibration can only classify unobserved areas when multiple properties are consider together.

The second type of calibration mechanism is a scale-based scheme. In these types of techniques, calibration is done by mapping the data values from the initial scale on to a new scale. Possible types of data-mapping are normalization against the highest or lowest value, against the median, or against the average value. We use a scheme where the smallest value on all instances is mapped to value 0, the largest value to value 1, and all other values are mapped according to the formula: $x_{new} = \frac{x_{init} - x_s}{x_l - x_s}$, where x_{init} is the initial value for the property, x_s is the smallest value, and x_l is the largest value prior to calibration.

The advantage of a scale-based scheme is, in principle, higher resolution and more expressive power than a rank order scheme. However, these types of approaches can be very sensitive to data outliers - a few exceptionally large or small values. For a scale-based scheme, each of the property values may be plotted on a segment after data-interpretation on the absolute values has been applied. Regions of the segment which are populated by a particular algorithm are defined as classification regions for these algorithms. Regions of the segment which are not populated by any algorithm are specified as unclassified.

5   Properties

There are two key benefits for developing properties in the generic form (0-1 ILP). The first is a conceptual benefit, while the second is software reuse. The conceptual benefit is that treating properties in a generic form greatly facilitates the process of identifying new properties for newly targeted optimization problems. The software reuse benefit lies in the fact that many properties that are developed for one optimization problem can be easily reused for forensic analysis of other optimization problems. Therefore, software for the extraction of these properties need only be written once.

Note that although many problems can be specified using the generic format, often a specific optimization problems have specific features. For example, depending on the problem, the generic formulation may or may not have an objective function. Specifically, the SAT problem contains an empty objective function; as long as all the constraints are satisfied, the value of the objective function is irrelevant. Other properties to consider include the types of variables that appear in the constraints (positive only, negative only, or both), the weights of the variables in the constraints (are they all the same or not), does the objective function contain all of the variables in the problem or only a subset, and so forth. The key is to identify the essential properties of the problem and develop a quantitative way to measure them.

Note that the solution properties can also be extracted in the generic form by mapping the solution output of the algorithms to the generic solution form, then computing the property values. We illustrate the steps in Figure 4.

The representative set of instances for the problem are used both in their standard representation and in generic form. On the right side of the Property Extraction phase, the instances are converted into generic form and then in this form the instance property extraction methods are applied. The instance

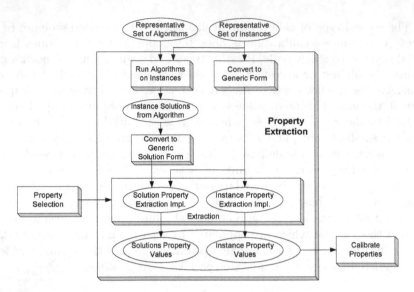

Fig. 4. Procedure for generic property extraction.

property values are collected and passed on to the calibration step. On the left side of Figure 4, the representative set of algorithms executes each of the instances in the representative set. The solutions for each algorithm on each instance are converted to the generic solution formulation, which is then given to the solution property extraction method along with the original instance in its generic formulation. The solution property values for the given algorithm and instance are collected and the data passes to the calibration phase.

We have developed a number of generic instance properties which we illustrate with their representative meaning for the SAT problem.

[I_1] **Constraint Difficulty.** Each constraint in the problem formulation contains coefficients for each variable appearing in the constraint and the value (b-value) on the right-hand side of the constraint. The goal of constraint difficulty is to provide a measure of how much effort and attention the algorithm places on a given constraint. For example, in the SAT formulation, each constraint represents a single clause, and therefore all variables have unit weight. The b-value of the constraint is dependent on the number of positive and negative literals in the constraint. Therefore, in this case this generic property summarizes information about the size of the clauses in the instance. The aggregate information about constraints can be expressed using statistical measures such as average and variance, which we actually used in our system.

[I_2] **Ratio of Signs of Variables.** The key observation is that some variables tend to appear in all constraints in a single form, while others variables will appear in multiple forms and have more balanced appearance counts. For this property, we assume, without loss of generality, that all coefficients b are positive. In the problem formulation, analysis of the positive, negative, and x-weighted, occurrences of a variable can be examined with respect to the total number of occurrences of the variable in the instance. In the SAT problem, we can use this property to identify the tendency of a variable in the instance to be assigned true or false. Again, various statistical measures can be used to aggregate this information. We use average and variance.

[I_3] **Ratio of Variables vs. Constraints.** This property can be applied to all or a subset of variables in all or a subset of the constraints in the instance. It provides insight into the difficulty of these constraints. A low number of variables in a large number of constraints can imply that the constraints are difficult to satisfy due to the fact that numerous constraints are dependent on the same variables.

[I_4] **Bias of a Variable.** We measure the bias of a variable to be assigned to either zero or one, based on the number of constraints which would benefit from the variable being assigned each way.

[I_5] **Probability of satisfying constraints.** This property considers the difficulty of satisfying each constraint based on the variables, weights of the variables, and its b-value. We define the probability of the constraint to be satisfied as shown below.

$$P(\text{constraint satisfied}) = 1 - [\bigcup_{v_i} P(\text{variable assigned opposite of constraints benefit})].$$

Solution properties analyze the relationship of the solution and structure of the problem instance. We have developed the following properties.

[S_1] **Non-important variables.** This property identifies variables that received an assignment which has no effect on the objective function or on the satisfiability of the constraints. Therefore, the goal is identify variables which are not crucial to the solution of the problem. Constructive and greedy algorithms tend to find solutions which have a high number of variables which are not crucial to the solution.

[S_2] **Variable(s) Flip with k% of Constraints still satisfied.** While the non-important variables property aims at identifying variables that have no bearing on the solution of the instance, this property attempts to measure the importance of the variables which impact the objective function and/or the constraints.

[S_3] **Constraint Satisfaction.** This property aims at identifying the extent to which the constraint was satisfied. For example, for constraints of the type $Ax \geq b$, we can define the property as the value of $\frac{Ax(sol)-b}{Ax(max)-b}$. This equation evaluates how much more the constraint was satisfied over the required level by considering the solution's Ax value less the required value against the maximum possible value less the requirement. This formulation is applied to each constraint in the SAT problem. In the case of SAT, this property translates to the level to which each clause is satisfied by the solution.

[S_4] **Variable Tendency.** In many cases, constructive algorithms follow the natural tendencies presented by the instance. More specifically, variables that have all positive coefficients have an intrinsic inclination to be assigned a value of 1, and vice versa. This property tries to quantify to what extent this tendency was followed by a particular type of algorithm. A measure of variable tendency is the number of variables which were assigned according to the ratio of its positive and negative appearances of a variable in the SAT problem.

6   Model Building and Validation

In this section, we discuss the modeling phase of the RGFE technique. We begin with a discussion concerning how clustering and classification of the property data for the tools is achieved. The Classification and Regression Trees (CART) model is adopted and generalized for classification, and we analyze the benefits of the model and its application. Finally, we present details on the use of SA to generate the CART model. The starting point for the development of the classification model is that each solution for each algorithm for a given problem is represented as a point in n-dimensional space, where n is the number of solution and instance properties. The goal of classification is to partition the space into subspaces that classify regions populated mainly, or in the ideal case only, by solutions produced by a particular algorithm. We define $A + 1$ classification classes, where A is the number of algorithms observed. The additional classification class, a unique addition to the standard classification problem, is reserved for subspaces that are not populated by solutions of any of the observed algorithms. If a given output falls into these spaces, the output is classified as produced by an unknown or unobserved tool. Our goal is to perform classification of the data with a model of low Kolmogorov complexity, yet high accuracy [2]. The low Kolmogorov complexity indicates that we did not overtune our model to the given data. Specifically, we follow the principle that for every parameter in the model, we have to have at least five points in the property space.

We adopt the CART model as a starting point for classification for a number of reasons. The model is intuitive, extensively proven to provide accurate classification in many situations, and provides an easy mechanism to enforce the principle of low complexity. The essence of the CART model can be conveniently summarized in the following way. From the geometric point of view, the CART model can be interpreted as partitioning of the n-dimensional space using $(n - 1)$-dimensional hyperplanes that are orthogonal on the axis of the space.

In order to develop the CART model of the n-dimensional data as required by the RGFE technique, we first define a standard grid. The resolution of the grid is determined by a user specified threshold for misclassification. We keep altering the resolution using binary search until the threshold is not achieved. Next, we examine each of the hypercubes, which the grid defines, for misclassifications, i.e. we identify regions which contain data from multiple algorithms.

Once the n-dimensional space has been sufficiently divided into hypercubes, the adjacent hypercubes are merged to represent regions of classification for each algorithm. For this task, we use a SA approach. The approach begins with a random classification of the space, which implies random merging of hypercubes into classification regions. Each merged classification solution is evaluated according to the following objective function: $OF = \alpha N_i + \beta P_m$, where N_i is the number of parameters needed to represent the defined classification in the CART model and P_m is the percentage of misclassification which can occur. The intuition behind the objective function is that the CART model will have smaller representation and complexity if fewer parameters are used. However, smaller representation implies higher misclassification levels. As a result, we try to balance both components in the objective function.

The SA algorithm requires specification of two additional key components: a basic move generation mechanism and a cooling schedule. The move generation mechanism specifies which changes can be made to the current solution in order to generate a new, so-called neighborhood, solution. In the case of the hypercubes, we define a change as either the movement of a single hyperplane of the hypercube by a single grid unit, or as the replacement of a single hypercube side with a new hypercube side in a different dimension.

The cooling schedule consists of a number of parameters which define the temperature decrement of the SA algorithm. These parameters are initial temperature, stop criterion, temperature decrement between successive stages, and the number of transitions for each temperature value. We define the initial temperature as the temperature on which 50% of the moves result in an increased OF. We stop searching if we visit s (s was 3 in our experimentations) temperatures without any improvement in solution. We decrement the temperature using a geometric schedule and at each temperature value, we consider 1000 generations. Validation was conducted using standard learn-and-test and resubstitution validation techniques.

7   Experimental Results

In this section, we present the results of the experimental evaluation of the RGFE technique on the boolean satisfiability and the graph coloring problem. The standard approach to solving the register assignment problem is to reduce the problem to the graph coloring problem (GC). We present experimental results for the register assignment problem in the form of graph coloring. For each problem, we discuss the instance and solution properties used for the developed generalized CART model, and the optimization algorithms for which were used to build the model. Furthermore, we provide experimental evidence of the importance of simultaneously considering both solution and instance properties using the SAT problem. Finally, the performance of the overall technique for classifying both observed and unobserved algorithm output for both problems is presented.

The final CART model used by the RGFE technique for the SAT problem used only five generic properties: two instance properties, and three solution properties. The properties which were selected are the following: [I_1] Weighted Average of "Short" Clauses, [I_3] Ratio of Variables vs. Number of Constraints, [S_1] Percentage of Non-important variables, [S_2] Average Variable Flip with 80% of Constraints still satisfied, and [S_3] Average Constraint Satisfaction.

These solution properties were used to analyze the outputs of four SAT algorithms: GRASP, nsat, sato and walksat. The GRASP algorithm [9], is a generic search algorithm which performs non-chronological backtracking with a conflict analysis procedure and tree pruning. The nsat algorithm is a simple backtrack search algorithm. Sato applies the David-Putnam approach and tries to speed up unit propagation [7]. Walksat is a stochastic search algorithm, which is incomplete, developed by Kautz and Selman. It is an iterative improvement approach which performs two separate types of moves: a flip of the current variable assignment of a variable appearing in an unsatisfied clause, or a greedy move. The SAT algorithm that we used for testing the classification ability of unobserved algorithms is the Satz algorithm. This approach is a systematic, complete SAT solver with randomized restarts.

The representative set of SAT instances used to build the CART model include instances from the DIMACS standard benchmark set. The first set, jnh*, are randomly generated instances of the constant density model. The problem distribution of these instances is Random P-SAT. The aim* instances are random 3-SAT instances. The third set of instances are propositional versions of parity learning problems, par8*. Lastly, the ii* set are instances of inductive interference problems. Additional information on these benchmark sets and others can be found at [11].

In order to demonstrate the importance of comparing properties of instances and solutions, we present data and comparisons using the SAT problem. We used a set of 55 SAT instances. In Figure 5, we present the dependency between instance property, $[I_1]$ weighted average of "short" clauses and solution property $[S_1]$ non-important variables. The solution property is calibrated using rank-order. A rank of one is given to the algorithm with the highest property value on a given instance, and a rank of 4 is the lowest rank. If two algorithms have the same property value on an instance, they are given the same rank number. The horizontal axis of the figure displays the name of each of the instances. The vertical axis indicates the value of instance property. The piece-wise linear line displays the values of property I_1 for each instance. Note that there are three distinguishable subsets of instances which have distinctly different I_1 values, approximately 0.06, 0.12, and 0.23. For each instance, the calibrated rank of the corresponding solution property values for each algorithm is displayed along the horizontal axis in bar format. For each of the distinguishable regions of I_1 values, a noticeable pattern in the algorithms ranks can be seen. For example, in the first region of I_1 values, 0.06, the GRASP algorithm is always ranked the lowest, the walksat algorithm is ranked highest in nine of the eleven instances, and sato is only ranked second and first in all cases. Similar ranking consistency can be seen in the results for solution property, S_2 in Figure 6. According to this property, for the instances in the highest instance property range, approximately 0.23, walksat is ranked the highest in all but two of the cases, sato is ranked second in all but three cases, and nsat and GRASP are tied in all cases. In the other two regions, patterns also exist.

In order to test the generalized CART model, we ran both new instances and new instances where the order of the inputs (variables) was subject to random permutation. All the instances were from the same class of selected benchmarks, and included instances which were not in the representative set. In total, we used the CART model to classify 1000 different solutions of each algorithm, including the unobserved algorithm satz. The results of the classification are shown in Table 7. The rows of the table present the solver used to generate the solution,

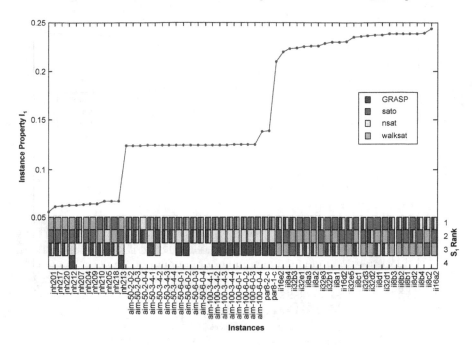

Fig. 5. SAT: Dependency between instance property (I_1) and solution property (S_1).

and the columns represent the algorithm for which the output was classified as by the CART model. The CART model had confidence interval of 92%.

We now present the properties and algorithms used for application of the RGFE technique on the graph coloring problem. The final CART model for classification of algorithms for the GC problem used the following instance and solution properties:[I_2] Variable Appearance vs. Average Variable Appearance, [I_3]Ratio of Variables vs. Number of Constraints on Edge Constraints, [S_1] Percentage of Non-important variables - nodes which can change coloring without increasing the number of colors used, [S_2] Average Variable Flip with 80% of Constraints Still Satisfied - average number of coloring possibilities per node, and [S_3] Constraint Satisfaction - percentage of nodes which can only be colored with a single color.

For the GC problem, we used four algorithms for building the CART model: dsatur, maxis, itrgrdy, and tabu. Additionally, we use the bkdsat algorithm as the unobserved algorithm. The dsatur algorithm, developed by Brelaz [12], selects the node to color at each step based on the degree of the node, and the number of colors which cannot be used to color the node due to conflicts with previously colored nodes. Nodes with the least number of coloring possibilities are colored first. Maxis is a recursive, large first algorithm (RLF) which applies exponential backtracking. The iterative improvement approach, itrgrdy, uses an iterative local improvement search to improve the current coloring assignment.

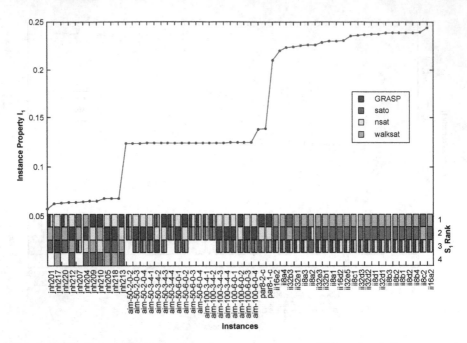

Fig. 6. SAT: Dependency between instance property (I_1) and solution property (S_2).

Tabu search is a probabilistic iterative improvement algorithm [13]. The original assignment of colors is applied randomly, and conflicts are attempted to be resolved by reassigning conflicting nodes to different colors. Lastly, the bkdsat algorithm is a greedy algorithm which attempts to color higher density regions of the graph.

For instances of the graph coloring problem, we use graphs from the DIMACS benchmark set, types of which include register allocation, leighton, scheduling, and quasi-random graphs. We select 100 instances to build our CART model. The resulting CART model had a confidence interval of 94%. The results for attempting classification on 50 additional instances and their permutations are

SAT						GC					
Solver	GRASP	nsat	sato	walksat	unobs	Solver	dsatur	maxis	itrgrdy	tabu	unobs
GRASP	993	5	0	0	2	dsatur	992	4	0	1	3
nsat	5	994	0	0	1	maxis	2	996	0	0	2
sato	0	1	995	3	1	itrgrdy	0	2	997	0	1
walksat	2	0	4	992	2	tabu	2	0	1	994	3
satz	3	4	2	1	990	bkdsat	1	3	0	0	996

Table 1. Experimental results for SAT and GC.

shown in Table 7. The table displays the classification of the solution generated by each of the algorithms on 1000 permutated instances from the DIMACS set. The model is capable of classifying the output with extreme accuracy.

8 Conclusion

We have introduced the RGFE technique for identifying which tool, if any, produced a particular solution to a given optimization problem. The new approach is capable of not only differentiation between outputs of known algorithms, but is able to determine if an unknown algorithm was used to produce the output. The new technique enables rapid retargeting to new optimization problems.

References

[1] Qu, G., Potkonjak, M.: Intellectual Property Protection in VLSI Design: Theory and Practice. Kluwer (2003)
[2] Breiman, L., et al.: Classification and Regression Trees. Chapman and Hall (1993)
[3] Kirkpatrick, S., et al.: Optimization by simulated annealing. Science **220** (1983) 671–680
[4] Wong, J., Kirovski, D., Potkonjak, M.: Non-parametrical statistical computational forensic techniques for intellectual property protection. In: 4th International Information Hiding Workshop. (2001) 71–86
[5] Marques-Silva, J., Sakallah, K.: Boolean satisfiability in electronic design automation. In: Cliques, Coloring, and Satisfiability. (2000)
[6] Hamzaoglu, I., Patel, J.: New techniques for deterministic test pattern generation. In: IEEE VLSI Test Symposium. (1998)
[7] Zhang, H.: Sato: An efficient propositional prover. In: Conference on Automated Deduction and LNAI 1249. (1997) 272–275
[8] Selman, B., Levesque, H., Mitchell, D.: A new method for solving hard satisability problems. In: AAAI. (1992) 440–446
[9] Marques-Silva, J., Sakallah, K.: Grasp: a search algorithm for propositional satisfiability. Transactions on Computers **48** (1999) 506–521
[10] Selman, B., Kautz, H.: Domain-independent extensions to gsat: Solving large structured satisfiability problems. In: International Conference on Artificial Intelligence. (1993) 290–295
[11] SATLIB: The satisfiability library. http://www.satlib.org (2004)
[12] Brelaz, D.: New methods to color the vertices of a graph. Comm. of the ACM **22** (1979) 251–256
[13] Hertz, A., de Werra, D.: Using tabu search techniques for graph coloring. Journal of Computing **39** (1987) 345–351

Syntax and Semantics-Preserving
Application-Layer Protocol Steganography*

Norka B. Lucena, James Pease, Payman Yadollahpour, and Steve J. Chapin

Systems Assurance Institute
Syracuse University
111 College Place 3-114, Syracuse, NY 13244
{norka,jmpease, pyadolla, chapin}@ecs.syr.edu

Abstract. Protocol steganography allows users who wish to communicate secretly to embed information within other messages and network control protocols used by common applications. This form of unobservable communication can be used as means to enhance privacy and anonymity as well as for many other purposes, ranging from entertainment to protected business communication or national defense. In this paper, we describe our approach to application-layer protocol steganography, describing how we can embed messages into a commonly used TCP/IP protocol. We also introduce the notions of syntax and semantics preservation, which ensure that messages after embedding still conform to the host protocol. Based on those concepts, we attempt to produce reasonably secure and robust stegosystems. To demonstrate the efficacy of our approach, we have implemented protocol steganography within the Secure Shell (SSH) protocol. Findings indicate that protocol steganographic system is reasonably secure if the statistical profile of the covermessages and the statistical profile of its traffic match their counterparts after embedding.

Keywords: steganography, application protocols, syntax, semantics, SSH

1 Introduction

Steganography, from the Greek "covered writing," refers to the practice of hiding information within other information [1]. Its purpose is to allow two parties to communicate in such a way that the presence of the message cannot be detected. While cryptography focuses on protecting the content of the message, steganography conceals the mere existence of the message. Classical steganography comprises a broad variety of methods and materials, ranging from tattooing messengers' heads to using invisible ink and microdots. Modern steganography involves digital media and techniques: images, formatted and written text, digital sounds, and video, as well as some others less orthodox such as storage devices

* This work was supported in part by the State of New York, the CASE Center's SUPRIA program at Syracuse University, and the Air Force Research Laboratory (AFRL).

J. Fridrich (Ed.): IH 2004, LNCS 3200, pp. 164–179, 2004.

and TCP/IP packets [2]. In recent years,the evolution of stegosystems has received particular attention, as have the security and robustness of their methods [3, 4, 5, 6, 7]. In this context, protocol steganography arises as a new means of hiding information in Internet messages to achieve secret communication.

Protocol steganography is the art of embedding information within messages and network control protocols used by common applications [8]. Protocol steganography takes advantage of existing application-layer network traffic to communicate privately, which could be a useful and important means of communication in many different areas. It can be effective in law enforcement for undercover investigations and espionage. For example, it could have been convenient for "Enron whistleblower" Sheron Watkins to have set up a private communication channel with the District Attorney's office that worked without having to deploy special anonymity frameworks, but utilizing the traffic generated by one of her regular web-browsing sessions. The business arena can also benefit from hiding the communication when doing important negotiations.

Early attempts at hiding information within network protocols were based on the discovery of covert channels—communication channels neither designed nor intended to transfer information at all [9]—in TCP/IP packets [10, 11, 12, 13]). In contrast, our approach of protocol steganography specifically targets application-layer protocols such SMTP (for email service), FTP (for file transfer), SSH (for secure login), LDAP (for distributed directory services), and HTTP (for web browsing, which alone accounted for over 53% of all Internet traffic in 2002 [14]). We aim to hide information within the format and structure of the protocol, and not in the transmitted content, such as images, sounds, text, or video. Information hiding within these content types can be achieve using well-known steganographic techniques before the content is sent across the network.

The most relevant feature of a steganographic system is how secure it is. At the moment, there is controversy in the field regarding the definition of a perfectly secure system [15, 16]. The most cited approaches are based on information theory and the ideas of security taken from cryptography definitions [17, 18, 19, 20]. There are other definitions such as the Ettinger's game-theoretical definition [21] and the complexity-theoretical definitions in [22, 23]. However, to the best of our knowledge, there is no record of any implemented stegosystem proven secure under those definitions. We recognize the enormous effort put behind producing an exact mathematical definition of security, but for this paper we limited our approach to produce an empirically and "reasonably secure" [24] stegosystem.

The remainder of this paper is organized as follows. Section 2 explains the concepts of security and robustness in terms of protocol steganography. Section 3 describes the model for secret communication considered in our approach and discusses its potential advantages. Section 4 presents a summary of the research to date and related work in relevant areas of steganography. Section 5 explores the concept of protocol steganography through the SSH protocol, describes a prototype implementation, and discusses consequences and important issues regarding security and robustness of the approach as well. Finally, Section 6 lists some conclusions and remarks of lessons learned.

2   Security and Robustness in Protocol Steganography

Steganographic systems are usually defined in terms of three elements: capacity, security, and robustness. *Capacity* is the amount of information that can be hidden in the cover. *Security* refers to the difficulty that a knowledgeable adversary (one who understands the stegosystem) has in obtaining evidence or even grounds for suspicion that a secret communication is taking place. *Robustness* is the amount of alteration a stegomessage can support without the hidden message being destroyed [1, 25]. For this study, we focus in examining both security and robustness of our steganographic methods against the threat of passive and active adversaries more than in increasing their capacity.

The protocol steganography model assumes prior knowledge of the distribution of the covers, standard practice when defining stegosystems. This allows to produce appropriate embedding and extraction methods which minimize or eliminate alterations in the statistical profile of the covermessages. Protocol steganography however needs to deal not only with the characteristics of the covermessage itself but also with the statistical profile of its traffic such as the distribution of the payload length. A *reasonably secure* protocol stegosystem is one in which the adversary cannot distinguish between a covermessage and a stegomessage by analyzing the meaning of the packet payload and the statistical properties of the protocol traffic. Stegomessages are *reasonably robust* if, after alterations from a malicious attacker, they are rendered inadequate regarding their protocol semantics. Stegomessages that are not semantically valid usually cause the interruption of the overt communication.

Seeking to produce both secure and robust stegosystems, we define two concepts for stegomessages: syntax preservation and semantics preservation. *Syntax preservation* guarantees that the stegomessage is well formed within the rules of the protocol; the actual meaning of the stegomessage may be different than the original cover. *Semantics preservation* means that, as observed at a point along the message's path through the network, the stegomessage has the same meaning as the original cover. Semantics preservation is stronger than, and implies, syntax preservation. Semantics preservation increases robustness—it reduces or eliminates the possibility for an active attacker to render the hidden message useless without causing substantial damage to the packet, thereby breaking the overt communication. The early work in covert channels was, in general, neither syntax nor semantics preserving, and depended on routers not performing tight checking against the protocol specification.

3   Framework for Secret Communication

Our model for protocol steganography involves two agents who wish to communicate secretly through arbitrary Internet traffic in a hostile environment (see

Figure 1). *Alice* and *Bob* [26] are two agents who wish to communicate secretly. To achieve that, they use a communication path already in place between themselves or two arbitrary communicating processes, the *sender* and *receiver*. Adversaries located between Alice and Bob can be both active or passive. A passive adversary, *Eve*, observes the communication to discover stegomessages. Eve's eventual goal is to find the embedded information, and prove its existence to a third party, if necessary. An active adversary, *Mallory* [27] attempts to remove the embedded message during the communication process, while preserving the integrity of the cover.

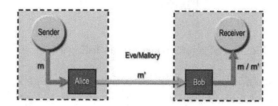

Fig. 1. Framework for Secret Communication.

Two scenarios are possible depending on whether or not Alice and Bob are the same as the sender and the receiver, respectively. In the first case, Alice and Bob are trying to hide secret information in some of their own harmless messages, as in traditional steganography models. They both run a modified version of the communicating software that allows them to convey the secret message. In the second case, Alice and Bob are placed somewhere along an arbitrary communication path, modifying messages in transit to hide meaningful information. In short, both the internal agent and the external confederate might be either end points of the communication or middlemen, acting to embed and extract the hidden message as the data passes them in the communication stream. In fact, the receiving middleman has the option of removing the hidden message, thus restoring and forwarding the original covermessage. The midpoints where Alice and Bob can alter the message might be within the protocol stack of the sending and receiving machines (which is still distinct from the sending process), or at routers along the communication path. These arbitrary boundaries are indicated by the dashed boxes in Figure 1.

Considering all combinations of internal agents and external confederates and all different points where the message can be altered yields six different combinations of roles for the agents, as shown in Figure 2. In this discussion, following the established information hiding terminology [28], Alice executes the *embedding* process and Bob the *extraction* process, represented in the picture as a circle and a diamond, respectively. As pointed out by Pfitzmann [28], the embedding and extracting processes may require the use of a *stegokey*, not shown in the picture. The *cover* (i.e. the original harmless message) is m, and the *stegomessage* (i.e. the message with steganographic content) is m'.

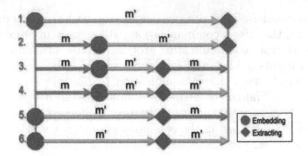

Fig. 2. Message Paths.

The six possible sets of agent roles are as follows:

1. *Alice* acts as sender and *Bob* as receiver—the message along the entire path is m'.
2. *Alice* is a middleman, embedding information to the message on its way, and *Bob* acts as *receiver*—the message from the *sender* to *Alice*'s location is m, while from there to the endpoint is m'.
3. Both agents are middlemen, and *Bob* restores the message to its original form—the message from the *sender*'s point to where *Alice*'s location is m, from *Alice*'s to *Bob*'s is m', and from there to the endpoint is m again, because extraction of the hidden content and restoration of the original cover message occurred at *Bob*'s location.
4. Both agents are middlemen, but *Bob* does not restore the message—the message from the *sender*'s point to the *Alice*'s location is m, and from *Alice*'s to the *receiver*'s point is m', with the hidden information extracted at *Bob*'s location while the message was in transit.
5. *Alice* is acting as *sender*, with *Bob* as a middleman extracting the embedded information and restoring the original message—the message from the initial point to *Bob*'s location is m', and from *Bob*'s location to the *receiver*'s point is m.
6. *Alice* is acting as sender and *Bob* is a middleman extracting the hidden information without restoring the message as it travels to the *receiver*—the message from end to end is m', but B gets the hidden content somewhere before the message reaches its destination.

Even though not every one of these scenarios might be realistic, cases 1 and 3 certainly are. Thus, they were the focus of this study. All the options where the hidden content is extracted but the message is not restored seem risky. In particular, case 4 wherein the message seen by the receiver is clearly different from that seen by the sender, neither of whom are the agents communicating secretly.

3.1   Issues with Middlemen

Having the agents acting as middlemen in the communication stream provides several advantages, because any packet that will flow past the locations where Alice and Bob are can be modified (as long as an embedding function that preserves both syntax and semantics is available for the transport or application protocol in that packet). That intermediate location lowers the susceptibility to traffic analysis, as there is no longer a single source/sink for the stegomessages, and there is no specific protocol used. It also allows us to achieve a higher bit rate as well as privacy, anonymity, and plausible deniability, in some cases. In the case of undercover operations, for example, an ideal situation would be that Alice is located on the last router inside the sender's domain (the egress router for that domain), and Bob is located on the first router outside the domain (the ingress router). In such scheme, m' will be "on the wire" for the minimum possible time, lowering the probability of detection.

Detection of packet modifications along the communication path might seem trivial for an observer monitoring the network. We argue that it is not. First of all, the modified packets at the embedding and the extraction points will be both syntax and semantics preserving, which evades routing and intrusion detection defense mechanisms. Secondly, individual packet comparison from both sides of an embedding/extraction point is resource intensive and not currently done by IDS systems to avoid the overhead incurred with large amounts of traffic. Lastly, routine network operations for most IPSs, for example, involve the collection of aggregate traffic statistics rather than individual packet analysis, because of the high volume [29].

IP fragmentation is another issue that can affect the reliability of the communication when the agents are middlemen. When the application-layer protocol uses TCP as transport protocol, we assume that the packets used as carrier are delivered reliably. If there still exist packet loses, they are treated as communication errors. Fragmentation rates in packets of TCP applications are minimal. In addition, most of them set the "don't fragment" bit on. In contrast, when the application-layer protocol uses UDP, additional mechanisms need to be implemented to guarantee that Bob actually receives the message sent by Alice.

4   Related Work

Handel and Sandford [11] reported the existence of covert channels within network communication protocols. They described different methods of creating and exploiting hidden channels in the OSI network model, based on the characteristics of each layer. In particular, regarding to the application layer, they suggested covert messaging systems through features of the applications running in the layer, such as programming macros in a word processor. In contrast, the protocol steganography approach studies hiding information within messages and network control protocols used by the applications, not inside images transmitted as attachments by an email application, for example.

Examples of implementation of covert channels in the TCP/IP protocol suite are presented by Rowland [13], Project Loki [12], Ka0ticSH [30], and more deeply and extensively by Dunigan [10]. These researchers focused their attention in the network and transport layers of the OSI network model. In spite of that, Dunigan [10] did point out in his discussion of network steganography that application-layer protocols, such as Telnet, FTP, SMTP, and HTTP, could possibly carry hidden information in their own set of headers and control information. However, he did not develop any technique targeting these protocols. Rowland [13] implemented three methods of encoding information in the TCP/IP header: manipulating the IP identification field, with the initial sequence number field, and with the TCP acknowledge sequence number field "bounce." Dunigan [10] analyzed the embedding of information, not only in those fields, but in some other fields of both the IP and the UDP headers as well as in the ICMP protocol header. He based his analysis mainly in the statistical distribution of the fields and the behavior of the protocol itself. Project Loki [12, 30] explored the concept of ICMP tunneling, exploiting covert channels inside of ICMP_ECHO traffic. All these approaches, without minimizing their importance, can be detected or defeated with the latest router and firewall technology.

One such mechanism is reported in Fisk et al. [31]. Their work defines two classes of information in network protocols: *structured* and *unstructured* carriers. Structured carriers present well-defined, objective semantics, and can be checked for fidelity en route (e.g., TCP packets can be checked to ensure they are semantically correct according to the protocol). On the contrary, unstructured carriers, such as images, audio, or natural language, lack objectively defined semantics and are mostly interpreted by humans rather than computers. The defensive mechanism they developed aims to achieve security without spending time looking for hidden messages: using active wardens they defeat steganography by making strong semantic-preserving alterations to packet headers (e.g. zeroing the padding bits in a TCP packet). The most important considerations to their work related to protocol steganography are the identification of the co-vermessages in used as structured carrier, and the feasibility of similar methods of steganalysis that target application-layer protocols.

Recently, researches are focusing more of their attention in the use of covert channels using specifically the HTTP protocol. Bowyer [32] described a theoretical example without implementation, wherein a remote access Trojan horse communicates secretly with its control using an HTTP GET request. Although this approach takes advantage of the semantics of regular HTTP messages, as we intent to do, it is different from our approach because it can be blocked by restricting access to certain websites, or by scanning images for steganographic content. Bauer [33] proposed the use of cover channels in HTTP to enlarge anonymity sets and provide unobservability in mix networks. He shares our view of using traffic generated by other subjects to hide communication.

5   A Case Study: SSH

The SSH protocol provides secure remote login and other secure network services over an insecure network [34]. It does so through mechanisms that supply server authentication, confidentiality, and integrity with perfect forward secrecy. There are several implementations of SSH, both commercial and open-source. The latest and most widely used version of the protocol is SSH2.

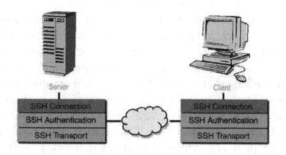

Fig. 3. SSH2 Protocol Architecture.

The SSH2 protocol consists of three major components shown in Figure 3:

- **Transport Layer Protocol**. Provides server cryptographic authentication, confidentiality through strong encryption, and integrity plus, optionally, compression. Typically, it runs over a TCP/IP connection listening for connections on port 22.
- **User Authentication Protocol**. Authenticates the client-side user to the server. It runs over the transport layer protocol.
- **Connection Protocol**. Multiplexes the encrypted tunnel into several logical channels. It runs over the user authentication protocol. It provides interactive login sessions, remote execution of commands, forwarded TCP/IP connections, and forwarded X11 connections.

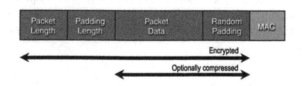

Fig. 4. SSH2 Binary Packet Protocol.

In particular, the Transport Layer protocol defines the *Binary Packet Protocol*, which establishes the format SSH packets follow (see Figure 4). It consists of five fields. *Packet length* is an unsigned 32-bit integer representing the length of the packet data in octets. *Padding length* is the number of octets representing the length of the padding. *Packet data* is the actual content of the message. *Random padding* is an arbitrary-length padding appended to the packet data, so the payload reaches the block cipher sizes specified by the protocol. *MAC* corresponds to the message authentication code, which is computed if previously negotiated. The packet length, padding length, packet data, and random padding fields are encrypted. The packet data and the random padding are compressed before encryption, if compression was specified during the connection setup.

SSH was selected as our first Protocol Steganography case of study for several reasons, with the randomness of the content of its packets being the most important. Encrypted traffic provides an appropriate cover for other messages with uniform distribution, e.g. additional encrypted data. We can blend hidden content securely within what is considered "normal" traffic, without altering the statistical properties of the payload. In addition to that, the fact that the SSH traffic is encrypted may deter adversaries from trying to analyze its content, as pointed out by Barrett and Silverman [35]. Lastly, SSH is widely used and use TCP as transport protocol, which guarantees delivery packets even when they are fragmented.

5.1   Prototype Implementation

We identified several potential possibilities of information hiding in the SSH protocol structure, but selected only two of them for implementation: generating a MAC-like message and adding additional encrypted content to the packet. Such methods of hiding information match, respectively, cases 1 and 3 of our framework of secret communication, described in Figure 2. Case 1 assumes that *Alice* is the sender and *Bob* is the receiver. In Case 3, both agents *Alice* and *Bob* are middlemen located along the communication path. Then, *Bob* needs to restore the stegomessage to the covermessage after extracting the hidden message embedded by *Alice*.

Both implementations were coded in C, tested under Red Hat 8.0, and each of them runs independently of the other. For implementing the first scenario of secret communication, generating a MAC-like message, we modified version 3.5 of Open SSH (http://www.openssh.org), a popular open-source SSH product. For the second scenario, adding encrypted content, we developed a kernel module to capture packets in transit and we tested the system using unmodified OpenSSH 3.5.

Generating a MAC-like Message. In this steganography scenario *Alice* (the sender) and *Bob* (the receiver) are running identically-modified software. At first sight, it might seem strange to pursue secret communication over an already encrypted channel. However, this example of protocol steganography is appropriate for environments where unobtrusive communications are required in the presence of traffic analysis, particularly the number and frequency of messages. In the military and intelligence agencies, even if the content of the communication is encrypted, a significant increase in communications between military units could signal an impending attack [1]. For example, *Alice* might be working at the Pentagon and *Bob* might be a high-level commander in the Middle East. To avoid eavesdropping by terrorists, they encrypt their messages using OpenSSH. It is not possible for the adversary to decipher the messages being sent, but the adversary can perform traffic analysis by studying the length and frequency of the messages exchanged. A sudden increase in traffic gives a clear indication that something "big" is going on.

As shown in Figure 4, the SSH2 specification defines a message authentication code field. The MAC is computed with a previously negotiated MAC algorithm using the key, the sequence number of the packet, and the unencrypted (but compressed, if compression is required) packet data. The MAC algorithms defined by the protocol are hmac-sha1, hmac-sha1-96, hmac-md5, and hmac-md5-96 whose digest lengths vary from 12 to 20 octets. Therefore, generating a MAC-like message will allows us to transmit up to 20 additional octets of per packet.

To simulate the randomness of the MAC, the embedded messages are previously compressed and then encrypted. The modified version of the SSH client reads the content to be embedded from a file compressed with GZip (http://www.gzip.org) and encrypted with the GNU Privacy Guard software (http://www.gnupg.org), using the Blowfish algorithm. It embeds and extracts exactly the same amount of octets reserved for computing the MAC in the selected algorithm. At the receiving end, the modified version of the SSH server ignores recomputing the MAC and comparing it with the one received from the client, because the server is action as *Bob*. Instead, *Bob* saves the MAC-like message into a file.

The drawback of this implementation is the impossibility of verifying whether the actual payload of the message was correctly transmitted or not, as a consequence of replacing the MAC. Information about the error rates in transmission of SSH packets will be useful for better understanding the validity of this approach. However, augmenting a short MAC might be a way of getting around this issue. Because the different MAC algorithms offered by SSH produce MACs of different lengths, it would still be possible to select an algorithm with a short MAC and pad the stegomessage to it. For example, if the hmac-md5-96 algorithm, which computes a 12-octet MAC is used, we can add 8 octets of secret information to each packet, bringing the pseudo-MAC up to the 20-octet limit. Of course, for this approach to work, *Alice* and *Bob* must agree in advance on what algorithm to use. That is trivial to set up through the SSH authentication mechanism. Moreover, when they are not planning to communicate secretly, *Alice* and *Bob* can choose to use the hmac-sha1 algorithm which computes a MAC of length 20, so the average total lengths of their SSH packets does not raise suspicion.

Because we are maintaining the randomness of the covermessage when creating a stegomessage as well as the distribution of the payload length, we consider this stegomethod to be reasonably secure. *Eve* cannot distinguish between two encrypted payloads (cover and stego) of the same size. Because of particular properties of the SSH protocol, embedding a MAC-like message is reasonably robust. SSH takes any change in the MAC at the receiving end as a signal of existence of an attacker somewhere in the middle of the communication stream. SSH issues a warning and the session will be interrupted (normal behavior of the protocol). *Mallory* cannot then recompute and substitute the MAC (besides that involves having knowledge of the encrypted packet payload, the keys, and the algorithms used). *Mallory* cannot make subtle changes to the packet either, such as switching some bits. Our implementation takes similar actions to the ones SSH takes when there when the hidden message is not meaningful to *Bob*.

Adding Additional Encrypted Content to the Packet. This prototype implementation works in the secret communication environments described in cases 2, 3, or 4. However, we will consider only case 3 in this discussion because it is the most challenging. Both *Alice* and *Bob* are middlemen located somewhere along the communication path. *Alice* intercepts a packet from the sender, embeds a portion of her secret message on it, and sends it on. *Bob* extracts the hidden content and restores the message as it originally was before it reaches its destination. *Alice* and *Bob* can be any two parties who wish to communicate secretly by taking advantage of available SSH traffic on the Internet.

This implementation intercepts the SSH traffic and inserts an additional encrypted message at the beginning of the already encrypted payload, as detailed in Figure 5. A 32-bit "magic" number marks the presence of a hidden message.

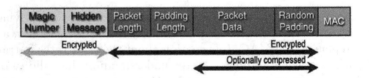

Fig. 5. Adding an encrypted portion with a hidden message to a regular SSH packet at the beginning of the encrypted payload.

To be able to intercept SSH traffic, we implemented a *Packet Transmogrifier*[1] (PT), written in C for Linux 2.4 kernels. The PT is a piece of software that captures arbitrary packets in transit, embeds secret messages into a stream of outgoing packets, and correspondingly extracts the hidden message when used downstream. It was implemented as a kernel module for deployment in Linux-based routers. In principle, the PT uses a combination of several individual

---

[1] With appropriate apologies and thanks to Bill Watterson, creator of "Calvin and Hobbes" [36].

protocol-specific packet transformers as plug-in modules (each of which could be used by an individual application to embed a message in a data stream). This approach gives us the flexibility of embedding hidden messages in packets of multiples types corresponding to different protocols, and with a variety of sources and destinations. The current implementation of the PT provides a series of default protocol-dependent embedder and extractor functions that are called based on the options selected by the user and the payload type of a particular IP packet. The corresponding functions for handling SSH packets are called sshEmbedder and sshExtractor.

When establishing an SSH session, the client and the server negotiate the algorithms to be used in the session, the MAC algorithm among them. Next, they initiate the key exchange. The number of messages exchanged till this point by the client and server are unencrypted, therefore, sshEmbedder and sshExtractor are not interested in modifying such packets. The analyze their content and discharge them if they are any of the plain-text packets. Once the key exchange is done, both sides, client and server, turn on encryption, perform authentication, and the secure connection is establish. From that particular stage, sshEmbedder begins altering the SSH packets, embedding encrypted hidden messages. Conversely, sshExtractor attempts to extract a secret message from every encrypted packet and reformats the SSH packet to its original form. The functions sshEmbedder and sshExtractor are semantics preserving. The SSH traffic reminds encrypted after embedding or extraction, hence both the cover and the stegomessage have the same semantic meaning to a third party observer.

From monitoring SSH traffic, we learned that the most common packet sizes in Telnet-like SSH session are 48 and 80 bytes, with each comprising approximately 23% of the recorded data. For testing the functionality of this implementation, we elected to embed data in chunks of at least 12 octets with a 32-bit (4-octet) CRC to verify the integrity of the message when transmitted. That is, the total length of the SSH payload is incremented by at least 16 octets after the embedding. Hence, a portion of the SSH packets with payload length 48 bytes are converted into 64-octet packets. Similarly, a portion of the SSH packets with payload length between 49 and 64 are transformed into 80-octet packets. Figure 6 shows a sample output of the PT when embedding messages.

If *Eve* is able to observe both sides of the communication at the location where the PT is placed, it would be trivial to notice the difference in the payload size. The scenario is nevertheless implausible because of the high volume traffic on the Internet and the multitude of potential insertion points along the communication path, which make packet-by-packet comparison impractical. Still, to avoid detection through automated tools when increasing the payload length of the packets, we need to simulate the packet length distribution of the SSH payload at any given time. We are currently adding capability to fit a given payload length distribution within a one-minute interval using the Chi-square test for goodness of fit. Therefore, we conclude that this stegomethod is not reasonably secure when *Eve* has knowledge of the covermessage payload length distribution.

```
IP Header:
        Version        : 4
        Header Length  : 20 bytes
        Type of Service: 0x0
        Total Length   : 100 bytes
        ID             : 0x24e1
        Time to Live   : 64
        Protocol       : TCP
        Source         : 192.168.1.1
        Destination    : 192.168.1.44
TCP header:
        Source Port        : 32795
        Destination Port   : 22
        Header Length      : 32 bytes
        Flags              : PSH ACK
        Sequence Number    : 788611435
        Acknowledgment Number: 2147254624
Data (48 bytes):
        55 d5 dd 8d aa bc 48 1d 54 9a 18 8f a5 95 77 dd    U.....H.T.....w.
        98 32 55 36 2b 73 15 82 56 4b 75 2f c0 04 11 7c    .2U6+s..VKU/...|
        5a a0 cb 1c 7e d8 16 56 62 b1 81 e5 9b 69 ee 10    Z...~..Vb....i..
Application protocol: ssh

Hidden message (12 bytes):
        d3 2e 1e e5 38 47 af 88 6d ba 11 a0                ....8G..m...
Data (64 bytes):
        58 0c 2e 8a d3 2e 1e e5 38 47 af 88 6d ba 11 a0    X.......8G..m...
        55 d5 dd 8d aa bc 48 1d 54 9a 18 8f a5 95 77 dd    U.....H.T.....w.
        98 32 55 36 2b 73 15 82 56 4b 75 2f c0 04 11 7c    .2U6+s..VKU/...|
        5a a0 cb 1c 7e d8 16 56 62 b1 81 e5 9b 69 ee 10    Z...~..Vb....i..
```

Fig. 6. Sample Output of the Packet Transmogrifier when Embedding Information in SSH Traffic where a 48-byte payload is enlarged to a 64-byte payload.

6   Conclusions and Lessons Learned

In this paper, we have described semantics-preserving application-layer protocol steganography, and have presented methods for embedding secret messages in an application-layer protocol. We have developed the notions of syntax and semantics preservation in accordance to the goal of achieving a reasonably secure and robust stegosystem. We raised issues that evidence the need for definition of new theoretical paradigms of security. They must involve not only fitting the statistical profile of the cover itself but also fitting the statistical profile of how the transmission of the covers. Our approach has several advantages over prior work:

– Because of its applicability to a wide range of protocols, we can theoretically embed messages in the vast majority of network traffic on the Internet.
– The use of non-source stego (en route embeddings and extractions) increases the available bandwidth and complicates traffic analysis because of the ability to choose traffic from a variety of senders and receivers.
– Semantics preservation dramatically increases the practical ability of producing secure and robust stegomethods in network protocols.

As a proof-of-concept, we implemented an end-to-end protocol steganography approach in the SSH2 protocol as well as one with agents as middlemen. The SSH approach is not general, but represents a step toward finding generalized methods of embedding which is the ultimate goal of protocol steganography. The packet transmogrifier is a valuable contribution from the SSH implementations. It allows us to perform on-the-fly message embedding and extraction while a packet of arbitrary network traffic is en route. The software may be obtained from the authors upon request. In the near future, we will expand our family of embedder/extractor functions to include HTTP as well as other protocols.

References

[1] Katzenbeisser, S., Petitcolas, F.A.: Information Hiding: Techniques for Steganography and Digital Watermarking. Artech House, Norwood, MA (2000)

[2] Johnson, N.F., Jajodia, S.: Steganalysis: The investigation of hidden information. In: Proceedings of the IEEE Information Technology Conference, Syracuse, New York, USA (1998) 113–116

[3] Anderson, R., ed.: Information Hiding: Proceedings of the First International Workshop. In Anderson, R., ed.: Lecture Notes in Computer Science 1174, Cambridge, U.K., Springer (1996)

[4] Aucsmith, D., ed.: Information Hiding: Proceedings of the Second International Workshop. In Aucsmith, D., ed.: Lecture Notes in Computer Science 1525, Portland, Oregon, U.S.A., Springer (1998)

[5] Moskowitz, I.S., ed.: Information Hiding: Proceedings of the Fourth International Workshop. In Moskowitz, I.S., ed.: Lecture Notes in Computer Science 2137, Pittsburg, PA, U.S.A., Springer (2001)

[6] Oostveen, J., ed.: Information Hiding: Preproceedings of the Fifth International Workshop, Noordwijkerhout, The Netherlands (2002)

[7] Pfitzmann, A., ed.: Information Hiding: Proceedings of the Third International Workshop. In Pfitzmann, A., ed.: Lecture Notes in Computer Science 1768, Dresden, Germany, Springer (1999)

[8] Chapin, S.J., Ostermann, S.: Information hiding through semantics-preserving application-layer protocol steganography. Technical report, Center for Systems Assurance, Syracuse University (2002)

[9] Kemmerer, R.: A practical approach to identify storage and timing channels: Twenty years later. In: Proceedings of the 18th Annual Computer Security Applications Conference (ACSAC 2002), San Diego, California (2002) 109–118

[10] Dunigan, T.: Internet steganography. Technical report, Oak Ridge National Laboratory (Contract No. DE-AC05-96OR22464), Oak Ridge, Tennessee (1998) [ORNL/TM-limited distribution].

[11] Handel, T., Sandford, M.: Hiding data in the OSI network model. In Anderson, R., ed.: Information Hiding: Proceedings of the First International Workshop, Cambridge, U.K., Springer (1996) 23–38

[12] route@infonexus.com, alhambra@infornexus.com: Article 6. Phrack Magazine, 49 (1996) Retrieved on August 27, 2002 from the World Wide Web: http://www.phrack.com/phrack/49/P49-06.

[13] Rowland, C.H.: Covert channels in the TCP/IP protocol suite. Psionics Technologies (1996) Retrieved on August 23, 2002 from the World Wide Web: http://www.psionic.com/papers/whitep03.html.

[14] CAIDA.org: Characterization of internet traffic loads, segregated by application - OC48 analysis (2002) Retrieved on October 15, 2003 from the World Wide Web: http://www.caida.org/analysis/workload/byapplication/oc48/20020305/ apps_perc_20020305/index.xml.

[15] Katzenbeisser, S., Petitcolas, F.A.: Defining security in steganographic systems. In: Electronic Imaging, Photonics West, (SPIE). Volume 4675 of Security and Watermarking of Multimedia Contents IV. (2002) 50–56

[16] Moskowitz, I.S., Longdon, G.E., LiWuChang: A new paradigm hidden in steganography. In: Proceedings of the New Security Paradigm Workshop 2000, Cork, Ireland (2000) 41–50

[17] Cachin, C.: An information-theoreic model for steganography. Technical Report Report 2000/028 (2002) http://www.zurich.ibm.com/ cca/papers/stego.pdf.
[18] Anderson, R.J., Petitcolas, F.A.: On the limits of steganography. IEEE Journal of Selected Areas in Communications **16** (1998) 474–481
[19] Mittelholzer, T.: An information-theoretic approach to steganography and watermarking. In Pfitzmann, A., ed.: Information Hiding: Proceedings of the Third International Workshop. Volume 1768 of Lecture Notes in Computer Science., Dresden, Germany, Springer (1999) 1–16
[20] Zöllner, J., Federrath, H., Klimant, H., Pfitzmann, A., Piotraschke, R., Westfeld, A., Wicke, G., Wolf, G.: Modeling the security of steganographic systems. In Aucsmith, D., ed.: Information Hiding: Proceedings of the Second International Workshop. Volume 1525 of Lecture Notes in Computer Science., Portland, Oregon, U.S.A., Springer (1998) 344–354
[21] Ettinger, J.M.: Steganalysis and game equilibria. In Aucsmith, D., ed.: Information Hiding: Proceedings of the Second International Workshop. Volume 1525 of Lecture Notes in Computer Science., Portland, Oregon, U.S.A., Springer (1998) 319–328
[22] Hopper, N., Langford, J., von Ahn, L.: Provably secure steganography. In Yung, M., ed.: Advances in Cyptology - CRYPTO 2002: Proceedings of the 22nd Annual International Cryptology Conference. Volume 2442 of Lecture Notes in Computer Science., Santa Barbara, California, U.S.A., Springer (2002) 77–92
[23] Reyzin, L., Russell, S.: More efficient provably secure steganography. Cryptology ePrint Archive: Report 2003/093 (2003) http://eprint.iacr.org/2003/093/.
[24] Fridrich, J., Goljan, M.: Practical steganalysis of digital images - state of the art. In: Proceedings of the SPIE Photonics West (Security and Watermarking of Multimedia Contents IV). Volume 4675., San Jose, California, USA (2002) 1–13
[25] Provos, N., Honeyman, P.: Hide and seek: An introduction to steganography. IEEE Security & Privacy Magazine **1** (2003) 32–44
[26] Simmons, G.J.: The prisoners' problem and the subliminal channel. In: Proceedings of CRYPTO '83, Plenum Press (1984) 51–67
[27] Schneier, B.: Applied Cryptography. John Wiley & Sons, Inc (1996)
[28] Pfitzmann, B.: Information hiding terminology. In Anderson, R., ed.: Information Hiding: Proceedings of the First International Workshop, Cambridge, U.K., Springer (1996) 347–349
[29] Korn, F., Muthukrishnan, S., Zhu, Y.: Ipsofacto: A visual correlation tool for aggregate network traffic data. In: Proceedings of the 2003 ACM SIGMOD International Conference on Management of Data, San Diego, California, ACM Press (2003) 677–677 Demonstration Session.
[30] Ka0ticSH: Diggin em walls (part 3) - advanced/other techniques for bypassing firewalls. New Order (2002) Retrieved on August 28, 2002 from the World Wide Web: http://neworder.box.sk/newsread.php?newsid=3957.
[31] Fisk, G., Fisk, M., Papadopoulos, C., Neil, J.: Eliminating steganography in Internet traffic with active wardens. In Oostveen, J., ed.: Information Hiding: Preproceedings of the Fifth International Workshop, Noordwijkerhout, The Netherlands, Springer (2002) 29–46
[32] Bowyer, L.: Firewall bypass via protocol steganography. Network Penetration (2002) Retrieved on January 05, 2003 from the World Wide Web: http://www.networkpenetration.com/protocol_steg.html.

[33] Bauer, M.: New covert channels in HTTP - adding unwitting web browsers to anonymity sets. In Samarati, P., Syverson, P., eds.: Proceedings of the 2003 ACM Workshop on Privacy in the Electronic Society, Washington, DC, USA, ACM Press (2003) 72–78 ISBN 1-58113-776-1.

[34] Secure Shell Working Group, I.E.T.F.I.: The secure shell. Retrieved on October 26, 2003 from the World Wide Web: http://www.ietf.org/html.charters/secsh-charter.html (2003)

[35] Barrett, D.J., Silverman, R.: SSH, The Secure Shell: The Definitive Guide. O'Reilly (2001)

[36] Watterson, B.: Something Under the Bed is Drooling. Andrews and McMeel, pp. 101–104, Kansas City, MO (1988)

A Method of Linguistic Steganography
Based on Collocationally-Verified Synonymy*

Igor A. Bolshakov

Center for Computing Research (CIC)
National Polytechnic Institute (IPN)
Mexico City, Mexico
igor@cic.ipn.mx

Abstract. A method is proposed of the automatic concealment of digital information in rather long orthographically and semantically correct texts. The method does not change the meaning of the source text; it only replaces some words by their synonyms. Groups of absolute synonyms are used in a context independent manner, while the groups of relative synonyms are previously tested for semantic compatibility with the collocations containing the word to be replaced. A specific replacement is determined by the hidden information. The collocations are syntactically connected and semantically compatible pairs of content words; they are massively gathered beforehand, with a wide diversity in their stability and idiomacity. Thus the necessary linguistic resources are a specific synonymy dictionary and a very large database of collocations. The steganographic algorithm is informally outlined. An example of hiding binary information in a Russian text fragment is manually traced, with a rough evaluation of the steganographic bandwidth.

1 Introduction

We define linguistic steganography as a set of methods and techniques that permit the hiding of any digital information within texts based on some linguistic knowledge [9]. To hide the very fact of hiding, the resulting text should not only remain inconspicuous (i.e. appear to be ordinary text, with fonts, orthography, lexicon, morphology, syntax, and word order outwardly corresponding to its meaning) but also conserve grammatical correctness and semantic cohesion.

We expect that the linguistic knowledge needed for this purpose should be non-trivially large, and thus we dissociate ourselves from all studies in special text formatting (cf. e.g., [17]). The nature of the information to be hidden is irrelevant for us; it is merely a string of binary digits.

The current situation in linguistic steganography, as it was defined above, does not seem well developed.

---

* Work done under partial support of Mexican Government (CONACyT, SNI) and CGEPI-IPN, Mexico. Many thanks to Prof. V. Korzhik who led me into the new domain, and to Dr. P. Cassidy who gave me many valuable suggestions.

J. Fridrich (Ed.): IH 2004, LNCS 3200, pp. 180-191, 2004.
© Springer-Verlag Berlin Heidelberg 2004

The series of the synonymy-oriented works [9, 10] render resulting texts syntactically correct, but potentially conspicuous, since semantically they are incoherent, leaving alone their original meaning.

The works [2, 3] proposed an original semantic representation of the carrier texts supposedly permitting their deep pseudo-synonymous transformations while IH. However, we are to expect some time before this method will be brought to perfection in the following aspects:

- The transformation 'text → its tree semantic representation' should be based on deep linguistic knowledge, especially that of synonymy between various syntactic constructions—to minimize the repertoire of labels on the semantic tree branches;

- The efficacious revealing of co-references and anaphoras should be based on huge extra-linguistic knowledge, polythematic and relevant, as well as on plausible reasoning. Otherwise the attempts to insert next bit sequence for steganographic use could graft upon semantically queer phrases like *Spy planes fly over Afghanistan, which they are attacking*, or liberally insert truisms from the fact DB like *Afghanistan borders Pakistan*, which can make the carrier text somewhat conspicuous.

The work [15] also supposes a special preprocessing of the carrier, but it is not clear if the resulting text really conserves the initial content.

In this paper, we propose a steganographic algorithm that replaces textual words by their synonyms, just as in [9]. However, we always conserve inconspicuousness, linguistic correctness, and the very meaning of the source text by verifying the possible replacements against the context of the word to be replaced.

The context of a word is a set of collocations it is in. We consider collocations as syntactically connected and semantically compatible pairs of content words. They need to be collected beforehand in very large numbers, with a wide diversity in their stability and idiomacity. Examples of English collocations are *full-length dress, well expressed, to briefly expose, to pick up the knife* or *to listen to the radio*, where the collocation components (content words) are underlined. The collocations can also contain auxiliary words (mainly prepositions) that link the collocation components and thus help to reveal the collocations while text processing.

More specifically, the objectives of our paper are:

- To touch upon the notion of synonymy in order to clarify that synonyms can be not only separate words but also multiwords, and that we divide all synonyms into absolute and relative ones, which are used in our algorithm in a different manner;
- To outline the most important features of DBs of collocations with components that can have synonyms;
- To outline rather informally our algorithm realizing a linguistic steganography method based on collocationally-verified synonymy;
- To develop a manually traced example of hiding a small portion of binary information within a typical fragment of text from Russian newswire, with evaluation of steganographic bandwidth of the method.

The idea of our method does not depend on language, but its implementation heavily depends on available language-specific resources. So we use English examples to illustrate our considerations in all cases we can, whereas a specific steganographic example is in Russian.

2 Absolute and Relative Synonymy

Basically we are interested in synonymous paraphrasing (SP). It is a modification of natural language text or its fragments that preserves the meaning of the whole text. Nearly every plain text allows SP—contrasting with lists of names, numerical data, poetry, and the like. Computational linguistics has always considered SP an important and difficult problem.

There exists a well developed linguistic theory—Meaning–Text Theory by I. Mel'čuk [12]—that takes SP as one of its basic principles. It considers NL something like a calculus of SP. A set of meaning-conserving rules for restructuring sentences was developed within the framework of this theory. In the process of SP the words making up a text, their morpho-syntactic features and the word order significantly change. However, program implementation for SP based on MTT thus far covers a rather limited fragment of natural language [1].

In this paper we only deal with local SP that conserves the structure and word order of a sentence, as well as the number of words (counting stable multiwords like *hot dog* as one unit, see later).

In their simplest definition, synonyms are words that can replace each other in some class of contexts with insignificant change of the whole text meaning. The references to 'some class' and to 'insignificant change' make this definition rather vague, nevertheless nearly all modern synonymy dictionaries are based on it.

A synonymy dictionary is a set of word groups, the words within each of them considered synonymous. Any word can be similar to the members of one group in a given aspect and of another group in other aspect, i.e. it can belong to several intersecting groups or to neither. (Here we exclude WordNet whose synsets are artificially constructed without intersections [11].) In many dictionaries, a title (dominant) member is selected for each group that expresses the group meaning in the most general and neutral way.

For our purposes, it proved to be insufficient to include only separate words in the synonymy groups; sometimes compactly co-occurring multiwords are necessary. An example of the English synonymy group is {*rollercoaster, big dipper, Russian mountains*}, where the unique single word member is the result of agglutination of the pair.

The only mathematically formal case of synonymy is when the compared units can replace each other in **any** context without **any** change in meaning. These are absolute synonyms, e.g., English {*sofa, settee*}. Within the group, absolute synonyms are connected by the mathematical relation of equivalence.

Unfortunately, absolute synonyms are extremely rare in any language. However, there exists another kind of equivalence—between various abbreviations and agglutinations. E.g., we can consider {*United States of America, USA, United States*} as an equivalence group. Such equivalents can occur in the same text without violation of the style. The admission of multiword synonyms provides a large number of new absolute synonyms like {*former president, ex-president*}.

In Russian, many noun-headed concepts are used in two equivalent forms: (1) a word pair consisting of a modifier with the stem S_1 plus its head noun with the stem S_2, or (2) a single noun containing both stems S_1 and S_2, or their initial parts, or only S_1: *detskij sad* 'kindergarten' = *detsad*; *električeskij tok* 'electrical current' = *elektrotok*; *fizičeskij fakul'tet* 'physical faculty' = *fizfak*; *komičeskij akter* 'comical actor' =

komik; *seismičeskaja stancija* 'seismic station' = *seismostancija*. The number of such agglutinations continues to grow, especially in newswire and everyday speech (several thousands of commonly used concepts), and now they are considered stylistically neutral in any genre of text. In academic dictionaries they are scarce, but this type of equivalence seems very important for wider lingware applications. Note that English agglutinations like *picture element* = *pixel* is a similar phenomenon, but both variants scarcely co-occur in the same text.

A small number of equivalence groups are the so-called morphological variants, e.g., Rus. *nul'* = *nol'* 'zero'; *mučat'* = *mučit'* 'to torture'; *tunnel'* = *tonnel'* 'tunnel'.

Hereafter, we presume the availability of a synonymy dictionary with the following specific features:

- Each synonymy group has a dominant.
- The equivalents of the dominant (if any) are specially labeled.
- Any member of the group including the dominant can be multiword.
- Any member of the group including the dominant can repeat in another group and/or be a homograph (homonym) of the member of another group.
- A group member can represent not a whole lexeme but its grammeme, i.e. a part of its morphological paradigms. For example, it can be either the singular or plural of a noun, or the infinitive of a verb or its participle taken separately.

Let us explain the last feature. It was quickly recognized that the singular and plural number variants of the same noun in any language may have their own sets of synonyms and their own set of associated components that may combine to form collocations. E.g., the synonymy group {*client, consumer, customer, user*} of singular number is opposable to the group {*clients, clientele, consumers, customers, users*} of plural. We use the collocation *numerous users* but not *numerous user*, and we can say *single user* but rarely *single users* (their proportion in Google is 73 to 1). As to the grammemes of verbs, in many languages participles may play the syntactic role of adjectives, while Russian and Spanish gerunds play the role of adverbs. Hence, various grammemes have different sets of synonyms and collocational supplements.

3   Collocations

For a long time collocations were studied in lexicography rather than in computational linguistics. The mainstream initiated by N. Chomsky usually treats collocations simply as a series of two or more words occurring together in a narrow window moving along a text.

There exist semantic links of two types in natural languages: paradigmatic and syntagmatic. WordNet [11] describes semantic links of only paradigmatic type; these are synonyms, hyponyms/hyperonyms, antonyms, etc. The links between components of collocations are syntagmatic. These are, for example, the link between a verb and a noun filling its valence (*play → the role*), or the link between noun and its adjective modifier (*new ← method*). A comprehensive collection of English collocations are now gathered in the Oxford collocation dictionary [16].

At this time, the only theory that gives a consistent description of all types of syntactically connected word combinations is the MTT [14]. Syntactical connectedness is understood in the MTT as in dependency grammars. The head component syntactically governs the dependent one, being adjoined to it directly or through an auxiliary word (cf. examples above). Sequentially, the components can be at any distance from each other in a sentence, but are nearby in the dependency tree.

To our knowledge, publicly available electronic databases of collocations did not exist until 1997, when the Advanced Reader's Collocation Searcher (ARCS) for English emerged [4], but it is now inferior to [16] in all aspects.

The only project in the recent decade to develop a very large collocation DB available now for local use was dedicated to Russian and it produced an interactive system called CrossLexica [5, 6, 7]. Its core part is a large database of Russian collocations, but it contains also something like a Russian WordNet. Particularly, the WordNet-like part contains a synonymy dictionary and a hyponymy/hyperonymy hierarchy.

Ideologically, CrossLexica is based on the MTT, but it does not describe collocations in terms of lexical functions; syntactic types of collocations in it are not as fine-grained as in the MTT; it adheres to the grammeme principle of word description in its dictionary; and it contains numerous free (non-idiomatic) word combinations, while the MTT did not consider them to be collocations.

The inclusion of free combinations proved to be of special importance for most of the applications of CrossLexica [5]. This is also very important for steganography, since components of free word combinations are to be mainly used for synonymous paraphrasing.

Hereafter, we can imagine the synonymy dictionary and the collocation DB as corresponding parts of CrossLexica-like system.

Additionally, the hyponym-to-hyperonym hierarchy could be involved to facilitate collocation testing. Hyperonyms are used to infer new collocations in the following way [7]: if the component C_1 has the hyperonym H, and H forms a collocation with the component C_2, then C_1 forms the collocation of the same type with C_2. If the hyperonym H of C_1 has no relevant collocations, a hyperonym of H is tested for the same purpose, etc.

4   Algorithm

The proposed steganographic algorithm has two inputs:

- The information to hide, in the shape of a bit sequence.
- The source text in natural language of the minimal length evaluated as approximately 250 times greater than of the information to hide. The text format can be arbitrary, but the text proper should be orthographically correct, to lessen the probability of unintended corrections during transmission. The corrections can change the number of synonymous words in the text or the conditions for their verification and thus can desynchronize the steganography *vs.* steganalysis. The text should not be semantically specific, i.e. not to be a mere list of names or sequence of numbers. In this respect newswire flow or political articles are quite acceptable. Any long fragments of inappropriate type increase the total length required for steganographic use.

The steps of the algorithm are as follows:

Search for dictionary entries The text is scanned, and single- and multiwords are extracted that are entries of the systemic dictionary. If a word sequence and its subsequence are found both conforming to the mentioned conditions, the longer entity is preferred. The operations are applied to text fragments independently whether the latter have synonyms or not, and they include reducing of separate words and parts of multiwords to corresponding dictionary forms. The operations are successful if there are no intersections between multiwords, when one or more sequent words enter to two or more different longer multiwords.

Formation of synonymy groups The synonymy groups are analyzed one by one. If a content word (multiword) has no synonyms, we consider it as a degenerate synonymy group of only one member. If a given group includes only absolute synonyms, it is taken as such for further steps. If the group includes at least one relative synonym, all of them are taken for the operation referred in mathematics as transitive closure.

Transitive closure means that each member of a group is tested to see if it also appears in another synonymy group. If so, the related group is joined to the former one without repetitions. The newly included synonyms are analyzed to determine if they are also members of yet another group and so forth, until the process of broadening stops.

Such operations are also made through homographs. The database is searched to determine if the textual word or its synonyms have homographs. If so, the homographs as well as their synonyms (if any) are joined to the set under formation. Each newly included member is analyzed against its synonyms and homographs, etc. The process is finite, but sometimes gives a rather large combined set. At each step, members with specific lexicographic labels (e.g., of idiomaticity or a low style) are omitted in the combined set.

Transitive closure is needed to ensure the same content of the resulting set on both steganographic and steganalytic stages. The cases when the resulting set is so broad that it contains absolutely unlike members usable in the same context are possible but seem extremely rare.

Collocational verification of synonyms The verification of synonyms is performed sentence by sentence and deals only with content words. Then for the sentence with content words $w_1, w_2 ... w_N$ the verification is as follows:

```
for i = 1...N
    for j = i+1...N
        if form_collocation(w_i, w_j, T)
            search ∀_{p,q} form_collocation(syn_p(w_i), syn_q(w_j), T)
```

where $syn_p(w)$ is pth synonym of w, and the function **form_collocation**(w_i, w_j, T) is true when w_i and w_j form collocation of the type T, with any direction of syntactic dependency between the collocation components. To put it in other words, a complete sub-bigraph is searched in the bigraph formed by links between synonyms of w_i on one side and of w_j on the other side. In Figure 1, the subsets {$syn_2(w_i)$, w_i, $syn_4(w_i)$} and {w_j, $syn_2(w_j)$} form the sought-for complete bigraph.

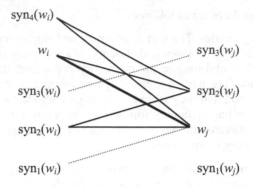

Fig. 1. Extraction of complete sub-bigraph

If the complete bigraph contains only w_i and/or only w_j, the corresponding degenerated group does not participate immediately in the IH. The members of each non-degenerate group are ordered in a predetermined manner (e.g., by alphabet) from 0 to $k-1$, where k is the set count.

Enciphering The sequence of the filtered synonymy groups is scanned from the left to the right. On this step, the decomposition of the carrier to sentences is not needed. Let the counts of synonyms in p sequential groups be $k_1, k_2... k_p$, with the total product $k_1 k_2...k_p = K$. We round down K to the nearest 2^N and take M_0 as N-bit syllable of the information to be hidden. The numbers $n_1, n_2... n_p$ of the replacing synonyms are then determined sequentially as

$$n_i = M_{i-1} \bmod k_i; \quad M_i = M_{i-1} \operatorname{div} k_i; \quad i = 1, 2... p-1;$$
$$n_p = M_{p-1};$$

where **div** is the integer division; **mod** is the *modulo* operation. In cases when all counts $k_1, k_2... k_p$ are powers of 2 or when we can be unsparing to round down any k_i to the nearest power N_i of 2, the numbers n_i of the replacing synonyms are equal to the sequential N_i-bit syllables of the information to be hidden.

Reagreement If grammatical features of a newcomer (its number, gender, case, person, etc., depending on specific language and on the part of speech) differ from the source synonym, operations of morphological reagreement are to be fulfilled.

The steganographic process continues until one of the inputs is exhausted. The text modified by synonyms is the unique output of the algorithm.

The reversibility of the algorithm at the stage of steganalysis is rather obvious. The addressee should have just the same versions of linguistic resources, as well as the algorithm. At the beta stage of the implementation, the steganographic and steganalytic operations should be done together on the sender's side, to ward off the cases of the wrong finding in the dictionary or the wrong filtering of synonyms. If any difference between input and output hidden bit sequence is found, some corrections in the linguistic resources or/and the algorithm should be introduced.

5 A Manually Traced Russian Example

For our tests, we have taken the flow of news in the Russian Web site *Gazeta.ru*. The flow consists of separate pieces generated by various Russian or foreign word-wide agencies, with the mean length of text ca. 600 Bytes and header of ca. 50 Bytes. It is well known that the first sentence of a news piece in many agencies repeats the title but with more detail and some extensions. In the case of *Gazeta.ru*, we have noticed many paraphrases in the first sentences, including synonymous modifications of the type under consideration.

We took a typical text fragment from this site:

(1) *Pjat' <u>podzemnyz tolčkov</u> <u>zaregistrirovano</u> **<u>za sutki</u>** na juge <u>Respubliki Altaj</u>. <u>Sila</u> <u>zemletrjasenij</u> <u>sostavljala</u> ot 2,2 do 3,1 balla po škale Rixtera, <u>soobščili</u> na Aktašskoj **<u>sejsmičeskoj stancii</u>** segodnja <u>posle poludnja</u>.*

It means: '(As many as) five <u>subterranean pulses</u> (are) <u>registered</u> **during 24 hours** in the south of <u>Altai Republic</u>. (The) <u>strength</u> (of the) <u>earthquakes</u> <u>amounts</u> from 2.2 to 3.1 points on Richter scale, (as they have) <u>informed</u> in (the) Aktash **seismic station** today <u>in the afternoon</u>.' The words in the parentheses are introduced into the translation, to conform to English grammar rules.

The single and multiwords of the Russian text having synonyms are underlined. The absolute synonyms are additionally highlighted with bold face.

Hereafter all synonymous options are ordered by the Russian alphabet and binary numbered for the steganographic use. Following are groups of absolute synonyms (in their dictionary forms):

    0. *za 24 časa* 'during 24 hours'   1. *za sutki* 'during 24 hours'
    0. *sejsmičeskaja stancija* 'seismic station' 1. *sejsmostancija* 'seismic station'

The relative synonym *za den'* 'during the day' in the second group is omitted, to have in this group only $2 = 2^1$ absolute members.

While performing the transitive closure for *zaregistrirovannyj*, the following five synonymy groups are found, with the dominants coming first:

zaregistrirovannyj 'registered', *zafiksirovannyj, otmečennyj*
zakreplennyj 'fastened', *zafiksirovannyj, prikreplennyj*
pomečennyj 'marked', *otmečennyj, vydelennyj*
zamečennyj 'noticed', *otmečennyj, podmečennyj, primečennyj, upomjanutyj*
otprazdnovannyj 'celebrated', *otmečennyj*

Thus the combined set without repetitions is

(2) *zakreplennyj, zamečennyj, zaregistrirovannyj, zafiksirovannyj, otmečennyj, otprazdnovannyj, podmečennyj, pomečennyj, prikreplennyj, primečennyj, upomjanutyj*

Here are other groups of relative synonyms not affected by transitive enclosure:

    0. *zemletrjasenija* 'earthquakes' 1. *podzemnye tolčki* 'subterranean pulses'
    0. *Altaj* 'Altai'   1. *Respublika Altaj* 'Republic Altai'
    0. *ravnjat'sja* 'to be equal'   1. *sostavljat'* 'to amount'
    0. *proinformirovat'* 'to inform' 1. *soobščit'* 'to communicate'
    0. *vo vtoruju polovinu dnja* 'in the second half of the day' 1. *posle poludnja* 'in the afternoon.'

The noun *sila* has two different senses, $sila_1$ and $sila_2$, with their own groups of synonyms:

00. *magnituda* 'magnitude'   00. *dejstvennost'* 'efficacy'
01. *moščnost'* 'power'   01. $sila_2$ 'potency'
10. *mošč'* 'might'
11. $sila_1$ 'force'

Let us now verify relative synonyms against the context.

The both member of synonymy group {*zemletrjasenija, podzemnye tolčki*} forms collocations only with the subset

00. *zamečennyj* 01. *zaregistrirovannyj* 10. *zafiksirovannyj* 11. *otmečennyj*

of the set (2), so all other members are to be discarded. These four options form collocations with the absolute synonym *za sutki* and are also compatible with the non-synonymous *jug*.

Among the two senses of *sila* only synonyms of $sila_1$ conform to members of the group {*zemletrjasenija, podzemnye tolčki*}.

The collocation DB does not contain collocations of the members of {*proinformirovat', soobščit'*} and the members of the absolute synonymy group {*sejsmičeskaja stancija, sejsmostancija*}, but the inference through the hyperonym *stancija* gives the following result: (*sejsmostancija* IS_A *stancija*) & (*soobščit' na stancii*) → (*soobščit' na sejsmostancii*).

The last tests are between the groups {*soobščit', proinformirovat'*} and {*posle poludnja, vo vtoruju polovinu dnja*}. All four tests are successful and thus none synonym is discarded.

Hence the synonymous words of the source text give the following amounts of bits for steganographic use:

podzemnye tolčki	1	*zemletrjasenija*	1
zaregistrirovannyj	2	*sostavljat'*	1
sutki	1	*soobščit'*	1
Respublika Altaj	1	*sejsmičeskaja stancija*	1
sila	2	*posle poludnja*	1

The total is 12 bits, i.e. we can hide in the given fragment, say, the string of two Latin letters with codes equal to the right 6-bit syllables of ASCII table. E.g., the hiding of the bigram *si* (Spanish 'yes') gives the following text (The differences from the source are highlighted.)

*Pjat' podzemnyz tolčkov **zafiksirovano za 24 časa** na juge Respubliki Altaj. Sila zemletrjasenij sostavljala ot 2,2 do 3.1 balla po škale Rixtera, **proinformirovali** na Aktašskoj sejsmičeskoj stancii segodnja posle poludnja.*

The meaning of the modified fragment remains the same, though the third difference created a minor stylistic infelicity. The hidden bigram *no* corresponds to the completely irreproachable fragment:

*Pjat' podzemnyz tolčkov zaregistrirovano za sutki na juge Respubliki Altaj. **Moščnost'** zemletrjasenij sostavljala ot 2,2 do 3.1 balla po škale Rixtera, soobščili na Aktašskoj **sejsmostancii** segodnja posle poludnja.*

Note that the steganalysis of the source fragment (1) gives an unintended result—in the shape of the bigram *om*.

The size of the hidden bigram is 1.5 Bytes, while the source text amounts 205 Bytes. Hence the ratio that measures the steganographic bandwidth (SB) equals .0073. In a few other manually traced examples taken at random from the same newswire, synonymous words were rarer with corresponding SB decrease. We could orient to the SB mean value about .004. That is why carrier texts should be 250 times longer than the hidden information.

As another measure of steganographic rate, we can take the ratio between the numbers of enciphered bits and encountered synonymy groups. The example above gives 1.2 bits per synonym.

6 Discussion, Conclusion, and Future Work

The proposed method of linguistic steganography totally conserves the meaning of the carrier text, as well as its inconspicuousness. The method is based on the two large linguistic resources: a large synonymy dictionary and a very large collocation database. The groups of absolute synonyms for words in a source text can be used immediately, whereas the groups of relative synonyms are broadened in a specific way and then filtered for conformity with the collocations textual words are in.

The mean value .004 of steganographic bandwidth reached with the local synonymous paraphrasing seems rather low. But let us compare the local SP with the global SP realized by methods of the Meaning–Text Theory. The French sentence in [12] of 200 bytes in 35 words (blanks and punctuation marks included) reveals ca. 50 million $= 2^{25.6}$ synonymous variants. It means that each paraphrase of the sentence can hide in itself 25.6 bits of information, thus giving the bandwidth of about .016. If to suppose that the local SP was not included in the global SP, the value reached by our method gives 20% of the maximally possible level, whereas if the local SP was already included, our method reaches 25% of the utmost level.

The main problem for implementation of our method is the limited availability of the abovementioned linguistic resources. Nowadays, the only language for which these resources are near to completion is Russian. Perhaps the potential for application in such a critical field as steganography will give an additional impetus toward creation of such lexical databases for English—the lingua franca of the modern sci-tech world.

The reachable value of SB evidently depends on saturation of the linguistic resources. Hence they are to be developed further, without any clear-cut limits of perfection.

As to our algorithm, we can hardly consider it faultless. The following issues seem now especially acute:

- In the contexts of the kind *the corporation's own resources* the algorithm can replace *own* by its relative synonym *personal*, but inspection of one step further node in the dependency tree context, i.e. *corporation's,* suggests that this would be inappropriate.
- It is necessary to search for a way to cut long synonymy/homography chains like Russian *osveščenie₁* 'coverage'—*osveščenie₂* 'illumination'—*svet₁* 'light'— *svet₂* 'world'—*mir₁* 'world'—*mir₂* 'peace'—*peremirie* 'armistice.' Otherwise we

could sometime find that the words at the chain extremities admit the same contexts and thus are evaluated as interchangeable, in spite of their major semantic differences. The simplest way is to totally exclude too long chains from steganographic process.

- Special precautions are needed while paraphrasing constructions with coordination. The stable coordination pairs like *comments and suggestions* are supposedly included in the collocation DB [8]. Local paraphrasing usually destroys such pairs and thus is prohibited in such cases. E.g., one can say in Russian *ran'še i teper'* but not *ran'še i sejčas,* though the both options have the same meaning 'earlier and today.' In constructions with freely coordinated synonyms or quasi-synonyms like *isolated subterraneous pulses and powerful earthquakes,* the paraphrasing *subterraneous pulses ↔ earthquakes* can results in repetitions violating the conventional literary style.

In the future, all these problems should be investigated in depth.

Let us consider now the measures against the possible actions of the adversary.

If the adversary possesses the same linguistic resources and the same algorithms, he can read the hidden information I. The tool to exclude this is a secret bit string K of the length comparable with I. The key K is applied to I on the sender's side (at the very beginning) and on the addressee's side (at the very end), as the bit-by-bit logical operation of equivalence. Note that SB keeps the same value after all.

As a tool to detect the adversary's tampering of I, it is worthwhile to use the secret mask M of mainly empty elements with some interspersed bit constants, 0 or 1. On the sending end, the bits of the original I are sent until next constant occurred in M, then the encountered constant is sent. These operations are repeated in a cycle. If n constants are already sent while the adversary changes each bit with randomly generated 0 or 1, the tampering is detected with the probability $1-2^n$. With this method, SB diminishes by $1-n/N$, where N is the whole length of the string already sent.

Nevertheless, we do not know thus far how to restore the hidden information mutilated by the abovementioned interference, at any expense of steganographic bandwidth.

References

1. Apresian, Ju. D., I.M. Boguslavsky, *et al.* ETAP-3 Linguistic Processor: a Full-Fledged NPL Implementation of the Meaning–Text Theory. Proc. First Int. Conf. Meaning–Text Theory, MTT 2003, Paris, Ecole Normale Supérieure, June 2003, p. 279-288.
2. Atallah, M.J., V. Raskin, M. Crogan, C. F. Hempelmann, F. Kerschbaum, D. Mohamed, S. Naik. Natural Language Watermarking: Design, Analysis, and a Proof-of-concept Implementation. In: I.S. Moskowitz (Ed.) *Information Hiding.* Proc. Int. Workshop IH'2001. LNCS 2137, Springer, 2001, p. 185-199.
3. Atallah, M.J., V. Raskin, C.F. Hempelmann, M. Karahan, R. Sion, U. Topkara, K.E. Triezenberg. Natural Language Watermarking and Tamperproofing. In: F.A.P. Peticolas. *Information Hiding.* Proc. Int. Workshop IH'2002, LNCS 2578, Springer, 2003, p. 196-212.
4. Bogatz, H. *The Advanced Reader's Collocation Searcher (ARCS).* ISBN 09709341-4-9, http:www.asksam.com/web/bogatz, 1997.

5. Bolshakov, I.A. Getting One's First Million... Collocations. In: A. Gelbukh (Ed.). *Computational Linguistics and Intelligent Text Processing*. Proc. 5th Int. Conf. CICLing-2004, Febrary 2004, Seoul, Korea. LNCS 2945, Springer, 2004, p.229-242.

6. Bolshakov, I.A., A. Gelbukh. A Very Large Database of Collocations and Semantic Links. In: M. Bouzeghoub *et al.* (Eds.) *Natural Language Processing and Information Systems*. Proc. Int. Conf. on Applications of Natural Language to Information Systems NLDB-2000. LNCS 1959, Springer, 2001, p. 103-114.

7. Bolshakov, I.A., A. Gelbukh. Heuristics-Based Replenishment of Collocation Databases. In: E. Ranchhold, N.J. Mamede (Eds.) *Advances in Natural Language Processing*. Proc. Int. Conf. PorTAL 2002, Faro, Portugal. LNAI 2389, Springer, 2002, p. 25-32.

8. Bolshakov, I.A., A. Gelbukh, S.N. Galicia-Haro. Stable Coordinated Pairs in Text Processing. In: V. Matoušek, P. Mautner (Eds.) *Text, Speech and Dialogue*. Proc. 6th International Conference TSD 2003, České Budějovice, Czech Republic, September 2003. LNAI 2807, Springer, 2003, p. 27-34.

9. Chapman, M., G.I. Davida. Hiding the Hidden: A Software System for Concealing Ciphertext as Innocuous Text. In: Yongfei Han, Tatsuaki Okamoto, Sihan Qing (Eds.) Proc. First Int. Conf. on Information and Communication Security ICICS 97. LNCS 1334, Springer, 1997, p. 335-345.

10. Chapman, M., G.I. Davida, M. Rennhard. A Practical and Effective Approach to Large-Scale Automated Linguistic Steganography. In: G.I. Davida, Y. Frankel (Eds.) *Information security*. Proc. of Int. Conf. on Information and Communication Security ICS 2001, LNCS 2200, Springer, 2001, p. 156-165.

11. Fellbaum, Ch. (Ed.) *WordNet: An Electronic Lexical Database*. MIT Press, 1998.

12. Mel'čuk, I. *Dependency Syntax: Theory and Practice*. SONY Press, NY, 1988.

13. Mel'čuk, I. *Cours de morphologie général*. Vol. 1, Montreal/Paris, Les Presses de l'Université de Montréal/C.N.R.S., 1993.

14. Mel'čuk, I. Phrasemes in Language and Phraseology in Linguistics. In: M. Everaert *et al.* (Eds.) *Idioms: Structural and Psychological Perspectives*. Lawrence Erlbaum Associates Publ., Hillsdale, NJ / Hove, UK, 1995, p. 169-252.

15. Michiharu Niimi *et al.* Linguistic Steganography Using SD-Form Semantics Model. IPSJ Journal. Vol. 44, No. 08.

16. *Oxford Collocations Dictionary for Students of English*. Oxford University Press. 2003.

17. Shingo Inoue et al. A Proposal on Information Hiding Methods Using XML. http://takizawa.gr.jp/lab/nlp_xml.pdf.

Graph Theoretic Software Watermarks: Implementation, Analysis, and Attacks

Christian Collberg, Andrew Huntwork, Edward Carter, and Gregg Townsend

The University of Arizona
{collberg,ash,ecarter,gmt}@cs.arizona.edu

Abstract. This paper presents an implementation of the novel watermarking method proposed by Venkatesan, Vazirani, and Sinha in their recent paper *A Graph Theoretic Approach to Software Watermarking*. An executable program is marked by the addition of code for which the topology of the control-flow graph encodes a watermark. We discuss issues that were identified during construction of an actual implementation that operates on Java bytecode. We measure the size and time overhead of watermarking, and evaluate the algorithm against a variety of attacks.

1 Introduction

This paper builds upon and elaborates a software watermarking scheme proposed by Venkatesan, Vazirani, and Sinha in *A Graph Theoretic Approach to Software Watermarking* [21]. We will refer to that paper as *VVS* and to its watermarking scheme as *GTW*. The present paper contributes:

- The first public implementation of GTW
- An implementation that operates on Java bytecode
- An example of an error-correcting graph encoding
- The generation of executable code from graphs
- Several alternatives for marking basic blocks
- Extraction (not just detection) of a watermark value
- Empirical measurements of an actual GTW implementation
- Experimental analysis of possible attacks

Graph theoretic watermarking encodes a value in the topology of a *control-flow graph*, or CFG [1]. Each node of a CFG represents a *basic block* consisting of instructions with a single entry and a single exit. A directed edge connects two basic blocks if control can pass from one to the other during execution. The CFG itself also has a single entry and a single exit.

A watermark graph W is merged with a target program's graph P by adding extra control-flow edges between them. Basic blocks belonging to W are *marked* to distinguish them from the nodes of P. These marks are later used to extract W from $P + W$ during the recognition process. The *GTW* process is illustrated in Figure 1.

J. Fridrich (Ed.): IH 2004, LNCS 3200, pp. 192–207, 2004.

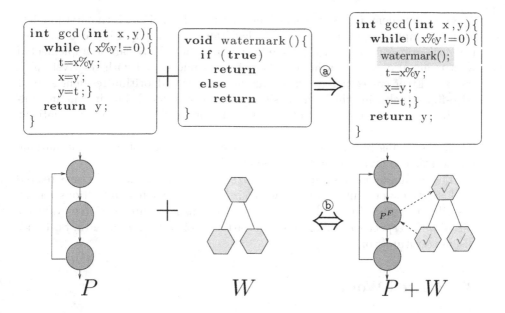

Fig. 1. Overview of graph theoretic watermarking. In ⓐ the code for watermark W is merged with the code for program graph P, by adding fake calls from P to W. In ⓑ the same process is shown using a control-flow graph notation. Part ⓑ also shows how the mark is later recovered by separating the marked ($\checkmark$) nodes of W from P with some tolerance for error.

The *VVS* paper hypothesizes that naively inserted watermark code is weakly connected to the original program and is therefore easily detected. Weakly connected graph components can be identified using standard graph algorithms and can then be manually inspected if they are few in number. Such inspection may reveal the watermark code at much lower cost than manual inspection of the full program.

The attack model of *VVS* considers an adversary who attempts to locate a *cut* between the watermark subgraph and the original CFG (dashed edges in Figure 1). The *GTW* algorithm is designed to produce a strongly connected watermark so that such a cut cannot be identified. The *VVS* paper proves that such a separation is unlikely. More formally, the *GTW* algorithm adds edges between the program P and the watermark W in such a way that many other node divisions within P have the same size cut as the division between P and W.

We have implemented the *GTW* algorithm in the framework of SAND-MARK [4], a tool for experimenting with algorithms that protect software from reverse engineering, piracy, and tampering. SANDMARK contains a large number of obfuscation and watermarking algorithms as well as tools for manually and automatic analysis and reverse engineering. SANDMARK operates on Java bytecode. It can be downloaded for experimentation from `sandmark.cs.arizona.edu`.

Our implementation of GTW, which we will call GTW_{SM}, is the first publicly available implementation of the GTW algorithm and this paper is the first empirical evaluation of the algorithm. We have found that GTW can be implemented with minimal overhead, a high degree of stealthiness, and with relatively high bit-rate. Error-correcting graph techniques make the algorithm resilient against edge-flip attacks, in which the basic blocks are reordered, but it remains vulnerable to a large number of other semantics-preserving code transformations. GTW's crucial weakness is its reliance on the reliable recognition of marked basic blocks during watermark extraction. We are unaware of *any* block marking method that is invulnerable to simple attacks.

The remainder of this paper is organized as follows. Section 2 surveys related work. Section 3 presents an overview of our implementation, and Sections 4 and 5 describe the embedding and recognition algorithms in detail. Section 6 evaluates GTW with respect to resilience against attacks, bit-rate, and stealth. Section 7 discusses future work.

2   Related Work

Davidson and Myhrvold [10] published the first software watermarking algorithm. A watermark is embedded by rearranging the order of the basic blocks in an executable. Like other order-based algorithms, this is easily defeated by a random reordering.

Qu and Potkonjak [17, 14] encode a watermark in a program's register allocation. Like all algorithms based on renaming, this is very fragile. Watermarks typically do not survive a decompilation/recompilation step. This algorithm also suffers from a low bit-rate.

Stern et al. [20] use a spread-spectrum technique to embed a watermark. The algorithm changes the frequencies of certain instruction sequences by replacing them with equivalent sequences. This algorithm can be defeated by obfuscations that modify data-structures or data-encodings and by many low-level optimizations.

Arboit's [2] algorithm embeds a watermark by adding special opaque predicates to a program. Opaque predicates are logical expressions that have a constant value, but not obviously so [8].

Watermarks are categorized as static or dynamic. The algorithms above are static markers, which embed watermarks directly within the program code or data. Collberg and Thomborson [5] proposed the first dynamic watermarking algorithm, in which the program's run-time behavior determines the watermark. Their algorithm embeds the watermark in the topology of a dynamically built graph structure constructed at runtime in a response to a particular key input sequence. This algorithm appears to be resilient to a large number of obfuscating and optimizing transformations.

Palsberg et al. [16] describe a dynamic watermarker based on that algorithm. In this simplified implementation, the watermark is not dependent on a key input sequence, but is constructed unconditionally. The watermark value is represented as a planted planar cubic tree. Palsberg et al. found the CT algorithm to be practical and robust.

3   An Overview of GTW_{SM}

Our implementation of GTW operates on Java bytecode. Choosing Java lets us leverage the tools of the SANDMARK and BCEL [9] libraries, and lets us attack the results using SANDMARK's collection of obfuscators. Like every executable format, Java bytecode has some unique quirks, but the results should be generally applicable.

The GTW embedding algorithm takes as input application code P, watermark code W, secret keys ω_1 and ω_2, and integers m and n. GTW_{SM} uses a smaller and simpler set of parameters. Values of m and n are inferred from P, W, and ω_1. The *clustering* step (Section 4.4) is unkeyed, so ω_2 is unused. Thus, our implementation takes as input application code P, a secret key ω, and a watermark value.

The GTW_{SM} embedding process proceeds through these steps:

1. The watermark value v is split into k values, $\{v_0, \ldots, v_{k-1}\}$ (Section 4.1).
2. The split values are encoded as directed graphs $\{G_0, \ldots, G_{k-1}\}$ (Section 4.2).
3. The generated graphs are converted into CFGs $\{W_0, \ldots, W_{k-1}\}$ by generating executable code for each basic block (Section 4.3).
4. The application's clusters are identified (Section 4.4).
5. The watermark is merged with the application by adding control-flow edges to the graphs (Section 4.5).
6. Each basic block is marked to indicate whether it is part of the watermark (Section 4.6).

The recognition process described in VVS has three steps: detection of watermark nodes, sampling of subsets of the watermark nodes, and computation of robust properties of these subsets. The set of robust property values composes the watermark. The process is as follows:

1. Marked nodes of the program CFG are identified (Section 5.1).
2. The recognizer selects several subsets of the watermark nodes for decoding (Section 5.2).
3. Each subset is decoded to compute a value, and the individual values are combined to yield the watermark (Section 5.3).

4   Embedding

The construction of a watermark graph W is not discussed in VVS. In GTW_{SM} we accept an integer value for transformation into a watermark CFG. The recognition process performs the inverse transformation from CFG to integer.

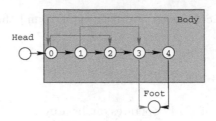

Fig. 2. Reducible permutation graph of the integer value 8

The embedding process involves several steps: splitting the watermark value into small integers; constructing directed graphs that encode these values; generating code that corresponds to the graphs; and connecting the code to the program.

4.1   Watermark Value Splitting

GTW_{SM} splits a watermark value v into a multiset S of k integers, $k \geq 2$. Empirically, we have determined that values of k between 5 and 15 produce watermark methods that are neither overly large nor overly numerous.

A watermark value v is split as follows:

1. Compute the minimum exponent l such that v can be represented using $k-1$ digits of base 2^l.
2. Split the value v into digits $v_0, v_1, \ldots, v_{k-2}$ such that $0 \leq v_j < 2^l$ and $v = \sum_{j=0}^{k-2} 2^{jl} v_j$.
3. Encode the digits in the multiset $\{s_0, s_1, \ldots, s_{k-1}\}$ where $s_0 = l - 1$ and $s_i = s_{i-1} + v_{i-1}$.

For a concrete example, consider splitting a watermark value of 31415926 with $k = 10$. The minimum radix is 8, so $l = 3$. This produces a list v_i of 6, 6, 1, 7, 5, 6, 7, 6, 1 and finally the multiset $\{2, 8, 14, 15, 22, 27, 33, 40, 46, 47\}$.

4.2   Encoding Integers as Graphs

Each integer is converted into a graph for embedding in the application. Several issues must be considered when choosing a graph encoding:

1. The graph must be a *digraph* (a directed graph) for use as a CFG.
2. The graph must have the structure of a valid CFG. It should have a header node with in-degree zero and out-degree one from which every node is reachable, and it should have a footer node with out-degree zero that is reachable from every node.

3. The graph should have a maximum out-degree of two. Basic block nodes with out-degrees of one or two are easily generated using standard control-structures such as if- and while-statements. Nodes with higher out-degree can only be built using switch-statements. These are relatively unusual in real code, and hence conspicuous.

4. The graph should be *reducible* [1], because true Java code produces only reducible graphs. Intuitively, a CFG is reducible if it is compiled from properly nested structured control constructs such as if- and while-statements. More formally, a reducible flow graph with root node r has edges that can be split into an acyclic component and a component of backedges, where each backedge (u, v) has the property that every path from r to u passes through v. In this case, v is said to *dominate* u.

5. The control structures represented by the graph should not be deeply nested, because real programs seldom nest deeply.

In GTW_{SM} each part of the split watermark is encoded as a *reducible permutation graph*, or RPG [3]. These are reducible control-flow graphs with a maximum out-degree of two, mimicking real code. They are resilient against edge-flip attacks and can be correctly decoded even if an attacker rearranges the basic blocks of a method.

An RPG is a reducible flow graph with a Hamiltonian path consisting of four pieces (see Figure 2):

A header node: The root node of the graph having out-degree one from which every other node in the graph is reachable. Every control-flow graph has such a node.

The preamble: Zero or more additional initial nodes from which all later nodes are reachable. Any node in the body can have an edge to any node in the preamble while preserving reducibility.

The body: The set of nodes used to encode a value. Edges within the body, from the body to the preamble, and from the body to the footer node encode a permutation that is its own inverse.

A footer node: A node with out-degree zero that is reachable from every other node of the graph. This node represents the method exit.

There is a one-to-one correspondence between self-inverting permutations and isomorphism classes of RPGs, and this correspondence can be computed in polynomial time. An RPG encoding a permutation on n elements has a bitrate of at least $\frac{1}{4} \lg n - 0.62$ bits per node [3].

For encoding integers we use only those permutations that are their own inverses, as this greatly reduces the need for a preamble. An integer n is encoded as the RPG corresponding to the nth self-inverting permutation, using the enumeration of Collberg et al. [3].

4.3 Generating Code from a Graph

A graph is embedded in an application by building a set of instructions that have a corresponding CFG. We want to generate code (in this case Java bytecode) that is stealthy, executable, and efficient. In VVS it is expected that watermark code be connected to the application by means of opaque predicates, and hence never executed. This leaves the watermarked application open to tracing attacks. In GTW_{SM}, we generate executable watermark code that has no semantic effect on the program.

Given a graph, our code generator produces a static method that accepts an integer argument and returns an integer result. Tiny basic blocks that operate on an integer are chosen randomly from a set of possibilities to form the nodes in the graph. The basic blocks are connected as directed by the graph, using conditional jumps and fall-through paths whenever possible. When used in combination with a graph encoder that mimics genuine program structures (such as our RPG encoder), the result is a synthetic function that is not obviously artificial.

If the graph has at least one leaf node (representing a return statement) then the generated function is guaranteed to reach it, so the function can safely be called. Furthermore, the generator can be instructed to guarantee a positive, negative, zero, or nonzero function result, allowing the function call to be used in an opaque predicate.

4.4 Clustering

GTW includes a clustering step before the edge addition step to increase the complexity of the graphs to which edges are added. If edges are added directly to control flow graphs, few original nodes will have more than two out-edges or a small number of in-edges, and high-degree nodes generated by edge adding will be conspicuous. The clustering step allows complex graphs to occur stealthily. VVS specifies a clustering step that proceeds by

> Partition[ing] the graph G into n clusters using ω as a random seed, so that edges straddling across clusters are minimized (approximately).

VVS also states that

> The clustering step (2) must have a way to find different clusterings for different values of ω, so that the adversary does not have any knowledge about the clustering used.

With Java bytecode, edges can be added only within methods or to entry points of other (accessible) methods. This constrains the usable clusterings. Fortunately, the natural clustering of basic blocks into Java methods is suitable for our needs. The proven difficulty of separating W from P does not rely on keyed clustering, so we have chosen in GTW_{SM} to simply treat each Java method as a cluster.

Each node in the cluster graph then represents an application or watermark method, and an edge between two nodes represents a method call. This clustering scheme is very likely to approximately minimize the number of edges between clusters, since two basic blocks in the same method are much more likely to be connected than two basic blocks in different methods. This scheme also allows us to implement edge addition stealthily, efficiently, and easily. We were unable to identify any substantially different clustering scheme with both of these properties.

4.5 Adding Control-Flow Edges

The GTW algorithm adds edges between clusters using a random walk, with nonuniform probabilities designed to merge the watermark code indistinguishably into the program. This process begins by choosing a random start node n, then repeatedly choosing another node l, creating an edge between n and l, and finally setting $n = l$. This process proceeds until m edges have been added between P and W.

To ensure that watermark code is not trivially detected as dead code, we then continue randomly adding edges until no watermark method has degree zero.

VVS does not address the issue of choosing m. Our implementation chooses m to make the average degree of the watermark nodes approximately the same as the average degree of the application nodes as follows.

Let p be the number of program clusters and w be the number of watermark clusters. Set $q_p = \frac{p-1}{p+w-1}$ and $q_w = \frac{w-1}{p+w-1}$. Let c be the number of edges in the original cluster graph. Then set

$$m = \frac{4ew(1 - q_w)(1 - q_p)}{p(2 - q_w)(1 - q_p) - w(2 - q_p)(1 - q_w)}. \tag{1}$$

Within the watermark cluster graph, q_w is the probability that the next node chosen in the random walk will also be a watermark node. The probability that one edge-ending is added to watermark nodes is $1 - q_w$, $q_w(1 - q_w)$ for two edge-endings, $q_w^2(1 - q_w)$ for three, and so on. The expected number of edge-endings to be added to watermark nodes before leaving to original program nodes is then $E_w = \sum_{n=1}^{\infty} nq_w^{n-1}(1 - q_w) = \frac{1}{1-q_w}$.

Similarly, q_p is the probability that the next node chosen after a cluster from the original program is another cluster from the original program. We obtain the analogous value $E_p = \frac{1}{1-q_p}$ for the expected number of edge-endings to be added to program nodes before leaving for watermark nodes.

For every two cross edges added, we expect to add $1 + E_w$ edge-endings to watermark nodes and $1 + E_p$ edge endings to program nodes. Let $m = 2k$. Since we want the average degree to be the same in original program nodes and watermark nodes, we have the formula

$$\frac{k(1 + E_w)}{w} = \frac{2e + k(1 + E_p)}{p}. \tag{2}$$

Solving (2) for m gives (1).

Because each method is a cluster, adding an edge from cluster A to cluster B means inserting code into method A that calls method B. The generated watermark methods are pure functions, so they can be executed without affecting program semantics. Therefore, the added method calls to watermark methods can actually be executed. However, application code may have arbitrary side effects, so the edge adding process must not change the number or order of executions of application methods. Therefore, added application method invocations are protected with opaquely false predicates to ensure that they are not actually executed. Additionally, application methods may be declared to throw checked exceptions. Preparing for and catching checked exceptions requires the addition to A of several blocks other than the method call block.

Also as a result of making each method a cluster, not every edge can be created. For example, private methods from different classes cannot call each other. In this case, the edge is simply not created and the process continues normally.

4.6   Marking Basic Blocks

Each basic block that corresponds to a node of the watermark must be individually marked for later recognition. The *VVS* paper does not provide an actual algorithm, but suggests that

> one may store one or more bits at a node that flags when a node is in W by using some padded data after suitable keyed encryption and encoding.

For marking purposes, the contents of a block can be changed as long as the modified code is functionally equivalent to the original. Here are some examples of possible block markers:

1. Add code that accomplishes no function but just serves as a marker, for example by loading a value that is never used or writing to a value that has no effect on overall program behavior.
2. Count the number of instructions in a block, and use the parity as a mark. Add a no-op instruction, or make a more subtle change, to alter the mark.
3. Count accesses of static variables to determine a mark. Add variables and accesses as necessary to produce the desired results.
4. Compute a checksum of the instructions and use one or more bits of that as a mark. Alter the code as necessary to produce desired results.
5. Transform the instruction sequence in each block to a canonical form, then vary it systematically to encode marks.
6. Add marks in the meta-information associated with each block. For example, alter or create debugging information that associates code locations with source line numbers.

All of these marking methods are easily defeated if an adversary's goal is to disrupt the watermark without necessarily reading it. We are not aware of any robust block marking technique; this remains an unsolved problem.

For our implementation we have adopted the checksum technique, computing the MD5 digest [18] of each block. Only instruction bytes and immediate constant values, such as those in `bipush`, contribute to the digest value. This makes the digest insensitive to some simple changes such as reordering of the Java "constant pool".

A block is considered marked if the low-order two bits of the checksum are zero. We expect, then, to alter $\frac{3}{4}$ of the blocks in the watermark set but only $\frac{1}{4}$ of the other blocks to get the right results. A real application will have many more application blocks than watermark blocks, so this is a desirable imbalance.

Marking is keyed by concatenating a secret value to the instruction sequence before computing the MD5 digest. The set of marks cannot be read, nor can it be counterfeited, without knowing the key.

5   Recognition

The recognition process in VVS has three steps: detection of watermark nodes, sampling of subsets of the watermark nodes, and computation of robust properties of these subsets. The set of robust property values composes the watermark.

5.1   Node Detection

A basic block that is part of the watermark code can be detected by computing its MD5 digest, as described in Section 4.6. A digest value ending in two zero bits indicates a mark. Attacks on the watermarked program may change the digest value of some blocks, but our recognizer uses "majority logic" to recover from isolated errors. If 60% of the blocks in a method are marked, the recognizer treats all the blocks in that method as marked. If fewer than 40% of the blocks are marked, all are considered unmarked. If the number is between 40% and 60%, the recognizer tries both possibilities.

5.2   Subset Sampling

GTW specifies that after the watermark nodes have been detected, several subsets of them should be sampled. GTW_{SM} uses method control flow graphs as samples, and every watermark node is contained in exactly one sample set, in particular, the control flow graph it belongs to.

5.3   Graph Decoding

The recognition process attempts to decode each sampled method control flow graph as a Reducible Permutation Graph [3] that encodes an integer. A valid RPG can be decoded into a self-inverting permutation. The decoder proceeds by first computing the dominance hierarchy of the graph and, once the graph is verified to be reducible, finding the unique Hamiltonian path in the graph. This Hamiltonian path imposes an order on the vertices, after which decoding the graph into a self-inverting permutation is relatively straightforward, as laid out in [3].

Each graph's permutation is mapped back to an integer, using the same enumeration as in Section 4.2. The combined set of integers S is combined to produce single integer v, the watermark. This calculation is as follows:

1. Let $k = |S|$. Write S as $\{s_0, s_1, \ldots, s_{k-1}\}$, where $s_0 \leq s_1 \leq \cdots \leq s_{k-1}$.
2. Set $l = s_0 + 1$. For each $0 \leq j \leq k - 2$, set $v_j = s_{j+1} - s_j$.
3. Then $v = \sum_{j=0}^{k-2} 2^{jl} v_j$.

5.4   Use in Fingerprinting

Because the recognizer returns a specific watermark value, as opposed to just a success/failure flag, GTW_{SM} can be used for fingerprinting. This is a technique where each copy of an application program is distributed with its own unique watermark value, allowing pirated copies to be traced back to a specific original.

6   Evaluation

Most software watermarking research has focused on the discovery of novel embedding schemes. Little work has been done on their evaluation. A software watermarking algorithm can be evaluated using several criteria:

Data rate: What is the ratio of size of the watermark that can be embedded to the size of the program?

Embedding overhead: How much slower or larger is the watermarked application compared to the original?

Resistance to detection (stealth): Does the watermarked program have statistical properties that are different from typical programs? Can an adversary use these differences to locate and attack the watermark?

Resilience against transformations: Will the watermark survive semantics-preserving transformations such as code optimization and code obfuscation? If not, what is the overhead of these transformations? How much slower or larger is the application after enough transformations have been applied that the watermark no longer can be recognized?

6.1   Data Rate and Embedding Overhead

A watermark of any size can be embedded in even the smallest of programs using this algorithm. Larger watermarks merely require larger watermark graphs, or a larger number of them, thus incurring larger overhead in terms of increased code size.

For non-trivial programs, there is little relationship between watermark size and code growth, as illustrated in Figure 3. Block marking and edge addition add code that proportional to the size and complexity of the application, not the watermark. For watermarks up to 150 bits, size increases varying between 40 and 75 percent were measured.

CaffeineMark [19] benchmark results show the effect of watermarking on execution time. Some programs were not affected significantly, while others took 20 to 36 percent longer, as shown in Table 1.

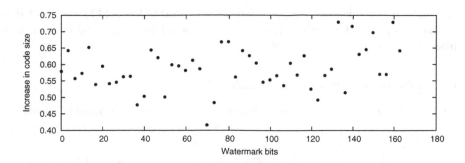

Fig. 3. Increase in code size for the machineSim program

6.2 Stealth

Some common attacks against watermarking systems, such as manual attacks and subtractive attacks, begin by identifying the code composing the watermark. To resist such attacks, watermarking could should be stealthy: It should be indistinguishable from the host code. Two useful measures of stealth are the similarity of the watermark code to the host code and the similarity of the watermark code to general application code.

GTW_{SM} introduces several new artificially-generated methods to an application. These methods are not stealthy in two respects. First, these methods include a very high percentage of arithmetic operations. While general Java bytecode includes approximately 1% arithmetic instructions, the methods inserted by GTW_{SM} contain approximately 20% arithmetic instructions. Second, the control flow graphs of the inserted methods are all reducible permutation graphs. While RPGs are designed to mimic the structure of real control flow graphs, only 2 of 3236 methods in the SpecJVM benchmarking suite have control flow graphs that are RPGs. Therefore, RPGs are not stealthy if an attacker is looking for them.

GTW_{SM} currently introduces unstealthy code to implement edge addition between clusters. Edges between application methods are protected using the

Table 1. CaffeineMark scores before and after embedding a watermark

Category	Original	Watermarked	Slowdown
Sieve	8676	6876	20.7%
Loop	25636	16344	36.2%
Logic	20635	13231	35.9%
String	19481	20198	-3.6%
Float	18657	18646	0%
Method	19106	12783	33.1%
Overall	17719	13816	22.0%

particularly conspicuous opaque predicate if (null != null). Also, GTW_{SM} passes a constant for each argument to the called function; real code is more likely to compute at least one of its arguments.

6.3 Semantics-Preserving Attacks

Automated attacks are the most serious threat to any watermark. Debray [13, 12, 11] has developed a family of tools that optimize and compress X86 and Alpha binaries. BLOAT [15] optimizes collections of Java class files. SANDMARK implements a collection of obfuscating code transformations that can be used to attack software watermarks.

We first tested the robustness of GTW_{SM} on a Java application *machineSim* which simulates a Von Neumann machine. Various SANDMARK obfuscations were applied to see if a watermark could survive. The watermark was successfully recognized after inlining, register re-allocation, local variable merging, array splitting, class inheritance modification, local variable splitting, and many others. It was destroyed by primitive boxing, basic block splitting, method merging, class encryption, and code duplication. These types of transformations are described in [6, 7, 8].

Method merging makes such large changes to control-flow graphs that there is really no hope of recovering the watermark value. Primitive boxing changes the instructions in many basic blocks in a method, and thereby changes the marks on the blocks. Code duplication and basic block splitting add nodes to the control flow graph of a method. While RPGs can survive some kinds of attacks on edges, they cannot survive node additions.

The attack model considered in *VVS* is a small number of random changes to the watermarked application. We have implemented an obfuscation that randomly modifies a parameterized fraction of blocks in a program. If fewer than about half of the blocks in a watermarked application are modified, the watermark survives. If more than that are modified, the watermark cannot be recovered.

6.4 False Positive Rates

For our implementation to detect a spurious watermark in an unmarked application, the application would have to have at least two methods with acceptable control-flow graphs in which the majority of basic blocks would produce MD5 digests with two low-order zero bits. The probability of finding a mark in a single basic block is only $\frac{1}{4}$. We examined a large group of methods from real programs and found the probability of a control-flow graph being a valid RPG to be 0.002. While there is a possibility of finding an RPG with only two or three nodes where all the nodes are marked in a real program, choosing watermark values from a sufficiently sparse set should be enough to prevent false positives.

7   Discussion and Future Work

Our implementation of the *GTW* watermarking system is fully functional and reasonably efficient. It is resilient against a small number of random program modifications, in accordance with the threat model assumed by *VVS*.

The system is more vulnerable to pervasive changes, including several obfuscations implemented in the SANDMARK system. Such vulnerabilities stem from issues left unaddressed by the *VVS* paper. These and other areas provide opportunities for future work.

Static marking of basic blocks is the fundamental mutation applied by the watermarker. Development of a robust marking method, capable of withstanding simple program transformations, is still an unsolved problem.

Another area of great potential is the encoding of values as graph structures. In particular, the development of other error-correcting graphs, as postulated by *VVS*, would greatly increase the strength of a watermark.

More sophisticated generated code and opaque predicates would improve the stealthiness of a watermark.

Implementations of *GTW* for other architectures besides Java would undoubtedly prove enlightening, because they would be likely to supply somewhat different challenges and opportunities.

One key feature of *GTW* is the algorithm for connecting new code representing a watermark into an existing application. This algorithm also adds branches within the pre-existing code and is interesting in its own right as a means of obfuscation. This also has potential for further research.

8   Summary

We have produced a working implementation of the Graph Theoretic Watermark described by Venkatesan et al. [21]. The implementation is faithful to the paper within the constraints of Java bytecode, and includes necessary components that were left unspecified by the original paper. While the *GTW* design protects against detection, its fundamental dependence on static block marking leaves watermarked programs vulnerable to distortive attacks.

References

[1] Alfred V. Aho, Ravi Sethi, and Jeffrey D. Ullman. *Compilers, Principles, Techniques, and Tools*. Addison-Wesley, 1986. ISBN 0-201-10088-6.

[2] Geneviève Arboit. A method for watermarking Java programs via opaque predicates. In *The Fifth International Conference on Electronic Commerce Research (ICECR-5)*, 2002.

[3] Christian Collberg, Edward Carter, Stephen Kobourov, and Clark Thomborson. Error-correcting graphs. In *Workshop on Graphs in Computer Science (WG'2003)*, June 2003.

[4] Christian Collberg, Ginger Myles, and Andrew Huntwork. SANDMARK — A tool for software protection research. *IEEE Magazine of Security and Privacy*. To appear.

[5] Christian Collberg and Clark Thomborson. Software watermarking: Models and dynamic embeddings. In *In Conference Record of POPL '99: The 26th ACM SIGPLAN-SIGACT Symposium on Principles of Programming Languages (Jan. 1999)*, 1999.

[6] Christian Collberg, Clark Thomborson, and Douglas Low. A taxonomy of obfuscating transformations. Technical Report 148, Department of Computer Science, University of Auckland, July 1997. http://www.cs.auckland.ac.nz/~collberg/Research/Publications/CollbergThomborsonLow97a.

[7] Christian Collberg, Clark Thomborson, and Douglas Low. Breaking abstractions and unstructuring data structures. In *IEEE International Conference on Computer Languages, ICCL'98*, Chicago, IL, May 1998. http://www.cs.auckland.ac.nz/~collberg/Research/Publications/CollbergThomborsonLow98b/.

[8] Christian Collberg, Clark Thomborson, and Douglas Low. Manufacturing cheap, resilient, and stealthy opaque constructs. In *Principles of Programming Languages 1998, POPL'98*, San Diego, CA, January 1998. http://www.cs.auckland.ac.nz/~collberg/Research/Publications/CollbergThomborsonLow98a/.

[9] Markus Dahm. Byte code engineering. In *The Scientific German Java Conference*, September 1999. ftp://ftp.inf.fu-berlin.de/pub/JavaClass/paper.ps.gz.

[10] Robert L. Davidson and Nathan Myhrvold. Method and system for generating and auditing a signature for a computer program. US Patent 5,559,884, September 1996. Assignee: Microsoft Corporation.

[11] Saumya Debray, William Evans, Robert Muth, and Bjorn De Sutter. Compiler techniques for code compaction. *ACM Transactions on Programming Languages and Systems*, 22(2):378–415, March 2000.

[12] Saumya Debray, Robert Muth, Scott Watterson, and Koen De Bosschere. ALTO: A link-time optimizer for the Compaq Alpha. *Software — Practice and Experience*, 31:67–101, January 2001.

[13] Saumya Debray, Benjamin Schwarz, Gregory Andrews, and Matthew Legendre. PLTO: A link-time optimizer for the Intel IA-32 architecture. In *Proc. 2001 Workshop on Binary Rewriting (WBT-2001)*, September 2001.

[14] Ginger Myles and Christian Collberg. Software watermarking through register allocation: Implementation, analysis, and attacks. In *International Conference on Information Security and Cryptology*, 2003.

[15] Nathaniel Nystrom. Bloat – the bytecode-level optimizer and analysis tool. http://www.cs.purdue.edu/homes/whitlock/bloat, 1999.

[16] Jens Palsberg, Sowmya Krishnaswamy, Minseok Kwon, Di Ma, Qiuyun Shao, and Yi Zhang. Experience with software watermarking. In *Proceedings of ACSAC '00, 16th Annual Computer Security Applications Conference*, pages 308–316, 2000.

[17] G. Qu and M. Potkonjak. Analysis of watermarking techniques for graph coloring problem. In *IEEE/ACM International Conference on Computer Aided Design*, pages 190–193, November 1998. http://www.cs.ucla.edu/~gangqu/publication/gc.ps.gz.

[18] Ronald Rivest. The MD5 message-digest algorithm. http://www.ietf.org/rfc/rfc1321.txt, 1992. The Internet Engineering Task Force RFC 1321.

[19] Pendragon Software. Caffeinemark 3.0. http://www.pendragon-software.com/pendragon/cm3/, 1998.

[20] Julien P. Stern, Gael Hachez, Francois Koeune, and Jean-Jacques Quisquater. Robust object watermarking: Application to code. In *Information Hiding*, pages 368–378, 1999.

[21] Ramarathnam Venkatesan, Vijay Vazirani, and Saurabh Sinha. A graph theoretic approach to software watermarking. In *4th International Information Hiding Workshop*, Pittsburgh, PA, April 2001.

Threading Software Watermarks

Jasvir Nagra and Clark Thomborson

Department of Computer Science, University of Auckland
Auckland, New Zealand
{jas,cthombor}@cs.auckland.ac.nz

Abstract. We introduce a new dynamic technique for embedding robust software watermarks into a software program using thread contention. We show the technique to be resilient to many semantic-preserving transformations that most existing proposals are susceptible to. We describe the technique for encoding the watermark as a bit string and a scheme for embedding and recognizing the watermark using thread contention. Experimental results with Java bytecode indicate that thread based watermarks have small impact on the size of applications and only a modest effect on their speed.

1 Introduction

Software watermarking is a technique for embedding an identifier into a piece of software in order to encode some identifying information about it. This identifying information can be used to demonstrate ownership; and in cases of piracy, may make it possible to trace software to the source of its illegal distribution. Watermarking has received an increasing amount of interest from the research community which has resulted in increasingly resilient techniques. However, no single watermarking algorithm has emerged that is effective against all existing and known attacks. In fact, it is generally agreed that it is not possible to devise a watermark that some sufficiently determined attacker would not be able to defeat. As a result, the goal of the watermarking community is to develop techniques that are sufficiently robust that the resources required to defeat the watermark are too expensive to be worth the attackers while.

In this paper, we propose a new technique for software watermarking, *thread-based watermarking*, for embedding and detecting a watermark using thread contention. Our premise is that multithreaded programs are inherently more difficult to analyse and the difficulty of analysis increases with the number of threads that are "live" concurrently [18].

Software watermarks can be used for different purposes and their desirable properties vary depending on their use [15]. For software piracy the two properties that interest us are "robustness" and "invisibility". "Robustness" ensures that the watermark is difficult for an attacker to remove and thus the watermark can act as a software intellectual property identifier. "Invisibility" means that the watermarks are designed to be non-apparent to the end-user and thus do not interfere with legitimate use of the program.

J. Fridrich (Ed.): IH 2004, LNCS 3200, pp. 208–223, 2004.

Our proposed technique embeds the watermark in the order and choice of threads which execute different parts of an application. The embedding is a two step process. Firstly, we increase the number of possible paths through the program by creating multiple threads of execution. The semantics of the old program are maintained by introducing locks. Secondly, we add other locks to ensure that only a small subset of the possible paths are in fact executed by the watermarked program. The particular paths that are executed encode the watermark.

The rest of the paper is organized as follows. In Section 2, we give an overview of the state-of-the-art in watermarking literature and other related work. In Section 3, we give an overview of the basic idea behind thread based watermarks. Section 4 describes how thread based watermarks can be implemented for Java bytecode. Section 5 gives experimental evaluation of our technique. Finally, Section 6 gives future directions and conclusions.

2 Related Work

There are several other published techniques for doing software watermarking, static watermarks and dynamic watermarks. The earliest software watermarks were static watermarks where the watermark was embedded in either the code section (eg. in variable names, order of exectuable statements) or in the static data sections (eg. in the strings, images, headers) of a program [8]. Moskowitz [14] describes such a scheme in which the watermark is embedded in an image or other digital media using any known media watermarking scheme. The image is in turn embedded in the static data section of the program, and the watermark is extracted at runtime. This fragile watermark is necessary for program correctness.

A more advanced kind of static code watermark was introduced by Davidson and Myhrvold [7]. The technique involved statically encoding the watermark in the ordering of basic blocks that constitute program. Another code watermark was introduced by Monden [13] which involved injecting dummy unexecuted methods into the program. These dummy methods contain an encoding of the watermark in the choice of opcodes and numerical operands. A comparable spread spectrum technique was introduced by Stern et al. [22] for embedding a watermark by modifying the frequencies of instructions in the program.

Instead of watermarking the code or data sections of a program, Sander and Tschudin [20] introduce a technique for watermarking a function by embedding information statically in the I/O interface between the client and the server.

Static watermarks are particularly susceptible to obfuscation attacks. Two such attacks described by Collberg et al. [4] involve breaking and scattering all strings and other static data around the program and/or replacing this static data with code that generates the same data at runtime. Both these attacks are extremely effective in making watermark detection impractical.

Perhaps the strongest known static watermark was introduced by Venkatesan et al. [23] which involves modifying a program so that its control flow graph encodes the watermark represented as a graph.

Dynamic data structure watermarks were introduced by Collberg and Thomborson [2]. These watermarks alter the original program so that a data structure that represents the watermark gets built whenever the program is run with the correct input. In order to implement these dynamic data structure watermarks, a system called SandMark [5] was designed jointly at the University of Auckland and the University of Arizona. Sandmark provides a framework to watermark Java programs by modifying the application bytecode to make it build a structure at runtime that encodes the watermark. This structure is recognized as the watermark by dumping and analyzing the Java heap.

Historically, watermarking has not been the only technique used for protection of intellectual property of software. Other techniques include the use of a registration database [9] [21], hardware cryptography [17], obfuscation [4] and tamper-proofing [1]. Furthermore, research has been conducted into using "software birthmarks", which are preexisting properties of a piece of software, to establish the authorship of a program [8] [11].

In Collberg et al. [5] the authors suggest using thread contention, but as a possible technique for obfuscating the execution of a program, not for watermarking. This paper gives the first practical method for software watermarking using thread contention.

3   Thread Based Watermarks

We describe a new watermarking algorithm, *thread based watermarking*, where the basic idea is to embed the mark in the threading behavior of the program. Our proposed technique relies on introducing new threads into single threaded sections of a program. In an unsynchronized multithreaded program, two or more threads may try to read or write to the same area of memory or try to use resources simultaneously. This results in a *race condition* - a situation in which two or more threads or processes are reading or writing some shared data, and the final result depends on the timing of how the threads are scheduled.

One technique that allows threads to share resources in a controlled manner is using a *mutual exclusion* object often called a mutex. A mutex has two states, *locked* and *unlocked*. Before a thread can use a shared resource, it must lock the corresponding mutex. Other threads attempting to lock a locked mutex will block and wait until the original thread unlocks it. Once the mutex is unlocked, the queued threads contend to acquire the lock on the mutex. The thread that wins this contention is decided by priority, order of execution or by some other algorithm. However, due to the nature of multithreaded execution and the number of factors that can affect the timing of thread execution, the particular thread that acquires the lock is difficult to predict and appears to be largely random [18].

In order to embed our watermark, we take advantage of the fact that although thread contention appears to be random, by carefully controlling the locks in a program, we can force a partial ordering on the order in which some parts of the program are executed.

```
void run () {                 boolean doneA = false;              boolean doneA = false;
  blockA();                   boolean doneB = false;              boolean doneB = false;
  blockB();                   Mutex mutex2 = new Mutex();         Mutex mutex2 = new Mutex();
}                             Mutex mutex1 = new Mutex();         Mutex mutex1 = new Mutex();
                              void run () {                       void run () {
                              Thread t0 = new Thread () {         Thread t0 = new Thread () {
                                public void run () {                public void run () {
                                  lock mutex1;                       lock mutex1
                                  if ( !doneA ) {                    if ( !doneA ) {
                                    blockA(); doneA=true;              blockA(); doneA=true;
                                  }                                  }
                                  unlock mutex1;                     lock mutex2;
                                  lock mutex2;                       unlock mutex1;
                                  if ( !doneB ) {                    if ( !doneB ) {
                                    blockB(); doneB=true;              blockB(); doneB=true;
                                  }                                  }
                                  unlock mutex2;                     unlock mutex2;
                                }                                  }
                              };                                 };
                              Thread t1 = new Thread (t0);        Thread t1 = new Thread(t0);
                              t1.start(); t0.start();             t1.start(); t0.start();
                              t1.join(); t0.join();               t1.join(); t0.join();
                              }                                   }

            a.                           b.                                 c.
```

Fig. 1. In **a.** we have the original program. **b.** shows a multithreaded but unconstrained version of the original program. There are four different correct paths through this program, all of which may be executed. **c.** shows a multithreaded and constrained version of the original program. In this version, although both threads contend to execute blockA which ever thread executes the first block also executes the second one because of the order of locks.

For example consider Figure 1a which shows a simple snippet of a program with a run() method that calls other methods blockA() and blockB(). We could introduce new threads into the program to execute each of the statements as show in Figure 1b. This version of the program remains correct and semantically equivalent to the original, however, there a several paths of execution with either t0 or t1 executing blockA() followed by either t0 or t1 executing blockB(). In order to embed information into a program, we manipulate the locks so that only a given subset of paths through the code is taken. In Figure 1c, we show one example of such manipulation. In this example, although the two new threads race to acquire a lock on mutex1 like before, in this case whichever thread locks this mutex is also guaranteed to lock mutex2 and thus executes both blockA() and blockB(). We can detect this scenario as distinct from the case where different threads execute blockA() and blockB() and thus we can use it to embed a bit of information.

The advantage of allowing some thread contention to remain is that although it allows a bit to be embedded, the actual path of execution still changes every time the program is executed. This makes the attackers task of determining which exact sequence embeds the mark more difficult. We discuss this resilience to attack more in the Section 5.

4 Watermarking Java Bytecode

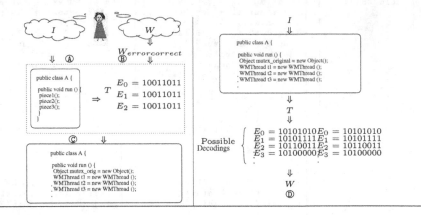

Fig. 2. Overview of thread based watermarking

We have implemented thread based watermarking for Java bytecode. This implementation consists of three stages. In the tracing phase, the dynamic behaviour of the program is captured by tracing its execution on a secret input, I. In the embedding phase, the watermark number W is selected by the user and embedded in the input code by modifying the behavior of the program on the secret input I. Finally, in the recognition phase, the program is traced again with input I, and the watermark is extracted from the trace.

Figure 2 illustrates the watermarking process. In Ⓐ the original program is annotated for tracing and executed with the secret input I that the user selects. In Ⓑ the user selects a watermark string and encodes it using some encoding scheme. In Ⓒ watermark code is inserted into the original program. When the watermarked program is executed with the special input sequence in Ⓓ, the resulting trace will contain the watermark.

4.1 Tracing

We begin the tracing phase by performing control flow analysis on the input program to build up a control-flow graph. This graph represents the possible paths through a program. The nodes of the graph represent basic blocks while the directed edges represent jumps from one node to another. A basic block is a piece of straight line code without any jumps or jump targets. We instrument the input program to write a program trace to a file and execute the program with the secret input I. The trace is a series of tuples (B_i, T_i) where B_i is the block id of every basic block executed and T_i is the id of the thread that executed B_i. The watermark is embedded in the execution behavior of input program and as such we select input I such that for a given thread T_n, the sequence $T = < B_0, B_1, ..., B_n >$ is reproducible on different runs.

The program trace serves two purposes. Primarily it is used to find the basic blocks that are executed by the input program when given the chosen input. These basic blocks are potential blocks to embed bits of the watermark. Secondarily, the program trace counts how often each basic block gets executed and thus helps identify tight loops, recursion and other program hotspots. There is a computational and thread switching runtime cost associated with inserting new threads into the program and to avoid excessive slow down, we avoid inserting watermarks in to these hotspots.

The secret input I acts as the key and the watermark will be expressed when this secret input is entered. Other inputs may express other watermarks. Keeping this input a secret impedes an attacker who gains access to the recognizer from mounting the so called Oracle attack [6] which can be used to create a non-watermarked program when a watermark recognizer is available.

4.2   Embedding

The embedding phase modifies the input code so that the watermark W can be extracted from a trace of basic blocks executed on the input sequence I, as described in Section 4.1.

In our prototype design, we encode a 24-bit watermark string W into a 48-bit string E, using a randomly chosen code. The extreme sparseness of this code gives us a strong error-detection property which we will use in our recognition step: if a 48-bit string is chosen uniformly at random from the set $\{0,1\}^{48}$, the probability of this string being a legal codeword is only 2^{-24}.

We split our 48-bit string into six 8-bit bytes $E = < E_0, E_1, ..., E_5 >$. Each byte is embedded separately. For each byte, we select a thread T_i at random and a subsequence of $T < (B_0, T_i), ..., (B_n, T_i) > $ - that is a set of n basic blocks executed by T_i in the order of execution. To simplify embedding we ensure that we select n distinct basic blocks - that is we select B_i such that $\forall i, j : i \neq j \rightarrow B_i \neq B_j$.

As mentioned earlier thread switching code is expensive in time. Basic blocks that are executed repeatedly are poor candidates for embedding as slowing them down will significantly deteriorate the overall performance of the program. Furthermore we select some of the basic blocks that are input dependent to make the value of the expressed watermark vary with I.

In order to embed our watermark we require our chosen thread to be able to execute an arbitrary piece of code that it is passed. Thus we first extend the java `Thread` class so that threads can be passed a closure to execute. A closure is a data structure that contains an expression and an environment of variable bindings in which the expression is to be evaluated. There is no direct support for closures in Java. However, several techniques for implementing closures in Java exist in literature. In particular, Pizza [16] describes two schemes for implementing closures in Java. In our implementation a closure is translated into a class that implements the `Runnable` interface. This interface contains a single `run()` method. The body of the closure is inserted into the `run()` method of the new class while the call location is replaced with an instantiation of the new class and an invocation of the run() method.

A closure allows the introduced threads to access and possibly alter the local variables used by the basic block. Unfortunately, formal parameters in Java are passed by value and we need some mechanism by which to pass updates out of the function body. In our implementation we construct a Locals class for every closure in which all variables used by the closure are captured. When the closure is instantiated we pass this environment to it.

We insert into each basic block B_i code that causes the threads to switch in such a way as to encode E_i. A simple implementation is shown in Figures 3 and 4.2.

In our implementation, a bit 0 is encoded as a sequence of three basic blocks executed by three different threads. A bit 1 is encoded as a sequence of three basic blocks, where the first and third basic blocks are executed by the same thread and the second basic block is executed by a different thread. The advantage of such an encoding scheme over one that explicitly uses named blocks and threads is that it is more resilient to renaming attacks.

We use Java monitors to control the ordering of locks. The only mechanism in the Java language for manipulating monitors is the **synchronized** statement which acquires a lock on an object before executing a block and then releasing it. The synchronized statement requires all lock and unlock calls to be fully nested and is not sufficiently expressive for our purposes. Thus to we use the macros **monitor_enter()** and **monitor_exit()** in the source code of our examples. These expand to **monitor_enter** and **monitor_exit** calls in Java bytecode, and have the advantage that they cannot be decompiled to synchronized statements in Java source. This provides some defense against decompilation attacks.

```
WMThread t1;
WMThread t2;
WMThread t3;
int[] wm = { 1,0,1,1,1,0,1,0 };
...
for ( int i=0; i < wm.length; i++ ) {
    embedBit_macro ( t1, t2, t3,
       Bit0_Closure );
} else {
    embedBit_macro ( t1, t2, t3,
       Bit1_Closure );
}
```

a.

```
embedBit_macro ( t1, t2, t3 , body ) {
    Object mutex_orig = new Object ();
    t1.setBody ( body );
    t2.setBody ( body );
    t3.setBody ( body );
    monitor_enter ( mutex_orig );
    t1.start(); t2.start(); t3.start();
    while ( t1.isAlive() &&
            t2.isAlive() &&
        t3.isAlive() )
        { Thread.yield() }
    monitor_exit ( mutex_orig );
    t1.join(); t2.join(); t3.join();
}
```

b.

Fig. 3. Part a shows the code inserted to embed the bits 10111010. The embed_bit_macro call is the macro that expands as shown in Part b. The setBody method takes a closure as its argument.

The problem with the simple implementation of Figures 3 and 4.2 is that the inserted threads do not in fact perform any computation and as such are conspicuous as well as easily removed. In order to tamperproof the watermark

```
boolean doneA , doneB , doneC , doneD ;
doneA=doneB=doneC=doneD=false;
Object mutex0 = new Object ();
Object mutex1 = new Object ();
monitor_enter ( mutex0 );
if ( !doneA ) {
  doneA = !doneA;
  monitor_enter ( mutex1 );
  monitor_exit ( mutex0 );
  monitor_enter ( mutex_orig );
  monitor_exit ( mutex_orig );
}
if ( !doneB ) {
  doneB = !doneB;
  monitor_exit ( mutex0 );
  monitor_enter ( mutex1 );
  monitor_enter ( mutex_orig );
  monitor_exit ( mutex_orig );
}
if ((!doneC && opaque_true) ||
   (( doneC && opaque_false) ||
    (doneD && opaque_false )) ) {
  doneC = !doneC;
  if ( doneD )
    monitor_exit ( mutex1 );
  else {
    monitor_exit ( mutex1 );
    doneD = !doneD;
  }
} else {
  doneC = !doneC;
  monitor_exit ( mutex0 );
}
```

```
boolean doneA , doneB , doneC , doneD ;
doneA=doneB=doneC=doneD=false;
Object mutex0 = new Object ();
Object mutex1 = new Object ();
monitor_enter ( mutex0 );
if ( !doneA ) {
  doneA = !doneA;
  monitor_enter ( mutex1 );
  monitor_exit ( mutex0 );
  monitor_enter ( mutex_orig );
  monitor_exit ( mutex_orig );
}
if ( !doneB ) {
  doneB = !doneB;
  monitor_exit ( mutex0 );
  monitor_enter ( mutex1 );
  monitor_enter ( mutex_orig );
  monitor_exit ( mutex_orig );
}
if ((!doneC && opaque_false) ||
   ((doneC && opaque_true) ||
    (doneD && opaque_true) ) {
  doneC = !doneC;
  if ( doneD )
    monitor_exit ( mutex1 );
  else {
    monitor_exit ( mutex0 );
    doneD = !doneD;
  }
} else {
  doneC = !doneC;
  monitor_exit ( mutex1 );
}
```

Fig. 4. Implementation of Bit0_Closure(left) and Bit1_Closure(right). The only differences between the implementations have been highlighted.

we use the new threads to perform the computation that was originally occurring in the basic block. Firstly we divide the selected basic block into three pieces, piece1(), piece2() and piece3() with each piece containing zero or more instructions and construct a closure around them. We then pass these new closures along with those that implement the watermarks to the new threads for execution as shown in our final implementation at Figure 5 and Figure 6.

In Figure 5 we embed a bit 0. The original thread T_{orig} locks $mutex_{orig}$ then forks of three new threads T_0, T_1 and T_2 which are executing identical closures. It then waits for these threads to terminate. The three new threads contend for $mutex_0$ and the winner proceeds to execute LA1 as shown in Figure 5. This causes piece1() to be executed by the winner while the other threads wait. The body of the threads are identical and because the cases are symmetric, let us assume T_0 wins the lock. T_0 proceeds to execute LA1 and lock $mutex_1$, unlock $mutex_0$ then blocks waiting for $mutex_{orig}$ which is owned by T_{orig}. Threads T_1 and T_2 now contend for the freed $mutex_0$ and one of them wins the lock.

Once again the cases are symmetric and we assume T_1 locks $mutex_0$. T_1 now executes LB1 and thus T_1 executes piece2(), unlocks $mutex_0$ and blocks waiting for $mutex_1$ owned by T_0. At this point T_0 is still waiting on $mutex_{orig}$.

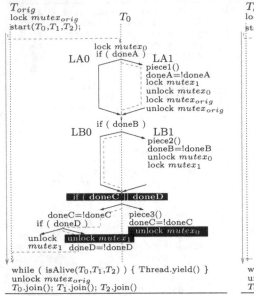

Fig. 5. Embedding a bit 0: A control flow diagram of T_{orig} and the three threads T_0, T_1 and T_2 executing an identical body. The threads T_1 and T_2 are identical to T_0 and are not shown. One possible path of execution of these threads is that T_0 executes LA1 and LB0; T_1 executes LA0 and LB1; and T_2 executes LA0 and LB0. Continuing this path T_2 will execute piece3().

Fig. 6. Embedding a bit 1: A control flow diagram of T_{orig} and the three new threads T_0, T_1 and T_2. To execute LA1' and LB0', T_1 executes LA0' and T_2 executes LA0' and LB0' Continuing this path T_0 will execute piece3(). This figure is identical to Figure 5 except where shown in reverseface .

Finally, T_2 locks $mutex_0$, executes piece3() unlocks $mutex_0$ and exits. At this point, T_{orig} is able to wake and unlock $mutex_{orig}$ allowing either T_1 or T_2 to wake up, release their locks and exit. Finally, T_{orig} waits until all three threads T_0, T_1 and T_2 have exited before continuing execution. As a result of this execution, three distinct threads have executed the three pieces thus embedding a bit 0.

In Figure 6 we embed a bit 1. The behavior of the threads is identical to embedding bit 0 until T_2 evaluates the third conditional marked ⌐!doneC⌐. In this case, T_2 skips evaluating piece3() and instead unlocks $mutex_0$ and exits. As a result, T_{orig} unlocks $mutex_{orig}$ and T_0 acquires it. T_0 then executes piece3() and exits allowing T_1 to also release its locks and exit. As a result of this execution, the same thread executes piece1() and piece3() while a different one executes piece2() thus embedding a bit 1.

The introduced code is carefully constructed so that the only differences between the embedding of bit 0 and bit 1 are the arguments to unlock and the third conditional as shown in Figure 6.

The first of these differences, the arguments to `unlock` is obscure to an attacker because in Java `monitor_enter` and `monitor_exit` are stack operations. Thus it is not possible to statically pattern match on the code to determine if a 0 or a 1 bit is being embedded. Furthermore, it is difficult given the stack operations to determine purely statically which object $mutex_0$ or $mutex_1$ will be on top of the stack when `unlock` is called.

The second of these differences may allow an attacker to pattern match on the conditional statements (⌜`!doneC`⌝ versus ⌜`(doneC || doneD)`⌝ to distinguish between an embedding of 0 and an embedding of 1. To prevent this, we use *opaque predicates* to fold the two different expressions into one. An opaque predicate [3,4] is an expression whose value is known to the watermarker at time of watermarking but which is difficult for the attacker to deduce.

An opaque false predicate is an opaque predicate which is always false whilst an opaque true predicate is one which is always true. We are able to construct a single expression of the form: ⌜`(!doneC &&` X_{opaque} `) || ((doneC &&` Y_{opaque}`)`
`|| (doneD &&` Z_{opaque}`))`⌝

To embed bit 0 as shown in Figure 4a, we set X to be opaquely true and Y and Z to be opaquely false, thus reducing the expression to ⌜`(!doneC)`⌝. Alternately, to embed bit 1 as shown in Figure 4b, we set X to be opaquely false and Y and Z to be opaquely true thus reducing the expression to (doneC || doneD) as required.

The opaque predicates can be selected from a large library of opaque predicates such as described by Collberg et. al. [4] which makes pattern matching or static analysis of this expression useless in distinguishing between an embedding of bit 0 or bit 1.

4.3   Recognition

Watermark recognition involves identifying our original watermark in a possibly tampered piece of code. As discussed in Section 3, in our scheme using dynamic watermarking, recognition involves replaying the watermarked program with key input and decoding the watermark from the threading behaviour of the application.

Watermark recognizers can be broadly classified as "detectors" - those that merely report the presence of a watermark and "extractors" - those that return the encoded value of the watermark. We can build a detector for our watermark by the following method.

First, we extract information about the threading behaviour of the watermarked program. We begin by collecting a trace of its execution on secret input I, using a technique similar the one described in Section 4.1. During detection, we are only interested in the transition from one thread to the next. Therefore given two consecutive tuples in the trace, $(B_i, T_i), (B_{i+1}, T_j)$, we only record a thread ID, T_i if $i \neq j$. This results in $T = <T_0, T_1, ..., T_m>$ which is a list of thread IDs in basic block execution order.

We select every combination of three distinct thread IDs that occur in T and form a subsequence with just these threads. Note that if there are 4 thread

IDs, then we form $\binom{4}{3} = 4$ subsequences. In general, we form $\binom{m}{3} = O(k^3)$ subsequences from a trace T containing m thread IDs. From these subsequences, we then reconstruct all possible 8-bit watermark bytes by extracting all thread-transition sequences of length 24; recall that we embed each bit of an 8-bit watermark code byte as a sequence of three thread-transitions. Our final step is to construct all possible 6-byte sequences, testing whether each of these is a legal codeword. We can quickly test whether each codeword is valid by hash-lookup of a 48-bit possibly-valid code in a table with approximately 16 million (2^{24}) valid 48-bit codes E. The appropriate 24-bit watermark signal W is stored with each valid code.

Two of our three benchmarks are single-threaded, so our extraction process is quite straightforward. During the extraction process on these benchmarks, almost all thread-transitions are due to our watermark, so our error-detection code is not heavily used. Our JFig benchmark is multi-threaded, however, with 7 threads and 47 thread-transitions when it is run on our secret input before watermarking. After watermarking, JFig has a total of 25 threads, because we add three threads for each byte in our 6-byte encoded watermark E. There are $\binom{25}{3} = 2300$ different ways to select three threads from twenty-five threads; only six of these thread-choices will reveal a valid byte from our encoded watermark. All other choices will give spurious signals, and most of these signals cannot be properly sequenced with five other bytes E_i to form a 48-bit possibly-correct codeword E. In our preliminary experimentation (although we are not confident of the correctness of our implementation) our reconstruction process generates less than 100 possible 48-bit codewords E for our watermarked JFig. This is well within the error-detection capacity of our encoding process: we'd estimate a false-extraction error rate of less than $100/2^{24}$ under the reasonable assumption, which has yet to be experimentally verified, that the spurious codewords are uncorrelated with our randomly-chosen encoding scheme.

4.4   Experimental Results

Experiments were performed on three pieces of software: TTT, a trivial tic-tac-toe program; JFig, a figure editor; and SciMark, a Java benchmark. This latter benchmark is a composite benchmark consisting of five computational kernels used for measuring the performance of numerical codes occurring in scientific and engineering applications. The programs were selected for experimentation because they categorize different types of Java programs that may be water-marked. TTT is a small GUI program (64 lines) with one major loop and all but 4 of the lines in the program are executed on our sample input. JFig is a much larger GUI program ($\approx$ 23000 lines) with most lines of code never being executed. The SciMark benchmark ($\approx$ 1300 lines) is a non-GUI application that consists of many tight loops optimized for numerical computations. A significant number of lines (5%) are run more than 50,000 times.

The two GUI programs have no bounds on running time and for our experiments were run for a fixed input. For TTT this consisted of two games of

Execution Frequency		Average Running Time
TTT	4 lines never run	30s
(64 lines)	34 lines run 1 time	
	0 lines run > 100 times	
	0 lines run $> 50,000$ times	
JFig	18678 lines never run	600s
(22,779 lines)	0 lines run 1 time	
	0 lines run > 100 time	
	0 lines run $> 50,000$ times	
SciMark	224 lines never run	26s
(1,279 lines)	105 lines run 1 time	
	146 lines run > 100 times	
	61 lines run $> 50,000$ times	

Table 1. Characteristics of benchmark programs measured on a Pentium(R) 4 - M CPU 2.40GHz running GNU/Linux Java HotSpot(TM) Client VM (build 1.4.2-beta-b19, mixed mode)

tic-tac-toe while for JFig it was the time taken to draw a simple figure. Table 1 summarizes the characteristics of these programs.

We measured the impact of embedding bits of a watermark on the running time of an application. SciMark performs no IO operations after it was started, hence it required no special timing harness.

For the two GUI applications, we used xnee, an X event recorder to record the X events sent to an application. After watermarking the application we replayed the X events and timed the entire procedure.

The original applications were timed 10 times and averaged to calculate initial speed. Following this they were watermarked and run ten times again to record how much they slowed down. The left-hand plot of Figure 7 shows the average slow down that results from embedding a watermark. In each of our ten timed tests the location at which the watermarks are embedded is selected randomly from the basic block trace which is produced during the trace step. It should be noted that although inserting a 48-bit watermark in SciMark results in a very significant slow down with a factor of ≈ 8, real world applications like TTT and JFig which have a GUI and wait for user interaction were observed to have very few time critical loops. For these applications, the resulting slow down was much less noticeable.

We also measured the size overhead of embedding our thread based watermark. The most significant contribution to the increased size of the application was the creation of closures. The right-hand plot of Figure 7 shows that thread based watermarks have a significant impact on the size of the small input application. Each embedding of a watermark bit caused the code size to increase by about 1.2 kilobytes.

5   Attacks

A software pirate attempting to steal a watermarked program may carry out several different attacks to prevent a watermark from remaining recognizable. To

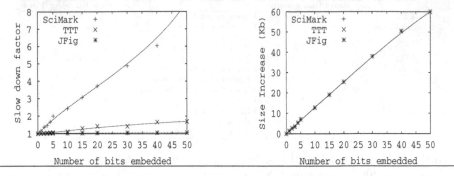

Fig. 7. Slow down of program execution, and Increase in the code size (in kilobytes), as a function of number of watermark bits embedded.

evaluate the resilience of our watermarking scheme we must know how resilient it is to these attacks.

5.1 Obfuscation Attacks

The simplest static attack that may remove a watermark is obfuscations that rename all variables and methods in a program, reorder blocks of code, or restructure data [2]. A more advanced obfuscation technique which attempts to obscure the identity of variables or methods is "inlining" or "outlining". Inlining is a common compiler optimization technique that involves replacing a method call with an instance of the method's body. Similarly, outlining is where a set of instructions is replaced with a call to a method containing those instructions.

Our proposed technique is completely resilient to all of these attacks. This is because the recognition relies on the executed behavior of the program and not on its static structure - and this executed behaviour is preserved by these static attacks.

5.2 Decompilation/Recompilation Attack

An advanced attack is one where the watermarked program is decompiled then recompiled. Decompilation of programs that contain our watermark is difficult because although the watermarked code is legal Java bytecode, the improperly nested monitor calls mean that it cannot be directly expressed in the Java language. In particular, it was found that of the three decompilers tried Jad [10], Homebrew [19] and Dava [12], only Dava successfully handled unnested monitor calls correctly. It uses a library that emulated Java monitors in pure Java. Unfortunately, other errors prevented it from correctly decompiling our watermarked program. Even if an attacker is given a decompiler able to handle unnested monitors, we believe the proposed technique will survive a decompilation attack because the watermark is embedded in the order of execution of threads. This will be maintained by any semantic preserving decompile-recompile transformation. The decompilation attack can be made even more difficult by obfuscating the watermarked program using additional thread switches that are not used for watermark encoding, but which are necessary for program correctness. This can be easily done by introducing straight-line code where one of the two threads executes a subtly different and buggy version of each statement in the original code.

5.3   Additive Attacks

The most potent attack against the proposed technique is one where the attacker succeeds in inserting random thread switches within a watermark piece. Note it is not enough for the attacker to simply insert new threads, or for him to insert new basic blocks such that an existing thread executes it. These types of errors are successfully corrected during our decoding process.

For an attacker to successfully destroy the watermark, they will need to cause at least two of the three threads involved in embedding a bit in a piece to switch. Such an attack need not be stealthy and thus can be achieved simply by inserting a `Thread.yield()` inside a basic block. However, the attacker cannot modify a large number of basic blocks in this way, because this may result in a large slowdown of the program. Alternately, unless an attacker can identify which thread switches are encoding watermarks, they will not know where to insert thread switches.

6   Conclusion

This paper has shown a novel technique for embedding watermarks using multiple threads, locks and thread contention. In particular, we showed how to encode the watermark in preparation for embedding, how to embed a single-bit and multi-bit watermark, and how to recognize the watermark.

Experimental results using an implementation to watermark Java bytecode indicate that the cost of watermarking is relatively small for real world applications. In addition, we looked at several classes of attacks against thread based watermarks, and we have proposed techniques for minimizing the effectiveness of these attacks.

References

[1] Ross J. Anderson, editor. *Tamper Resistant Software: An Implementation*, Cambridge, U.K., May 1996. Springer-Verlag. Lecture Notes in Computer Science, Vol. 1174.

[2] Christian Collberg and Clark Thomborson. Software watermarking: Models and dynamic embeddings. In *Symposium on Principles of Programming Languages*, pages 311–324, 1999.

[3] Christian Collberg, Clark Thomborson, and Douglas Low. A taxonomy of obfuscating transformations. Technical Report 148, Department of Computer Science, University of Auckland, July 1997.

[4] Christian Collberg, Clark Thomborson, and Douglas Low. Manufacturing cheap, resilient, and stealthy opaque constructs. In *Proc. 25th ACM SIGPLAN-SIGACT Symposium on Principles of Programming Languages 1998, POPL'98*, pages 184–196, San Diego, CA (USA), January 1998.

[5] Christian Collberg and Gregg Townsend. Sandmark: Software watermarking for java, 2001. http://www.cs.arizona.edu/sandmark/.

[6] Ingemar Cox and Jean-Paul Linnartz. Some general methods for tampering with watermarks. *IEEE Journal on Selected Areas in Communications*, 16(4):587–593, May 1998.

[7] Robert L. Davidson and Nathan Myhrvold. Method and system for generating and auditing a signature for a computer program. US Patent number 5,559,884, September 24 1996.

[8] Derrick Grover. *The Protection of Computer Software: Its Technology and Applications*, chapter Program Identification. The British Computer Society Monographs in Informatics. Cambridge University Press, second edition, 1992.

[9] Keith Holmes. Computer software protection. US Patent number 5,287,407 , Assignee: International Business Machine, February 1994.

[10] Pavel Kouznetsov. Jad - the fast java decompiler, version 1158e for Linux on Intel platform. Avaliable http://kpdus.tripod.com/jad.html, 5 august, 2001.

[11] Ivan Krsul. Authorship analysis: Identifying the author of a program. Technical Report CSD-TR-94-030, Computer Science Deparment, Purdue University, 1994.

[12] Jerome Miecznikowski. Dava decompiler, part of SOOT, a Java optimization framework, version 7.1.09. Avaliable http://www.sable.mcgill.ca/software/soot/ 17 December, 2003.

[13] Akito Monden, Hajimu Iida, et al. A watermarking method for computer programs (in japanese). In *Proceedings of the 1998 Symposium on Cryptography and Information Security, SCIS'98*. Institute of Electronics, Information and Communication Engineers, January 1998.

[14] Scott A. Moskowitz and Marc Cooperman. Method for stega-cipher protection of computer code. US Patent number 5,745,569, April 28 1998.

[15] Jasvir Nagra, Clark Thomborson, and Christian Collberg. Software watermarking: Protective terminology. In *Proceedings of the ACSC 2002*, 2002.

[16] M. Odersky and P. Wadler. Pizza into Java: Translating theory into practice. In *Proceedings of the 24th ACM Symposium on Principles of Programming Languages (POPL'97), Paris, France*, pages 146–159. ACM Press, New York (NY), USA, 1997.

[17] Rafail Ostrovsky and Oded Goldreich. Comprehensive software system protection. US Patent number 5,123,045, June 16 1992.

[18] John K. Ousterhout. Why threads are a bad idea (for most purposes). Invited Talk at 1996 Usenix Technical Conference, 1996. Slides avaliable at http://www.sunlabs.com/~ouster/.

[19] Peter Ryland. Homebrew decompiler, version 0.2.4. Avaliable http://www.pdr.cx/projects/hbd/, 15 february, 2003.

[20] Tomas Sander and Chrisitan F. Tschudin. Protecting mobile agents against malicious hosts. In *Mobile Agents and Security*, pages 44–60, 1998. Springer-Verlag, Lecture Notes in Computer Science 1419.

[21] Narayanan Shivakumar and Héctor García-Molina. Building a scalable and accurate copy detection mechanism. In *Proceedings of the First ACM International Conference on Digital Libraries DL'96*, Bethesda, MD (USA), 1996.

[22] Julien P. Stern, Gael Hachez, Francois Koeune, and Jean-Jacques Quisquater. Robust object watermarking: Application to code. In Andreas Pfitzmann, editor, *Information Hiding (Proceedings of the Third International Workshop, IH'99), LNCS 1768*, Germany, 2000. Springer.

[23] Ramarathnam Venkatesan, Vijay Vazirani, and Saurabh Sinha. A graph theoretic approach to software watermarking. In *4th International Information Hiding Workshop*, Pittsburgh, PA, April 2001.

Soft IP Protection: Watermarking HDL Codes

Lin Yuan, Pushkin R. Pari, and Gang Qu

Department of Electrical and Computer Engineering
and Institute for Advanced Computer Studies
University of Maryland, College Park, MD 20742
{yuanl,pushkin,gangqu@eng.umd.edu}

Abstract. Intellectual property (IP) reuse based design is one of the most promising techniques to close the so-called design productivity gap. To facilitate better IP reuse, it is desirable to have IPs exchanged in the soft form such as hardware description language (HDL) source codes. However, soft IPs have higher protection requirements than hard IPs and most existing IP protection techniques are not applicable to soft IPs. In this paper, we describe the basic requirements, make the necessary assumptions, and propose several practical schemes for HDL code protection.

We protect the HDL codes by hiding author's signature also called as watermarking, similar to the idea for hard IP and multimedia data protection. But the new challenge is how to embed watermark into HDL source codes, which must be properly documented and synthesizable for reuse. We leverage the unique feature of Verilog HDL design to develop several watermarking techniques. These techniques can protect both new and existing Verilog designs. We watermark SCU-RTL & ISCAS benchmark Verilog circuits, as well as a MP3 decoder. Both original and watermarked designs are implemented on ASICs & FPGAs. The results show that the proposed techniques survive the commercial synthesis tools and cause little design overhead in terms of area/resources, delay and power.

1 Introduction

Design reuse and reuse-based design have become increasingly important and are widely considered as the most efficient way to close the design productivity gap between silicon capacity and designer's ability to integrate circuits onto silicon [27]. For reuse to be successful, the reusable building blocks, also known as macros, cores, intellectual properties (IPs), or virtual components, must be easily accessible and integrable. Several industry organizations such as the San Jose-based "Virtual Socket Interface Alliance", the "design and reuse" in Europe, and "IP highway" in Japan have already started building libraries and tools that can be shared by designers all over the world. More importantly, they are working on the specification of various IP design standards for IP integration. But how to guarantee IP provider's IP rights and royalties remains one of the major obstacles for design reuse.

J. Fridrich (Ed.): IH 2004, LNCS 3200, pp. 224–238, 2004.

IP exchange and reuse normally takes the forms of hard, firm, or soft. Hard IPs, delivered as GDSII files, are optimized for power, size, or performance. Soft IPs are delivered in the form of synthesizable HDL codes. Firm IPs, such as placement of RTL blocks or fully placed netlist, are a compromise between hard and soft IPs [24]. From security point of view, hard IPs are the safest because they are hard to be reverse engineered or modified. But this one-fits-all solution does not give IP users any flexibility other than the built-in configuration options. Soft IPs, on the other hand, are preferred by IP users due to their flexibility of being integrated with other IPs without much physical constraints. On some occasions, IP provider may also prefer releasing soft IPs to leave customer-dependent optimization process to the users. Not surprisingly, it has been recognized that the IP market will be dominated by soft IPs [10]. However, the flexibility makes soft IPs hard to trace and therefore difficult to prevent IP infringements from happening. IP providers are taking a high risk in releasing their IPs in the soft form without protecting their HDL codes with techniques that are effective, robust, low-complexity, and low-cost. Unfortunately, such techniques or tools are not available and their development is challenging.

Most existing VLSI design IP protection mechanisms, such as physical tagging, digital watermarking and fingerprinting, target the protection of hard/firm IPs. Traditional software obfuscating and watermarking methods are not applicable to HDL code either. In this paper, we 1) analyze the challenges in HDL code protection; 2) describe the basic requirements and necessary assumptions; 3) develop the first set of Verilog source code protection methods. Our approaches can be easily integrated with the design process to protect a new design. They can also be applied to protect existing designs, which give IP providers the option of releasing the (protected) source code for their hard/firm IPs that are already in the IP market to make them more competitive.

We propose three watermarking techniques to protect Verilog source code. The first method takes advantage of the don't-care conditions inherently existing in the modules by enforcing them to have specific values corresponding to designer's signature. A separate test module can be easily constructed to retrieve such information. The second one utilizes the fact that many logic units can be implemented in different ways. Instead of using one fixed structure, we build multiple functionally identical modules with different implementations in the same Verilog code. We then selectively instantiate these duplicated modules for information hiding. The third technique splits the implementation of one module into two phases in such a way that designer's signature will be mixed with the module's input and output information. We implement and test the proposed protection schemes on SCU-RTL and ISCAS benchmark circuits using Synopsys' design analyzer and Xilinx FPGA CAD tool. The results show that our watermark survives the synthesis and optimization tools. We measure the area/resources, delay, and power of the designs before and after watermarking, and find that our methods introduce little overhead in these three key aspects.

2   Previous Work

HDL codes describe VLSI design IPs in the style and structure similar to general C/C++ programs. Hence, it is natural to investigate whether the existing design IP protection techniques and software watermarking and obfuscating methods can be extended for HDL code protection.

2.1   VLSI Design IP Protections

According to the IP protection white paper released by VSIA, there are three approaches to secure an IP: **deterrent approach** like patents, copyrights, and trade secrets; **protection** via licensing agreements or encryption; **detection mechanism** such as physical tagging, digital watermarking and fingerprinting [23]. Legal enforcement (copyright, licensing agreement, etc.) can be used to protect HDL codes. But it is always hard to enforce such protection, particularly for the flexible soft IPs. Encryption can be used for soft IP protection [21,22]. But it makes IP reuse inconvenient and there are security holes from which the un-encrypted IP information may leak. Recently, Kahng et al. [8] established principles for constraint-based watermarking techniques in the protection of VLSI design IPs [16,17].

The protection is achieved by tracing unauthorized reuse and making untraceable unauthorized reuse as difficult as re-designing the IP from scratch. The essence of their approach is to introduce watermark-related additional constraints into the input of a black-box design tool such that the design will be rather unique and the embedded watermark can be revealed as proof of authorship. This approach is generic and has been applied to various stages of the VLSI design process, from behavioral and logic synthesis to standard cell place and route algorithms, to FPGA designs [7,8,9,10,11,14].

It is possible, but never easy, to extend the idea of constraint-based watermarking directly into the context of HDL code protection. RT-level HDL source codes normally describe a design in a program-like manner. The constraints are the abstract description of the system's functionality. One can introduce new constraints as watermark. However, any additional constraint at the top abstract level description usually can be easily identified and thus removed or modified. Another concern is the design overhead incurred by adding constraints at this level. If we add constraints at such early stage, it may have large impact to the design quality.

2.2   Software Watermarking and Obfuscating

Watermarking, tamper proofing, and obfuscating are the typical source code protection methods to prevent software piracy [3,2,6,15,19,20]. Watermarking is a technique that embeds a secret message into the program to discourage IP theft by enabling the establishment of IP ownership [5,12]. Tamper-proofing technique protects software from being tampered by making the software with any unauthorized modification into a nonfunctional code. Obfuscating method makes the program "unintelligible" while preserving its correct functionality.

Obfuscating and tamper-proofing techniques are not suitable for HDL code protection. First, they make programs less readable and harder (if not impossible) to modify, which are all against the incentive to release soft IPs for better design reuse. Secondly, the continuous push for HDL design standards reduces the power of such protections.

Software watermarking methods embed a structure or a function into the program such that it can be reliably located and extracted even after the program has been translated, optimized, and obfuscated. Existing software watermarking schemes are either static or dynamic [4]. Static schemes embed watermark only in the executable and are vulnerable to many attacks. HDL program does not have any executables, so this approach cannot be applied. Dynamic watermark is constructed at run time and stored in dynamic state of the program. The quality of a watermarking scheme depends on how well it stands up to different types of attacks and how successfully the watermark can be retrieved.

To sum up, HDL source codes are soft IPs in the form of program. They have more reuse value than hard/firm IPs because of their flexibility and easy accessibility. However, existing hard/firm IP protection techniques cannot be directly used to prevent designers from losing control of their IPs once HDL source codes are released. On the other hand, HDL code is different from other programming languages like C/C++ and Java [1,13,18]. Current software protection is not applicable for HDL code protection due to the following two reasons: 1) design reuse methodology requires HDL code to be developed and documented following industrial standards; 2) there are no executables associated with HDL programs.

3   HDL Code Watermarking Techniques

3.1   Goals and Assumptions

The sole objective of HDL code watermarking is to hide designer's digital information into the HDL source code for ownership protection. However, a good HDL watermarking technique (at RT-level) must also meet the following goals: (1) Strong proof of authorship. (2) Low design overhead. (3) Survivability from re-synthesis. (4) Resilience. (5) Preserve IP's I/O interface.

To achieve the above goals, we make two necessary assumptions:

Documentation Assumption: designer must document the HDL modules properly and give sufficiently detailed information on each reusable module's input, output, and functionality. However, other details on how each module is implemented are not required.

This assumption has been widely accepted in the HDL design community. It is critical for HDL code watermarking. Without this assumption, designers will be forced to document everything including their watermark implementation. This makes watermark visible and further increases the difficulty of watermarking.

Verification Assumption: all HDL design should follow the hierarchical modular fashion and complicated gate-level HDL code should not be mixed with RT-level description.

We focus on the protection of soft IP at HDL source code level and consequently we restrict the watermark verification problem to be within the context of HDL code as well. The verification assumption prohibits the following attack: obtain the gate-level HDL codes for certain modules from the netlist and use them to replace their equivalent modules. We mention that our proposed techniques are robust against the attack of replacing a single RT-level module by its equivalent gate-level code. However, if the attacker constructs a new module by flattening and combining several modules in gate-level code, then the problem of identifying a watermark is equivalent to sub-circuit isomorphism which is NP-hard. The verification assumption requires hierarchical modular design and discourages designs with only a single module. This is not vital to our approach, but rather a common practice in large real life designs. Attackers can verify the functionality of each module, but they cannot afford to extract all the modules from the HDL source code and re-synthesize them and their combinations. In fact, such attempt is more expensive than redesign from the top-level description given in the documentation.

Next, we will use Verilog as the framework to illustrate three HDL code watermarking approaches. We mention that since Verilog share many common features as hierarchical modular design fashion, code documentation and reused-based design with other HDL languages, VHDL for example, we can easily extend the proposed watermarking techniques for the protection of general HDL code.

3.2   Verilog Watermarking Approaches

Module Watermarking: In this method, we extend the concept of constraint-based watermarking to the Verilog design of a module. A module takes certain input signals and produces output based on the logical functionality to be implemented. The input-output relationship, known as truth table, constrains the module's implementation. To embed additional constraints, we take advantage of the don't care conditions inherently existing in the module. Consider the design of an encoder that converts radix-4 numbers into binary. The useful inputs for this module are 0001, 0010, 0100 and 1000, which produce outputs 00, 01, 10 and 11 respectively. The other twelve combinations of the 4-bit input are don't care conditions as they will not occur in the circuit. Now we show how to embed into the design of this encoder a 15-bit stream $b_{14}b_{13}\dots b_1b_0 = 100010010000010$ ('DA' in binary with the last bit as the parity bit). First we order the 12 don't cares in ascending order and make a cyclic list: 0000,0011,0101,,1111. Then we repetitively pick don't cares one- by-one and assign them specific output values to embed the above bit-stream following the algorithm in Figure 1.

More specifically, we take 3, the value of $\lfloor log_2 12 \rfloor$, bits $b_2b_1b_0 = 010$ from the given bit-stream (line 4 and 5). This gives us the binary 2 and we thus select the third (0 offset) don't care 0101 from the list of don't cares. Next we assign a specific value, $00 = b_4b_3$, to this input (line 7) and delete it from the list of don't cares (line 10). Now there are 11 don't cares left and we restart from the top don't care 0110 which is the one after 0101. We repeat this process and assign don't care 1011 output $00=b_9b_8$ and 1101 output $10=b_{14}b_{13}$, where the two don't cares are selected based on $b_7b_6b_5$ and $b_{12}b_{11}b_{10}$. As a result, we implement this encoder based on the watermarked truth table (Figure 2(b)) instead of the original truth table (Figure 2(a)).

Input: cyclic list of n don't cares L, number of output bits m, and bit-stream b_i to be embedded.
Output: list of selected don't cares and their assigned output W.

Algorithm:

1. i = 0; // start with the last bit b0 of the bit-stream
2. j = 0; //start with the top don't care in list L
3. do
4. $s = \lfloor log_2 n \rfloor$; //bits to pick don't care
5. $(d)_{10} = (b_{s+i-1} \ldots b_{i+1}b_i)_2$;
6.   i = s + i; // update the position in the bit-stream
7.   add {the (d+j) (mod n) don't care, its assigned output $b_{m+i-1} \ldots b_{i+1}b_i$} to the output list W;
8.   i = m + i;
9.   j = (d+j+1) mod n;//update the top don't care in list L
10.   delete the (d+j) (mod n) don't care from L;
11.   n = n - 1; // delete the selected don't care from L
12. while (bit-stream embedding not done)

Fig. 1. Pseudo-code for module watermarking with don't cares.

	INPUT	OUT
	1000	00
(a)	0100	01
	0010	10
	0001	11

INPUT	OUT
1000	00
0100	01
0010	10
0001	11
0110	00
1011	00
0000	10

(b)

Fig. 2. (a) Original truth table. (b) Watermarked truth table.

To retrieve the bit-stream, we can conveniently write test module forcing these selected don't cares to be the inputs of the watermarked module. We then use Verilog simulation tools to re-establish the bit-stream from the mapping between the don't cares and their corresponding outputs.

Now we briefly analyze this technique. First, watermark's strength, P_c, can be defined as the probability that a random truth table implementation for the original assigns same values to our selected don't cares. Small P_c indicates strong watermark. Let n be the total number of don't cares in the module, k be the number of don't cares that we choose to embed our watermark and m be the number of output bits. P_c can be roughly estimated as:

$$P_c = \frac{k!.(n-k)!}{n} \cdot (\frac{1}{2})^{m.k} \tag{1}$$

$$k = |b|/(\lfloor log_2 n \rfloor + m) \tag{2}$$

However, to embed b bits information, we must choose at least don't care conditions and give them specific values accordingly. This may introduce design overhead. For example, the original encoder in Figure 2(a) can be implemented by two OR gates and four literals, but the watermarked one needs one NOR gate, one OR gate, one AND gate, and a total of five literals. To reduce this overhead, we break long watermark into multiple short ones and embed them into different modules.

Finally, we mention that this method is robust and it is unique for circuit design protection. To remove or alter the watermark, one need to change the values that we have assigned to the selective don't cares. But, in the final circuit implementation of the design, every input pattern will produce a deterministic output. One cannot distinguish whether this output is the original requirement, or comes from the watermark, or simply a value assigned to a don't care condition during the logic synthesis and minimization.

Module Duplication: Despite the possible overhead, the module watermarking method can be easily implemented before the start of Verilog coding. However, it cannot be applied to protect an existing module in Verilog unless we know all original don't cares and redesign the module. The second approach avoids this problem by duplicating some modules and selectively instantiating either the original module or one of its 'duplicates' to hide information.

In Verilog code, there usually exist basic functional modules that are instantiated multiple times by the top-level module or other modules in a higher hierarchy. The functionality of these modules normally can be implemented in different ways. We thus build duplicates for these modules with a 'different look'. That is, they all perform the same function as the original one but synthesis tools will not identify them as identical copies and therefore they will stay in the final design. The simplest way is by assigning different values to don't cares in the original module every time we duplicate it. In this way, the synthesis tool will not delete the duplicates to optimize the design. In the absence of don't cares, normally we can find alternative implementation for the module. Consider an '1101' pattern detector example which receives one bit input data during each clock cycle. It sets output to be '1' whenever it detects a consecutive inputs pattern '1101'; otherwise, the output is always '0'. This module is implemented in Verilog in two different ways. Module detector_0 in Figure 3(a) uses finite state machine while module detector_1 in Figure 3(b) uses a shift register. However, these two modules are functionally equivalent.

Suppose the detector module has been instantiated multiple times in another module P. Now, with the presence of duplicates, we will have option of which module to instantiate. Instead of instantiating one randomly, we can embed information behind the selection. For example, one scheme is to pick the original Verilog module detector_0 for bit '0' and instantiate module detector_1 for a bit '1'. This is shown in Figure 4 below:

Verifying the signature involves a simple equivalence checking of the module and its duplicates, as well as the evidence of their instantiations. This method provides a strong protection for the Verilog IP as it is highly unusual for an optimized design to have two or more modules that are functionality equivalent. The implementation challenge of this method, however, is how to disguise the duplicates to survive from synthesis. In practice, we have discovered a set of tricks to successfully fool the synthesis tools. One of them, for example, is to assign different values to the same don't care for the original module and its duplicate. The method is robust against attackers who attempt to remove the duplicates or change the module instantiations. Attackers face the (sub-) circuit verification problem and they need to detect the duplicates that have already survived the synthesis optimization tools! Frequent module instantiations in large hierarchical Verilog designs not only provide us a large space for signature embedding, but also make the watermark resilient as we can duplicate modules throughout the design. Another advantage is that it is applicable to existing Verilog codes.

Module Splitting: This approach is usually applied to fairly large modules. It basically splits a large module into several smaller modules. As shown in Figure 5, we use two modules: $\mathcal{A}(X_1, Y_1, Z_1)$ and $\mathcal{B}(X_2, Y_2, Z_2)$, to implement a single-module $\mathcal{M}(X, Y, Z)$, where X is the set of inputs, Y is the set of outputs and Z are optional test outputs. Module splitting is performed as follows:

- First, the watermarking module $\mathcal{A}$ takes input $X_1 \subset X$ and produces 1) part of the functional outputs in $Y_1 \subset Y$, 2) part of the optional test outputs in $Z_1 \subset Z$, and 3) the intermediate watermarking outputs W. W is defined according to our signature on specific input pattern of X_1.
- Next, the correction module $\mathcal{B}$ takes inputs $X_2 \subset W \cup X$ and produces the rest of the required outputs in Y_2 and Z_2. That is, $Y_2 = Y - Y_1$ and $Z_2 = Z - Z_1$.

The above module splitting method is functionally correct because the two modules $\mathcal{A}$ and $\mathcal{B}$ combined to generate signals Y and Z, same as the signals generated by $\mathcal{M}$. To verify the signature, one only needs to feed module $\mathcal{A}$ the input pattern that we define our watermarking signal W, which will be observable from $\mathcal{A}$'s output. To make the watermark robust against both synthesis tools and attackers, we use watermarking signal W from A and as few as possible inputs from X as input for module $\mathcal{B}$. In such way, the watermarking signal W becomes part of the design. Otherwise, they will most likely be removed immediately by

```
module detector_0 (clk, reset, dataIn, out);
    input clk, reset, dataIn;
    output out;
    reg     out;
    reg     [1:0] currentState, nextState;
    always @(dataIn or currentState) begin
        case (currentState)
        2'b00: begin
                    nextState = (dataIn == 1) ? 2'b01 : 2'b00;
                    out = 0;end
        2'b01: begin
                    nextState = (dataIn == 1) ? 2'b10 : 2'b00;
                    out = 0;end
        2'b10: begin
                    nextState = (dataIn == 0) ? 2'b11 : 2'b10;
                    out = 0;end
        2'b11: begin
                    nextState = 2'b00;
                    out = (dataIn == 1);end
        endcase
    end
    always@(posedge clk) begin
        if(~reset) begin
            currentState <= 2'b00;
            out <= 0;
        end
        else currentState <= nextState;
    end
endmodule
```

(a) FSM implementation

```
module detector_1 (clk,reset,dataIn,out);
    input dataIn,clk,reset;
    output out;
    reg out;
    reg [3:0] pattern;
    always@(posedge clk) begin
        if( reset) begin
            pattern = 0;
            out = 0;end
        else begin
            pattern[0]=pattern[1];
            pattern[1]=pattern[2];
            pattern[2]=pattern[3];
            pattern[3]=dataIn;
            if(pattern==4'b1101) out=1;
            else out=0;
        end
    end
endmodule
```

(b) Shift register implementation

Fig. 3. '1101' Patern Detector

```
module P;
    reg clk, reset;
    reg data1,data2,data3;
    wire out1, out2, out3;
    detector_0 d1(clk, reset, data1, out1);// signature bit 0
    detector_1 d2(clk, reset, data2, out2);// signature bit 1
    detector_0 d3(clk, reset, data3, out3);// signature bit 0
    ...        ...        ...
endmodule
```

Fig. 4. Instantiation of module detector

optimization tools. The strength of the watermark relies on the rarity of implementing module $\mathcal{M}$ by constraining the intermediate signal W. Although it is secure as watermark is integrated into the design, we mention that this method may considerably increase design complexity particularly for the second module and will be vulnerable to attacks if the verification assumption is not made.

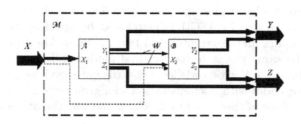

Fig. 5. The idea of module splitting

4 Experimental Results

We apply the proposed techniques to benchmark Verilog circuits and demonstrate that they meet the watermarking objectives. Verilog designs include circuits such as controllers, adders, multipliers, comparators, DSP cores, ALUs (from SCU-RTL and ISCAS benchmarks [26,27], and a MP3 decoder [25]. The MP3 design and SCU-RTL benchmarks [28] are original designs while the RT-level ISCAS Verilog codes are obtained from netlists by reverse engineering [25]. The SCU-RTL and the MP3 benchmarks are perfect examples for the module duplication technique because of the multiple single module instantiations or function calls. The first module watermarking method can also be applied to these designs if the original detailed functional description of each module is available. However, they are not good for the module splitting method because the modules are small. For the ISCAS benchmarks, because they are reversed engineered, we cannot identify the original don't cares and they have only a few modules, almost all of which are instantiated only once. Consequently, both module watermarking and duplication are not applicable for these benchmarks. But we can use module splitting technique to protect these moderate sized modules with known functionality. We are currently developing a set of Verilog designs to test the first module watermarking method, which we are unable to test over these two existing benchmarks due to the unavailability of their original detailed design specifications. We optimize each original design by Synopsys' design analyzer and then map them to the CLASS library. After that, we collect the following design metrics: area, power, and delay through the design analyzer report. Next, we apply the proposed Verilog watermarking techniques to these designs and repeat the above design process for the watermarked design. As we have described, SCU-RTL benchmark is watermarked by module duplication, and ISCAS circuits by module splitting.

After optimization, we can clearly identify from the schematic view in the Synopsys design analyzer window, both the duplicated modules in the module duplication method and the watermark module in the module splitting method. This insures that our watermarks survive the synthesis tools. Figure 6 gives the gate-level views of ISCAS 74181 circuit (a 4-bit ALU) before and after watermarking, where a 9-letter message (corresponding to author's affiliation, hidden for anonymous review) in ASCII is embedded by splitting the CLA module, which has 3 inputs and 4 outputs, into two modules. We document these two modules in the same way as other original modules. To test the watermark's resilience at both the Verilog code level and the gate level, we showed the watermarked Verilog codes with documentation to a group of our colleagues together with Figure6. None of them could tell which one was the original.

Benchmark Circuits		Original	Watermarked	Overhead
FIR	Area (λ^2)	4083	4557	11.6 %
(2264 gates, 16 bits	Power (μ W)	34.49	35.33	2.4 %
embedded)	Delay (ns)	48.7	48.7	0 %
IIR	Area (λ^2)	16419	16431	0.07 %
(15790 gates, 15 bits	Power (μ W)	35.33	35.06	-0.76 %
embedded)	Delay (ns)	49.15	49.15	0 %
IDCT	Area (λ^2)	20755	21271	2.5 %
(17341 gates, 16 bits	Power (μ W)	23.31	23.5	0.8 %
embedded)	Delay (ns)	49.2	49.2	0 %
MP3	Area (λ^2)	16955	17297	4.9 %
(>20000 gates, 20 bits	Power (μ W)	67.49	70.82	2.0 %
embedded)	Delay (ns)	49.15	49.15	0 %

Table 1. Watermarking SCU-RTL & MP3 Verilog benchmark circuit.

Table 1 reports the design overhead on SCU-RTL benchmarks by module duplication. As expected, there is little area overhead due to the duplicated modules. However, the average area overhead is about 4.76% (and this percentage is mainly caused by the small FIR Design). The watermarked design does not introduce any additional delay and consumes only 1% more energy on an average than the original design.

Benchmark Circuits		Original	Watermarked	Overhead
74181	Area (λ^2)	86	94	9.3 %
(61 gates, 56 bits	Power (μ W)	102.41	111.84	9.2 %
embedded)	Delay (ns)	9.26	10.38	12.1 %
C432	Area (λ^2)	176	192	9.1 %
(160 gates, 56 bits	Power (μ W)	230.87	249.89	8.2 %
embedded)	Delay (ns)	20.44	19.63	-4.0%
C499	Area (λ^2)	400	410	2.5 %
(202 gates, 56 bits	Power (μ W)	14.75	11.71	2.5 %
embedded)	Delay (ns)	14.75	11.71	-20.6 %
c1908	Area (λ^2)	574	598	4.1 %
(880 gates, 56 bits	Power (μ W)	581.43	612.47	5.3 %
embedded)	Delay (ns)	21.82	22.54	3.3 %
C7552	Area (λ^2)	4489	4525	0.8 %
(61 gates, 56 bits	Power (μ W)	5778.1	5808.5	0.5 %
embedded)	Delay (ns)	65.57	65.57	0 %

Table 2. Watermarking on ISCAS benchmark circuits.

Table 2 reports the results of watermarking ISCAS benchmarks by module splitting. In this technique, we enforce the watermark into design's functionality. In general, this should cause design overhead. For example, we see that both average area and power overhead are slightly over 5 %. Interestingly, the circuit delay may decrease after watermarking. This might be possible, for example, if we split a module that has a signal on the critical path, this signal may be generated by the simpler watermarking module and thus reduce the delay. From tables 1 and 2, we can see that large design overhead often occurs for small designs (FIR, 74181, and C432). Although it is premature to claim, given the limited set of experiments, we anticipate that all design overhead will decrease for large designs and eventually become negligible for real life designs.

FPGA designs occupy a significant part of the integrated circuit market these days, and our watermarking techniques are easily applicable to them as well. We implement the original and watermarked Verilog benchmarks on certain Xilinx Virtex-II devices. Most of the Verilog code written for ASIC implementation can be synthesized by FPGA synthesis tools with little or no modifications. Some Verilog code had some technology dependent features, such as instantiating some gates from a particular library that could not be mapped to the FPGA devices using our FPGA synthesis tool. Therefore a subset of all the designs was chosen and synthesized using the Xilinx ISE5.1. (This is the reason why in Table 3, the gate counts for the same benchmark increase.) The synthesizable Verilog benchmarks include: the IIR circuit from the SCU-RTL benchmark suite and 74181, C432 and C499 circuits from the ISCAS benchmark suite. These designs are mapped to Xilinx Virtex-II devices and the implementation results show

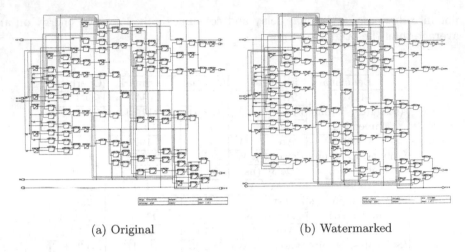

(a) Original   (b) Watermarked

Fig. 6. Gate-level view of circuit 74181

that the embedded watermarks survive synthesis and optimization performed by the design tool. Figure 7 displays the fully placed and routed original and watermarked IIR design on the Xilinx Virtex II FPGA. We have embedded a 15-bit signature in the watermarked Verilog source code. However, it is not easy to locate the watermark by reverse engineering at the chip-level as there is no information available at that level, specific to the watermark.

In FPGAs, the two main design criteria are speed and resource utilization in terms of the number of slices and LUTs used. Table 3 reports the Maximum combinational path delay and resource utilization in both original and watermarked designs generated by the Xilinx tool.

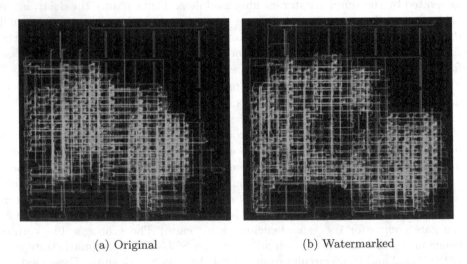

(a) Original   (b) Watermarked

Fig. 7. Floor plan view of IIR targeted to Xilinx Virtex-II.

Benchmark Circuits		Original	Watermarked	Overhead
IIR (27572 gates,	♯ Slices	286	329	18.71 %
15 bits embedded	Max. Path Delay (ns)	11.1	11.1	0 %
C432 (420 gates,	♯Slices	40	44	10.1 %
56 bits embedded	Max. Path Delay (ns)	29.791	29.137	-2.2 %
C499 (696 gates,	♯Slices	67	74	10.45 %
56 bits embedded	Max. Path Delay (ns)	16.326	17.908	9.69 %
74181 (132 gates,	♯Slices	13	13	0 %
56 bits embedded	Max. Path Delay (ns)	13.71	13.71	0 %

Table 3. Benchmarks targeted to Xilinx Virtex-II FPGA.

5   Conclusions

We propose the first set of non-traditional protection mechanisms for soft IPs
(HDL codes). These codes describe circuits at the software level and therefore their protection has different requirements and challenges, from those for
hard/firm VLSI IP or software protection. We use Verilog as the framework and
leverage Verilog's unique role between hardware and software to embed the watermark message into the source code for protection. We evaluate the strength,
resilience, and design overhead of these watermarking techniques both analytically and by simulation over benchmark Verilog circuits available in the public
domain. We demonstrate the applicability of these techniques for FPGA and
ASIC designs and evaluate the overhead. The proposed techniques can be used
to protect both new and existing Verilog designs as well as VHDL designs. We
are currently collecting and building more Verilog and VHDL circuits to test our
approach. We are also planning to develop CAD tools for HDL protection.

References

1. G. Arboit, "A Method for Watermarking Java Programs via Opaque Predicates
   (Extended Abstract)", The Fifth International Conference on Electronic Commerce
   Research (ICECR-5), 2002.
2. C. Collberg and G. Myles and A. Huntwork, "SANDMARK — A Tool for Software
   Protection Research", IEEE Magazine of Security and Privacy, vol. 1, aug, 2003.
3. C.S. Collberg and C. Thomborson, "Watermarking, tamper-proofing, and obfuscation – tools for software protection", IEEE Transactions on Software Engineering,
   Vol. 8, **8**, 2002.
4. C.S. Collberg, C. Thomborson, "Software Watermarking Models and Dynamic Embeddings," ACM Symposium on Principles of Programming Languages, Jan 1999.
5. P. Cousot and R. Cousot, "An Abstract Interpretation-Based Framework for Software Watermarking", ACM Principles of Programming Languages, 2004.
6. R.L. Davidson and N. Myhrvold, "Method and System for Generating and Auditing
   a Signature for a Computer Program", US Patent 5,559,884, Assignee: Microsoft
   Corporation,1996.

7. I. Hong and M. Potkonjak. "Behavioral Synthesis Techniques for Intellectual Property Protection", 36th ACM/IEEE Design Automation Conference Proceedings, pp. 849-854, June 1999.
8. A.B. Kahng, et al.. "Watermarking Techniques for Intellectual Property Protection", 35th ACM/IEEE Design Automation Conference Proceedings, pp. 776-781, June 1998.
9. D. Kirovski, Y. Hwang, M. Potkonjak, and J. Cong. "Intellectual Property Protection by Watermarking Combinational Logic Synthesis Solutions," IEEE/ACM International Conference on Computer Aided Design, pp. 194-198, November 1998.
10. M. Keating and P. Bricaud. "Reuse Methodology Manual, For System-On-A-Chip Designs," Second Edition, 1999.
11. J. Lach, W.H. Mangione-Smith, and M. Potkonjak. "FPGA Fingerprinting Techniques for Protecting Intellectual Property," Proceedings of the IEEE 1998 Custom Integrated Circuits Conference, pp. 299-302, May 1998.
12. G. Myles and C. Collberg, "Software Watermarking Through Register Allocation: Implementation, Analysis, and Attacks", International Conference on Information Security and Cryptology, 2003.
13. A. Monden and H. Iida and K. Matsumoto and K. Inoue and K. Torii, "A practical method for watermarking Java programs", 24th Computer Software and Applications Conference, 2000.
14. A.L. Oliveira. "Robust Techniques for Watermarking Sequential Circuit Designs," 36th ACM/IEEE Design Automation Conference Proceedings, pp. 837-842, June 1999.
15. J. Palsberg and S. Krishnaswamy and M. Kwon and D. Ma and Q. Shao and Y. Zhang, " Experience with Software Watermarking", Proceedings of ACSAC'00, 16th Annual Computer Security Applications Conference, pp. 308-316, 2000.
16. G. Qu and M. Potkonjak, "Analysis of watermarking techniques for graph coloring problem", Proceedings of the 1998 IEEE/ACM international conference on Computer-aided design, pp. 190–193, 1998.
17. G. Qu and M. Potkonjak, "Fingerprinting intellectual property using constraint-addition", Design Automation Conference, pp. 587-592, 2000.
18. J. P. Stern and G. Hachez and F. Koeune and Jean-Jacques Quisquater, "Robust Object watermarking: Application to code", Information Hiding, pp. 368-378, 1999.
19. R. Venkatesan and V. Vazirani and S. Sinha, "A Graph Theoretic Approach to Software Watermarking", 4th International Information Hiding Workshop, Pittsburgh, PA, april, 2001.
20. R. Venkatesan and V. Vazirani, "A Technique For Producing, Through Watermarking, Highly Tamper-Resistant Executable Code And Resulting "Watermarked" Code So Formed", International Patent WO 01/69355 A1, 2001.
21. Altera Corporation. San Jose, California. http://www.altera.com/
22. Xilinx Inc. San Jose, California. http://www.xilinx.com
23. Virtual Socket Interface Alliance. "Intellectual Property Protection White Paper: Schemes, Alternatives and Discussion Version 1.0," September 2000.
24. Virtual Socket Interface Alliance. "Architecture Document Version 1.0," March 1997.
25. http://www.ece.cmu.edu/~ee545/s02/10/fpga_1813.txt
26. http://www.eecs.umich.edu/~jhayes/iscas.
27. International Technology Roadmap for Semiconductors. http://public.itrs.net/Files/2001ITRS/
28. http://www.engr.scu.edu/mourad/benchmark/RTL-Bench.html

An Asymmetric Security Mechanism for Navigation Signals

Markus G. Kuhn

University of Cambridge, Computer Laboratory,
15 JJ Thomson Avenue, Cambridge CB3 0FD, United Kingdom
http://www.cl.cam.ac.uk/~mgk25/

Abstract. Existing navigation services, such as GPS, offer no signal-integrity (anti-spoof) protection for the general public, especially not with systems for remote attestation of location, where an attacker has easy access to the receiver antenna. With predictable broadcast signals, the antenna can be replaced with a signal generator that simulates a signal as it would be received elsewhere. With a symmetrically encrypted broadcast signal, anyone who can build or reverse engineer a receiver will know the secret key needed to spoof other receivers. Such encryption is only of use in closed user communities (e.g., military) or with highly tamper-resistant modules protecting the common key. In open user communities without common secret keys, integrity protection is needed instead, with properties similar to digital signatures. The ability to verify a navigation signal must be separate from the ability to generate a new one or to apply selective-delay attacks; but simply signing the broadcast signals will not protect their exact relative arrival times. This paper introduces a practical solution based on short-term information hiding.

1 Introduction

Alice runs a transport company for high-valued goods. Her armoured lorries are equipped with satellite navigation receivers. These are queried via radio every few minutes by her computer. If one of her lorries deviates from the planned route or loses contact without plausible explanation, she can take action immediately to prevent it being stolen.

Bob runs a prison service. Some of his "clients" live and work outside the prison, but have to remain within a specified area. Others are offenders on probation who must stay outside certain areas or just have their location monitored continuously. Bob attaches a navigation receiver to their ankles and his prison computer queries that via radio (e.g., GSM) several times per hour.

Several such systems for remote attestation of location via the Global Positioning System (GPS) have been fielded, in particular for vehicle tracking [1]. The use of trusted GPS receivers has also been proposed for location-based network authentication [2]. Radio tagging of offenders to control a curfew is now practised

J. Fridrich (Ed.): IH 2004, LNCS 3200, pp. 239–252, 2004.
© Springer-Verlag Berlin Heidelberg 2004

in several countries [3].[1] Other potential applications include road-charging and tachograph systems.

These are examples of security systems that use a navigation-signal receiver as a trusted component. Such a receiver may end up in the hands of an attacker with a strong incentive to manipulate the system such that it reports a *pretended position* **r**′ instead of its *actual position* **r**.

Section 2 below very briefly reviews the operating principles of modern positioning systems, Sect. 3 describes different classes of attacks on trusted positioning receivers, and Sect. 4 reviews briefly the symmetric security mechanisms available to military users of GPS and a technique proposed by Denning and MacDoran [2]. Section 5 then presents a new information-hiding based defense against the selective-delay attack from Sect. 3. Unlike previously proposed techniques, it adds to navigation signals an asymmetric security property known from digital signatures, namely that those able to verify the integrity of an antenna signal are not able to synthesize one that could pass the same verification process. Sect. 6 discusses a variant of the selective-delay attack involving directional antennas and how to defend against it, and Sect. 7 finally illustrates how some of the parameters involved might be chosen in a practical implementation.

2   Conventional Pseudorange Positioning Systems

Modern positioning systems use a number of transmitters X_i located at known coordinates $\mathbf{x}_i \in \mathbb{R}^3$. Each transmitter is equipped with a synchronized clock and knows the exact system time t. A receiver R is located at the coordinates $\mathbf{r} \in \mathbb{R}^3$ (to be determined). If each transmitter X_i broadcasts a navigation signal $s_i(t)$ that propagates through space in all directions with speed c, then we will receive at position $\mathbf{r}$ the signal

$$g(\mathbf{r}, t) = \sum_i A_i \cdot s_i \left(t - \frac{|\mathbf{x}_i - \mathbf{r}|}{c} \right) + n(\mathbf{r}, t) \tag{1}$$

where A_i is the attenuation the signal suffers on its way from X_i to R, and $n(\mathbf{r}, t)$ is background noise (see Fig. 1). With carefully chosen functions $s_i(t)$ (low auto- and cross-correlation, include timestamps and information on transmitter position), the receiver can separate the individual terms of this sum, identify the time delay $|\mathbf{x}_i - \mathbf{r}|/c$ for each and infer from it the "range"

$$d_i = |\mathbf{x}_i - \mathbf{r}| \ . \tag{2}$$

With three known ranges d_i to known transmitter positions $\mathbf{x}_i$, three equations (2) can be solved unambiguously for $\mathbf{r}$ (unless all three $\mathbf{x}_i$ are located on a line).

---

[1] Due to the difficulties of receiving satellite signals indoors, most offender tagging systems still rely on a base station installed in the monitored person's home. However, future global positioning systems with increased transmitter power, lower carrier frequencies and improved receiver technology (e.g., long integration times) may well work reliably enough indoors to be used in such applications.

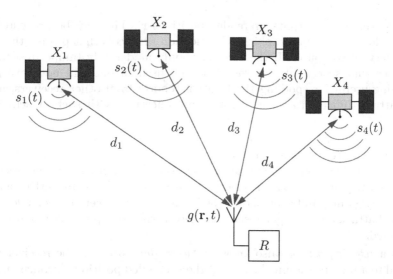

Fig. 1. A pseudorange navigation receiver R works by observing at its position $\mathbf{r}$ the delayed broadcast signals $s_i(t - d_i/c)$ from at least four transmitters X_i. Their relative delays can be used to solve four equations that determine the 3-dimensional position $\mathbf{r}$ and the time t.

Highly stable clocks (e.g., caesium oscillators) are costly and pure receivers cannot participate in two-way clock synchronization. Therefore, in practice, R will only have access to an imprecise estimate $t_R = t + u_R$ of the exact system time t. It therefore receives the signal

$$g(\mathbf{r}, t_R) = \sum_i A_i \cdot s_i \left(t - \frac{|\mathbf{x}_i - \mathbf{r}|}{c} + u_R \right) + n(\mathbf{r}, t_R) \qquad (3)$$

and can infer from the delays $|\mathbf{x}_i - \mathbf{r}|/c - u_R$ only the "pseudoranges"

$$\tilde{d}_i = |\mathbf{x}_i - \mathbf{r}| - c \cdot u_R \ . \qquad (4)$$

The clock error u_R adds a fourth unknown scalar. With pseudorange measurements to at least four transmitters X_i, the resulting system of equations (4) can be solved for both $\mathbf{r}$ and u_R, providing both the exact position and time, without requiring a precise local clock.

3 Attacks on Navigation Receivers

We now consider an attacker of a system for remote attestation of location who has access to its navigation receiver (for example, because it was tied to her ankle following a court order). There are two points to manipulate.

The first is the output of the receiver or the channel over which it reports the position of its antenna. The receiver could be substituted with a device that continuously outputs pretended positions $\mathbf{r}'$. This can be prevented with well-understood cryptographic authentication protocols that protect the link to the querying computer. If the receiver is only moderately tamper-resistant, an attacker who successfully extracts the key used in one will not have gained anything useful for spoofing the location reports from other receivers, making this attack difficult to scale. We are not concerned with such attacks in this paper.

The second point of attack is the navigation antenna, or more generally speaking, the connection of the receiver with the electromagnetic environment specific to its location. An attacker can separate the antenna from the receiver, or equivalently place it into a shielded enclosure along with a transmitting antenna, either way gaining full control over the input of the receiver. This enables several types of attack on a tamper-resistant receiver whose output is cryptographically protected.

In a *relaying attack* (also known as *worm-hole attack*), the receiver is connected to a remote antenna located at the pretended position $\mathbf{r}'$.[2] Such an attack may be logistically complex (arrangements may have to be made to move the remote antenna around in a plausible way) and the remote antenna can easily be located. One possible countermeasure might involve the use of a high-bandwidth signal, to maximize the cost of forwarding it. Another might use a highly stable clock in the receiver, to detect the signal delay introduced by a relaying attack. We are not concerned with relaying attacks in the rest of this paper.

In a *signal-synthesis attack*, the receiver is connected to a device that generates the navigation broadcast signal $g(\mathbf{r}', t)$ as it can be expected to be found at the pretended location. With fully-standardized plaintext broadcast signals, where all aspects of the message format and modulation are publicly known, a modest amount of hardware can simulate the signal to be expected at any point in time and space.

The obvious countermeasure against the signal-synthesis attack is to encrypt the individual broadcast signals $s_i(t)$, such that the attacker cannot predict the waveform $g(\mathbf{r}', t)$ that the receiver needs to see before it can report its position as $\mathbf{r}'$.

Carefully implemented encryption can guarantee the integrity and confidentiality of transmitted data, but this alone is not sufficient in the case of a navigation signal. Here the security-critical aspect of the signals $s_i(t)$ lies not only in the data they carry, but also in their exact relative arrival times at the receiver.

This is exploited in the *selective-delay attack*, in which the attacker uses the signal $g(\mathbf{r}, t)$ received at the actual position $\mathbf{r}$, converts it into a prediction of the signal $g(\mathbf{r}', t - \Delta t)$ that would have been received at the pretended position $\mathbf{r}'$ a short time Δt earlier, and feeds that into the receiver. To accomplish this, the attacker needs to be able to separate the signal $g(\mathbf{r}, t)$ into the individual terms of equation (1), that is

---

[2] for example via a real-time radio link that transmits the entire radio band used by the positioning system, shifted into another band

$$g(\mathbf{r}, t) = \sum_i A_i \cdot g_i(\mathbf{r}, t) + n(\mathbf{r}, t) \tag{5}$$

with

$$g_i(\mathbf{r}, t) = s_i \left(t - \frac{|\mathbf{x}_i - \mathbf{r}|}{c} \right) . \tag{6}$$

This can then be reassembled into

$$g(\mathbf{r}', t - \Delta t) = \sum_i A_i \cdot g_i \left(\mathbf{r}, t + \frac{|\mathbf{x}_i - \mathbf{r}| - |\mathbf{x}_i - \mathbf{r}'|}{c} - \Delta t \right) + n'(t) \tag{7}$$

after choosing

$$\Delta t \geq \max_i \{|\mathbf{x}_i - \mathbf{r}| - |\mathbf{x}_i - \mathbf{r}'|\}/c \tag{8}$$

to preserve causality.[3]

4   Symmetric Security

The 24 orbiting satellites of the GPS constellation emit two separate broadcast signals $s_i(t)$, known as the C/A and Y signals. They both carry the same 50 bit/s data stream. It includes information on the current time and the exact orbital parameters of each satellite, which receivers need to calculate the time-dependent transmitter positions $\mathbf{x}_i(t)$. This data is transmitted using direct-sequence spread-spectrum (DSSS) modulation. The civilian C/A signal is modulated using a relatively short published spreading function. It can therefore not only be demodulated by the general public, but is also vulnerable to a signal-synthesis attack.

The military Y signal is produced by multiplying the 50 bit/s data signal with a secret and very long 10.23 MHz pseudo-random spreading sequence. This not only encrypts the signal like a stream cipher; it also spreads the 100 Hz mainlobe bandwidth of the data signal by a factor of 2×10^5 to 20 MHz. As a consequence, its peak power-spectral density is reduced by the same factor (53 dB) and ends up (according to [4]) roughly 28 dB below the thermal noise density seen by a typical receiver.

The original reason for this design were international regulations that protect microwave telephone links in the same frequency band from interference [4, p. 59]. Various tactical low-probability-of-intercept communication systems use DSSS modulation in a similar way to keep the power-spectral density of the transmission signal below the noise densities at expected eavesdropper sites.

---

[3] If the receiver forwards some unpredictable information received from each of the transmitters (for example their message-authentication codes) in real-time and the querying side has a means to verify these, then this creates another requirement for a selective-delay attack to succeed. At least four of the transmitters visible at the pretended position also have to be visible at the actual position. For GPS satellites (altitude: 20 200 km), this is usually the case within a few thousand kilometers.

In both the time and frequency domain, the Y signal disappears in the noise. Someone trying to manipulate the GPS Y code will therefore find it difficult to split $g(\mathbf{r}, t)$ up as in equation (5). As the shape of the waveforms is not known, correlation techniques cannot be applied to extract the phase of the Y signal from the noise.

It would therefore be very difficult to apply even a selective-delay attack on a GPS Y signal received with an omnidirectional antenna. The only option left to an attacker is to separate individual transmitters by using high-gain antennas. The use of at least four tracking dish antennas or a phased array may be feasible in some particularly well-funded attacks, but in most situations we would expect an attacker to be mobile and only be able to operate an omnidirectional antenna to capture $g(\mathbf{r}, t)$.

The problem with the GPS Y signal is of course that, since it is based on a single secret key, anyone in its possession can not only decode the Y signal to determine their position, but is also able to perform a signal-synthesis attack on any other Y-signal receiver. As a result, encrypted spread-spectrum navigation signals are so far used only in closed, mutually trusting user communities, in the case of the GPS Y signal the US military.

Another protection against signal-synthesis attacks has been proposed by Denning and MacDoran [2]. Their "location signature sensor" not only decodes the GPS C/A navigation signal in order to report its position to a remote authentication peer. It also detects and records a number of unpredictable attributes of the GPS signal, for example the clock noise added by the selective availability (SA) function of GPS to reduce the quality of service to the general public, as well as short-term fluctuations in the relative orbital positions that are not reported in the broadcast data. As long as the location signature sensors at both ends of the authenticated communication can see the same satellites, they can convince each other of being within a few thousand kilometers.

Again, this system only provides symmetric authentication and anyone able to verify the output of a location signature sensor in a geographical region will also be able to fake the output of such a sensor from anywhere within the same region.

5   Asymmetric Security

We now describe a new navigation-signal scheme that offers protection against signal-synthesis and selective-delay attacks comparable to that of an encrypted broadcast signal, that is one where the spreading sequence is a shared secret. However, the new scheme described in this section achieves this protection without the need to distribute and share any long-term secret keys among receivers. There is no information available to any receiver that would enable it to attack others. This approach is therefore particularly suited for open, international, civilian applications, where receivers are available in many forms to the general public and where some deployed receivers can be expected to be reverse engineered successfully by potential attackers.

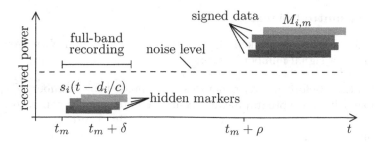

Fig. 2. In the proposed navigation-signal structure, first each transmitter X_i emits simultaneously from time t_m to $t_m + \delta$ its *hidden marker* $s_i(t)$. These pseudo-random waveforms overlap in the time and frequency domain. Their power is reduced significantly below the receiver noise level. The waveforms $s_i(t)$ are kept secret until time $t_m + \rho$ (typically a few seconds later). Then, signed information packets $M_{i,m}$ that describe the hidden markers are broadcast at normal power. Only after receiving these can receivers separate the markers from the recorded radio signal and determine their exact arrival times by detecting peaks in the cross-correlation function.

5.1   Hidden Markers

At regular preannounced times $t_1, t_2, \ldots$, for example every few seconds (or fractions thereof), all transmitters in the navigation system broadcast what we will call a *hidden marker*. We will discuss here only the transmission of hidden marker number m in this series, starting at system time t_m, understanding that this entire process will be repeated soon afterwards, starting at another time t_{m+1}, and so on.

The hidden marker is a rectangular pulse of duration δ, broadcast with DSSS modulation using a previously unpublished spreading sequence. Its power-spectral density is chosen such that it is at least 20 dB below the thermal noise when it arrives at the receiver. At the time at which this marker is transmitted, all the receivers and attackers can do is to digitize and buffer the entire antenna signal (filtered to the transmission band). This preserves in each receiver the information about the exact arrival time of the hidden marker, but it cannot be accessed yet. To determine this arrival time, the recorded noise has to be cross-correlated with the spreading sequence, in order to despread the marker and recover it from the noise.

However, the necessary information about the spreading sequence is not yet available at that time to any receiver. It is broadcast only after a delay ρ. Once this has been received, both regular receivers and attackers can identify and separate the markers in the recorded antenna signal. But any signal-synthesis or selective-delay attack can now be performed only with a delay $\Delta t > \rho$. By choosing ρ large enough, we can ensure that this delay can easily be detected by any receiver, even using an only loosely synchronized low-cost crystal clock. See also Fig. 2.

5.2   Transmitted Signal

In more detail, the steps taken at each broadcasting station X_i to generate the hidden-marker signal number m are:

1. Some time before t_m, X_i generates an unpredictable number $N_{i,m}$, for example using a cryptographically secure random-number generator.
2. This $N_{i,m}$ is used to seed a cryptographically secure pseudorandom bit-sequence generator $P(N_{i,m}, j) \in \{-1, +1\}$ that outputs a sequence of bits with indices $j = \{0, 1, 2, \ldots\}$.
3. From time t_m to $t_m + \delta$, X_i transmits the hidden marker, a sinusoidal carrier wave that is multiplied with the output of the seeded pseudorandom-bit generator, in order to spread its frequency spectrum[4]:

$$s_i(t) = A \cdot \sin[2\pi f_c \cdot (t - t_m)] \cdot P(N_{i,m}, \lfloor f_s \cdot (t - t_m) \rfloor), \quad t_m \leq t < t_m + \delta \quad (9)$$

Here f_c is the chosen center frequency of the resulting signal and f_s is the bit rate of the spreading sequence, which is equivalent to half the mainlobe bandwidth of the resulting spectral power-density distribution

$$|S(f)|^2 = (A/f_s)^2 \cdot \frac{\sin^2[\pi(f - f_c)/f_s]}{[\pi(f - f_c)/f_s]^2} \quad (10)$$

The parameters t_m, f_c and f_s are identical for all transmitters (in other words, this is CDMA, not FDMA or TDMA), and the amplitude A is chosen low enough to bring the received signal well below the noise level.

4. At time $t_m + \rho$ (where $\rho \gg \delta$), X_i broadcasts a data packet of the form

$$M_{i,m} = \text{Sign}_{K^{-1}}[t_m, X_i, \mathbf{x}_i(t_m), N_{i,m}] \quad , \quad (11)$$

which is a message that is cryptographically signed with the private key K^{-1} of the navigation system and that reveals a full description of the previously transmitted hidden marker, including its transmission time t_m, the identifier X_i and exact location $\mathbf{x}_i(t_m)$ of the transmitter, and finally the unpredictable number $N_{i,m}$ used by that transmitter to spread the spectrum of this particular marker signal. Parts of this message may be transmitted earlier, as long as no information about $N_{i,m}$ is revealed until the nonce-release time $t_m + \rho$ has been reached.

5.3   Verification at the Receiver

By going through the following steps, each receiver R can use the hidden marker scheme to determine its position in a way that is robust against signal-synthesis and selective-delay attacks:

---

[4] We use here binary phase-shift keying (BPSK) to modulate the hidden marker signal, but many other modulation schemes could be used equally, including the binary offset carrier (BOC) modulation techniques used in some more recent navigation systems.

1. The implementation of the receiver's local clock $t_R(t)$ must not be influenced in any way by information received through navigation signals. We assume that it has a known maximum relative frequency error ε_f, such that

$$\left| \frac{t_R(t + \tau) - t_R(t)}{\tau} \right| \leq \varepsilon_f \;.$$

We also assume that t_R was last adjusted by an authenticated two-way clock synchronization from a trusted source at system time $\hat{t}$ such that $|t_R(\hat{t}) - \hat{t}| \leq \varepsilon_s$. The error $u_R(t)$ of the local clock $t_R(t)$ is then bounded by

$$|u_R(t)| \leq \varepsilon_f \cdot (t - \hat{t}) + \varepsilon_s, \quad \text{for } t \geq \hat{t} \;. \tag{12}$$

Simple crystal oscillators offer $\varepsilon_f < 10^{-5}$ and authenticated two-way clock synchronization over wireless computer networks usually offers $\varepsilon_s < 100$ ms.

2. During a time interval slightly larger than $[t_m, t_m + \delta]$, the receiver digitizes the entire frequency band $[f_c - f_s, f_c + f_s]$ with a sampling rate of at least $4f_s$ and stores it in a RAM buffer $B(t_R)$.

3. It then waits for the arrival of the broadcast messages $M_{i,m}$ and discards those whose signature cannot be verified using the navigation system's well-known public key K or whose marker time t_m does not match the marker time for which the receiver initiated the wide-band recording in the previous step.

4. For each $N_{i,m}$ extracted from a message $M_{i,m}$ that passed these checks, the receiver now generates the spreading sequence $s_i(t_R)$ from equation (9). These are then cross-correlated with the RAM buffer B^5:

$$C_{i,m}(\tau) = \int_t B(t) \cdot s_i(t + \tau)\, \mathrm{d}t \tag{13}$$

5. For each cross-correlation result $C_{i,m}$, the position $\hat{\tau}_{i,m}$ of the largest peak in it is recorded, together with the relative amplitude $w_{i,m}$ of any second-largest peak.

6. Of the recorded tuples $(i, \hat{\tau}_{i,m}, w_{i,m})$ the receiver now discards all where the second-largest peak is not attenuated by at least a configurable security factor W relative to the largest peak. (The reason for this step will become clear in Sect. 6.)

7. The remaining peak-positions $\hat{\tau}_{i,m}$ are then used as pseudoranges

$$\tilde{d}_i = c \cdot \hat{\tau}_{i,m} = |\mathbf{x}_i - \mathbf{r}| - c \cdot u_R \tag{14}$$

and the resulting set of equations, which use the received digitally signed transmitter positions $\mathbf{x}_i$, is solved for $\mathbf{r}$ and u_R.

8. The result is accepted, if the u_R value remains within the clock uncertainty allowed by inequality (12) and is smaller than the time delay ρ for the publication of the spreading-sequence seed values.

---

[5] In a practical implementation, recording and cross-correlating the hidden marker may be done after conversion from f_c down to a lower intermediate frequency.

This scheme utilizes the fact that there are now low-cost analog-to-digital converters available, with sampling rates of more than 100 MHz. This, together with falling RAM prices, has made it feasible to record in battery-operated low-cost devices at an intermediate frequency of up to 50 MHz for several seconds entire RF bands that are 20 MHz or more wide, as they are occupied by the GPS Y signal.

5.4   Optimized Broadcast Data

Existing navigation systems operate with comparatively low bit rates for the transmission of data (e.g., 50 bit/s for GPS). Therefore, a concern may be the length of the cryptographically authenticated message $M_{i,m}$, which releases the number $N_{i,m}$ and binds it securely to the transmission parameters of the corresponding hidden marker. A digital signature alone consists of several hundred bits, so the length of $M_{i,m}$ might become a limiting factor for the rate at which hidden markers can be transmitted. Fortunately, there are several optimizations of the scheme possible, which reduce the required bit rate.

The individual messages $M_{i,m}$ can be consolidated into a single system-wide message M_m. In particular, M_m could contain only a single unpredictable number N_m, from which then the individual seed numbers $N_{i,m} = g(N_m, i)$ can be derived in a predictable way. The function g could be something as simple as addition. Individual transmitters can also vary the order in which they transmit the elements of M_m, such that receivers can compile the complete M_m faster from the parallel reception of several transmitters than from listening to merely a single one.

Instead of including N_m in M_m as a separate data field, it could also be derived from M_m's digital signature, which is already unpredictable. The transmitters would then have to commit to the content of M_m before time t_m is reached, and would lose their ability to update position and time using the latest measurements, in return for eliminating the need to transmit N_m. Where the values of t_m and $\mathbf{x}(t_m)$ can be predicted well in advance, only the marker serial number m itself needs to be signed in each M_m. The parameters for predicting t_m and $\mathbf{x}(t_m)$ from m can then be broadcast as a separate message much less frequently.

Alternatively, it is also possible to avoid the addition of a digital signature to each M_m entirely by using a symmetric *stream-authentication method*, such as the one proposed in [5]. Such schemes operate on a principle very similar to the hidden-marker system presented here. They replace the digital signature with a symmetric message-authentication code, and release the – for the receiver unpredictable – authentication key only after a delay (equivalent to ρ above) that is longer than the clock uncertainty of the receiver. Only the first message in such a stream needs to be digitally signed. The message-authentication keys used in all further packets are derived from their respective successor, using a secure one-way function. They can therefore be verified from their respective predecessor, as soon as they are released.

If we used a standard stream-authentication method, such as [5], directly to protect the messages M_m, the authenticity of the hidden marker could only be verified after *two* delay periods ρ, one to protect N_m and the other to protect the message-authentication key. This problem can be avoided by eliminating the message-authentication code, and instead making all the values N_m directly parts of a one-way chain.

In more detail, here is how we can combine the hidden markers number $m_0, m_0 + 1, \ldots, m_0 + n$ into a single marker stream that requires only one single digital signature:

1. The transmitters pick at random an unpredictable final number N_{m_0+n} for the stream, and then generate a number N_m for each of the n previous markers, via the recursion $N_m = h(N_{m+1})$ (for $m_0 \leq m < m_0 + n$). This way, the first number will be $N_{m_0} = h^n(N_{m_0+n})$. Here, h is a secure one-way function, that is a function for which, given a value y, it is computationally infeasible to find a preimage x with $h(x) = y$.

2. The transmitters then broadcast some time before t_{m_0} the message

$$M_{m_0} = \text{Sign}_{K^{-1}} [m_0, h(N_{m_0}), D] \quad , \tag{15}$$

where D is a parameter set that describes how the values t_m and $\mathbf{x}_i(t_m)$ can be calculated from a given station number i and marker number m.

3. Finally, the transmitters broadcast from time t_m to $t_m + \delta$ their respective hidden markers, generated from $N_{i,m} = g(N_m, i)$, and they broadcast at time $t_m + \rho$ the message N_m, and this for each $m \in \{m_0, \ldots, m_0 + n\}$, as described in Sect. 5.2.

The receivers follow the same steps as described in Sect. 5.3, except that a digital signature is now verified only for the first message M_{m_0} in each stream. The subsequently released value N_{m_0} is verified against the signed value $h(N_{m_0})$ in M_{m_0}. All the subsequently released values N_m (for $m_0 < m \leq m_0 + n$) are then verified with the test $h(N_m) = N_{m-1}$. The parameters t_m and $\mathbf{x}_i(t_m)$ are calculated from the signed parameter set D (which in a satellite navigation system, for example, would include the orbital parameters).

This way, apart from the signed message M_{m_0} that precedes a stream of $n+1$ consecutive markers, only a single number N_m needs to be broadcast per marker. It will not have to be longer than 60–80 bits in practice, just enough bits to make a brute-force inversion of h infeasible within the time interval $t_{m+1} - t_m$.

The length $n + 1$ of these marker streams is limited by the requirement that newly activated receivers, and those that missed one of the values N_m, should not have to wait long until they can restart the authentication chain with the start of a new stream.

6   Selective-Delay Using High-Gain Antennas

There is an alternative way of separating the right side of equation (5) into the terms contributed by the individual transmitters, which does not depend on knowing the spreading functions. If the approximate positions of transmitters are predictable, at least four of them can be targeted with directional antennas.

If the gain of these antennas is high enough to lift the broadcast signals out of the background noise, demodulation and threshold operations can be applied in order to free the signal of one station completely from any interference by the others, enabling a selective-delay attack that cannot be detected. The only protection against this attack appears to be to keep the signal strength enough below the noise limit to require antennas so large that their use during a practical attack becomes infeasible.

If the signal-to-noise ratio achievable with directional antennas is not sufficient for separating and decoding the signals directly, then the attacker can still delay the raw antenna signals and mix them together for the receiver. In practice, no directional antenna will be able to suppress the signals from all other transmitters completely. This will cause weaker shadow peaks to show up in the cross-correlation results for each transmitter station, picked up and contributed by an antenna pointing to another station, at the relative delay applied there. The security parameter W in the receiver algorithm from the previous section defines, how sensitively the receiver should react to such shadow peaks. This sensitivity could be made dependent on the distance in time from the main peak, such that a selective-delay attack with directional antennas is not confused with secondary peaks caused by plausible multi-path propagation.

7   Example Parameters

The technique presented in Sect. 5 is particularly suited for navigation systems that transmit from medium-earth-orbit (MEO) satellites, such as GPS, Glonass or Galileo. In this setting, there are clear lower and upper bounds for the ranges between receivers and visible transmitters (e.g., 20 000–26 000 km for GPS), which helps to ensure a uniform received signal strength, at least outdoors. The transmitters also move fast enough to complicate the use of directional antennas. For other types of pseudo-range navigation systems, such as land-based long-wave transmitters (e.g., LORAN-C) or short-range ultrasonic or ultra-wideband-radio positioning systems, more complex schemes may be needed that involve hidden markers broadcast at a wide range of power levels.

The security of the scheme is based on the assumption that at any receiver position, the time intervals during which hidden markers arrive from the various transmitters will overlap substantially. With MEO transmitters, ranges can vary by up to 6000 km. This corresponds to 20 light milliseconds, and the duration of the hidden marker will have to be at least one or two orders of magnitude longer than that. A typical value may be $\delta = 1$ s.

We need to chose the signal strength, such that a clear peak appears after the cross-correlation with the correct spreading sequence in a receiver, while keeping on the other hand the power spectral density of the broadcast signal well below thermal noise. Integrating during a cross-correlation for an entire second is roughly equivalent to filtering the noise bandwidth of a signal down to 1 Hz.

As a very simple example, if we quantify (pessimistically) the thermal background noise to be expected by a receiver with an equivalent antenna temperature of 290 K (including atmospheric noise, cosmic background radiation, antenna temperature noise, transmission line losses, amplifier noise [4,6]), this corresponds (after multiplication with the cross-correlation bandwidth of 1 Hz and Boltzmann's constant) to a noise power level of about -204 dBW. If the transmission power of each hidden marker is selected such that about -170 dBW reach the receiver, then the 34 dB signal-to-noise ratio obtained this way ensures that spurious peaks in the cross-correlation output caused by noise will remain much smaller than the peak caused by the hidden marker.

If we use, as the GPS Y-code does, a spreading frequency of $f_s = 10$ MHz, then an attacker who does not know yet the spreading sequence will have to work with the full 20 MHz mainlobe bandwidth of the broadcast signal. Even with a much better omnidirectional antenna, with an equivalent noise temperature of only 100 K, this still leaves -136 dBW received noise power, which is 34 dB above the signal energy and therefore will render the broadcast signal unrecognizable.

A 20 MHz wide intermediate frequency signal can be recorded comfortably with a sampling frequency of 200 MHz. With a signal-to-noise ratio of -34 dB, there is little point in storing more than one or two bits per sample after analog-to-digital conversion, as the quantization noise would still be small compared to the thermal noise. Therefore, the entire hidden marker can be practically stored in not more than 25 MB of RAM.

The choice for the delay time ρ after which the information about the spreading sequence is released depends on how frequently a receiver is assumed to get in contact with a trusted source of the system time t, and how stable its local clock is. If we take as an example a maximum time between resynchronizations of $t - \hat{t} < 1$ week, a local clock frequency error of $\varepsilon_f < 10^{-5}$, and a synchronization error of $\varepsilon_s < 1$ s, then from equation (12), $\rho = 10$ s $> u_R$ would appear to be a suitable choice. Where no single value for ρ can be found that suits all applications, it is possible to broadcast hidden markers with a range of different time delays.

8   Conclusions

This paper considered an aspect of the security of pseudoranging positioning systems, such as GPS, namely how a receiver can be misled about the position of its antenna if an attacker is allowed to insert a signal-manipulation device between the receiver and the antenna. We have shown that positioning systems currently offer no defense against signal-synthesis or selective-delay attacks without the receiver obtaining all the information necessary to mount these attacks on others.

We outlined a new signal structure and the corresponding verification algorithm for receivers that solves this problem. A weak spread-spectrum broadcast signal is temporarily hidden in background noise while receivers buffer the entire radio band in RAM. The despreading key is only published after a time that is larger than the uncertainty of the local clock in the receiver, at which time both a signal-synthesis and a selective-delay attack can easily be detected. Such keys can be authenticated efficiently by making them part of a one-way chain.

The system is still based on the pseudoranging principle and uses only a low-cost local clock in the receiver. It can therefore still be defeated by relaying attacks. Against these, we see no solution other than using a more expensive highly-stable oscillator in the receiver, or using authenticated two-way ranging, both of which would be able to detect the added delay.

The system is also vulnerable to selective-delay attacks involving at least four high-gain directional antennas. A security parameter that limits the height of shadow peaks in the cross-correlation result can be used to control the minimum antenna gain needed for this attack to succeed, thereby limiting its practicality.

References

1. Paul Kallender: Omron uses GPS to catch a car thief. EE Times, 12 June 2001.
   http://www.eetimes.com/at/news/OEG20010612S0059
2. Dorothy E. Denning, Peter F. MacDoran: Location-based authentication: Grounding cyberspace for better security. Computer Fraud & Security, Elsevier, February 1996, pp. 12–16.
   http://www.cosc.georgetown.edu/~denning/infosec/Grounding.txt
3. Electronic tagging: A virtual prison? BBC News Online, 7 January, 2000.
   http://news.bbc.co.uk/1/hi/special_report/1999/02/99/e-cyclopedia/594314.stm
4. J.J. Spilker Jr.: GPS signal structure and theoretical performance. In B.W. Parkinson and J.J. Spilker Jr.: Global Positioning System: Theory and Applications – Volume I, Progress in Astronautics and Aeronautics, Volume 163, American Institute of Aeronautics and Astronautics, Washington DC, 1996, ISBN 1-56347-106-X.
5. Adrian Perrig, Ran Canetti, J.D. Tygar, Dawn Song: The TESLA broadcast authentication protocol. CryptoBytes, Vol. 5, No. 2, pp. 2–13, RSA Laboratories, Summer/Fall 2002.
6. Radio noise. Recommendation ITU-R P.372-7, International Telecommunication Union, Geneva, 2001.

Analysis of COT-based Fingerprinting Schemes: New Approach to Design Practical and Secure Fingerprinting Scheme*

Jae-Gwi Choi[1], Ji-Hwan Park[1], and Ki-Ryong Kwon[2]

[1] Department of Information Security, Pukyong National University. 599-1 Daeyeon-dong
Nam-ku Busan, 608-810, Korea
jae@mail1.pknu.ac.kr, jpark@pknu.ac.kr
[2] Department of Electronic and Computer Engineering, Pusan University of Foreign Studies,
55-1 Uam-dong Nam-ku Busan, 608-738, Korea
krkwon@taejo.pufs.ac.kr

Abstract. Digital fingerprinting schemes deter people from illegal copying of digital contents by enabling the seller to identify the original buyer of a copy that was redistributed illegally. What is important in designing fingerprinting scheme is to make it more practical and efficient. However, the complexity of existing schemes is too high to be implementable. Recently, oblivious transfer protocol-based schemes to consider practicality were proposed. These are significant in the sense that there are completely specified from a computation point of view and are thus readily implementable. But these schemes have the serious problem that they cannot offer the security of sellers and buyers. In this paper, we first show how to break the existing oblivious transfer-based fingerprinting schemes and then suggest how to make secure fingerprinting schemes against the dishonesty of a sellers and buyers. We use oblivious transfer protocol with two–lock cryptosystem to make it practical and secure. All computations are performed efficiently and the security degree is strengthened in our proposal.

1 Introduction

Digital fingerprinting schemes are cryptographic methods deterring buyers from illegally redistributing digital contents. It enables sellers to identify the traitor / copyright violator by providing each buyer with a slightly different version.

Classical Fingerprinting protocol [GCG86][Ne83] is symmetrical in the sense that the seller knows the fingerprint with the buyer. Thus, if another copy with this fingerprint turns up, one cannot really assign responsibility about redistribution to one of them. This problem is overcome by asymmetric protocol [PS96]. Here, because only the buyer can obtain the exact fingerprinted copy, if an unauthorized copy is found, the

---

* This work is partly supported by grant No.01-2002-000-00589-0 from the Basic Research Program of the Korea Science & Engineering Foundation and by University IT Research Center Project, MIC, Korea.

J. Fridrich (Ed.): IH 2004, LNCS 3200, pp. 253-265, 2004.

seller can obtain a means to prove to a third party that the buyer redistributed it and he can identify a traitor. However the drawback of this solution is that it did not provide a buyer's anonymity. To protect buyer's privacy [PW97] has been suggested. The idea is that the seller can know neither the fingerprinted contents nor the buyer's real identity. Nevertheless the seller can identify the traitor later. This possibility of identification will only exist for a traitor, whereas honest buyers will remain anonymous.

Requirements of anonymous fingerprinting schemes can be listed as follows [PW97]:

1. **Anonymity**: A buyer should be able to purchase digital contents anonymously.
2. **Unlinkability**: Given two digital contents, nobody can decide whether or not these two contents were purchased by the same buyer.
3. **Traceability**: The buyer who has distributed digital contents illegally can be traced.
4. **No Framing (Buyer's security)**: An honest buyer should not be falsely accused by a malicious seller or other buyers.
5. **No Repudiation (Seller's security)**: The buyer accused of redistributing an unauthorized copy should not be able to claim that the copy was created by the seller.
6. **Collusion Tolerance**: Attacker should not be able to find, generate, or delete the fingerprint by comparing the copies, even if they have access to a certain number of copies.
7. **Practicality[1]**: All computations should be performed efficiently so that it can be readily implementable.

The most important point of designing anonymous fingerprinting scheme is to make it more practical and efficient. [Do99] scheme based on committed oblivious transfer from fingerprinting (fingerprinting step) point of view and [PS00] scheme based on digital coin from registration and identification point of view were highly valued among existing schemes.

The first proposal to pay attention to practical fingerprinting scheme was [Do98][2][Do99] scheme. The previous scheme [PW97] is inefficient and impractical because it is based on secure two-party computations [CDG87] (It uses general theorems like "every NP-language has a zero-knowledge proof system" without presenting explicit protocols) with high complexity. On the contrary, [Do99] scheme is based on the committed oblivious transfer (COT) that is completely specified from a computational point of view and is thus readily implementable. But it is pointed out that it allows the seller to cheat honest buyers [Sa01]. Later, [Sa01] made several constructive proposals to repair some flaws of [Do99] scheme and [PS00] suggested an efficient method without secure two party computations, which is based on the

---

[1] Note that we add practicality to the requirement of anonymous fingerprinting scheme from [PW97]

[2] In [Do98], an anonymous fingerprinting algorithm is proposed which avoids secure multiparty computation and is based on 1-out-of −2 oblivious transfer. However, this approach also relies on a unspecified general zero-knowledge proof.

principles of digital coins. But [Sa01] scheme also has security problems that buyers and sellers can cheat each other. We prove it clearly in the section 2.

[PS00] scheme is also impractical because it uses [BS95] code as a building block for collusion resistance. In [BS95] scheme, their code needed for embedding is so long that the overall system cannot be practical. High complexity fingerprinting step also remains unsettled in [PS00].

1.1 Our Contribution

In this paper, we propose a practical and secure anonymous fingerprinting scheme based on the oblivious transfer (OT) with two-lock cryptosystem. We first show the shortcomings of the previous schemes [Do99][Sa01] based on the COT. Then we show how to solve their security problems and improve their computational complexity. As a result, our proposal brings anonymous fingerprinting far nearer to practicality. We compare the features of our proposal with the previous schemes in Table 1.

Table 1. Comparison of our proposal with the previous schemes

Features	[Do99]	[PS00]	[Sa01]	Our Proposal
Anonymity	Offer	Offer	Offer	Offer
No Framing	No Offer	Offer	No Offer	Offer
No Repudiation	No Offer	Offer	No Offer	Offer
Collusion Tolerance	No Offer	Offer	No Offer	Offer
Participators of the Identification	All buyers, Seller, Registration Center	Seller, Registration Center	All buyers, Seller, Registration Center	Seller, Registration Center
Methodology	COT*	Digital Coin	COT	OT*

* COT/OT: Committed Oblivious Transfer/ Oblivious Transfer with Two-lock Cryptosystem

The most undesirable issue of [Do99][Sa01] schemes is that they do not offer the security of buyer and seller (No Framing and No Repudiation) because the seller can know the buyer's fingerprint if he abuses flows of COT in the [Do99] scheme, or buyers can know both versions of contents' each bit in the [Sa01] scheme. On the contrary, our proposal offers the security of buyer and seller even if it is based on OT protocol.

[Do99] scheme does not offer collusion-tolerance that is an important property a fingerprinting scheme should possess and [Sa01] also does not solve this problem. In fact, [Do99] introduced the approach to use tamper-proof device such as smart card to provide collusion-tolerance. But [Do99] just sketched it and leaves some problems such that the buyer and the seller have complete trust in the smart card and this is difficult to justify because the tamper-resistance of smart cards provide only limited security [Sa01]. [Sa01] just pointed out problems of [Do99] and did not suggest any solutions. So we describe that collusion-tolerance in the two schemes was not offered.

A further critical problem in [Do99] is that during the identification step the seller must contact all buyers (This problem has reported in the [Sa01] scheme, but [Sa01] has not suggested its solution).

[PS00] scheme and our scheme offer collusion-tolerance but [PS00] scheme has the problem that the length of code used is too long (the code needed for embedding is so long that the overall system cannot be called practical). On the other hand, our scheme uses Cox's scheme [CK97] for collusion-tolerance that is estimated to be highly resistant to collusion attacks [KT98]. The most meaningful feature of our scheme is practicality. Since we remove interaction between the buyer and the seller in the fingerprinting step and exclude the buyer's participation from identification step.

1.2 Our Approach

The main idea of our scheme is to use an oblivious transfer with two-lock cryptosystem in order to prevent the seller's illegal transaction such as input of same values and remove interaction between buyers and sellers in the fingerprinting step.

In our scheme, the seller sends the fingerprinted contents to the buyer but he cannot know which contents the buyer chose. The buyer can also verify that the seller does not embed the same fingerprint, but she cannot know all fingerprinted contents that the seller sent. Thus we solve the security problem of the [Do99] scheme that the seller can cheat the buyer by inputting the same version of each bit and that of the [Sa01] scheme that the buyer can know all versions of contents' each bit.

The second idea is that we use Cox algorithms [CK97] which has high resistant at collusion attack instead of [BS95] code as a building block for collusion tolerance in order for efficient identification process. Thus sellers can identify the traitor by estimating fingerprint's correlations between the redistributed copy and assigned fingerprint without the help of buyers in our scheme.

The rest of this paper is organized as follows. First, the previous COT-based schemes [Do99][Sa01] are described briefly and its shortcomings are discussed in Section 2. Next, OT with two-lock system as our methodology is described in Section 3. Then the proposed anonymous fingerprinting scheme is described in detail in Section 4 and various features of the proposed scheme are analyzed in Section 5. Finally, we conclude in Section 6.

2 Overview of the Attacked Schemes

In this section we briefly review the construction proposed in [Do99][Sa01]. For simplicity we use the same notations.

2.1 Domingo's Scheme [Do99]

System Setup: The digital contents *item* is assumed to be n bit long. There are two possible versions of each contents, a marked version and an unmarked version. For each bit $item_i$ $(i = 1,2,...,n)$ the seller creates two versions $item_i^0, item_i^1$ of $i-th$ bit $item_i$. For $i = 1$ to n, the seller commits, using BCXs (bit commitment with XOR), to $item_i^0$ and to $item_i^1$ to get com_i^0, com_i^1. The seller sends to the registration center a signed and time-stamped message containing a short description of *item* as well as a list of the $l < n$ bit positions in *item* containing a mark.

Buyer Registration: Registration center chooses a random nonce $x_r \in Z_p$ and sends $y_r = g^{x_r}$ to buyer. Then buyer chooses secret random s_1 and s_2 in Z_p such that $s_1 + s_2 = x_B \pmod{p}$ and sends $S_1 = y_r^{s_1}$ and $S_2 = y_r^{s_2}$ to registration center. In here, x_B is the secret key of the buyer and $y_B = g^{x_B} \pmod{p}$ is the public key corresponding with it. The buyer convinces the registration center in zero-knowledge of possession of s_1 and s_2. The buyer computes an ElGamal public key $y_1 = g^{s_1}$ and sends it to the registration center. Next, the registration center checks $S_1 S_2 = y_B^{x_r}$ and $y_1^{x_r} = S_1$. The registration center returns to the buyer a certificate $Cert(y_1)$. The certificate states the correctness of y_1.

Fingerprinting: The following steps are executed for $i = 1,...,n$.

1. The seller permutes the pairs $(item_i^0, item_i^1)$ and stores the result $(item_i^{(0)}, item_i^{(1)})$ in his purchase record.
2. The seller and the buyer run a Committed Oblivious Transfer Protocol (COT) from [CGT95]. At the beginning of this protocol the seller inputs commitments $com(item_i^{(0)}), com(item_i^{(1)})$ of his two secret bits $item_i^{(0)}, item_i^{(1)}$ and the buyer inputs the commitment $com(b_i)$ to a bit b_i which indicates the secret she wants to learn. The protocol should not reveal any information on the other secret to the buyer. It also should not leak any information on b_i to the seller. The output of the protocol to the buyer is the fingerprinted sub-item $item_i^* := item_i^{(b_i)}$ and its commitment $com_i^* = com(item_i^*)$.
3. The buyer signs com_i^* using the secret s_1 and sends it together with the certificate $cert(y_1)$ to the seller who verifies them.

Identification: After finding a redistributed copy $item^{red}$,

1. The seller retrieves all signed commitments corresponding to the contents sold that is similar enough to $item^{red}$.
2. The seller sends a signed copy of $item^{red}$ to registration center and to all pseudonymous buyers who have bought a copy of this contents.

3. All suspected pseudonymous buyers execute the following until he finds a traitor:

   (1) Using a coin-flipping protocol the seller and the pseudonymous buyer agree on $l_1 \leq i < n$ bit positions. If the resulting positions contain less than $l_2 \leq l_1$ marks, then seller requests the buyer to start again the coin flipping protocol to agree on a new set of positions. The procedure is repeated until the resulting positions contain l_3 marks with $l_2 \leq l_3 \leq l_1$.

   (2) The pseudonymous buyer opens her commitments corresponding to l_1 bit positions agreed upon. If all l_3 opened commitments match with the corresponding bit values in $item^{red}$, the seller takes this as proof of redistribution. Otherwise the buyer is declared innocent and gets new fingerprinted contents.

4. The seller presents the opened signed commitments to the registration center requesting for identification. The proof of redistribution consists of opened commitments, the signed $item^{red}$ sent to the registration center in step 2 and the mark positions sent to the registration center in system setup.

2.2 Sadeghi's Scheme [Sa01]

Sadeghi's scheme made several constructive proposals to repair some flaws of [Do99] scheme. This scheme is very similar to Domingo's one except for the buyer registration and fingerprinting (dispute) steps. So we describe only both the buyer registration and fingerprinting steps below.

Buyer Registration: In general, if sellers can collude with a registration center, he can easily know the real identity of honest buyers. Since the pseudonym of buyers is provided by a registration center in anonymous fingerprinting schemes. [Sa01] suggested a k out of m trust model in order to reduce the chance of a dishonest seller to identify the buyer (real identity of the buyer). It means that k out of m registration centers perform the registration of the buyer. So the seller must collude with k out of m registration centers in order to succeed in revealing the honest buyer's real identity. The case $k = m$ is trivial and similar to the case with a single registration center, since one can simply establish a certificate chain among the registration center.

Fingerprinting: Fingerprinting step of [Sa01] is the same that of [Do99] except adding the following process.

During the fingerprinting (or a dispute) step the buyer requests the seller to open some pairs of commitments input to COT in a cut and choose manner and verifies whether the seller has behaved properly or not. However not all pairs can be opened and the identification-relevant parameters such as l_3 must be adapted accordingly.

2.3 Observations on Security

[Do99] scheme is significant in the sense that it presented the first construction for anonymous fingerprinting which is completely specified from a computational point of view and is thus readily implementable. [Sa01] scheme is also significant since it raised the efficiency and security of [Do99] scheme. But the most undesirable issue of both schemes is that they did not offer the security of buyers and sellers, because the seller knows the buyer's fingerprinted contents if he abuses flows of COT in the [Do99] scheme and buyers can know both versions of contents' each bits in the [Sa01] scheme.

- **Attack I against [Do99]**

We refer [Sa01] scheme that pointed out the security problem of [Do99]. The fingerprinting step of [Do99] scheme is insecure because the seller can always cheat the buyer by inputting the same version of the $item_i$ (e.g., $item_i^0$) to the COT-protocol for each i. Thus the seller will always know the output of COT, i.e., he knows which fingerprinted contents is assigned to which buyer. This allows a dishonest seller to wrongly accuse an honest buyer of treachery. Hence [Do99] does not satisfy with the requirements 4, 5 mentioned in section 1, because an honest buyer is falsely accused by a malicious seller and the buyer accused of reselling an unauthorized copy can also claim that the copy was created by the seller.

- **Attack II against [Sa01]**

[Sa01] insisted that his scheme solved security problem of [Do99] to open some pairs of commitments inputs to COT in the fingerprinting step or a dispute one.
Let's consider the following case. There are two buyers, Alice and Bob. They intend to collude in order to recreate another contents. So Alice will request to open special bits (for example even bits) and Bob will also request to open special bits (for example odd bits). The seller cannot know they will collude. Of course Alice and Bob may be the same person. In this case the seller also cannot know it, because buyers use the different anonymous identity using one-time registration in the anonymous schemes. Then Alice knows all versions of even bits, and Bob knows those of odd bits. Thus the buyers can obtain two versions of all bits and can create another contents that are not assigned to her/him. Of course the collusion of over two buyers makes it possible.

After all, both schemes based on the COT are weak against our attack and did not offer the security of buyer and seller.

2.4 Observations on Efficiency

One of the requirements for anonymous fingerprinting is to reduce the computational complexity. However both schemes have complexity of $O(nm)$ plain oblivious transfers and $O(nm^2)$ plain bit commitments (digital contents consists of n bits and m is a security parameter) in the fingerprinting step [CGT95] (See [Do99]). [Sa01] scheme has to use cut and choose manner additional for opening bits (Cut and choose protocol needs much computation and many pass numbers). These schemes are unrealistic, because round complexity of them is linear in the square number of bit-length of contents.

[Do99] scheme also has 5 exponent, 1 zero-knowledge proof, and 4-pass number in the registration protocol. A further critical issue in [Do99] is that the seller must contact all pseudonymous buyers during the identification step. This is again an unrealistic approach that all other proposals on anonymous fingerprinting try to avoid. Of course [Sa01] did not solve it.

3 Preliminaries

3.1 Oblivious Transfer Using Two-Lock Cryptosystem

We introduce discrete logarithm problem-based oblivious transfer using two-lock cryptosystem in order to prevent the dishonesty of buyers or sellers. The discrete logarithm based $t - out - n$ oblivious transfer of Qian-Hong Wu et al. is applied to the fingerprinting step of our scheme. To our best knowledge, a more efficient protocol for OT was presented as "Oblivious Transfer Using Two-Lock Cryptosystem" in [WZ03]. We assume that this protocol is secure, and the security proof is given in the same paper [WZ03].

Let Alice possess n (string) secret $m_1, m_2, ..., m_n$ and be willing to reveal t secret of them to Bob. Suppose Bob is interested in secrets $m_{i1}, m_{i2}, ..., m_{it}$. Assume that Alice chooses her random secret key k and Bob chooses secret keys $s_1, s_2, ..., s_t$. It is convenient to implement $t - out - n$ OT using two-lock cryptosystem as follows.

1. Alice sends Bob: $Y_1 = A_k(m_1), ..., Y_n = A_k(m_n)$.
2. Bob sends Alice: $Z_1 = Bs_1(Y_{i_1}), ..., Z_t = Bs_t(Y_{i_t})$.
3. Alice sends Bob: $C_1 = A_k^{-1}(Z_1), ..., C_t = A_k^{-1}(Z_t)$.
4. Bob decrypts: $m_{i_1} = B_{s_1}^{-1}(C_1), ..., m_{i_t} = B_{s_t}^{-1}(C_t)$.

Here, $A_k(.), B_s(.)$ are the different encryption algorithm and $A_k^{-1}(.), B_s^{-1}(.)$ denotes the decryption of $A_k(.), B_s(.)$. Bob can decrypt the cipher text C and reveal the message $m = B_k^{-1}(C)$. In case that $A = B$, it is also known as commutative encryption [BD00].

To achieve sending privacy, Alice's encryption algorithm should meet the security requirements: given $C_1, Z_{i_1}, ..., C_t, S_{i_t}$, it is infeasible to find k' satisfying $C_1 = A_{k'}^{-1}(Z_1), ..., C_t = A_{k'}^{-1}(Z_t)$. On the other hand, if Bob's encryption is semantically secure, then receiving ambiguity is guaranteed. In our protocol, we use this protocol based on discrete logarithm, which is secure unless an adversary could compute discrete logarithm.

4   Proposed Anonymous Fingerprinting Scheme

In this section, we describe practical and secure anonymous fingerprinting scheme using OT with two-lock cryptosystem, which is an improved scheme of [Do99][Sa01].

[Outline]
The proposed scheme consists of the following steps: Buyer registration step for buyer's pseudonym, fingerprinting step for making a fingerprinted contents and identification step for identification of the traitor.

[Preprocessing]
Let $p(\le n\ bits)$ be a large prime such that $q = (p-1)/2$ is also a prime. Let G be a group of order $p-1$, and let g be a generator of G such that computing discrete logarithms to the base g is difficult.

[Notations]
We assume that the content being sold is a still image, though in general the protocol is also applicable to audio and video contents for ease of exposition. We establish some notation as follows.

- *item* : Original image.
- $F = \{F_0, F_1,..., F_t\}$: Fingerprint (watermark) as a vector of "fingerprint elements",
  $F_i = \{f_{i_1},..., f_{i_k}\}$.
- x_B / y_B : Secret key / Public key corresponding with x_B of a buyer.
- $item_i^*$: Fingerprinted image embedded F_i .
- $A_a(.), B_b(.) / A_a^{-1}(.), B_b^{-1}(.)$: Encryption/Decryption algorithm with secret key a, b .

STEP 1. Buyer Registration
The buyer (Bob) chooses secret random x_1, x_2 in Z_p such that $x_1 \cdot x_2 = x_B \in Z_p$. Bob sends y_B, y_B^* $(y_B^* = g^{x_1})$ and x_2 $(E_{y_{Ron}}(x_2))$ encrypted by using the Registration Center's (Ron) public key y_{Ron} . Bob convinces Ron of zero-knowledge of possession of x_1 . The proof given in [Ch87] for showing possession of discrete logarithms may be used here. Ron decrypts $E_{y_{Ron}}(x_2)$ and checks that $y_B = (y_B^*)^{x_2}$. If it is verified, Ron returns to Bob a certificate $Cert(y_B^*)$. The certificate states the correctness of y_B^* .

STEP 2. Fingerprinting
Bob sends $Cert(y_B^*)$ to a seller (Alice). If it is verified, Alice generates valid n fingerprint $(F_0, F_1,..., F_{n-1})$ randomly. She must generate different n fingerprints to all

buyers. Each fingerprint F_i of our protocol and W of Cox scheme[3] has the same property. Then she makes n copies to embed each fingerprint F_i. All copies differ embedding information (fingerprint). Alice stores records $Cert(y_B^*), y_B^*, F_0, F_1, ..., F_{n-1}$ at her table $Table_A$. Next, Alice and Bob execute OT with two-lock cryptosystem as follows.

1. Alice encrypts n copies (fingerprinted contents) with her own secret key k and sends Bob: $Y_0 = A_k(item_0^*), ..., Y_{n-1} = A_k(item_{n-1}^*)$.

   Remark 1: Here, Alice generates $n(\geq 2)$ fingerprints, where Bob would choose one out of n fingerprinted contents. The choice of n implies a trade off between correctness and efficiency. In such case, probability of Alice knowing which fingerprinted contents Bob chose would be equal to $1/n$.

   Remark 2: We use a specific construction which introduced a spread-spectrum watermarking techniques proposed by Cox et al [CK97] for collusion-tolerance.

2. Bob chooses one among them. Suppose Bob chose $Y_2 = A_k(item_2^*)$. Then he re-encrypts it with his secret key s and sends it back to Alice: $Z = B_s(Y_2)$. Now Bob cannot know the hidden fingerprint because they are encrypted with Alice's key but he can verify that Alice did not encrypt the same contents (i.e., Bob can verify that Alice did not embed the same fingerprint into the contents).

3. Alice stores records Z at her table $Table_A$ and sends Bob: $C = A_k^{-1}(Z)$. Alice also cannot know which fingerprinted contents Bob chose because it is encrypted with Bob's secret key.

4. Bob decrypts and uses: $item_2^* = B_s^{-1}(C)$.

STEP 3. Traitor Identification

After finding a redistributed copy $item^{red}$, Alice extracts the unique fingerprint G in $item^{red}$. For robust fingerprint embedding algorithm, by computing correlations of extracted fingerprint G and every fingerprint stored in $Table_A$, Alice finds F_i with the highest correlation and obtains the transaction information involving F_i from the table. The information consists of $Cert(y_B^*), y_B^*, Z$. Alice sends them and the redistributed copy to an arbiter. The arbiter verifies the presence of F_i in the $item^{red}$, if it is checked, he asks the real identity of the traitor to Ron. Thus the seller can identify the traitor.

If the accused buyer cannot agree with the arbiter's decision, he sends his own contents to arbiter (or the arbiter asks the buyer Z and the buyer must open Z). If the

---

[3] Cox et al., embed a set of independent real numbers $W = \{w_1, ..., w_n\}$ drawn from a zero mean, variance 1, Gaussian distribution into the m largest DCTAC coefficients of an image. Results reported using the largest 1000 AC coefficients show the technique to be remarkably robust against various image processing operations and after printing and rescanning and multiple-document (collusion) attack.

same F_i indeed present in the accused buyer's contents or Z , he is found guilty otherwise he is innocent.

5 Features and Security Analysis

We discuss and analyze features and security of the proposed scheme according to the list of requirements (Section 1). We assume that all of the underlying primitives are secure. Security of our scheme relies on that of the underlying watermarking algorithm and cryptosystem.

1. **Anonymity**: We assume that the registration center does not reveal the buyer's real ID if the buyer is honest. In fingerprinting step, the seller knows y_B^*. Finding y_B would require knowledge of x_2. However, if the encryption algorithm is secure, attacker (seller) cannot know x_2. Thus buyer anonymity is guaranteed.

2. **Unlinkability**: Because our scheme executes one-time registration generation protocol whenever the buyer buys a contents (By going through the registration step several times, the buyer can obtain several different certified keys y_B^*). This implies that the buyer's purchases are unlinkable.

3. **Traceability**: Due to the properties of the underlying encryption, we can assume that a malicious buyer cannot change or substitute a fingerprint generated by the seller. Further a detecting function in the fingerprint detection must guarantees that the seller can extract the unique fingerprint F_i that belong to a traitor. Besides, the buyer cannot remove the fingerprint F_i because he does not know F_i. Thus the buyer who has distributed digital contents illegally can be traced in our scheme.

4. **No Framing**: Since, to forge Y with the special fingerprint F_i, the seller must know the buyer's private key s. In our proposal, only the buyer knows his secret key s if computing discrete logarithm is hard and encryption algorithm (underlying primitives) is secure. Since we use secure oblivious transfer with two-lock cryptosystem in the fingerprinting step, the seller cannot know which fingerprinted contents buyers selected. And the seller cannot input the same values in the execution of OT because all inputs are received to the buyer and the buyer checks them. Thus an honest buyer should not be wrongly identified as a traitor, because the others cannot recreate the buyer's copy with specific fingerprint.

5. **No Repudiation**: The buyer accused of reselling an unauthorized copy cannot claim that the copy was created by the seller or a security breach of the seller's system. Since only the buyer know his secret key s and his unique fingerprinted contents $item_i^*$, the others cannot recreate the buyer's copy.

6. **Collusion Tolerance**: Our scheme has used [CK97] as a building block. We assumed that this algorithm is secure. And this algorithm is estimated to be highly resistant to collusion attacks [KT98]. Our protocol is secure only as much as the underlying watermarking techniques are secure and robust.

7. **Practicality**: While computation complexity of both schemes [Do99][Sa01] of fingerprinting step is $O(nm)$ plain oblivious transfers and $O(nm^2)$ plain bit commitments, that of our protocol is just $t+1$ encryption and 2 decryption, where t is

the number of contents to be copied/fingerprinted for a contents. It is not liner in the length of contents. Doing this in sequence is unrealistic in the [Do99][Sa01], because the round complexity of the algorithm is linear in the bit-length n of the contents (one should think of the size of an image). And [Do99] has 5 exponentiations, a zero knowledge proof and 4-pass number in the registration step, but our protocol has just 4 exponentiations, a zero knowledge proof and 2-pass. Besides all buyers must take part in the identification step in [Do99][Sa01]. On the contrary, the seller can identify the traitor without the help of buyer in our protocol. In the event, our scheme[4] first reduces the round complexity and computational complexity from both schemes. Furthermore we improve the identification step to remove the participation of the buyers (all buyers). We design anonymous fingerprinting scheme that removes interaction property between buyers and sellers in the fingerprinting step (embedding procedure).

6 Concluding Remarks

To perform fingerprinting protocol efficiently, some schemes [Do99][Sa01][PS00] were proposed. But [Do99][Sa01] schemes have the serious problem that sellers can recreate the buyer's copy when he abuses the general oblivious transfer. Besides the seller must contact all buyers in the identification step in the [Do99][Sa01] schemes. [PS00] scheme has the problem that used collusion-secure code is too long and fingerprinting step has high complexity.

In this paper, we proposed practical and secure anonymous fingerprinting protocol with lower computational complexity. For it, we applied oblivious transfer with two-lock cryptosystem to the fingerprinting step. Accordingly, our protocol is secure against the seller's illegal transaction though we use oblivious transfer. But drawback of our scheme is that our transmission overhead is linear in the number of generated fingerprinted contents though we improved the computational complexity. A further direction of this study will be to reduce the transmission overhead.

References

[BD00]   F.Bao, R.Deng, and P.Feng, "An Efficient and Practical Scheme for Privacy Protection in E-commerce of Digital Goods", ICICS'00, LNCS 2836, Springer-Verlag, 2000. pp.167-170.

[BS95]   D.Boneh and J.Shaw, "Collusion-secure Fingerprinting for Digital Data", Crypto'95, LNCS 963, Springer-Verlag, 1995, pp. 452-465.

[CD98]   J.Camenisch and I.Damgard, "Verifiable Encryption and Applications to Group Signatures and Signatures Sharing", Technical Report RS 98-32, Brics, Department of Computer Science, University of Aarhus, Dec.1998.

---

[4] The security of our scheme relies on the parameter t. Thus, for robust security of our protocol, t should be large. But, if t is very large, our scheme may be impractical. Thus it implies a trade off between practicality and security.

[CDG87]   D.Chaum, Ivan Bjerre Damgard and Jeroen van de Graaf., "Multiparty Computation Ensuring Privacy and Each Party's Input and Correctness of the Result",
Crypto'87, LNCS 293, Springer-Verlag, 1987, pp.86-119.

[CGT95]   Claude Crupeau, Jeroen van de Graaf, and Alain Tapp, "Committed Oblivious
Transfer and Private Maulti-Party Computation", Crypto'95, LNCS 963, Springer-
Verlag, 1995. pp. 110-123.

[Ch87]   D.Chaum, "An Improved Protocol for Demonstrating Possession of Discrete
Logarithms and Some Generalizations", Eurocrypto'87, LNCS 304, Springer-
Verlag, 1987, pp.127-141.

[CK97]   I.J. Cox, J.Kilian, T.Leighton, and T.Shamnon, "Secure Spread Spectrum Watermarking for Image, Audio and Video", IEEE Transactions on Image Processing,
vol.6, no 12, pp.1673-1678, 1997.

[Do98]   Josep Domingo-Ferrer and J.Herrera-Joancomarti, "Efficient Smart-card Based
Anonymous Fingerprinting", CARDIS'98, LNCS 1820, Springer-Verlag, 2000,
pp.221-228.

[Do99]   Josep Domingo-Ferrer, "Anonymous Fingerprinting Based on Committed Oblivious Transfer", PKC99, LNCS 1560, Springer-Verlag, 1999, pp. 43-52.

[GCG86]   G.R.Blakley, C.Meadows and G.B.Purdy, "Fingerprinting Long Forgiving Messages", Crypto'85, LNCS 218, pp.180-189, 1986.

[KT98]   Joe Killian, F. Thomson Leighton, Lasely R. Matheson, Talal G. Shannon, Robert
E. Tarjan, and Francis Zane, "Resistance of Digital Watermarks to Collusive
Attacke", Proceedings of 1998 IEEE ISIT, pp.271, 1998.

[Ne83]   Neal.R.Wanger, "Fingerprinting", IEEE Symposium on Security and Privacy
1983, IEEE Computer Society Press, pp.18-22, 1983.

[PS96]   B.Pfitzman and M.Schunter, "Asymmetric Fingerprinting", Eurocrypto'96, LNCS
1070, Springer-Verlag, 1996, pp. 84-95.

[PS00]   B.Pfitzman and A-R. Sadeghi, "Coin-Based Anonymous Fingerprinting",
Eurocrypto'99, LNCS 1592, Springer-Verlag, 2000, pp. 150-164.

[PW97]   B.Pfitzman and W.Waidner, "Anonymous Fingerprinting", Eurocrypto'97, LNCS
1233, Springer-Verlag, 1997, pp. 88-102.

[Sa01]   Ahmad-Reza Sadeghi, "How to Break a Semi-anonymous Fingerprinting
Scheme", Information Hiding 2001, LNCS 2137, Springer-Verlag, 2001, pp.384-
394.

[WZ03]   Qian-Hong Wu, Jian-Hong Zhang, and Yu-Min Wang, "Practical t-out-n Oblivious Transfer and Its Applications", ICICS2003, LNCS 2836, Springer-Verlag,
2003. pp.226-237.

Empirical and Theoretical Evaluation of Active Probing Attacks and Their Countermeasures*

Xinwen Fu[1], Bryan Graham[1], Dong Xuan[2], Riccardo Bettati[1], and Wei Zhao[1]

[1] Department of Computer Science, Texas A&M University
{xinwenfu, bwg7173, bettati, zhao}@cs.tamu.edu
[2] Department of Computer and Information Science, Ohio State University
xuan@cis.ohio-state.edu

Abstract. A variety of remote sensing attacks allow adversaries to break flow confidentiality and gather mission-critical information in distributed systems. Such attacks are easily supplemented by active probing attacks, where additional workload (e.g., ping packets) is injected into the victim system. This paper presents statistical pattern recognition as a fundamental technology to evaluate the effectiveness of active probing attacks. Our theoretical analysis and empirical results show that even if sophisticated approaches of link padding are used, sample entropy of probing packets' round trip time is an effective and robust feature statistic to discover the user payload traffic rate, which is important for maintaining anonymous communication. Extensive experiments on local network, campus network, and the Internet were carried out to validate the system security predicted by the theoretical analysis. We give some guidelines to reduce the effectiveness of such active probing attacks.

1 Introduction

This paper analyzes a class of active attacks on traffic flow confidentiality. In particular, we are interested in attacks that disclose the traffic rate on a network link. Traffic rate is critical information in many scenarios. For example, if Alice communicates with Bob through an anonymous communication network[3], an attacker may infer this communication relationship (sender and receiver) if he determines that the rate of output traffic from Alice roughly equals the rate of input traffic to Bob. In [2], Serjantov and Sewell give more examples about the importance of hiding traffic rates in Mix networks, and the authors of NetCamo [3] show examples in other mission-critical applications.

To hide traffic rate, dummy traffic is typically used to pad the original traffic, i.e., user payload traffic. As a result, the padded traffic has a different rate from the original

---

* This work was supported in part by the National Science Foundation under Contracts 0081761 and 0324988, by the Defense Advanced Research Projects Agency under Contract F30602-99-1-0531, and by Texas A&M University under its Telecommunication and Information Task Force Program. Any opinions, findings, and conclusions or recommendations in this material, either expressed or implied, are those of the authors and do not necessarily reflect the views of the sponsors listed above.

[3] Anonymous communication networks use *Mix* techniques pioneered by Chaum [1] and are often denoted as Mix networks.

J. Fridrich (Ed.): IH 2004, LNCS 3200, pp. 266–281, 2004.
© Springer-Verlag Berlin Heidelberg 2004

traffic, so that we achieve traffic rate hiding. Traffic padding[4] can be end-to-end padding (in which sender and receivers control the padding) and link padding (in which the intermediate hops control the padding). In either case, the original traffic is often padded to have a constant rate using a periodic timer; this technique is denoted as CIT (constant interval time) padding. The original traffic can also be padded to have a variant rate using a non-periodic timer, and this technique is denoted as VIT (variable interval time) padding. However, traffic padding is not a cure-all. Traffic analysis attacks have been developed to obtain the information about the traffic rate even if traffic padding is used.

In terms of techniques, traffic analysis attacks can be passive and active. (a) In a *passive traffic analysis attack*, an adversary passively collects traffic data and performs analysis on it. The authors of [4] describe statistical traffic analysis attacks to estimate the user payload traffic rate if CIT padding is used and how the effectiveness of this type of attack can be significantly reduced with the use of appropriate VIT padding. (b) In an active traffic analysis attack, the adversary interferes with the normal activity of a victim network in a seemingly innocuous way and tries to acquire critical information by analyzing the victim network's response to the interference.

One specific kind of active traffic analysis attack is an active probing attack, in which an adversary injects probing traffic (e.g., FTP/TELNET/Ping/etc.) into the victim network and analyze the network's response on the probing traffic. Wei Dai [5] briefly describes cases of active probing attacks aimed at getting traffic rate between pairs of users to break Freedom anonymity systems [6] by insiders, such as malicious users.

This paper analyzes active probing attacks by *outsiders* and develops countermeasures against these forms of attacks for systems that use VIT traffic padding. As an illustrative example, we use a simple *ping-based* probing attack, where the adversary *pings* various locations in the network in order to gain information, such as the payload traffic rate. We define *detection rate* as the probability that the adversary correctly recognizes the payload traffic rate and use it to evaluate the information assurance of a security system. We systematically evaluate the detection rate of various statistical methods which the adversary can then use to analyze the probing traffic. Specifically, using statistical pattern analysis as the framework, we find that sample mean, sample variance, and sample entropy of the round trip time (RTT) of probing packets can help the adversary track the payload traffic rate's changing pattern and obtain the payload traffic rate. Of those statistics, sample entropy is robust (i.e., not sensitive to outliers) and effective in terms of detection rate.

We also report results from extensive experiments in various situations, including local area network in a laboratory, campus networks, and wide area networks. Our data consistently demonstrates the usefulness of our analytic model and correctness of detection rates predicted by the closed-form formulae.

As with countermeasures, active probing attacks can generally be made ineffective through simple means, for example, by randomly delaying all non-payload traffic. We will empirically and analytically evaluate the effectiveness of such countermeasures by

---

[4] We distinguish traffic padding from packet padding. Packet padding hides the *length* of individual packets by adding padding data to packets. Traffic padding hides the temporal characteristics, for example rate, of a flow of packets. Traffic padding relies on packet padding and encryption to render dummy packets indistinguishable from real packets.

measuring to what extent they reduce the effectiveness of probing attacks. We note that the methodology of delaying outgoing traffic from security gateways may be desired for security contexts in addition to the context described here.

The rest of this paper is organized as follows. Section 2 reviews traffic padding as the countermeasure to traffic analysis attacks and recent practical traffic analysis attacks in different scenarios. We present the network model, padding mechanism, and an adversary's analysis strategies in Section 3. In Section 4, we develop a theoretical model and derive closed-form formulae for detection rates for different statistics. Section 5 validates our theory through experiments. Based on empirical and analytic techniques, Section 6 gives countermeasures to active ping probing attacks. Section 7 summarizes this paper and discusses possible extensions.

2   Related Work

Shannon [7] describes his perfect secrecy theory, which is the foundation for the ideal countermeasure system against statistical analysis attacks. Traffic padding is a major class of countermeasures that researchers have proposed to counter traffic analysis attacks. Baran [8] proposes the use of heavy unclassified traffic to interfere with the adversary's tampering of the links of a security network system used for communicating classified information. He also suggests adding *dummy*, i.e. fraudulent, traffic between fictitious users of the system to conceal the true amount of traffic.

A survey of countermeasures for traffic analysis is given in [9]. To mask the frequency, length and origin-destination patterns of an end-to-end communication, dummy messages are used to pad the traffic to a predefined pattern. It is evident that such a predefined pattern is sufficient but not necessary based on the perfect secrecy theory [7].

The authors in [10, 11, 12] give a mathematical framework to optimize the bandwidth usage while preventing traffic analysis of the end-to-end traffic rates. Timmerman [13] proposes an adaptive traffic hiding model to reduce the overhead caused by traffic padding, in which the link padding rate is reduced with the decrease of real traffic rate. This renders large-scale variations in traffic rates still observable. The authors of Net-Camo [3] provide the end-to-end prevention of traffic analysis while guaranteeing QoS (the worst case delay of message flows) in time constraint communication networks.

To protect the anonymity of email transmissions, Chaum [1] proposes the use of a *Mix* - a computer proxy. One technique used by a Mix is to collect a predefined number of fixed-size message packets from different users and to shuffle the order of these packets before sending them out. Many researchers suggest using constant rate padding (i.e., make the traffic rate appear as constant) between the user and the first proxy (e.g., [14]). Raymond in [15] gives an informal survey of several *ad hoc* traffic analysis attacks on systems providing anonymous services. For example, by correlating traffic rate or volume, attackers may discover the end points of a communication. One of his conclusions is that traffic padding is essential to achieve communication anonymity. The authors of [16] list many possible attacks in Freedom [6] anonymous communication system. The authors of [17] give a list of attacks to anonymity systems. Most of those attacks are only briefly discussed and lack systematic analysis. Tarzan [18] provides anonymity in a peer-to-peer environment by using link padding to counter possible attacks.

Recently researchers have disclosed some advanced statistical traffic analysis attack techniques. Song *et al.* [19] describe how SSH 1 and SSH 2 can leak user passwords under a passive traffic analysis attack. The authors illustrate how the inter-packet times in a SSH session accurately reflect the typing behavior of the user by exposing the inter-keystroke timing information. This in turn can be used to infer plaintext as typed on the keyboard. To prevent this, the authors propose padding traffic on the SSH connections to make it appear to be a constant rate. When there are not enough packets to maintain the constant rate, fake (dummy) packets are created and sent.

Felten and Schneider [20] develop an active timing attack based on browsing a malicious web page. This malicious web page is able to determine if a user has recently browsed a different target web page. The malicious web page contains embedded attack codes, which try to download a web file from the target webpage. If the user has recently browsed the target webpage, it is highly possible that the target webpage is cached locally, in which case, the access time will be very small, otherwise it will be much larger. The malicious code reports the access timing to the attacker, and then the attacker can decide if the user has recently browsed the target webpage by this access timing. The malicious codes can be Javascript codes, or with a little more effort, time measurement HTML codes. Clearly this attack is very difficult to prevent, and the only perfect countermeasure is to turn off the cache.

SafeWeb [21] is a web service, that uses anonymizing servers, which in turn behave like mixes and act as proxies between users and the web servers. The proxy downloads the requested webpage on behalf of the user and forwards it to the user in an encrypted form. Hintz [21] shows how observers can take advantage of the HTML weakness of using a separate TCP connection for each HTML object (such as HTML texts, image files, audio annotations, etc.) to deploy passive traffic analysis attacks. The number of TCP connections and the corresponding amount of data transferred over each connection form a fingerprint, which allows an observer to identify the accessed webpage by correlating fingerprint data with traffic observed between the user and the anonymizing server. To invalidate these fingerprints, we have to merge all the connections into a single connection or add noise (fake messages, etc.) to the web traffic flows. Sun *et al.* [22] use many experiments to show the possibility and efficiency of the above exploit.

3   System Models

This section first presents the network model and then discusses link padding mechanisms used as countermeasures for passive traffic analysis attacks. Finally, we define the model of adversary who uses statistical pattern recognition strategies for active *ping* probing attacks on these security systems, which employ link padding mechanisms.

3.1   Network Model

In this work, we assume that the network consists of *protected subnets* interconnected by *unprotected networks* and assume that traffic within protected subnets is shielded from observers. Unprotected networks can be public ones (e.g., the Internet) or networks deployed over an easily accessible broadcast medium. These networks are accessible to observation by third-parties, and limited services such as ping are available.

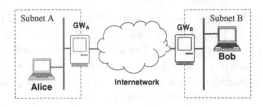

Fig. 1. Network Model

Thus, these networks are open to traffic analysis and other limited probing attacks. This model captures a variety of situations, ranging from battleship convoys (where the large-scale shipboard subnets are protected and the inter-ship communication is wireless) to communicating PDAs (where the protected subnets consist of single nodes).

Figure 1 illustrates the network setup. Two security gateways GW_A and GW_B are placed at the two boundaries of the unprotected network and provide the link padding necessary to prevent traffic analysis of the payload traffic exchanged between the protected subnets A and B.

Note that gateways can be realized either as stand-alone boxes, modules on routers, switches, software additions to network stacks, or device drivers at end hosts. In this paper, we assume that they are stand-alone boxes. (**Please note:** In an anonymous communication network such as Onion Routing [14], the link padding function can be implemented as device drivers at the end hosts (Alice's and Bob's machines), who connect to onion routers. Our result and analysis in this paper are valid in this case since the mechanism causing the problem of information leaking is similar.) To simplify the discussion, the communication is one-way from Subnet A to Subnet B. Consequently, GW_A and GW_B are also called *sender gateway* and *receiver gateway* respectively.

3.2   Link Padding Mechanism

The motivation of link padding is to ensure traffic flow confidentiality, i.e., to prevent the adversary from performing traffic analysis and inferring critical characteristics of the payload traffic exchanged over unprotected networks. We limit the adversary's interest to *payload traffic rate*, that is, the rate at which payload traffic is exchanged between protected subnets. Specifically, we assume that there is a set of discrete payload traffic rates $\{\omega_1, \cdots, \omega_m\}$. At a given time, the rate of payload traffic from the sender will be one of those m rates. Consequently, the objective of the adversary is to identify at which of the m rates the payload is being sent. But, we will also demonstrate how the adversary may use the approaches in this paper to track the continuous changing pattern of the payload traffic.

One way to counter the traffic analysis attacks is to "pad" the payload traffic, that is, to properly insert "dummy" packets in the payload traffic stream so that the real payload status is camouflaged. There are many possible implementations of link padding algorithms on the two gateways in Figure 1. The most common method uses a timer to control packet sending and works as follows: (a) On GW_A, incoming payload packets from the sender Alice are placed in a queue. (b) An interrupt-driven timer is set up on

GW_A. When the timer times out, the interrupt processing routine checks if there is a payload packet in the queue: (1) If there are payload packets, one is removed from the queue and transmitted to GW_B; (2) Otherwise, a dummy packet is transmitted to GW_B. This timer can be a constant interval timer (CIT), which is a periodic one with a constant interval between two consecutive timeouts. This is the most commonly used method for traffic padding, i.e., the constant rate traffic padding. The timer can also be a variable interval timer (VIT) with a variable amount of time between two consecutive timeouts, where the interval is picked from a probability distribution. We denote padding using these two different timers as CIT padding and VIT padding, respectively.

3.3 Adversary Strategies

Recall that we assume that the objective of the adversary is to identify at which of the m possible rates the payload is being sent. We need to discuss the adversary's power before we proceed further.

We assume an external adversary, who is not a participant of either Subnet A or B and does not compromise sender and receiver gateways. The adversary can only get access to the two subnets in seemingly legal ways such as pinging the two gateways.

Traffic flow confidentiality is ensured in the system in Figure 1 by VIT padding under passive traffic analysis attack. Packet contents are perfectly encrypted, all packets have a constant size (padded or manipulated), and dummy packets cannot be distinguished from payload packets. The authors of [4] proposed using VIT padding as an alternative to the commonly used CIT padding and show how CIT padding is extremely difficult to implement in practice and how minute disturbances make CIT padding subject to a sophisticated passive traffic analysis attack that measures the packet interarrival time of packets on the unprotected link.

We also assume that the adversary has complete knowledge about the gateway machines and the countermeasure algorithms used for preventing traffic analysis. Thus, the adversary can simulate the whole system, including the gateway machines, to obtain *a priori* knowledge about traffic behavior. In many studies on information security, it is a convention that we make worst-case assumptions like this. But, we will also show in this paper, even without the capability of simulating the system, the adversary can also track the traffic rate changing pattern by the method introduced in this paper.

Based on these assumptions, the adversary may deploy a sophisticated ping probing attack aimed at determining the payload traffic rate from $\{\omega_1, \cdots, \omega_m\}$. In the attack, the adversary pings the sender gateway GW_A, analyzes the statistics of round trip time of these ping packets and tries to figure out Subnet A's payload traffic rate even if GW_A uses VIT padding (If the padding is implemented as a device driver on Alice's host, the ping probing is aimed at getting Alice's real payload traffic rate). We use this ping attack as a model to analyze a much larger class of active probing attacks.

The adversary can analyze his sample of ping RTT data based on Bayes decision theory [23]. The entire attack strategy consists of two parts: Off-line training and run-time classification. We now describe them below.

Off-line training

The off-line training component can be decomposed into the following steps:
(1) The adversary selects a statistic of the RTT sample of size n. This statistic is called *a feature* and will be used for traffic rate classification. Possible features we study in this paper are *sample mean*, *sample variance*, and *sample entropy*.
(2) The adversary emulates the entire link padding system and collects RTT information at different payload traffic rates. From this information, the adversary derives the *Probability Density Functions* (PDF) of the selected statistical feature. As histograms are usually too coarse for the distribution estimation, we assume that the adversary uses the *Gaussian kernel estimator of PDF* [24], which is effective in our problem domain.
(3) Based on the PDFs of statistical features for different payload traffic rates, Bayes decision rules are derived. Recall that there are m possible payload traffic rates $\omega_1, \cdots, \omega_m$. The Bayes decision rule can be stated as follows:
The sample represented by feature s corresponds to payload rate ω_i if

$$\forall j \in [1, m], p(\omega_i|s) \geq p(\omega_j|s) \tag{1}$$

That is,

$$p(s|\omega_i)Pr(\omega_i) \geq p(s|\omega_j)Pr(\omega_j) \tag{2}$$

Here $Pr(\omega_i)$ is the *a priori* probability that the payload traffic is sent at rate ω_i, and $p(\omega_i|s)$ is the *a postireori* probability that the payload traffic is sent at rate ω_i when the collected sample has the measured feature s.

Run-time Classification

Once the adversary completes his training phase, he can start the classification at run-time. We assume the adversary has some means to ping the gateways GW_A and GW_B. In particular, when he wants to determine the current payload rate, the adversary collects a sample of ping RTTs. He calculates the value of the statistical feature from the collected sample and then uses the Bayes decision rules derived in the training phase to match the collected sample to one of the previously defined payload traffic rates.

4   Derivation of Detection Rate

Given models described in the previous section, we'd like to evaluate the security of the system in Figure 1 in terms of detection rate. *Detection rate* is defined as the probability that the adversary can correctly classify the payload traffic rate protected by security gateways. In this section, we derive the closed-form formulae for detection rates when the adversary uses sample mean, sample variance, or sample entropy, as the statistical feature, respectively. Our formulae will be approximate ones due to the complexity of the problem. Nevertheless, these formulae do correctly reflect the impact of various system parameters, including the type of padded traffic, sample size, and statistical feature used. These relationships are very useful in understanding the nature of the attack and designing effective countermeasures. In the next section, we will see that experimental data well matches the detection rate predicted by our approximation formulae.

Let $\{X_1, X_2, \cdots, X_n\}$ be a sample of ping RTT with sample size n. The *sample mean* $\bar{X}$, sample variance Y, and sample entropy $\widetilde{H}$ are defined below:

$$\text{Sample Mean: } \bar{X} = \sum_{i=1}^{n} X_i/n \tag{3}$$

$$\text{Sample Variance: } Y = \sum_{i=1}^{n} (X_i - \bar{X})^2/(n-1) \tag{4}$$

$$\text{Sample Entropy: } \widetilde{H} \approx -\sum_i k_i/n \log(k_i/n) + \log \Delta x \tag{5}$$

where in (5) we use the histogram-based entropy estimation developed in [25]. k_i is the number of sample points in the ith bin, and Δx is the histogram's bin size. In Appendix A, we provide a way to calculate the optimal bin size for the estimation of entropy.

Using sample mean, sample variance, and sample entropy as defined above, our experiments show that an adversary can continuously track the changing pattern of the user payload traffic rate (Figure 4 (d)). Below we give close-form formulae for simple cases in which the user payload traffic has two statuses: low rate ω_l and high rate ω_h.

4.1 Detection Rate for Recognizing Two Payload Traffic Rates

Because of the page limit, we just list the major theorems about sample mean, sample variance, and sample entropy. Interested readers can refer to [26] for details. Before introducing these theorems, let's first investigate the reason of the failure of VIT padding against the ping probing attack, which is demonstrate below. The reason for this failure lies in the subtle interaction between the traffic padding system and the probing traffic. While GW_A's network subsystem processes payload packets from Subnet A in Figure 1, the processing of ping packets is delayed. A higher rate of payload traffic causes more possible delay on ping packets. This means that sample mean, sample variance, and sample entropy of the RTT of the probing packets at a given sample size n are changed, and there is some kind of correlation between the user payload traffic rate and sample mean, sample variance, and sample entropy of the RTT of the probing packets. The adversary can explore this correlation to discover the user payload traffic rate.

The ping RTT can be represented as a random variable RTT. As analyzed above, under different user payload traffic rates, i.e., low rate and high rate in our illustrative case, we will have random variables RTT_{low} and RTT_{high}, whose means are denoted as μ_l and μ_h respectively, and whose variances are denoted as σ_l^2 and σ_h^2 respectively. Also we define r as the ratio between σ_h^2 and σ_l^2.

$$r = \sigma_h^2/\sigma_l^2 \tag{6}$$

The following theorem provides closed-form formulae for estimation of detection rate when sample mean, sample variance, and sample entropy are used as feature statistics.

Theorem 1. *The detection rate by sample mean,* $v_{\bar{X}}$ *can be estimated as follows:*

$$v_{\bar{X}} \approx 1 - (e^{-(\mu_h - \mu_l)^2/(4\sigma_h^2 + 4\sigma_l^2)})^n / \sqrt{2(1/\sqrt{r} + \sqrt{r})} \tag{7}$$

The detection rate by sample variance, v_Y, can be estimated as follows:

$$v_Y \approx \max(1 - C_Y/(n-1), 0.5) \tag{8}$$

where C_Y is calculated by

$$C_Y = 1/(2(1 - 1/(r-1)\log r)^2) + 1/(2(r/(r-1)\log r - 1)^2) \tag{9}$$

The detection rate by sample entropy, v_H, can be estimated as follows:

$$v_{\tilde{H}} \approx \max(1 - C_H/n, 0.5) \tag{10}$$

where $C_{\tilde{H}}$ is calculated by

$$C_{\tilde{H}} = 1/(2(\log(\frac{r}{r-1}\log r))^2) + 1/(2(\log(\frac{r-1}{\log r}))^2) \tag{11}$$

We have a few observations from the above Theorem:

(1) For sample mean, the detection rate is exponentially increasing with sample size n. This implies that a small difference between μ_h and μ_l may cause detection rate to dramatically increase with the increase of sample size. Furthermore, the detection rate decreases with an increase in variance σ_h^2 and σ_l^2.

(2) For sample variance, the detection rate is an increasing function in terms of sample size n. When $n \to \infty$, the detection rate is 100%. This means that if the payload traffic lasts for sufficient time at one rate, and the adversary can get a sample of a sufficiently large size, he may detect the payload traffic rate by sample variance of ping RTT. Furthermore, the detection rate is an increasing function of r in (6), where $r \geq 1$. That is, the smaller r, the closer the two variances under different payload traffic rates, and intuitively the lower the corresponding detection rate. When $r = 1$, the detection rate is 50%. That is, the probing attack using sample variance will fail.

(3) For sample entropy, the detection rate is also an increasing function in terms of sample size n. Also, the detection rate is also an increasing function of r in (6), where $r \geq 1$. When $r = 1$, the detection rate reaches 50%.

4.2 Detection Rate for Payload Traffic with Periodically Changing Rate

In practice, the rate of payload traffic from Subnet A in Figure 1 changes with time. Here, we consider the case in which the payload rate changes periodically and deduce the detection rate in Theorem 2 and its corollary. For a rigorous proof of these formulae, please refer to [26]. Here we briefly introduce the principle. To deploy probing attacks, an adversary pings the sender gateway and collects a sample of n RTTs of probing packets. This sample may be partitioned into a few segments, e.g., the first l RTTs are collected when the user payload traffic rate is low and the other $n-l$ RTTs are collected when the user payload traffic rate is high. Assuming that we have L possible partitions: $\{Partition_i : 1 \leq i \leq L\}$. For $Partition_i$, we can derive its occurrence probability $P(Partition_i)$ and the average recognition error rate conditioned on this partition case, $Pr(error|Partition_i)$. We also assume that the correct recognition is the one matching the user payload traffic rate when the first packet of the sample is collected. Then we have the general form of detection rate formula in Theorem 2.

Theorem 2. *The detection rate v_d for payload traffic with periodically changing rate is*

$$v_d = 1 - \sum Pr(error|Partition_i)P(Partition_i) \qquad (12)$$

For the case of two payload traffic rates, assuming traffic of each rate lasts for half of a single period, M is the number of ping RTT sample point in half of a period (ping packets are sent out at a constant rate) and n is the sample size, we have the following corollary from Theorem 2.

Corollary 1. *In case of $n < M$, a closed form of detection rate is given in (13),*

$$v_d = 1 - \epsilon(M - n + 1)/M - (n - 1)/(2M) \qquad (13)$$

where ϵ is the classification error: $\epsilon = 1 - v$, where v can be calculated in (7), (9) and (10) for different features.

Please refer to Appendix B for the proof. From Corollary 1, we can see that when the ping packet rate is fixed, the larger the payload rate changing period, the larger M and thus the bigger v. This is intuitive. v has a complicated relation with n because of ϵ's relation with n. Given M, v has maximum value at some n.

5   Evaluations

In this section, we evaluate how the theoretical analysis of detection rate from the previous section compares to results from experiments designed to reflect real-life situations.

In the experiments, we assume that the adversary uses a high-performance network analyzer, such as Agilent's J6841A, to dump ping packets. A series of experiments were carried out. In terms of experimental environments, we consider the following cases: lab (LAN), campus network (MAN), and wide area network (WAN).

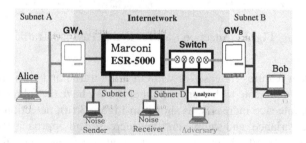

Fig. 2. Experiment setup in laboratory

GW_A and GW_B in Figure 1 run TimeSys Linux/Real-Time. To counter traffic analysis attacks, VIT padding is used. The timer interval satisfies a normal distribution $N(10ms, 3ms^2)$, which is a very powerful setting for resisting passive traffic analysis attacks [4]. Thus, the average rate of padded traffic between the two security gateways is 100 packets per second (pps). The payload has two average rate states: 10 pps and 40pps. We assume both rates occur in equal probability. Note that for such a system with two possible payload traffic rates, the detection rate for the adversary is lower-bounded at 50% corresponding to random guessing. For all the experiments, the adversary uses an appropriate rate of ping packets whose size is 512 bytes.

5.1   Experiments in a Laboratory Environment

Our experiment setup is shown in Figure 2. The advantage of experimenting in a lab environment is that we can control the cross traffic over the network. The disadvantage is that the generated cross traffic may not reflect the characteristics of a real network.

The two gateways are connected by a Marconi ESR-5000 enterprise switching router. Subnet C is connected to the router as the cross traffic (noise) generator while the cross traffic receiver is located in Subnet D. The cross traffic shares the outgoing link of the router, creating a case where the cross traffic makes an impact on the padded traffic. The adversary pings sender gateway GW_A behind the Marconi router.

Results of Probing Attacks on Stable Payload Traffic

By stable payload traffic, we mean that the traffic from user subnets lasts for a relatively long time at a roughly constant rate. Figure 3 (a) and (b) shows the detection

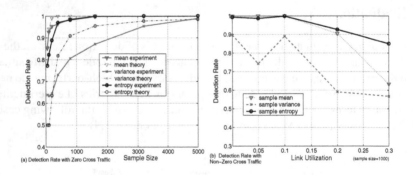

Fig. 3. Detection Rate for Stable Payload Traffic

rate by different features for cases of without cross traffic and with cross traffic (users in Subnet C communicate with users in Subnet D). We have the following observations:
(1) As the sample size increases, as shown in Figure 3 (a), detection rates for sample mean, sample variance, and sample entropy increase and approach 100%. This shows that when payload traffic lasts for enough time at some rate, these three features can determine the payload traffic rate with 100% accuracy, even if the powerful VIT padding is used. **Security systems using padding fail under probing attacks**. Furthermore, the trend of theoretical detection rate curves coincides well with the trend of empirical curves for the three features.
(2) From Figure 3 (a) and (b), sample entropy is a fairly robust feature in detecting the user payload traffic rate. This is because sample entropy defined in (5) is not sensi-

tive to outliers, which influence the performance of sample mean and sample variance, especially when there is cross traffic.

(3) In Figure 3 (b), overall, as the link utilization increases, the detection rates of the three features decrease. Intuitively, this is because the cross traffic between Subnet C and Subnet D interferes with ping traffic. In theory, compared to the ping RTT variances σ_l^2 and σ_h^2 in the no cross traffic case, both these variances in case of with cross traffic are increased by a quantity caused by cross traffic. This will cause a decrease in r. As Theorem 1 predicts, the detection rate by all three features drops.

Results of Probing Attacks on Payload Traffic with Periodically Changing Rate

Figure 4 (a), (b) and (c) give detection rates for payload traffic with periodically changing rate. Payload traffic of 10pps lasts for 1 minute and traffic of 40pps lasts for the next 1 minute. Figure 4 (d) illustrates how the adversary can track continuously changing payload traffic rate by probing attacks. We have the following observations.

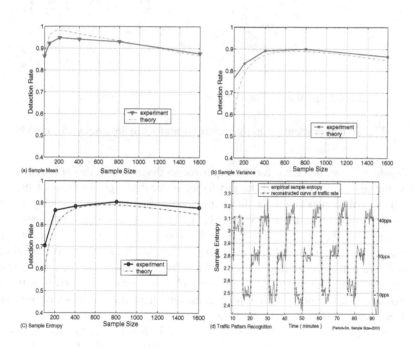

Fig. 4. Detection Rate for Payload Traffic with Periodically Changing Rate

(1) The theoretical curves well match the empirical curves. This validates Theorem 2 and its Corollary 1.

(2) As Corollary 1 predicts, there exists a maximum detection rate at some sample size. So, in practice, when the ping probing attack is deployed, the adversary has to choose an appropriate sample size to get an optimal detection rate. A large sample size for payload traffic with small rate changing period may cause a bad detection rate because a sample includes mixed rates of payload packets.

278   Xinwen Fu et al.

(3) In Figure 4 (d), sample entropy (sample size = 2000) is used to track the changing pattern of the user payload traffic rate while the user payload traffic rate has three
statuses: 0 pps, 10 pps, and 40 pps. The rate changes for 5 minutes on average. It is
clear that the adversary can use sample entropy to reconstruct the payload traffic rate's
changing pattern very well. This further validates probing attacks' validity in the general problem of tracking user payload traffic pattern.

5.2 Experiments over Campus and Wide Area Networks

In this subsection, we examine the detection rate when the adversary's ping traffic traverses a campus network and the internet respectively.

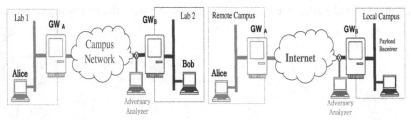

(a) Experiment Setup within Local Campus Network   (b) Network Setup between Remote and Local Campus

Fig. 5. Experiment setup over campus and wide area networks (WAN)

Figure 5 shows the setup for the experiments discussed in this subsection. In both
cases, the observation point of the adversary is located right in front of the receiver
gateway and thus maximally far from the sender. Figure 5 (a) is a setup for experiments over our local campus network[5]. That is, the ping traffic goes through our local
campus network before it reaches the sender's gateway. Figure 5 (b) is a setup for experiments over the Internet between a remote campus network and our local campus
network. Here, the sender workstation and the sender gateway are located at the remote
campus network. The ping traffic goes through the Internet and arrives at the remote
campus network. We note that in this case, the path from the sender's workstation to the
receiver's workstation spans 15 or more routers.

In each case, we collect data continuously for 24 hours. The data for the case of our
local campus network was collected on July 16, 2003 while the data for the wide area
network case was collected on July 14, 2003.

Figures 6 (a) and (b) display the detection rate throughout the observation period.
We have the following observations:

(1) When ping traffic traverses just our local campus network, the detection rates of
sample entropy and sample mean can approach about 75%. This means that over a
medium-sized enterprise network like our local campus network, the cross traffic does
have an influence on the ping traffic, but systems using VIT padding scheme alone still
cannot resist ping probing attacks effectively.

---

[5] Because the requirement of anonymous submission, related institute information is dropped.

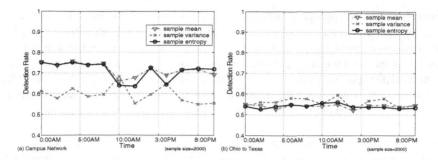

Fig. 6. Empirical detection rates for experiments over campus and WAN (sample size=2000)

(2) When the padded traffic traverses more network elements, such as the Internet between the remote campus network and our local campus network, the detection rates are much lower. This is because ping traffic has a low scheduling priority at a large number of routers and switches, and the RTT of ping packets is seriously distorted.

6 Countermeasures

To counter the active traffic analysis attacks, there are several possible approaches. The first approach is to disable the ping service on security gateways, but the disadvantage of this is that ping often is a useful service for debugging a network, e.g., to check if GW_A is alive. Sometimes we cannot sacrifice functionality for the sake of security.

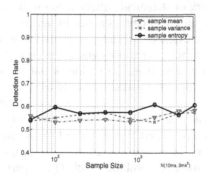

Fig. 7. Detection Rate by RTT of Delayed Ping Packets with Zero Cross Traffic

The second approach is inspired by our theories and experiments. We know that the smaller r and the bigger σ_l^2 and σ_h^2 in (6), the smaller the detection rate. To reduce r and increase σ_l^2 and σ_h^2, we intentionally introduce a random delay to ping packets. This is similar to adding noise to the RTT of ping packets and has the same effect as cross traffic does in Figure 3 (b). This delay satisfies a normal distribution $N(\mu_T, \sigma_T^2)$. It can be perceived that an appropriate selection of μ_T and σ_T will dramatically reduce the detection rate. To validate this approach, we again use the configuration in Figure 1 as the experiment network setup. There is no cross traffic. Figure 7 gives the detection rate by different statistics when ping packets are delayed by a random interval, which satisfies a normal distribution $N(10ms, 3ms^2)$. We can see that even though the attacker has the best-case (no cross traffic) the detection rate by different feature statistics approaches 50% (the minimum detection rate for two classes recognition) at a large sample size.

A third guideline for countering active ping probing attacks is that we should avoid the case in which user traffic possibly lasts for a long time at a roughly constant rate. For example, in a peer-to-peer anonymous file sharing system, the file should be split into small pieces before uploading and downloading.

7   Conclusions and Final Remarks

In this paper, we evaluate the security of sophisticated traffic padding schemes under active probing attacks. To demonstrate the threat from such attacks, we use ping probing attacks aimed at deriving user payload traffic rates. We found that by measuring statistics of the round trip time of ping packets injected into security gateways, the adversary can break the padding system, track the user payload traffic changing pattern, and discover exactly the payload traffic rate that security gateways try to protect even if a strong link padding scheme such as VIT padding is used by these gateways.

Of the possible statistics, sample entropy is an effective and robust feature statistic to explore the correlation between user payload traffic rate and the round trip time of probing ping packets. The reason for the success of the exploit is that users' payload traffic causes small disturbances to the RTT of ping packets. Moreover, the higher the user traffic rate, the larger this disturbance, therefore the bigger the entropy.

Under the framework of statistical pattern recognition, we formally model different statistics' detection rates. Our empirical results match our theoretical analysis. This framework can be easily extended to analyze other statistical analysis attacks because of statistical pattern recognition's maturity and abundance of analytical techniques. We also conducted extensive experiments in various situations including LAN in a laboratory, MAN such as campus networks, and wide area networks and found that for a MAN, the ping probing attack can still obtain a good detection rate. These extensive empirical data consistently demonstrates the usefulness of our formal model and correctness of detection rate predicted by the closed-form formulae.

Following our theory, after a careful analysis we propose randomly delaying the ping packets to counter the active probing attack. Our experiments and theories validate the effectiveness of this scheme. Other guidelines are also provided.

References

[1] Chaum, D.L.: Untraceable electronic mail, return addresses, and digital pseudonyms. Communications of the ACM **24** (1981)
[2] Serjantov, A., Sewell, P.: Passive attack analysis for connection-based anonymity systems. In: European Symposium on Research in Computer Security (ESORICS). (2003)

[3] Guan, Y., Fu, X., Xuan, D., Shenoy, P.U., Bettati, R., Zhao, W.: Netcamo: Camouflaging network traffic for qos-guaranteed critical allplications. In: IEEE Transactions on Systems, Man, and Cybernetics Part A: Systems and Humans, Special Issue on Information Assurance. Volume 31 of 4. (2001) 253–265

[4] Fu, X., Graham, B., Bettati, R., Zhao, W.: On effectiveness of link padding for statistical traffic analysis attacks. ICDCS (2003)

[5] Dai, W.: Freedom attacks. http://www.eskimo.com/ weidai/freedom-attacks.txt (1998)

[6] Back, A., Goldberg, I., Shostack, A.: Freedom systems 2.1 security issues and analysis. White paper, Zero Knowledge Systems, Inc. (2001)

[7] Shannon, C.E.: Communication theory of secrecy systems. Bell Sys. Tech. J. **28** (1949) 656–715

[8] Baran, P.: On distributed communications: Ix security, secrecy, and tamper-free considerations. Memo RM-3765-PR, Rand Corp. (1964)

[9] Voydoc, V., Kent, S.: Security mechanisms in high-level network protocols. ACM Computing Surveys (1983) 135 – 171

[10] Newman-Wolfe, R.E., Venkatraman, B.R.: High level prevention of traffic analysis. Computer Security Applications Conference, Seventh Annual (1991) 102 –109

[11] Newman-Wolfe, R.E., Venkatraman, B.R.: Performance analysis of a method for high level prevention of traffic analysis. Computer Security Applications Conference, Eighth Annual (1992) 123 –130

[12] Venkatraman, B.R., Newman-Wolfe, R.E.: Performance analysis of a method for high level prevention of traffic analysis using measurements from a campus network. Computer Security Applications Conference, 10th Annual (1994) 288 –297

[13] Timmerman, B.: a security model for dynamic adaptive traffic masking. New Security Paradigms Workshop (1997)

[14] Syverson, P.F., Goldschlag, D.M., Reed, M.G.: Anonymous connections and onion routing. In: IEEE Symposium on Security and Privacy, Oakland, California (1997) 44–54

[15] Raymond, J.: Traffic analysis: Protocols, attacks, design issues and open problems. In: PET. (2001)

[16] Back, A., Muller, U., Stiglic, A.: Traffic analysis attacks and trade-offs in anonymity providing systems. IHW2001 (2001)

[17] Danezis, G., Dingledine, R., Mathewson, N.: Mixminion: Design of a Type III Anonymous Remailer Protocol. In: the 2003 IEEE Symposium on Security and Privacy. (2003)

[18] Freedman, M.J., Morris, R.: Tarzan: A peer-to-peer anonymizing network layer. In: CCS. (2002)

[19] Song, D.X., Wagner, D., Tian, X.: Timing analysis of keystrokes and timing attacks on ssh. 10th USENIX Security Symposium (2001)

[20] Felten, E.W., Schneider, M.A.: Timing attacks on web privacy. CCS (2000)

[21] Hintz, A.: Fingerprinting websites using traffic analysis. http://guh.nu/projects/ta/safeweb/safeweb.html (2002)

[22] Sun, Q., Simon, D.R., Wang, Y., Russell, W., Padmanabhan, V.N., Qiu, L.: Statistical identification of encrypted web browsing traffic. IEEE Symposium on Security and Privacy (2002)

[23] Duda, R.O., Hart, P.E.: Pattern Classification. John Wiley & Sons (2001)

[24] Silverman, B.W.: Density estimation for statistics and data analysis. Chapman and Hall, London, New York (1986)

[25] Moddemeijer, R.: On estimation of entropy and mutual information of continuous distributions. Signal Processing **16** (1989) 233–246

[26] Fu, X., Graham, B., Xuan, D., Bettati, R., Zhao, W.: Active probing attacks. Technical Report TR2003-8-8, Texas A&M University (2003)

Optimization and Evaluation of Randomized c-Secure CRT Code Defined on Polynomial Ring

Hirofumi Muratani

Corporate Research & Development Center, Toshiba Corporation,
1, Komukai-Toshiba-cho, Saiwai-ku, Kawasaki, Japan,
hirofumi.muratani@toshiba.co.jp

Abstract. An improved construction of a binary fingerprinting code is evaluated. The c-secure CRT code, a variant of the c-secure code, has shorter code length than the original construction by Boneh and Shaw. Recently, two improvements to this code have been proposed. We provide conditions determining the code length of the construction combined with these two improvements and provide the optimal setting of parameters. We compare the code length of the improved construction with that of the original construction. For any size of collusion, the code length is improved. In particular, for the collusion size $c \geq 32$, the code length of the improved code becomes about a tenth of the original c-secure CRT code.

1 Introduction

The purpose of this study is to analyze constructions of a c-secure code providing short code length. The c-secure code is a binary fingerprinting code proposed by Boneh and Show[1], which is robust against collusion attacks if the size of the collusion is not greater than c. In order to make this code more practical, several modified constructions of the code have been proposed[1, 2, 3, 4, 5, 6, 7, 8, 9, 10, 11, 12, 13, 14, 15, 16, 17].

A c-secure CRT code[9], which is a variant of the c-secure code, provides a considerably shorter code length, based on the Chinese Remainder Theorem(CRT). Several improvements to this code have been proposed[13, 14, 15, 10, 11, 12, 16, 17]. In this paper, we analyze how short the code length of the c-secure CRT code can be made by some combinations of these improvements.

The original c-secure CRT code is constructed based on the CRT which holds for the ring of rational integers $\mathbb{Z}$. Kim et al. extended the construction to the CRT which holds for the polynomial ring $\mathbb{F}_q[x]$ and demonstrated that this construction can provide shorter code lengths than the original[13, 14, 15]. Watanabe and Kitagawa[17] proposed an improvement on the security of Yoshioka and Matsumoto's random-error-resilient version of the c-secure CRT code[10, 11, 12]. We apply Watanabe and Kitagawa's approach, but for a different purpose, namely, reduction of the code length of the original c-secure CRT code. In this paper, we evaluate the effect on code length reduction of a combination of these improvements. First, we provide the conditions determining the code length in the

J. Fridrich (Ed.): IH 2004, LNCS 3200, pp. 282–292, 2004.

combined construction, compare the code length of the improved construction with that of the original construction, and evaluate the effect of this improvement on the code length.

2 Approach

2.1 c-Secure Code

The c-seucre code with ϵ-error was proposed by Boneh and Shaw[1]. Let $U = \mathbb{Z}/n\mathbb{Z}$ be a set of all user IDs. A fingerprinting code is defined by $(\mathcal{C}, \mathcal{G}, \mathcal{E}, \mathcal{T})$. $\mathcal{C}$ is a set of codewords. In this paper, we assume $\mathcal{C}$ is a binary code whose code length is L, that is $\mathcal{C} \subset \{0,1\}^L$. $\mathcal{G}$ is an algorithm generating a random string s used in encoding and tracing, $\mathcal{E}$ is an encoding algorithm taking an input $(u \in U, s)$ and making an output $w \in \mathcal{C}$, and $\mathcal{T}$ is a tracing algorithm taking an input $(X \in \{0,1\}^L, s)$ and making an output of an element in 2^U. Let $\mathcal{E}(C, s) = \{\mathcal{E}(u, s) \mid u \in C\}$ for any $C \subseteq U$.

A collusion attack is modeled as an algorithm $\mathcal{A}$ which takes a subset $\mathcal{W}$ of $\mathcal{E}(U, s)$ as an input and produces an output $X \in \mathcal{F}(\mathcal{W})$, where $\mathcal{F}(\mathcal{W})$ is a feasible set of $\mathcal{W}$. In general, $\mathcal{A}$ is a probabilistic algorithm generating any codeword in a feasible set of $\mathcal{W}$. The feasible set of $\mathcal{W}$, $\mathcal{F}(\mathcal{W})$, is defined by

$$\mathcal{F}(\mathcal{W}) = \left\{ X \in \mathcal{C} \mid \forall i \in \{0, \cdots, L-1\} \left[\left[\forall W \in \mathcal{W} \; W_{[i]} = b \right] \to X_{[i]} = b \right] \right\},$$

where the suffix $[i]$ means the i-th bit position of those codewords. The distribution of X depends on a marking assumption which $\mathcal{A}$ is based on.

Definition 1. *The c-secure code with ϵ-error[1] is defined as $(\mathcal{C}, \mathcal{G}, \mathcal{E}, \mathcal{T})$ satisfying*

$$\Pr \left[s \leftarrow \mathcal{G}; \mathcal{W} \leftarrow \mathcal{E}(C, s); X \leftarrow \mathcal{A}(\mathcal{W}); C' \leftarrow \mathcal{T}(X, s) \; : \; C' \subseteq C \wedge C' \neq \emptyset \right] > 1 - \epsilon,$$

for any $\mathcal{A}$ satisfyng a marking assumption and for any $C \subseteq U$ satisfying $|C| \leq c$, where the probability in the left-hand side of the inequality is taken over random coin tosses of $\mathcal{G}$, $\mathcal{E}$, $\mathcal{A}$ and $\mathcal{T}$.

2.2 c-Secure CRT Code

We briefly review the c-secure CRT code[9].

Modulus Let N, k and l be positive integers satisfying $\lfloor 2N/c \rfloor = (k + l)$. Let $p_0, \ldots, p_{N-1}$ be positive integers which are pairwise relatively prime and satisfy

$$p_0 < \cdots < p_{N-1}, \tag{1}$$
$$p_0 \times \cdots \times p_{k-1} \geq n. \tag{2}$$

We call these integers *moduli*.

Residue Let $u \in \mathbb{Z}/n\mathbb{Z}$ be an ID. We call an integer $r_i \in \mathbb{Z}_{p_i}$ such that $r_i \equiv u \bmod p_i$ as a *residue* of u modulo p_i, where $i \in \mathbb{Z}/N\mathbb{Z}$.

Inner Code Corresponding to each $i \in \mathbb{Z}/N\mathbb{Z}$, we use a code $\Gamma_0(p_i, t)$ as an inner code, which is the same as that defined in [1]. The codeword of $\Gamma_0(p_i, t)$ is given as follows.

$$w_i^{(j)} = \underbrace{00\cdots\cdots0}_{t \times j}\underbrace{11\cdots\cdots1}_{t \times (p_i - j - 1)} \quad \text{for } j \in \mathbb{Z}/p_i\mathbb{Z}.$$

Each t-bit portion is called a *block*.

Outer Code We define a c-secure CRT code as a concatenated code of the above inner codes and denote it by $\Gamma(p_0, \ldots, p_{N-1}; n, t)$. A codeword $W^{(u)}$ corresponding to an ID, u, is given as follows.

$$W^{(u)} = w_0^{(r_0)} \| w_1^{(r_1)} \| \cdots \| w_{N-1}^{(r_{N-1})} \quad \text{for } u \in \mathbb{Z}/n\mathbb{Z},$$

where $r_i \equiv u \bmod p_i$ for $i \in \mathbb{Z}/N\mathbb{Z}$. Its code length is $L = t \sum_{i=0}^{N-1}(p_i - 1)$.

Tracing Algorithm A tracing algorithm of the c-secure CRT code is a sequence of two algorithms: a tracing algorithm of the inner codes and a searching algorithm. The tracing algorithm of the inner code, $\Gamma_0(p_i, t)$, is that of $O(n)$ n-secure code[6]:

Algorithm 1 (Tracing $\mathcal{T}$)
```
1:  input X;
2:  decompose X into x₀‖x₁‖···‖xₙ₋₁;
3:  for ( i = 0 ; i < N ; i++ ){
4:      for ( rᵢ⁽⁻⁾ = 0 ; rᵢ⁽⁻⁾ < pᵢ − 1 ; rᵢ⁽⁻⁾++ )
5:          if ( H_{rᵢ⁽⁻⁾}(x) > 0 ) break;
6:      for ( rᵢ⁽⁺⁾ = pᵢ − 1 ; rᵢ⁽⁺⁾ > rᵢ⁽⁻⁾ ; rᵢ⁽⁺⁾-- )
7:          if ( H_{rᵢ⁽⁺⁾−1}(x) < t ) break;}
8:  C = ∅;
9:  for ( u = 0 ; u < n − 1 ; u++ ){
10:     count D(u);
11:     if ( D(u) ≥ D_th ) C = C ∪ {u}; }
12: output C;
```

Here, $x \in \{0,1\}^{(p_i-1)t}$ is a portion corresponding to the i-th inner code in a detected codeword X, and $H_j(\cdot)$ is a Hamming weight of the j-th block, where $j \in \mathbb{Z}/(p_i - 1)\mathbb{Z}$. The pair $\langle r_i^{(-)}, r_i^{(+)} \rangle$ is called a *residue pair*. And

$$\mathcal{D}(u) = \left| \left\{ i \in \mathbb{Z}/N\mathbb{Z} \middle| (u \equiv r_i^{(-)} \bmod p_i) \vee (u \equiv r_i^{(+)} \bmod p_i) \right\} \right|,$$
$$\mathcal{D}_{th} = k + l,$$

and l is determined by Eq.(6) in Theorem 1. In Algorithm 1, the steps from 1 through 7 are corresponding to the tracing algorithm of the inner codes and the steps from 8 through 12 are corresponding to the searching algorithm of the outer code.

Marking Assumption The marking assumption of the c-secure CRT code is as follows:

1. The collusion algorithm $\mathcal{A}$ cannot generate any codeword which does not belong to the feasible set[1].
2. The collusion algorithm $\mathcal{A}$ generates any codeword in its feasible set randomly with equal probability.
3. We suppose that a coalition is organized randomly. By this assumption, we mean that the residues can be treated as random variables, which take a value $\alpha \in \mathbb{Z}/p_i\mathbb{Z}$ with the following probabilities.

$$\Pr\left[r_i^{(-)} = \alpha\right] = \left(1 - \frac{\alpha}{p_i}\right)^c - \left(1 - \frac{\alpha+1}{p_i}\right)^c, \tag{3}$$

$$\Pr\left[r_i^{(+)} = \alpha\right] = \left(\frac{\alpha+1}{p_i}\right)^c - \left(\frac{\alpha}{p_i}\right)^c. \tag{4}$$

The third assumption, originally given in [9], conflicts with Definition 1 because Definition 1 requires that, for any collusion, tracing succeeds with high probability. In this paper, we consider that, depending on the random choices s taken by $\mathcal{G}$, the algorithm $\mathcal{E}$ permutes U randomly, and the algorithm $\mathcal{T}$ permutes U inversely. This random permutation of the user IDs for a fixed collusion has the same effect as the generation of a random collusion. Then, no contradiction remains with Definition 1.

Condition for c-Secureness The code length of the c-secure CRT code is determined by the following theorem[9].

Theorem 1. *Let $N = \lceil c(k + l)/2 \rceil$. The code $\Gamma(p_0, \ldots, p_{N-1}; n, t)$ is a c-secure code with ϵ-error, if the following inequalities are satisfied.*

$$t \geq -\log_2\left[1 - (1 - \epsilon_1)^{\frac{1}{2N}}\right], \tag{5}$$

$$\left[1 - \prod_{i=k}^{k+l-1}\left\{1 - \left(1 - \frac{1}{p_i}\right)^c\right\}\right]^{{}_NC_{k+l}\times 2^{k+l}} \geq 1 - \epsilon_2, \tag{6}$$

where ϵ_1 and ϵ_2 satisfy $0 < \epsilon_1 < 1$, $0 < \epsilon_2 < 1$ and $(1 - \epsilon_1)(1 - \epsilon_2) > 1 - \epsilon$.

The code length of this construction is $L = t\sum_{i=0}^{N-1}(p_i - 1)$. Here, L implicitly depends on c, because it is a function of variables t and N which depend on c.

2.3   Construction on Polynomial Ring

Let $\mathbb{F}_q$ be a finite field of cardinality q. Let $\mathbb{F}_q[x]$ be a polynomial ring. It is known that the Chinese Remainder Theorem holds for $\mathbb{F}_q[x]$ because it is a unitary commutative ring. A construction of the c-secure CRT code on $\mathbb{F}_q[x]$ was proposed by Kim et al.[13, 14, 15]. The moduli in such construction are polynomials, $p_i(x) = a_{i,d}x^{d_i} + a_{i,d-1}x^{d_i-1} + \cdots + a_{i,0}$, which are pairwise relatively prime. Let $|p_i(x)|$ denote the number of all possible remainders. That is, $|p_i(x)| = q^{d_i}$. The equations (1) and (2) are modified as follows:

$$d_0 \leq \cdots \leq d_{N-1}, \tag{7}$$
$$q^{d_0 + \cdots + d_{k-1}} \geq n. \tag{8}$$

Let a user ID $u \in \mathbb{Z}/n\mathbb{Z}$ be expressed as $u = \sum_{i=0}^{d-1} u_i q^i$, where $d = \sum_{i=0}^{N-1} d_i$. Then, a polynomial $u(x)$ corresponding to u is defined as $u(x) = u_{d-1}x^{d-1} + u_{d-2}x^{d-2} \cdots + u_0$. Let $r_i(x)$ denote a remainder of $u(x)$ divided by $p_i(x)$. Let r_i be an integer corresponding to $r_i(x)$, where if $r_i(x) = \sum_{j=0}^{d_i-1} r_{i,j}x^j$, then $r_i = \sum_{j=0}^{d_i-1} r_{i,j}q^j$.

2.4   Randomization

Next the residues are transformed by random permutations. This randomization is introduced by Watanabe and Kitagawa[17] to enhance the security of a modified version of the c-secure CRT code proposed by Yoshioka and Matsumoto[11].

For each modulus, a random permutation $P_i : \mathbb{Z}/|p_i(x)|\mathbb{Z} \to \mathbb{Z}/|p_i(x)|\mathbb{Z}$ is chosen. Each r_i is mapped to $q_i = P_i(r_i)$. We assume that for any i, for any $\alpha \in \mathbb{Z}/|p_i(x)|\mathbb{Z}$, and for any $\beta \in \mathbb{Z}/|p_i(x)|\mathbb{Z}$, $\Pr[P(\alpha) = \beta] = 1/|p_i(x)|$. The q_i's are encoded by the inner codes. Therefore, pairs $\langle q_i^{(-)}, q_i^{(+)} \rangle$'s are traced from the inner codes, and instead of $\langle r_i^{(-)}, r_i^{(+)} \rangle$'s, $\langle q_i^{(-)}, q_i^{(+)} \rangle$'s follow Eq. (5) and Eq. (6). Because of this randomization, $\langle r_i^{(-)}, r_i^{(+)} \rangle$'s satisfy the following equations:

$$\Pr\left[r_i^{(-)} = \alpha\right] = \sum_\beta \Pr[P_i(\alpha) = \beta]\left\{ \left(1 - \frac{\beta}{|p_i(x)|}\right)^c - \left(1 - \frac{\beta+1}{|p_i(x)|}\right)^c \right\},$$
$$= \frac{1}{|p_i(x)|}, \tag{9}$$
$$\Pr\left[r_i^{(+)} = \alpha\right] = \sum_\beta \Pr[P_i(\alpha) = \beta]\left\{ \left(\frac{\beta+1}{|p_i(x)|}\right)^c - \left(\frac{\beta}{|p_i(x)|}\right)^c \right\},$$
$$= \frac{1}{|p_i(x)|}. \tag{10}$$

Theorem 2. *Let* $N = \lceil c(k+l)/2 \rceil$. *The code* $\Gamma(|p_0(x)|, \ldots, |p_{N-1}(x)|; n, t)$ *is a c-secure code with ϵ-error, if the following inequalities are satisfied.*

$$t \geq -\log_2\left[1 - (1 - \epsilon_1)^{\frac{1}{2N}}\right], \tag{11}$$

$$\left[1 - \prod_{i=k}^{k+l-1}\left\{\frac{1}{|p_i(x)|}\right\}\right]^{NC_{k+l}\times 2^{k+l}} \geq 1 - \epsilon_2, \tag{12}$$

where ϵ_1 and ϵ_2 satisfy $0 < \epsilon_1 < 1$, $0 < \epsilon_2 < 1$ and $(1 - \epsilon_1)(1 - \epsilon_2) > 1 - \epsilon$.

The code length of this construction is $L = t\sum_{i=0}^{N-1}(|p_i(x)| - 1)$.

2.5   Optimal Construction

In this construction, $d_0 = d_1 = \cdots = d_{N-1}$ is optimal.

Proposition 1. *In the construction of Theorem 2, the minimum of the code length L approximately resides on $d_0 = d_1 = \cdots = d_{N-1}$. Here, the approximation means that the parameters in the code design are considered to be continuous variables.*

Proof. We derive the optimal condition providing the minimum code length under the conditions of Theorem 2. Let $|p_i(x)| = q^{d_i}$ for $i = 0, \cdots, N - 1$. The (in)equalities that d_i's satisfy can be rewritten as

$$d_0 \leq d_1 \leq \cdots \leq d_{N-1}, \tag{13}$$

$$q^{\sum_{i=0}^{k-1} d_i} \geq n, \tag{14}$$

$$\left[1 - q^{-\sum_{i=k}^{k+l-1} d_i}\right]^{NC_{k+l}\times 2^{k+l}} \geq 1 - \epsilon_2, \tag{15}$$

$$t \geq -\log_2[1 - (1 - \epsilon_1)^{\frac{1}{2N}}], \tag{16}$$

$$L = t\sum_{i=0}^{N-1}(q^{d_i} - 1), \tag{17}$$

where $N = \frac{c(k+l)}{2}$. In the following derivation of the optimal solution, the variables in the above equations are regarded as continuous.

The variables $d_0, d_1, \cdots, d_{k-1}$ appear only in Eq. (13), (14) and (17). In order to minimize L, it is required that $d_0 = d_1 = \cdots = d_{k-1} = (\log_q n)/k$. Similarly, the variables $d_{k+l}, d_{k+l+1}, \cdots, d_{N-1}$ appear only in Eq. (13) and (17). In order to minimize L, it is required that $d_{k+l} = d_{k+l+1} = \cdots = d_{N-1} = d_{k+l-1}$.

The variables $d_k, d_{k+1}, \cdots, d_{k+l-1}$ appear in Eq. (13), (15), and (17). If $d_k + d_{k+1} + \cdots + d_{k+l-1}$ is constant, Eq. (15) does not change the value of l on varying $d_k, d_{k+1}, \cdots, d_{k+l-1}$. Under this condition, $d_k = d_{k+1} = \cdots = d_{k+l-1}$ minimizes L.

Thus, let $Q_A = q^{d_0} = \cdots = q^{d_{k-1}} = n^{1/k}$ and $Q_B = q^{d_k} = \cdots = q^{d_N-1}$. By Eq. (13), $Q_A \le Q_B$. Assume equalties hold in Eq. (15) and (16) to minimize L. Differentiating Eq. (17) by Q_B,

$$\frac{\partial L}{\partial Q_B} = \frac{\partial t}{\partial Q_B}(k(Q_A - 1) + (N - k)(Q_B - 1)) + t\frac{\partial N}{\partial Q_B}(Q_B - 1) + t(N - k),$$

$$= \frac{c}{2}\Big\{-(k(Q_A - 1) + (N - k)(Q_B - 1))\frac{\log_2(1 - \epsilon_2)}{2N^2}\cdot\frac{(1 - \epsilon_2)^{1/2N}}{1 - (1 - \epsilon_2)^{1/2N}}$$

$$+t(Q_B - 1)\Big\}\frac{\partial l}{\partial Q_B} + t(N - k), \tag{18}$$

By differentiating the equality of Eq. (15),

$$\frac{\partial l}{\partial Q_B}\ln(1 - Q_B^{-l})\Big\{\frac{\partial \ln(_NC_{k+l})}{\partial l} + \ln 2\Big\} = -\frac{lQ_B^{-l-1}}{1 - Q_B^{-l}}. \tag{19}$$

By using a formula of the digamma function $\psi(z) \equiv \ln \Gamma(z)/dz$:

$$\psi(z) = -C + \sum_{n=0}^{\infty}\Big(\frac{1}{n+1} - \frac{1}{z+n}\Big), \tag{20}$$

where C is Euler's constant, the positivity of the differential of logarithm of combination is obtained:

$$\frac{\partial \ln(_NC_{k+l})}{\partial l} = \sum_{n=0}^{\infty}\frac{N^2 + 2(N - K)(n + 1)}{(N - K + 1 + n)(N + 1 + n)(K + 1 + n)} > 0, \tag{21}$$

where $K = k + l$. By Eq. (19) and the above inequality, we obtain $\frac{\partial l}{\partial Q_B} > 0$. By Eq. (18) and $\frac{\partial l}{\partial Q_B} > 0$, we get $\frac{\partial L}{\partial Q_B} > 0$. Thus, L is minimized when $Q_A = Q_B$.
□

In this case, the code length is provided by parameters satisfying the following theorem, because $|p_i(x)| = q^{d_i} = q^{d_0}$:

Theorem 3. *Let* $N = \lceil c(k+l)/2\rceil$. *The code* $\Gamma(q^{d_0}, \ldots, q^{d_N-1}; n, t)$ *is a c-secure code with ϵ-error, if the following inequalities are satisfied.*

$$t \ge -\log_2\Big[1 - (1 - \epsilon_1)^{\frac{1}{2N}}\Big], \tag{22}$$

$$\big[1 - q^{-d_0l}\big]^{_NC_{k+l}\times 2^{k+l}} \ge 1 - \epsilon_2, \tag{23}$$

where ϵ_1 and ϵ_2 satisfy $0 < \epsilon_1 < 1$, $0 < \epsilon_2 < 1$ and $(1 - \epsilon_1)(1 - \epsilon_2) > 1 - \epsilon$.

The code length of this construction is $L = tN(q^{d_0} - 1)$.

Proof. We can prove the theorem by proving the following statements:

1. At least one colluder is traced with probability 1.
2. No innocent user is traced with probability larger than $1 - \epsilon$.

The first statement is proved as follows: The number of the residues traced by the inner-code tracing is at least $2\lceil \frac{c(k+l)}{2} \rceil$. Therefore, at least one colluder has at least $(k+l)$ residues in the set of the traced residues. The searching algorithm of the outer code certainly traces the person.

The second statement is proved as follows: There are two possibilities that an innocent user is traced:

1. Accidentally, a false residue is traced in the inner-code tracing.
2. Accidentally, an innocent user has enough residues to be traced in the outer-code searching.

The probability of the first possibility is limited to at most ϵ_1 by Eq. (11) and the marking assumptions 1 and 2. The probability of the second possibility is limited to at most ϵ_2 as follows: The number of combinations of $(k+l)$ residues in the traced tuple of residue pairs is $_NC_{k+l} \times 2^{k+l}$. For each combination, the probability that an ID exists which is congruent to every residue in the combination is q^{-d_0l} because of the CRT and Eq. (9) and (10). Therefore, the probability that no such combination exists is limited to at most ϵ_2 by Eq. (3).

$\square$

We have to note that another constraint exists on the optimal construction of the randomized c-secure CRT code on a polynomial ring. The conditions in Theorem 3 require N polynomials which have the same degree and are relatively prime to each other. The number of monic irreducible polynomials of degree d is given by $N_q(d) = \frac{1}{d}\sum_{m|d}\mu(m)q^{d/m}$ if q is prime, where $\mu(\cdot)$ is Möbius function. For example, $N_q(1) = q$, $N_q(2) = \frac{1}{2}q(q-1)$, $N_q(3) = \frac{1}{3}q(q^2-1)$, and $\cdots$. Let $\hat{N}_q(d)$ denote the maximum number of all monic polynomials which are relatively prime and whose degree is d. Then $\hat{N}_q(1) = N_q(1) = q$, $\hat{N}_q(2) = N_q(2)+N_q(1) = \frac{1}{2}q(q+1)$, $\hat{N}_q(3) = N_q(3) + \min\{N_q(1), N_q(2)\} = \frac{1}{3}q(q^2+2)$, $\cdots$. In general, the number $\frac{\hat{N}_q(d)}{q^d}$ decreases as d increases. If $|p_i(x)| = q^d$ and $N > \hat{N}_q(d)$, we cannot construct the code. In such case, smaller d and larger q should be chosen, because N, therefore L also, does not change while q^d remains constant. If $N > \hat{N}_q(d)$ even when $d = 1$, we cannot construct such code and have to choose larger q. In general, the optimal choice is $d = 1$ and $q \geq N$.

3   Results

Fig. 1 shows a code length comparison between the original c-secure CRT code and the improvement. The vertical axis is the collusion size and the horizontal axis is the code length. The symbols, $\bigcirc$, $\triangle$ and $\square$ represent examples of constructions of the original c-secure CRT code, the c-secure CRT code on the polynomial ring $\mathbb{F}_q[x]$, and the randomized c-secure CRT code on the polynomial ring $\mathbb{F}_q[x]$, respectively. In every construction, we assumed that the number of users n is at least 10^9 and the tracing error ϵ is less than 10^{-6}. In the latter two codes, we assumed that $p_i(x)$ are all monic irreducible polynomials of degree 1.

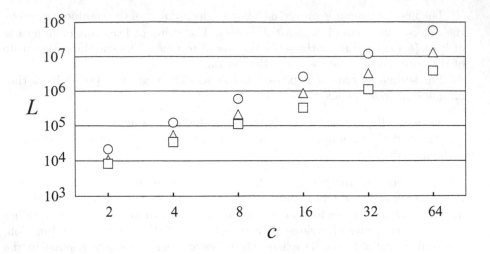

Fig. 1. Code Lengths Comparison: The symbols $\bigcirc$, $\triangle$ and $\square$ shows the construction examples of the original c-secure CRT code, the variant on a polynomial ring, and the randomized variant on a polynomial ring, respectively.

In the calculations of L, given n, c and ϵ, the other parameters are determined so that they satisfy the inequalities in the respective theorems and minimize the value of L.

We see from Fig. 1 that the c-secure CRT code on the polynomial ring also has shorter code length than the original for any collusion size. It alse demonstrates that, by combining the randomization, the improved code has much shorter code length for any collusion size c. In particular, for $c \geq 32$, the code length is a tenth of the original.

4   Discussion

We derived analytic conditions which the improved code has to satisfy, provided concrete code lengths for several parameter settings, and compared them with those of the original construction of the c-secure CRT code. We demonstrated that the improved code has shorter code than the original c-secure CRT code for any collusion size c. This code reduction has the following practical implication. Suppose an ID is embedded in a two-hour movie which has thirty frames per second and 10 bits are embedded per frame. Then, the total number of embedded bits is 2.16×10^6 bits. In the case of $n = 10^9$, this can accommodate a codeword of the original c-secure CRT code for up to $c = 8$. On the other hand, as for the improved code, it can accommodate a codeword for $c = 32$.

Finally, we have to analyze a relation of our result to the results in [18, 19]. In [19], a lower bound for a binary c-secure code is provided, which states that there exists a binary c-secure code whose code length is $O(c^2 \log n)$, and a construction satisfying such bound is provided. Compared to the construction, we confirmed that our construction still has shorter code length. However, the construction in [19] is based on a more general assumption concerning the attack algorithm $\mathcal{A}$ than is ours, which requires only the marking assumption 1. To clarify the relation between the marking assumption and the lower bound of the code length is an interesting remaining problem.

References

[1] Boneh, D., Shaw, J.: Collusion-Secure Fingerprinting for Digital Data. In: CRYPTO'95. Volume 963 of LNCS., Springer-Verlag (1995) 452–465

[2] Lindkvist, T.: Fingerprinting digital document. PhD thesis, Linköping University (1999)

[3] Löfvenberg, J.: Codes for Digital Fingerprinting. PhD thesis, Department of Electrical Engineering, Linköpnig University (2001)

[4] Suzuoki, M., Watanabe, H., Kasami, T.: A scheme of marking collusion-secure watermark. In: SCIS'97. (1997) 31B

[5] Watanabe, H., Kasami, T.: A Secure Code for Recipient Watermarking against Conspiracy Attacks by All Users. In: Information and Communication Security. (1997) 414–423

[6] Yoshida, J., Iwamura, K., Imai, H.: A coding method for collusion-secure watermark and less decline. In: SCIS'98. Number 10.2A (1998)

[7] Guth, H.J., Pfitzmann, B.: Error- and Collusion-Secure Fingerprinting for Digital Data. In Pfitzmann, A., ed.: Information Hiding, 3rd International Workshop, IH'99. Volume 1768 of LNCS., Springer-Verlag (2000) 134–145

[8] Yacobi, Y.: Improved Boneh-Shaw content fingerprinting. In: Topics in Cryptology – CT-RSA 2001. Volume 2020 of LNCS., Springer-Verlag (2001) 378–391

[9] Muratani, H.: A Collusion-Secure Fingerprinting Code Reduced by Chinese Remaindering and Its Random-Error Resilience. In Moskowitz, I.S., ed.: Information Hiding, 4th International Workshop, IH 2001. Volume 2137 of Lecture Notes on Computer Science., Springer-Verlag (2001) 303–315

[10] Yoshioka, K., Matsumoto, T.: Random-error-resilient tracing algorithm for collusion-secure fingerprinting code. Technical Report of IEICE **ISEC2001-52** (2001) 247–254

[11] Yoshioka, K., Matsumoto, T.: Random-Error-Resilient Tracing Algorithm for Collusion-Secure Fingerprinting Code (part 2). In: SCIS 2002. Volume II. (2002) 1021–1026

[12] Yoshioka, K., Matsumoto, T.: Random-Error-Resilience of a Short Collusion-Secure Code. IEICE Trans. on Fundamentals **E86-A** (2003) 1147–1155

[13] Kim, M., Shikata, J., Muratani, H., Imai, H.: Constructing c-secure codes using polynomials over finite fields. In: SITA2001 – The 24th Symposium on Information Theory and Its Applications. Number W-B-1-3 (2001) 27–30

[14] Kim, M., Shikata, J., Muratani, H., Imai, H.: On the c-Secure CRT Codes. In: SCIS 2002. Volume II. (2002) 1015–1019

[15] Kim, M., Shikata, J., Muratani, H., Imai, H.: Constructing c-Secure CRT Codes Using Polynomials over Finite Fields. IEICE Trans. on Fundamentals **E86-A** (2003) 3256–3266

[16] Watanabe, H., Kitagawa, T.: An attack for a fingerprinting code and its success probability. In: ISITA 2002. (2002) 555–558
[17] Watanabe, H., Kitagawa, T.: An ID coding scheme for fingerprinting, randomized c-secure CRT code. In: ICICS 2002. Volume 2513 of LNCS., Springer-Verlag (2002) 173–183
[18] Peikert, C., Shelat, A., Smith, A.: Lower Bounds for Collusion-Secure Fingerprinting. In: Proceedings of the 14th Annual ACM-SIAM Symposium on Discrete Algorithms (SODA) 2003. (2003) 472–479
[19] Tardos, G.: Optimal Probabilistic Fingerprinting Codes. In: STOC'03, ACM (2003) 116–125

Statistical Disclosure or Intersection Attacks on Anonymity Systems

George Danezis and Andrei Serjantov

University of Cambridge, Computer Laboratory,
William Gates Building, 15 JJ Thomson Avenue,
Cambridge CB3 0FD, United Kingdom.
George.Danezis@cl.cam.ac.uk   Andrei.Serjantov@cl.cam.ac.uk

Abstract. In this paper we look at the information an attacker can extract using a statistical disclosure attack. We provide analytical results about the anonymity of users when they repeatedly send messages through a threshold mix following the model of Kesdogan, Agrawal and Penz [7] and through a pool mix. We then present a statistical disclosure attack that can be used to attack models of anonymous communication networks based on pool mixes. Careful approximations make the attack computationally efficient. Such models are potentially better suited to derive results that could apply to the security of real anonymous communication networks.

1   Introduction

Intersection attacks take advantage of repeated communications between two parties to compromise the anonymity offered to them by anonymous communication systems. While it is possible to manage their impact within the anonymous communication infrastructure, they can be devastating when the anonymous communication system is abstracted as a single mix and attacked. In this case the adversary observes a victim sending messages and notes all their potential receivers. By aggregating and processing such information, Berthold, Pfitzmann and Standtke [2] observe, that an attacker is able to deduce some information about who is communicating with whom.

In this paper we are extending previous work done on a simple model of an anonymity system — users sending messages at random through a threshold mix. The idea of using such model for evaluating the anonymity of repeated communication is due to Kesdogan, Agrawal and Penz [7, 1]. They propose an expensive attack which aims to identify senders when they can be proved (within the assumptions of the model) to have sent a particular message. Later, Danezis showed that an efficient probabilistic attack is also possible [5] which is approximate, but still provides good results. In the first part of this paper we will revisit the original model and present new analytical results about the information that can be inferred by observing the mix.

Anonymous communication systems cannot in many cases be modelled as abstract threshold mixes, since a set of messages is likely to remain in the network across any chosen division in rounds. We therefore propose a statistical

J. Fridrich (Ed.): IH 2004, LNCS 3200, pp. 293–308, 2004.
© Springer-Verlag Berlin Heidelberg 2004

attack that applies to an anonymous communication channel modelled as a pool mix [12]. Such a mix retains a number of messages every round that are mixed with the messages injected in the network in the following round. This model can be used more effectively to study the limit of how much anonymity anonymous communication networks can provide. The attack presented is very efficient, and allows the adversary to judge the confidence of the results. The set of careful approximations that make this attack very efficient are explained as part of this work.

2   Previous Work

Anonymous communications over information networks were introduced in his seminal paper by David Chaum [3]. The basic building block that such systems use to provide the required anonymity properties is the *mix*, a node that takes a batch of input messages and outputs them all in such a way that their correspondence is hidden. Cryptographic techniques are used to hide the correlation between the input and output message bit patterns, and reordering of the messages is used to disrupt the timing patterns within each batch of messages. This mixing strategy is called a *threshold mix*. Other mix strategies have also been suggested that may make the mix node more resilient to active attacks [8, 12], and a body of work has concentrated on measuring the anonymity they provide [11, 6, 13].

Although the mix was originally conceived as a real network node, Kesdogan, Agrawal and Penz model [7] observe that any anonymity system that provides unlinkability (rather than unobservability) to its participants could be modelled as an abstract threshold mix. They then examine the anonymity offered by such a network to a sender that uses the mix across many rounds to communicate with a set of recipients. He describes the *disclosure attack* that can be used to deduce the set of recipients of a target sender. An analysis of the performance of the attack is further investigated by Agrawal, Kesdogan and Penz [1].

Such attacks were previously described as *intersection attacks* [2] or *partitioning attacks*, both when applied to single mixes and when performed against the whole anonymous network. When applied to single mixes, the attack can be eliminated by requiring each message travelling through the network to follow a different path, as originally proposed by Chaum [3], or by restricting the routes that messages can take out of each node [4]. On the other hand, given that senders will be communicating with a persistent set of parties, such attacks will always yield information when applied to the whole network. The Onion Routing project was the first to draw attention to such attacks performed at the edges of the network, and named them *traffic confirmation* attacks [10].

The main disadvantage of the disclosure attack is that its exact nature makes it computationally very expensive. Danezis [5] proposed a statistical attack based on a set of carefully selected approximations that allows an attacker observing the same model of a network to estimate a victim's set of receivers. As we will see, one of the main advantages of the statistical disclosure attack is that it can be generalised and applied against other anonymous communication network models. In particular [7] assumes that an anonymous network can be abstracted as a large threshold mix where batches of messages are anonymized together and sent out to their respective recipients.

A related idea is presented by Moskowitz *et al* in [9] where they assess how much information is leaked to an adversary by a malicious user using an anonymous channel. It is likely that analysing systems from that perspective will also provide results about the information leakage.

We will illustrate how the statistical disclosure attack can be generalised to anonymous communication mechanisms that can be modelled as pool mixes, or in other words where some messages are fed forward to the next mixing rounds of the model.

3 Formal Account of the Attack on the Threshold Mix

We follow the model considered by Danezis in [5]. The anonymity system is considered as a threshold mix with threshold $B + 1$. Thus, at each round $B + 1$ messages are processed. The victim of the attack, Alice, is known to the adversary to send one message at every round to a receiver chosen uniformly at random from a set M. Naturally, if Alice does not send a message during a round, we simply ignore it altogether. The other B senders whom we collectively call Steves send one message each to a receiver chosen independently and uniformly at random from a set N, $M \subseteq N$. The attacker knows $|M|$ (and $|N|$), and wishes to determine M.

We now define some notation. Let p_r be the probability that one of the other senders, a Steve, sends a message to a particular receiver r. Naturally, if they pick their recipients uniformly, $\forall r \in N$. $p_r = \frac{1}{|N|}$. Let $q_r = 1 - p_r$ be the probability Steve does not send a message to r.

Let us now start with some very simple cases and build up a technique for analysing how much information the attacker gains from observing Alice send messages via the anonymity system modelled as a threshold mix.

3.1 One Round, Alice Sends to One Receiver

Suppose $M = \{r\}$. Now consider the attacker observing one round of communication. The probability that we see r receiving exactly one message is q_r^B — Alice definitely sends her message to r, the other senders must send their messages to other receivers. The probability of any other receiver $r'(r' \in N \setminus \{r\})$ receiving exactly one message is $Bp_{r'}q_{r'}^{B-1}$.

Now define event X as "A particular user k receives one message" and an event Y as "$M = \{k\}$", i.e. k is the user Alice sends messages to. The event $Y|X$ is then "k is Alice's receiver given that k receives one message". Now note that what we calculated above is the probability of k receiving one message if he was Alice's receiver and the probability of k receiving one message if he was not. Thus, $\Pr[X|Y] = q_r^B$. Let us now look at the probability of Y being true. For this we need to consider what the adversary knows about the set M. We stated above that the attacker knows how many elements there are in M. If he knows nothing else, it is reasonable that he regards all possible sets of $|M|$ elements as equally likely. Thus, in our example here $\Pr[Y] = \frac{1}{|N|}$.

Now,

$$\Pr[X] = \Pr[X|Y]\Pr[Y] + \Pr[X|\neg Y]\Pr[\neg Y] = q_k^B \frac{1}{|N|} + Bp_k q_k^{B-1} \frac{|N|-1}{|N|}$$

We can now use Bayes' theorem to work out $\Pr[Y|X]$.

$$\Pr[Y|X] = \frac{\Pr[X|Y]\Pr[Y]}{\Pr[X]} = \frac{q_k^B \frac{1}{|N|}}{q_k^B \frac{1}{|N|} + Bp_k q_k^{B-1} \frac{|N|-1}{|N|}} =$$

$$= \frac{q_k}{q_k + Bp_k(|N|-1)} = \frac{1 - \frac{1}{|N|}}{1 - \frac{1}{|N|} + B - B\frac{1}{|N|}} = \frac{1}{1+B}$$

This is, of course, exactly what one would expect — after all, the attacker knew that M contains one receiver out of N with equal probability, and then observed that during one round of the mix (in which he knows Alice has participated) some particular receiver r has received one message. Without taking any further information into account (notably without knowing where all the other messages went), he can say that the probability that r is Alice's receiver is $\frac{1}{B+1}$.

A similar derivation shows that if all the messages during a round went to different receivers, the probability of any of them being Alice's receiver is still, as expected, $\frac{1}{B+1}$.

Now let us consider how much information the attacker gets if he observes someone receiving c messages, denote this event X_c.

The probability that r receives exactly c messages is

$$\binom{B}{c-1} p_r^{c-1} q_r^{B-c+1}$$

Note that c can be as high as $B+1$ requiring all the messages to go to the receiver r.

The probability of any other receiver $r'(r' \in N \setminus \{r\})$ receiving exactly c messages is:

$$\binom{B}{c} p_{r'}^c q_{r'}^{B-c}$$

Note that this becomes zero in the case of $c = B + 1$ – the receiver who is not r cannot possibly receive all the messages from the mix as Alice sends her message to r. We calculate the probability that k who receives c messages is Alice's receiver r. From above:

$$\Pr[X_c|Y] = \binom{B}{c-1} p_r^{c-1} q_r^{B-c+1}$$

$$\Pr[X_c] = \binom{B}{c-1} p_r q_r^{B-c+1} \frac{1}{|N|} + \binom{B}{c} p_r^c q_r^{B-c} \frac{|N|-1}{|N|}$$

$$\Pr[Y|X_c] = \frac{\Pr[X_c|Y]\Pr[Y]}{\Pr[X_c]} = \frac{\binom{B}{c-1}}{\binom{B}{c-1} + \binom{B}{c}} = \frac{c}{B+1}$$

For example, if we have a system with ten potential receivers and B=10, i.e. the mix processes 11 messages during a round, then if the attacker sees two messages being sent to Bob during a round can deduce that Alice sent a message to Bob with probability $\frac{10}{55} = \frac{2}{11} = 0.1818$.

3.2   Several Rounds, Alice Sends to One Receiver

We now generalise this to any number of rounds l.

From before, we know that $\Pr[X|Y] = q_r^B$. Now, for many independent rounds (let X_l be "k receives exactly one message during each of the l rounds"), $\Pr[X_l|Y] = q_r^{Bl}$ and $\Pr[X_l|\neg Y] = B^l p_r^l q_r^{(B-1)l}$. A derivation very similar to above yields:

$$\Pr[Y|X_l] = \frac{q_r^l}{q_r^l + B^l p^l(|N|-1)} = \frac{(|N|-1)^{l-1}}{(|N|-1)^{l-1} + B^l}$$

This, of course, subsumes (and is consistent with) the above case for $l = 1$.

An example is in order. If everyone chooses uniformly from 10 different receivers (and Alice always sends to the same person), then just from the fact that Alice participated in two rounds of a threshold mix with threshold of five and Bob receives exactly one message during each of the two rounds, the attacker can deduce that Alice is talking to Bob with probability 0.36.

Of course, we have merely given the probability of Y given a very specific event X_l, but it is clear that the probability of Y given any event Z_l can be computed by merely multiplying the probabilities of Y given the event corresponding to each round. This is justified as the rounds are independent.

3.3   Several Rounds, Alice Sends to Many Receivers

If Alice may send messages to more than one receiver, the situation changes slightly. We define the event X to be "there is a set K such that exactly one member of K receives one message during every round" and the event Y to be "Alice's set of receivers is the same as K or $M = K$". If the attacker knows the size of the set M then the number of possible sets K is $\binom{|N|}{|M|}$.

Now a simple derivation shows:

$$\Pr[Y|X] = \frac{q_r^l}{q_r^l + B^l p^l \left(\binom{|N|}{|M|} - 1 \right)} = \frac{(|N| - |M|)^l}{(|N| - |M|)^l + B^l(|M|)^l \left(\binom{|N|}{|M|} - 1 \right)}$$

Note that because M contains more than one element, $\Pr[Y]$ is $\dfrac{1}{\binom{|N|}{|M|}}$.

The set of Alice's receivers is equally likely to be any of the sets of that size. Of course, if the attacker knew nothing about the size of M, the situation would have been rather different. The reader is invited to consider it[1].

We have shown how to calculate the probability of any set K of being Alice's receiver set, or, in other words, a probability distribution over all possible K. This can be used to compute the anonymity of M *as a whole* – following [11], one just computes the entropy of this probability distribution.

Modifying the example from the previous section shows us what effect increasing the size of M has. If Alice sends to one of two people at each round, then the probability of Alice's receiver set being $\{r, r'\}$ where r got a message during the first round and r' got a message during the second round is merely 0.009!

3.4   Some Generalisations and Remarks

The reader may have observed that confining Alice to choosing her receivers from a uniform distribution over M and the other senders – from a uniform distribution over N is rather restrictive. Indeed, as long as all the other senders (Steves) choose their receivers using *the same* probability distributions, we may substitute different values for p_r and q_r in the equations above.

If the Steves send messages to receivers picked from different probability distributions (which are known to the attacker) the situation becomes more complicated. We consider it for the case of the pool mix in Section 4.

The attacker may well know more or fewer things about Alice's receiver set M. As we mentioned above, he may not know $|M|$, but assume that every possible M is equally likely. Alternatively, he may know a set N' such that $M \subseteq N' \subseteq N$. This knowledge too can be incorporated into the above calculations (but is a tedious exercise).

We have now given an account of the statistical disclosure attack on a anonymity system modelled by the threshold mix formally, giving a rigorous analysis underlying the attacks presented by Danezis [5] and Kesdogan et al [7, 1]. We go on to show how similar techniques can be used to derive similar results for a pool mix.

---

[1] Naturally, the probability of any particular set K being Alice's set of receivers decreases and one might like to consider the probability that a receiver r is a member of Alice's set of receivers. We leave this for future work.

4   Formal Account of the Attack on the Threshold Pool Mix

We now turn our attention to the pool mix. During each round a number b of messages are input into the mix from the previous round. We call these messages the pool. A number B of messages are input from the senders. Out of the $B + b$ messages in the mix a random subset of size B is sent to their respective receivers. The remaining b messages stay in the pool for the next round. The operation of the mix is shown in Figure 1.

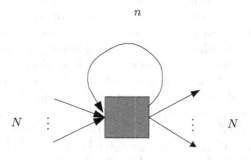

Fig. 1. A Pool Mix

Unlike in the case of a threshold mix, the rounds of a pool mix are not independent. Therefore we must consider a complete run of the pool mix as one observation and try to extract information from it. A complete run starts when the mix comes online and its pool is empty and finishes when the mix is about to be shut down and has sent out all the messages in its pool out to the receivers.

We follow our running example of Alice choosing her receivers uniformly at random from M (call this probability distribution[2] $\boldsymbol{v}$) and all the other senders choosing uniformly from N, call this $\boldsymbol{u}$, $M \subseteq N$.

We make several assumptions:

- The messages which are in the pool at the beginning of the operation of the mix are distributed according to $\boldsymbol{u}$. We may think of the mix operator inserting these messages.
- The attacker is able to observe an entire run of the pool mix, from the very first round, 0, to the very last, k (when no messages remain in the pool). This may seem unrealistic; indeed any real attack of this form will rely on a smaller run and will necessarily yield an approximation to the results presented below. We take the "pure" case merely as an illustration.

---

[2] Bold will consistently be used to indicate that the quantity is a vector describing a probability distribution.

First of all, let us define an observation of a pool mix over l rounds. Call O_i (for outputs) the multisets of receivers of round i and S_i the set of senders of round i[3]. One of the senders is Alice. Define S_0 to include all the initial messages in the pool and O_l to include all the messages which ended up in the pool in the last round and got set out to receivers. Observe that $|S_0| = |O_l| = B + b$ and $i \neq 0 \Rightarrow |S_i| = B$ and $j \neq l \Rightarrow |O_j| = B$. Now construct $O = \cup_{i=0}^l (O_i \times i)$ and $S = \cup_{i=0}^l (S_i \times i)$. Given an observation Obs $= (S, O)$, there are many possible scenarios of what happened inside the anonymity system which would have been observed as Obs by the attacker. Indeed, a *possible scenario* λ is a relation on $S \times O$ such that each member of the S and O occurs in the relation exactly once and $(s_i, r_j) \in \lambda \Rightarrow i \leq j$. The relation λ represents a possible way senders could have sent messages to receivers which is consistent with Obs.

We illustrate this with a simple example. Suppose we have a pool mix with a threshold of two messages and a pool of one message which functioned for two rounds. The message which was in the pool initially came from the sender m, the mix itself, the other two messages came from A (Alice) and q. Thus, $S_0 = \{m, A, q\}$. $O_0 = \{r, r'\}$. At the next round which happens to be the last, messages from Alice and s arrived and messages for r, r'' and r''' were sent, leaving the mix empty. Hence, $S_1 = \{A, s\}$, $O_1 = \{r, r'', r'''\}$, $S = \{m_0, A_0, q_0, A_1, s_1\}$ and $O = \{r_0, r'_0, r_1, r''_1, r'''_1\}$. A possible scenario λ consistent with the observation (S, O) is: $\lambda = \{(m_0, r'''_1), (A_0, r_0), (q_0, r'_0), (A_1, r_1), (s_1, r''_1)\}$.

We can now compute the set of all possible scenarios which are compatible with the observation Obs. Call this set Λ. Take a $\lambda \in \Lambda$ and a set K such that $|K| = |M|$. Define event Y as "$M = K$". If the possible scenario λ happened, then the attacker observes Obs — λ was observed by the attacker as Obs by definition — hence $\Pr[\text{Obs}|\lambda, K] = 1$. What is the probability of the possible scenario λ occurring if K was Alice's set of receivers? The possible scenario occurs if two things hold: if all the senders involved in this scenario picked their receivers in the same way as specified in λ and the mixing happened is such a way that the messages are sent to the receivers in accordance to λ. Hence

$$\Pr[\lambda|Y] = \left(\prod_{s \in S} p_s \right) \frac{1}{\left(\dfrac{B+b}{b} \right)^l}$$

where p_s is the probability of sender s sending a message to the receiver r such that $(s, r) \in \lambda$. Naturally, in the case we are considering above, $p_s = \frac{1}{|N|}$ if $s \neq$ Alice or $p_s = \frac{1}{|M|}$ if $s =$ Alice $\wedge r \in M \wedge (s, r) \in \lambda$ or $p_s = 0$ if $s =$ Alice $\wedge r \notin M \wedge (s, r) \in \lambda$. However, this approach is also applicable if the senders have different probability distributions p_s over N which are known to the attacker.

Having obtained $\Pr[\lambda|M]$, we can calculate $\Pr[\text{Obs}|M]$ and then, using Bayes' theorem as above, $\Pr[M|\text{Obs}]$. First,

---

[3] Until now we have not distinguished individual senders as all but Alice sent messages to receivers chosen according to the same probability distribution.

$$\Pr[\text{Obs}|Y] = \sum_{\lambda \in \Lambda} \Pr[\text{Obs}|\lambda, M] \times \Pr[\lambda|M] = \sum_{\lambda \in \Lambda} \Pr[\lambda|M]$$

$$\Pr[\text{Obs}] = \sum_{K s.t. |K|=|M|} \sum_{\lambda \in \Lambda} \Pr[\text{Obs}|\lambda, Y] \Pr[Y]$$

Now,

$$\Pr[Y|\text{Obs}] = \frac{\Pr[\text{Obs}|Y] \Pr[Y]}{\Pr[\text{Obs}]} = \frac{\sum_{\lambda \in \Lambda} \Pr[\lambda|M] \binom{|N|}{|M|}}{\sum_{K s.t. |K|=|M|} \sum_{\lambda \in \Lambda} \Pr[\lambda|Y] \binom{|N|}{|M|}}$$

This enables us to compute the probability of a set K being Alice's receiver set. Unfortunately, this calculation requires generating all the possible scenarios, Λ. The number of these is clearly at least exponential in Bk. Hence a calculation which is based on all possible scenarios which could have happened inside the mix is not feasible for any practical run of a pool mix. In the next section we make some simplifying assumptions and show that it is possible to extract some information out of this scenario efficiently.

5   Efficient Statistical Attack on the Pool Mix

This attack is a modification of the attack presented in [5] to apply in the case of the pool mix. It is worth noting that the threshold mix is a special example of a pool mix, with no messages feeding forward to the next mixing round. Figure 2 illustrates the model used for the attack.

As before, one of the senders, Alice, is singled out to be the victim of the attack. Each time she has to send a message, she selects a recipient randomly out of a probability distribution described by the vector v over all possible N receivers in the system. Alice does not send in each round (as was the case in the model described in [5]) but only sends at rounds described by the function $s(k)$. Depending on whether it is a round when Alice sends or not, $B - 1$ or B other senders respectively, send a message. They each choose the recipient of their messages independently, according to a probability distribution u over all possible recipients N. The initial b messages present in the pool at round 1 are also destined to recipients chosen independently according to the same probability distribution u.

6   Approximating the Model

We are going to define a series of approximations. These approximations distance the generalised statistical disclosure attack from other exact attacks, but allow the adversary to make very quick calculations and to decrease the anonymity of Alice's set of recipients.

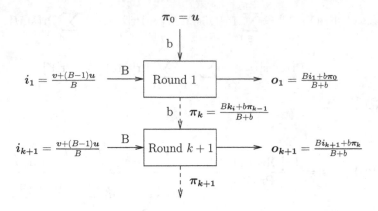

Fig. 2. The pool mix model and the probability distributions defined

We will first model the input distribution i_k of recipient of messages of each round k as being a combination of the distributions u and v. Depending on whether Alice sends a message or not the component v will be present.

$$i_k = \begin{cases} \frac{v+(B-1)u}{B} & \text{if } s(k) = 1 \\ u & \text{if } s(k) = 0 \end{cases} \tag{1}$$

i_k is a vector modelling the distribution of messages expected after a very large number of rounds with the input characteristic of input round k. Depending on whether Alice is sending at round k, ($s(k)$ being equal to one), the appropriate distribution is used to model this input.

At the same time we model the output of each round k, and name it o_k. This output is the function of the input distribution at the particular round k and the distribution of recipients that is forwarded to the present round via the pool. We call the distribution of recipients that are in the pool π_{k-1}. The output distribution of each round can then be modelled as

$$o_k = \frac{Bi_k + b\pi_{k-1}}{B + b} \tag{2}$$

By definition $\pi_0 = u$ and for all other rounds the distribution that represents the pool has no reason to be different from the distribution that represents the output of the round. Therefore $\pi_k = o_k$.

The attacker is able to observe the vector s describing the rounds at which Alice is sending messages to the anonymous communication channel. The adversary is also able to observe for each round the list O_k of receivers, to whom messages were addressed.

The generalised statistical disclosure attack relies on some approximations:

- The set of receivers at round O_k can be modelled as if they were each independently drawn samples from the distribution o_k as modelled above.

– The outputs of the rounds are independent from each other, and can be modelled as samples from the distribution o_k.

Note that these approximations are discarding information available in observations, and are likely to lead to a less powerful attack. Despite this we use them since they lead to very computationally efficient attacks.

Using the samples O_k we will try to infer the the distributions o_k and in turn infer the distribution v of Alice's recipients.

One can solve Equation 2 for a given function $s(k)$ and calculate o_k for all rounds k. Each distribution o_k is a mixture of u, the other senders' recipients, and v Alice's recipients. The coefficient x_k can be used to express their relative weights.

$$o_k = x_k v + (1 - x_k)u \tag{3}$$

By combining Equations 1 and 2 one can calculate x_k as:

$$x_k = \sum_{i \le k, s(i)=1} \left(\frac{b}{B+b}\right)^{(i-1)} \frac{B}{B+b}\frac{1}{B} \tag{4}$$

This x_k expresses the relative contribution of the vector v, or in other words Alice's communication, to each output in O_k observed during round k. When seen as a decision tree, each output contained in O_k has a probability $(1 - x_k)$ of being unrelated to Alice's set of recipients, but instead be drawn from another participant's distribution u.

6.1   Estimating v

The aim of the attack is to estimate the vector v that Alice uses to choose the recipients of her messages. Without loss of generality we will select a particular recipient Bob, and estimate the probability v_{Bob} Alice selects him as the recipient.

We can calculate the probability of Bob being the recipient of Alice for each sample we observe in O_k. We denote the event of Bob receiving message i in the observation O_k as $O_{ki} \rightarrow$ Bob. Given our approximations we consider that the particular message O_{ki} was the outcome of sampling o_k and therefore by using equation 3 we can calculate the probabilities.

$$\Pr[O_{ki} \rightarrow \mathrm{Bob}|v_{\mathrm{Bob}}, u_{\mathrm{Bob}}, x_k] = (x_k v_{\mathrm{Bob}} + (1 - x_k)u_{\mathrm{Bob}}) \tag{5}$$

$$\Pr[\neg O_{ki} \rightarrow \mathrm{Bob}|v_{\mathrm{Bob}}, u_{\mathrm{Bob}}, x_k] = 1 - (x_k v_{\mathrm{Bob}} + (1 - x_k)u_{\mathrm{Bob}}) \tag{6}$$

As expected, Bob being the recipient of the message is dependent on the probability Alice sends a message v_{Bob} (that is Bob's share of v), the probability others have sent a message u_{Bob} (which is Bob's share of u) and the relative contributions of Alice and the other's to the round k, whose output we examine.

Now applying Bayes' theorem to Equations 5 and 6 we estimate p.

$$\Pr[v_{\mathrm{Bob}}|O_{ki} \rightarrow \mathrm{Bob}, u_{\mathrm{Bob}}, x_k] =$$
$$\frac{\Pr[O_{ki} \rightarrow \mathrm{Bob}|v_{\mathrm{Bob}}, u_{\mathrm{Bob}}, x_k]\Pr[v_{\mathrm{Bob}}|u_{\mathrm{Bob}}, x_k]}{\int_0^1 \Pr[O_{ki} \rightarrow \mathrm{Bob}|v_{\mathrm{Bob}}, u_{\mathrm{Bob}}, x_k]\Pr[v_{\mathrm{Bob}}|u_{\mathrm{Bob}}, x_k]\mathrm{d}v_{\mathrm{Bob}}}$$
$$\sim (x_k v_{\mathrm{Bob}} + (1 - x_k)u_{\mathrm{Bob}})\Pr[\mathrm{Prior}\ v_{\mathrm{Bob}}]$$

$$\Pr[v_{\mathrm{Bob}}|\neg O_{ki} \rightarrow \mathrm{Bob}, u_{\mathrm{Bob}}, x_k] =$$
$$\frac{\Pr[\neg O_{ki} \rightarrow \mathrm{Bob}|v_{\mathrm{Bob}}, u_{\mathrm{Bob}}, x_k]\Pr[v_{\mathrm{Bob}}|u_{\mathrm{Bob}}, x_k]}{\int_0^1 \Pr[\neg O_{ki} \rightarrow \mathrm{Bob}|v_{\mathrm{Bob}}, u_{\mathrm{Bob}}, x_k]\Pr[v_{\mathrm{Bob}}|u_{\mathrm{Bob}}, x_k]\mathrm{d}v_{\mathrm{Bob}}}$$
$$\sim (1 - (x_k v_{\mathrm{Bob}} + (1 - x_k)u_{\mathrm{Bob}}))\Pr[\mathrm{Prior}\ v_{\mathrm{Bob}}]$$

Note that we choose to ignore the normalising factor for the moment since we are simply interested in the relative probabilities of the different values of v_{Bob}. The $\Pr[\mathrm{Prior}\ v_{\mathrm{Bob}}]$ encapsulates our knowledge about v_{Bob} before the observation, and we can use it to update our knowledge of v_{Bob}. We will therefore consider whether each message observed has been received or not by Bob and estimate v_{Bob} considering in each step the estimate of v_{Bob} given the previous data as the *a priori* distribution[4]. This technique allows us to estimate the probability distribution describing v_{Bob} given we observed R_k messages sent to Bob in each round k respectively.

$$\Pr[v_{\mathrm{Bob}}|(x_1, R_1) \ldots (x_l, R_l), u_{\mathrm{Bob}}]$$
$$\sim \prod_k (x_k v_{\mathrm{Bob}} + (1 - x_k)u_{\mathrm{Bob}})^{R_k}(1 - (x_k v_{\mathrm{Bob}} + (1 - x_k)u_{\mathrm{Bob}})))^{(B - R_k)}$$

The calculation above can be performed for each receiver in the system to estimate the likelihood it is one of Alice's receivers. The resulting probability distributions can be used as an indication of who Alice is communicating with, and their standard deviations can be used to express the certainty that this calculation provides.

7   Evaluation of the Attack

Figure 3 shows the set of probability distributions for 60 receivers. In this case we take the the probability distribution u to be uniform over all receivers and Alice to be choosing randomly between the first two receivers and sending messages for a thousand consecutive rounds (the mix characteristics in this case were $B = 10, b = 0$, namely it was a threshold mix). Figure 4 shows the same data for a pool mix with characteristics $B = 30, b = 15$. Note that the receivers 1 and 2 are Alice's and their respective v_1 and v_2 have different characteristics from the other receivers.

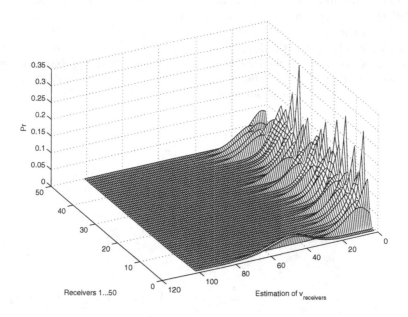

Fig. 3. Comparing the distributions of v_{receiver} for $B = 10, b = 0$

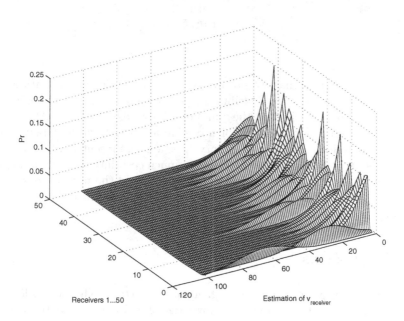

Fig. 4. Comparing the distributions of v_{receiver} for $B = 30, b = 15$

The same information can be more easily visualised if we take the average of all the distributions of receivers that do not belong to Alice, and compare them with the receivers of Alice. Figures 5(a) and 5(b) show the distributions of Alice's receivers and the averaged distributions of other receivers. The curves can be used to calculate the false positive rates, namely the probability a receiver has been attributed to Alice but is actually not in Alice's set, and false negative, namely a receiver wrongly being excluded from Alice's set of receivers.

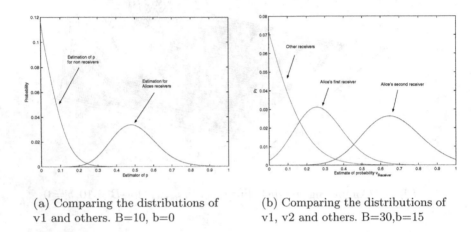

(a) Comparing the distributions of v1 and others. B=10, b=0

(b) Comparing the distributions of v1, v2 and others. B=30,b=15

Fig. 5.

It is unfortunate that we do not yet have analytic representations for the means and variances of the distribution describing $v_{receiver}$. Such representations would allow us to calculate the number of rounds for which Alice can send messages, given a particular set of mix characteristics, without being detected with any significant degree of certainty. The attack presented allows an attacker to understand where they stand, and how much certainty the attack has lead to, by numerically calculating them. On the other hand the network designer must simulate the behaviour of the network for particular characteristics to get some confidence that it does not leak information.

8   Conclusions

In this paper we presented a thorough account of attacks which consider repeated communication and the attacker's knowledge of it. First we gave some analytical

---

[4] Since we are calculating relative probabilities we can discard the *a priori* since it is the uniform distribution over $[0, 1]$

results which enable the attacker to compute the probability of a set being Alice's set of receivers, and therefore the anonymity of that set of receivers. Then we presented a similar result for the pool mix. However, computing the probabilities in this case is expensive, and we resorted to using approximations to yield an efficient attack against a pool mix. The approximations were validated by simulations; the results show that the attack is powerful as well as efficient. This is an important and unfortunate result for the designers of anonymity systems.

References

[1] Dakshi Agrawal, Dogan Kesdogan, and Stefan Penz. Probabilistic Treatment of MIXes to Hamper Traffic Analysis. In *Proceedings of the 2003 IEEE Symposium on Security and Privacy*, May 2003.

[2] Oliver Berthold, Andreas Pfitzmann, and Ronny Standtke. The disadvantages of free MIX routes and how to overcome them. In H. Federrath, editor, *Proceedings of Designing Privacy Enhancing Technologies: Workshop on Design Issues in Anonymity and Unobservability*, pages 30–45. Springer-Verlag, LNCS 2009, July 2000.

[3] David Chaum. Untraceable electronic mail, return addresses, and digital pseudonyms. *Communications of the ACM*, 4(2), February 1981.

[4] George Danezis. Mix-networks with restricted routes. In Roger Dingledine, editor, *Proceedings of Privacy Enhancing Technologies Workshop (PET 2003)*. Springer-Verlag, LNCS 2760, March 2003.

[5] George Danezis. Statistical disclosure attacks. In Samarati Katsikas Gritzalis, Vimercati, editor, *Proceedings of Security and Privacy in the Age of Uncertainty, (SEC2003)*, pages 421–426, Athens, May 2003. IFIP TC11, Kluwer.

[6] Claudia Diaz and Andrei Serjantov. Generalising mixes. In Roger Dingledine, editor, *Proceedings of Privacy Enhancing Technologies Workshop (PET 2003)*. Springer-Verlag, LNCS 2760, March 2003.

[7] Dogan Kesdogan, Dakshi Agrawal, and Stefan Penz. Limits of anonymity in open environments. In Fabien Petitcolas, editor, *Proceedings of Information Hiding Workshop (IH 2002)*. Springer-Verlag, LNCS 2578, October 2002.

[8] Dogan Kesdogan, Jan Egner, and Roland Büschkes. Stop-and-go MIXes: Providing probabilistic anonymity in an open system. In *Proceedings of Information Hiding Workshop (IH 1998)*. Springer-Verlag, LNCS 1525, 1998.

[9] Ira S. Moskowitz, Richard E. Newman, Daniel P. Crepeau, and Allen R. Miller. Covert channels and anonymizing networks. In *Proceedings of the Workshop on Privacy in the Electronic Society (WPES 2003)*, Washington, DC, USA, October 2003.

[10] Michael G. Reed, Paul F. Syverson, and David M. Goldschlag. Anonymous connections and onion routing. *IEEE Journal on Selected Areas in Communication Special Issue on Copyright and Privacy Protection*, 1998.

[11] Andrei Serjantov and George Danezis. Towards an information theoretic metric for anonymity. In Roger Dingledine and Paul Syverson, editors, *Proceedings of Privacy Enhancing Technologies Workshop (PET 2002)*. Springer-Verlag, LNCS 2482, April 2002.

[12] Andrei Serjantov, Roger Dingledine, and Paul Syverson. From a trickle to a flood: Active attacks on several mix types. In Fabien Petitcolas, editor, *Proceedings of Information Hiding Workshop (IH 2002)*. Springer-Verlag, LNCS 2578, October 2002.

[13] Andrei Serjantov and Richard E. Newman. On the anonymity of timed pool mixes. In *Proceedings of the Workshop on Privacy and Anonymity Issues in Networked and Distributed Systems*, pages 427–434, Athens, Greece, May 2003. Kluwer.

Reasoning About the Anonymity Provided by Pool Mixes That Generate Dummy Traffic

Claudia Díaz and Bart Preneel

K.U.Leuven Dept. Electrical Engineering-ESAT/COSIC
Kasteelpark Arenberg 10, B-3001 Leuven-Heverlee, Belgium
claudia.diaz@esat.kuleuven.ac.be, bart.preneel@esat.kuleuven.ac.be
http://www.esat.kuleuven.ac.be/cosic/

Abstract. In this paper we study the anonymity provided by generalized mixes that insert dummy traffic. Mixes are an essential component to offer anonymous email services. We indicate how to compute the recipient and sender anonymity and we point out some problems that may arise from the intuitive extension of the metric to take into account dummies. Two possible ways of inserting dummy traffic are discussed and compared. An active attack scenario is considered, and the anonymity provided by mixes under the attack is analyzed.

1 Introduction

The Internet was initially perceived as a rather anonymous environment. Nowadays, we know that it is a powerful surveillance tool: anyone willing to listen to the communication links can spy on you, and search engines and data mining techniques are becoming increasingly powerful. Privacy does not only mean confidentiality of the information; it also means not revealing information about who is communicating with whom. Anonymous remailers (also called *mixes*) allow us to send emails without disclosing the identity of the recipient to a third party. They also allow the sender of a message to stay anonymous towards the recipient.

In this paper, we extend previous results [DS03b, SD02, DSCP02] in order to obtain equations to compute sender and recipient anonymity, expressed using the model of generalised mixes. Then, we reason about the anonymity provided by these mixes when dummy traffic is inserted in the network. We point out that the intuitive way of computing the anonymity when dummy traffic is inserted by the mix presents some problems. We also analyze the anonymity offered by the mixes when an active attacker is capable of deploying an $n-1$ attack. Some side aspects are discussed, in order to provide a good understanding of the anonymity metric. The paper also intends to be an intermediate step towards the quantification of the anonymity provided by the whole mix network.

The structure of the paper is as follows: in Sect. 2 we give an overview on mixes. In Sect. 3 the concept of dummy traffic is introduced. Anonymity metrics are discussed in Sect. 4. Sections 5 and 8 provide results for recipient anonymity,

J. Fridrich (Ed.): IH 2004, LNCS 3200, pp. 309–325, 2004.
© Springer-Verlag Berlin Heidelberg 2004

first without dummy traffic and then with dummy traffic. Sender anonymity is analyzed in Sect. 6 and Sect. 7. Sect. 9 analyzes recipient anonymity under an active attack. Finally, Sect. 10 presents the conclusions and proposes topics of future work.

2   Mixes

Mixes are the essential building block to provide anonymous email services. A mix is a router that hides the correspondence between incoming and outgoing messages. A taxonomy of mixes can be found in [DP04]. The mix changes the appearance and the flow of the messages. In order to change the appearance of the messages, the mix uses some techniques, such as padding and encryption, thus providing bitwise unlinkability between inputs and outputs. Techniques like reordering and delaying messages, and generating dummy traffic are used to modify the flow of messages. This modification of the traffic flow is needed to prevent timing attacks that could disclose the relationship between an input and an output messages by looking at the time the message arrived to and left from the mix.

The idea of mixes was introduced by Chaum [Cha81]. This first design was a *threshold mix*, a mix that collects a certain number of messages and then flushes them. Since then, variants on this first design have been proposed in the literature [DS03b, MC00, Cot, Jer00]. One of the design strategies used to increase the anonymity of the messages and prevent some simple attacks is sending only part of the messages, while keeping others for later rounds. These are called *pool mixes* or *batching mixes*. Chaum's original design is a particular case of a pool mix, that keeps 0 messages in the pool when it flushes.

Another type of mixes, *synchronous* or *Stop-and-Go* mixes, were proposed by Kesdogan *et al.* in [KEB98]. These mixes modify the traffic flow just by delaying messages. They cannot be expressed as generalized mixes [DS03b], and their analysis is outside the scope of this paper. Some practical measurements on continuous mixes have been presented by Díaz *et al.* in [DSD04].

2.1   Generalized Mixes

The concept of generalized mixes was introduced by Díaz and Serjantov in [DS03b]. Here, we summarize the basic concepts of the generalized mixes model. Pool mixes are expressed in this model by a function, instead of a detailed algorithm. The mix is represented at the time of flushing, making abstraction of the event that triggers the flushing: it may be the expiration of a timeout (*timed mixes*) or the arrival of a message (*threshold mixes*). However, in Sect. 4.1 we point out some properties of threshold mixes which are worth discussing.

A *round* represents a cycle of the mix; during a round, the mix collects input messages that are placed in the pool, the last event of the round is the flushing of messages. The function $P(n)$ represents the probability of the messages being sent in the current round, given that the mix contains n messages in the pool.

An example of a timed pool mix that keeps 20 messages in the pool and flushes the rest is shown in Fig. 1. In this case: $P(n) = 0$ for $n \leq 20$ and $P(n) = 1 - 20/n$ for $n > 20$.

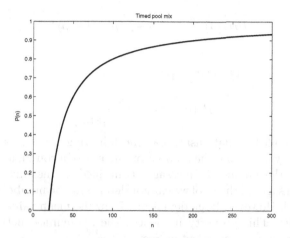

Fig. 1. Representation of a generalized mix

Note that all messages contained in the pool have the same chance of being selected for sending. This uniformity maximizes the randomness of the selection. Reducing this randomness leads to leaking more information about the outputs.

2.2   Deterministic Vs. Binomial Mixes

$P(n)$ denotes the probability of sending every message. There are two ways of dealing with this probability. We distinguish between *deterministic* and *binomial* mixes. Note that the value of the function $P(n)$ is independent of the mix being deterministic or binomial.

Deterministic Mixes. If a mix is deterministic then the number of messages sent is determined by the number of messages contained in the pool; the mix sends $s = nP(n)$ messages. The only randomness present in the flushing algorithm is the one used to select *which* messages will be sent, but not *how many*. Classical pool mixes fall into this category. Note that, for these mixes, once the number of messages in the pool (n) is known, the number of messages sent (s) is determined, and vice versa.

Binomial Mixes. Binomial mixes were introduced in [DS03b]. In these mixes, an independent decision is taken for every message in the pool. A biased coin (being the bias the value of $P(n)$) is thrown for each message, so it is sent with probability $P(n)$. The number of selected messages follows a binomial distribution with respect to the number of messages in the pool. The probability of sending s messages, given that the pool contains n messages is (note that p is the result of the $P(n)$ function for the current round):

$$Pr(s|n) = \frac{n!}{s!(n-s)!} \cdot p^s \cdot (1-p)^{n-s} \ .$$

The probability of having n messages in a pool of maximum size N_{max}, given that the mix sends s messages is [DS03b]:

$$Pr(n|s) = \frac{p(s|n)}{\sum_{i=s}^{N_{\max}} p(i|n)} \ .$$

This probabilistic relationship has the following effects: as it was shown in [DS03b], just by observing the number of outputs of a round, an observer cannot know *exactly* the number of messages contained in the mix; by knowing the number of messages in the pool we cannot determine the number of messages that will be flushed. However, large deviations from the mean values occur with very low probability. This property influences the anonymity metric under certain circumstances, as it is remarked in Sect. 4.2.

3   Dummy Traffic

Inserting dummy traffic (see [Jer00] for a discussion on the topic and [DP04] for a taxonomy of dummy traffic) in a mix network is a technique that hides the traffic patterns inside the mix network, making traffic analysis more difficult. As shown in Sect. 8, the generation of dummy traffic increases the anonymity of the messages sent through the mix network. Dummies also reduce the latency of the network by keeping a minimum traffic load (a low traffic load increases the latency of the mix network).

A dummy message is a "fake" message created by a mix, instead of a user. The final destination is also a mix, instead of a recipient; the dummy is discarded by the last mix, that may be the one that created it. Observers of the network and intermediate mixes cannot distinguish the dummy from a real message. In this paper, we make abstraction of the specific purpose of the dummy (link padding, ping traffic, etc.) and its path-length; we focus on the impact of these dummies in the anonymity provided by the mix that creates the dummies (note that dummies are treated as real messages by the other mixes, except for the last in the path, that discards them).

Creating and transmitting dummies has a cost. We need to find a tradeoff between the anonymity we want to offer and the cost of adding dummy traffic. In this paper we present formulas to compute the anonymity, taking into account the number of dummies produced by mixes. One possibility is that the dummies created by a mix are sent to itself through a path in the network. Therefore, every mix will discard its own dummies, and no mix is able to distinguish real messages from the dummies created by another mix. This strategy was already proposed by Danezis and Sassaman in [DS03a] in order to detect and prevent active attacks against a mix.

We assume that the mix generates dummies following a probability distribution. The creation of a fixed number d of dummies per round is a particular case, in which $\Pr(d_k = d) = 1$. The probability distribution that determines the number of dummies created should be independent of the traffic of real messages. Otherwise, an active attacker could develop an attack strategy which minimizes the number of dummies sent during his attack.

We consider two possible scenarios. First, we assume that the mix inserts the dummy messages into the output link at the time of flushing. If the mix flushes after a timeout (timed mix), the mix could add dummies even in the case in which no real messages are sent. In this case, the pool contains only real messages (note that dummies created by other mixes are considered real messages at the intermediate mixes).

In the second scenario, a number of dummies is added to the pool of the mix. In this case, the number of dummies present at the output depends on the random selection of messages from the pool. The function $P(n)$, that defines the probability with which messages are going to be sent, is computed taking into account the dummies present in the pool. Otherwise, in the case of low traffic, the mix would accumulate dummies that are flushed at a very low rate. Besides, the goal of keeping traffic above a minimum would not be achieved.

We also assume that the number of inserted dummies is independent of the number of dummies already present in the pool, in order to keep the mix design *stateless*, that is, that the decisions of one round are not constrained by the events of previous rounds. A setting in which the mix keeps, for instance, a constant number of dummies in the pool would need a different analysis.

4   Anonymity Metrics

In this section we introduce the anonymity metrics for mixes. We remark the particularities of some mix designs (binomial mixes and threshold mixes). Also, we present the attack model considered.

Anonymity was defined by Pfitzmann and Köhntopp [PK00] as *"the state of being not identifiable within a set of subjects, the anonymity set"*.

The use of the information theoretical concept of entropy as a metric for anonymity was simultaneously proposed by Serjantov and Danezis in [SD02] and by Díaz *et al.* in [DSCP02]. The difference between the two models for measuring anonymity is that in [DSCP02] the entropy is normalized with respect to the number of users. In this paper we will use the non-normalized flavour of the metric.

The anonymity provided by a mix can be computed for the incoming or for the outgoing messages. We call this *sender anonymity* and *recipient anonymity*.

Sender anonymity. In order to compute the sender anonymity, we want to know the effective size of the anonymity set of senders for a message output by the mix.

Therefore, we compute the entropy of the probability distribution that relates an outgoing message of the mix (the one for which we want to know the anonymity set size) with all the possible inputs.

Recipient anonymity. If we want to compute the effective recipient anonymity set size of an incoming message that goes through the mix, we have to compute the entropy of the probability distribution that relates the chosen input with all possible outputs.

Note that in the two cases, the metric computes the anonymity of a *particular* input or output message; it does not give a general value for a mix design and it is dependent on the traffic pattern. The advantage of this property is that mixes may offer information about the *current* anonymity they are providing. The disadvantage is that it becomes very difficult to compare theoretically different mix designs. Nevertheless, it is possible to measure on real systems (or simulate) the anonymity obtained for a large number of messages and provide comparative statistics. This has been done by Díaz *et al.* in [DSD04], where we can see that the anonymity offered by a mix can be analyzed through simulations.

4.1   Remarks on Threshold Mixes

If an active attack is deployed (see Sect. 9), the attacker is able to empty the mix of previous messages much faster, because he is able to trigger the flushings by sending many messages. Also, the attacker may have another advantage: when a dummy arrives to the last mix of the path it is discarded and it does not trigger the flushing if only one message more is required to reach the threshold. This way, the attacker may be able to know whether a message is a dummy or not. For these reasons, timed mixes should be preferred to threshold mixes.

4.2   Remarks on Binomial Mixes

There are two ways of computing the anonymity metric for binomial mixes. If the number n_k of messages in the mix (at round k) and the number s_k of messages sent from the pool are observable, this information can be used in the computation of the entropy. We would use s_k/n_k instead of $P(n_k)$. The anonymity obtained is the one that corresponds to a particular realisation of the mix. Note that the same pattern of incoming traffic fed several times into a binomial mix may result in different values of the metric.

If this is not observable (dummy traffic can hide this number), or if we want to compute the *average*[1] anonymity offered by a mix, then we have to use the

---

[1] This *average* may be different of the one obtained by considering e possible scenarios (binomial output combinations), each of them providing an entropy $H_i, (i = 0 \ldots e)$, happening with probability $p_i, (i = 0 \ldots e)$. We have checked on a simple numerical example that the average entropy that we obtain by summing the entropies H_i ponderated by their probabilities p_i is different from this *average*, that corresponds to the *a priori most probable case*.

a priori probability, $P(n)$. In this case, we obtain a fixed result for a given incoming traffic.

4.3   Attack Model and Dimensions of Uncertainty

The anonymity metric computes the uncertainty about the sender or the recipient of a message, given that some information is available. We compute the metric from the point of view of an attacker, whose powers must be clearly specified.

The attacker considered in the paper is a *permanent global passive observer*. The attacker knows the number of messages that arrive to the mix in every round (a_k) and the number of messages sent by the mix in every round (s_k). We assume that the function of the mix $P(n)$ is publicly known. Moreover, the attacker "has always been there" and "will always be there", that is, the attacker knows the whole history of the mix. This way we give a lower bound for anonymity, given that an attacker with less power will only obtain less information, and the users will be more anonymous towards him. In Sect. 9 we consider an active attacker, capable of deploying an $n - 1$ attack.

When the mix does not generate dummy traffic, the attacker has all the information needed to compute the anonymity (a_k, s_k and $P(n_k)$), because he can determine the number of messages in the pool, n_k. When the mix generates dummies, we can find some differences between deterministic and binomial mixes. If the mix is deterministic, then the attacker can find out n_k, regardless of the dummy policy. If the mix is binomial, then for a deterministic dummy policy he will also be able to determine n_k (note that the attacker is *permanent* and knows all the history). But for a random dummy policy the value n_k cannot be determined, and therefore $P(n_k)$ remains unknown. This means that the attacker cannot compute with certainty the anonymity of the messages. He may be able to estimate it; the estimation is more accurate when the number of dummies or the randomness of the dummy distribution decreases.

It is important to note that this uncertainty is, in most cases, independent of the anonymity provided by the mix. The cases in which this uncertainty increases the anonymity are indicated in the appropriate sections.

Another sort of uncertainty arises if the attacker starts observing the system when it has been running for some time (non permanent attacker), or if the mix starts with an unknown number of messages in the pool. This type of attacker has been considered in the literature (see, for example, [SN03]). In this case, the uncertainty about the number of unknown messages contained in the pool (arrived before the attacker started observing) decreases with every round, as the probability of any of them still being there does.

4.4   Anonymity Provided by a Mix Network

In this paper, we compute the anonymity of a single mix. Nevertheless, we assume that the mix is a node of a mix network (otherwise, it would not make sense to create dummy traffic). The goal of the analysis of the impact of dummy traffic on the anonymity provided by a mix is to go a step further towards a metric that computes the anonymity provided by a mix network, when dummy traffic is inserted by the nodes.

Without the results provided in this paper, it would not be clear the way of computing the anonymity of a mix network whose nodes insert dummy traffic. As we show in Sect. 7 and Sect. 8, we must be careful when applying the information theoretical anonymity metrics to mixes that generate or discard dummies.

Danezis [Dan03] has proposed a method to measure the anonymity provided by a mix network (in the absence of dummy traffic). The method can be applied to compute the recipient anonymity as follows: one measures the anonymity of a mix network as the entropy of the distribution of probabilities that relates a message m entering the network with all the possible outputs of the network, o_{ij} (being i the mix that outputs the message and j the message number). These probabilities are expressed as the product of two terms: first, the probability of the target input m being output o_{ij} conditioned to the fact that the m left at the same mix M_i as output o_{ij}; second, the probability of the target having been left from mix M_i.

The first term, $\Pr(m = o_{ij}|m$ left at $M_i)$ corresponds to the anonymity provided by mix M_i (i.e., the formulas presented in this paper are suited to compute this value). The second quantifies how effectively the traffic from different nodes is mixing together; it is dependent of the topology of the network and on the path selection of the messages and dummies. In order to effectively enhance the anonymity provided by the mix network, the dummy traffic should maximize the number and the probabilistic uniformity of the possible destinations for every outgoing message.

Although the computation of the second term when mixes create dummy traffic may not be obvious, the results provided in Sect. 8 and Sect. 7 may be useful to measure the impact of dummy traffic on anonymity at network scale.

5   Recipient Anonymity Without Dummy Traffic

In this section, we compute the effective recipient anonymity set size of an incoming message that goes through the mix. We need to compute the entropy of the probability distribution that relates the chosen input with all possible outputs.

We summarize the notation needed for this section:

- a_k: number of messages arrived to the mix in round k.
- n_k: number of messages in the mix in round k (before flushing).
- s_k: number of messages sent by the mix in round k.
- $P(n)$: characteristic function of a generalized mix [DS03b]. It represents the probability of a message that is in the pool of being flushed as a function of the number of messages contained in the mix.
- $p(O_i)$: probability of linking the chosen input with an output O that left the mix in round i.
- H_r: effective recipient anonymity set size. Also *recipient anonymity*.

Computing the recipient anonymity has a shortcoming: instead of needing the past history of the mix, we need to know the *future history*. In theory, we should wait infinite time before we can compute the entropy of an input. In practice, we can give an approximation of this value once the probability of the message still staying in the mix is very low (we can choose the probability to be arbitrarily small, and get as close to the real entropy as we want). Note that the approximation is still giving a lower bound for anonymity, because the approximated entropy is lower than the real one.

From [DS03b], we know that if a message arrived to the mix in round r, the probability of this message going out in round i is:

$$p(round_i) = P(n_i), \quad r = i.$$

$$p(round_i) = P(n_i) \prod_{j=r}^{i-1}(1 - P(n_j)), \quad r < i.$$

The probability of matching our target input message of round r to an output of round i, O_i, is (note that it is uniformly distributed over all outputs of round i, s_i):

$$p(O_i) = \frac{P(n_i)}{s_i}, \quad r = i.$$

$$p(O_i) = \frac{P(n_i) \prod_{j=r}^{i-1}(1 - P(n_j))}{s_i}, \quad r < i.$$

This result only makes sense if $s_i > 0$. Otherwise, $p(O_i) = 0$, and this term should not count in the computation of the entropy. The recipient anonymity of the input, assuming that the probability of it still being in the mix is negligible after round R, is:

$$H_r = -\sum_{i=r}^{R} s_i \cdot p(O_i) \log(p(O_i)) \ . \tag{1}$$

6   Sender Anonymity Without Dummy Traffic

In order to compute the sender anonymity, we want to obtain the effective size of the anonymity set of senders for a message output by the mix. Therefore, we compute the entropy of the probability distribution that relates an outgoing message of the mix (the one for which we want to know the anonymity set size) with all the possible inputs.

The notation we need for this section, in addition to the one presented previously, is:

- $p(I_i)$: probability of linking the chosen output with an input I that arrived to the mix in round i.
- H_s: effective sender anonymity set size. Also *sender anonymity*.

Given that the mix treats all messages in the same way, the probability for an input to correspond to the chosen output depends on the round in which the input arrived to the mix. If a message arrived in the current round r, it is certain that it is in the pool. Therefore, the probability is uniformly distributed among all the messages contained in the mix:

$$p(I_r) = \frac{1}{n_r} .$$

For the messages that have arrived in previous rounds, we need to take into account that they might have already been sent by the mix. Therefore, we need to multiply the previous result by the probability of that input still being inside the mix. If the message arrived in round i, the probability of staying each round is $1 - P(n_j)$. Taking into account that the decisions of different rounds are independent, the probability of the chosen output corresponding to an input of round i is:

$$p(I_i) = \frac{1}{n_r} \prod_{j=i}^{r-1}(1 - P(n_j)), \quad i < r .$$

Note that the result only makes sense if the number of inputs of the round we are considering is greater that zero, otherwise $p(I_i) = 0$, and this term should not be taken into account when computing the entropy. The measure of the sender effective anonymity set size, given by the entropy, is:

$$H_s = -\sum_{i=1}^{r} a_i \cdot p(I_i) \log(p(I_i)) . \tag{2}$$

Note that we start at round 1 because we assume that the attacker has been permanently observing the system. From a practical point of view, if a program to measure the anonymity is embedded in the mix to evaluate the anonymity performance, this program will be started at the same time as the mix, and will also "know" the whole history of it.

7 Sender Anonymity with Dummy Traffic

In this section we discuss the sender anonymity metric when dummy traffic is generated by the mix. We consider two scenarios: dummies inserted at the output and in the pool. We reason that the intuitive way of computing this anonymity results in a metric that does not reflect the actual increase in the anonymity of the users.

7.1 Dummies Inserted at the Output

We encounter the first limitation of the metric when trying to measure the sender anonymity in a setting in which the mix is producing dummies.

In order to compute the sender anonymity provided by the mix when dummy traffic is being inserted at the output link, we would first choose an output, and then compute the probability of this message being one of the inputs or one of the dummies. There is a conceptual difference between these two cases: if the output is a real message, we want to know *which one*; if it is a dummy, we do not really care whether it is "dummy number 1" or "dummy number 7": the fact of the message being a dummy contains only one bit of information (dummy/no dummy). We show that treating the two cases analogously would lead to a metric that is not meaningful in terms of anonymity.

Let us consider a distribution of probabilities p_i that relates the chosen output with every possible input I_i when no dummies are generated by the mix. The entropy of this distribution is H_s. If the mix adds d_k messages to every output round, then the new probability distribution is:

- Probability of being a dummy: $p_d = d_k / s_k$.
- Probability of being input I_i: $(1 - p_d) \cdot p_i$

The entropy of the new distribution is:

$$H = -p_d \log_2(p_d) - \sum_i (1 - p_d) \cdot p_i \log_2((1 - p_d) \cdot p_i) \ .$$

$$\cdot \quad H = -p_d \log_2(p_d) - (1 - p_d) \log_2(1 - p_d) + (1 - p_d) \cdot H_s \ .$$

From the formula, we observe that for high values of H_s and p_d, the value of the new entropy H (with dummies) may be lower than H_s (entropy with no dummies).

The decrease in the entropy is consistent with the concept associated with it: the *uncertainty*. If $p_d \gg 1 - p_d$, the attacker has little uncertainty about the output, he may guess that it is a dummy and he will be right with probability p_d. Nevertheless, the attacker is not gaining much with this guess because the uncertainty about the inputs that corresponds to real outputs stays the same.

We should conclude that it is not straighforward to use the metric H to compute the sender anonymity of a mix with dummy traffic. In order to get meaningful results, we should assume that the attacker chooses a real message, and never a dummy. As complementary information about the chances of the attacker of choosing a real message at the output of a mix, we suggest to provide, together with the metric H_s, the probability of success choosing a real message, $1 - p_d$.

On the other hand, we should note that the incoming dummies that are discarded by the mix do contribute to the sender anonymity.

7.2   Dummies Inserted in the Pool

The same problem pointed out in the previous section about the relevance of the metric applies to this scenario, hence the same solution is suggested. We propose as metric the entropy conditioned to the event that a real message is chosen, together with the probability of choosing a real message, $1 - p_d$ - as in the previous case.

The main difference witht he previous case is that for binomial mixes the number of dummies flushed by the mix follows a binomial distribution with respect to the number of dummies contained in the pool. The average number of dummies contained in the pool at round r is:

$$D_r = d_r + \sum_{i=1}^{r-1} d_i \prod_{j=i}^{r-1} (1 - P(n_j)) \ .$$

The proportion of dummies at the output is, on average, the same as in the pool (the dummies are selected to be sent with the same probability as real messages). The probability of selecting a real message at the output is: $1 - p_d = 1 - D_r/n_r$.

Note that the entropy in this scenario must be computed taking into account the actual value of $P(n)$ (where n includes the dummies). The value is higher than in the case in which dummies are inserted at the output. Therefore, the mix may provide less anonymity and less delay. Note that the value of the function $P(n)$ depends not only on the number of real messages contained in the pool, but also on the number of dummies. This implies that n_k will be bigger that in the other analyzed cases. $P(n)$ is a function that grows with n (a function that decreases with n would not make sense: the mix would send less messages as the traffic increases). From the expression of the entropy, we can conclude that for the same traffic load, the anonymity and the delay decrease when this policy is used instead of inserting the dummies at the output (note that higher values of $P(n)$ provide less anonymity and less delay). Eventually, we could reach a situation in which a real message is only mixed with dummies. Note that if the function $P(n)$ does not increase its value ($P(n)$ may reach a maximum value), the anonymity would not be affected.

8   Recipient Anonymity with Dummy Traffic

A similar problem arises for the case of recipient anonymity as for sender anonymity. In this case, we must assume that the attacker choses to trace a real input. This is a reasonable assumption when the message comes from the user. But in certain circumstances, the attacker may want to trace a message that comes from another mix (trying to find the path of the target message in the network). In this case, the attacker may choose a message that is actually a dummy that will be discarded by the mix. It does not seem easy to model the dummy traffic that arrives to a mix for being discarded, given that it depends on the whole network and the path of the dummy.

In order to effectively apply the anonymity metric, we must assume that the attacker computes the recipient anonymity for a message that will not be discarded by the mix (that is, a message that matches an output). Analogously to the case of sender anonymity, we may provide as complementary information to the recipient anonymity, the probability of choosing an input message that is not discarded by the mix.

In this section we discuss the impact of the dummy traffic created by the mix on the recipient anonymity. We show that a simple extension of the metric allows us to take into account dummy traffic generated by this mix (the input dummy traffic getting to the mix cannot be considered). We compare the two possible ways of inserting dummies: at the output and in the pool. The number of dummies inserted at round k is d_k. The number of dummies inserted follows a distribution $\Pr(d_k = d)$. We make abstraction of this distribution.

8.1   Dummies Inserted at the Output

The mix inserts d_k messages at the output link in round k. The recipient anonymity when dummy traffic is being inserted at the output of the mix is computed using (1). The only difference in this case is that s_k has a component of real messages, m_k, and another one of dummy messages, d_k ($s_k = m_k + d_k$). Therefore, the impact of the dummy traffic is equivalent to an increase in the traffic load.

This simple result is consistent with the fact that real messages which are not the one we want to trace act as cover traffic for the target message, just as dummy messages do. Whenever there is at least one real message in the output of a round, the probabilities of matching our target input message are distributed over the messages output by the mix in that round.

Nevertheless, it is important to note that if m_k and d_k are known by the attacker (deterministic mix or deterministic dummy policy), the rounds in which $m_k = 0$ (only dummy messages sent) can be discarded by the attacker. These dummy messages do not increase the recipient anonymity provided by the mix. This is not the case when the attacker has uncertainty about d_k and m_k (binomial mix with random dummy policy); therefore he has to take into account dummies sent in rounds in which no real message is flushed.

We can conclude that binomial mixes with random dummy policy offer more anonymity when the traffic is low (in particular, when $m_k = 0$), because the uncertainty of the attacker about the existence of real messages in the output increases the recipient anonymity: messages of rounds that would be discarded by the attacker in a deterministic mix cannot be discarded in a binomial mix.

8.2   Dummies Inserted in the Pool

The mix inserts in the pool d_k dummies in round k. The recipient anonymity provided by a mix implementing this dummy policy is computed using (1). The difference in this case is that the value of the function $P(n)$ depends not only on the number of real messages contained in the pool, but also on the number of dummies, with the same consequences on the anonymity as mentioned in Sect. 7.2.

9 Recipient Anonymity Under $n - 1$ Attack

The $n - 1$ or *blending* attack (analyzed in detail by Serjantov *et al.* in [SDS02]) is a method to trace a message going through a mix. The goal of this attack is to identify the recipient of a message (the attack only affects recipient anonymity, not sender anonymity). In order to deploy an $n - 1$ attack, the attacker fills the mix with his own messages and the target message (he must be able to delay the other incoming messages). Assuming that the attacker can recognize his messages at the output, then he is able to trace the target message. In this attack model, the adversary is able to delay messages and to generate large numbers of messages from distributed sources (so that the flooding of the mix cannot be distinguished from a high traffic load).

If no dummy traffic is being generated by the mix, then the attacker can successfully trace the target (with probability 1 for a deterministic mix and with arbitrarily high probability for a binomial mix).

9.1 Deterministic Mix with Dummy Traffic Inserted at the Output

In this case, the attacker knows d_k and m_k. Therefore, he knows when the target message is being sent by the mix (it is the round in which the number of unknown messages sent is $d_k + 1$). The anonymity will be that provided by the dummies in the round in which the target is flushed (round i):

$$H_r = - \sum_{j=1}^{d_i+1} \frac{1}{d_i + 1} \log_2(\frac{1}{d_i + 1}) = \log_2(d_i + 1) \ .$$

Note that although the attacker can detect the round in which the target message is flushed, he still cannot distinguish between the target message and the dummies.

9.2 Binomial Mix with Random Dummy Traffic Inserted at the Output

In this case, the attacker cannot observe in which round the message is flushed, because he does not know d_k and m_k, and he cannot distinguish between the dummies and the target message. We assume that after round R the probability of the target message being inside the mix is negligible.

The mix flushes s_k messages per round. The attacker can recognize m_k messages. He does not know whether the $s_k - m_k$ remaining messages are just dummies or if the target is among them.

The attacker fills the mix with his own messages and lets the target in at round r. From that round on, the probability of every unknown output of round i of being the target is:

$$p(O_i) = \frac{P(n_i)}{s_i - m_i}, \quad r = i.$$

$$p(O_i) = \frac{P(n_i)}{s_i - m_i} \prod_{j=r}^{i-1}(1 - P(n_j)), \quad r < i.$$

The entropy is given by:

$$H = -\sum_{i=r}^{R}(s_i - m_i) \cdot p(O_i) \log(p(O_i)) .$$

This means that all the dummies sent in the rounds in which there is a probability of sending the target (this includes the rounds before and/or after the actual sending of the target) contribute to the anonymity, in contrast with the previous case, in which the round that includes the target is observable and only the dummies sent in that particular round contribute to the recipient anonymity of the message.

9.3 Dummies Inserted in the Pool

If the dummies are inserted in the pool, then the attacker has uncertainty about the round in which the target message is flushed. This is independent of the type of mix (deterministic or binomial) and the dummy distribution (deterministic or random dummy policy): the attacker can neither distinguish at the output between unknown real messages and dummy messages, nor know which of the messages of the pool will be selected.

The anonymity provided in this case is computed as in the case of binomial mixes with random dummy policy. The only difference is that the pool will contain more messages (n grows due to the dummies). This increases $P(n)$, unless $P(n)$ reaches at a certain point a maximum (as it is the case in some practical designs, as Mixmaster) and the attacker sends enough messages to make it reach this maximum. An increase in the result of the function $P(n)$ would help the attacker to force the target to leave the mix in fewer rounds with a high probability.

10 Conclusions and Future Work

We have computed the sender and recipient anonymity provided by generalized mixes. The formulas provided are compact and easy to evaluate and implement. We have indicated how to measure the sender and recipient anonymity when the mix inserts dummy traffic in the pool or at the output. Given that the intuitive extension of the metric for this scenario provides confusing results, we have clearly explained how it should be applied. We have analyzed the anonymity provided by a mix that sends dummy traffic, when it is subject to an $n - 1$ attack, and provided the equations that express this anonymity.

We summarize the main conclusions of the paper:

- The dummies generated by the mix contribute to recipient anonymity, but not to sender anonymity. The dummies discarded by the mix contribute to sender anonymity but not to recipient anonymity. Much attention must be paid when implementing this metric to nodes that generate dummy traffic.
- Binomial mixes in combination with a random dummy policy provide more anonymity than deterministic mixes (regardless the dummy policy) or binomial mixes with deterministic dummy policy.
- Inserting the dummies in the pool provides less anonymity and less latency that inserting them at the output.
- When dummies are inserted at the output, binomial mixes with a random dummy policy offer more protection against the $n-1$ attack than deterministic mixes.
- Inserting dummies in the pool protects deterministic mixes better than inserting them at the output, when an $n-1$ attack is deployed.

Some of the topics that are subject of future work are:

- Find a metric that expresses the sender and recipient anonymity provided by a mix network with dummy traffic.
- Compare the anonymity achieved with different distributions of dummy traffic. Obtain quantitative results.
- Compare the anonymity provided by pool mixes to the anonymity provided by *Stop-and-Go* mixes, with dummy traffic.

Acknowledgments

Claudia Díaz is funded by a research grant of the K.U.Leuven. This work was also partially supported by the IWT STWW project on Anonymity and Privacy in Electronic Services (APES), and by the Concerted Research Action (GOA) Mefisto-2000/06 of the Flemish Government.

The authors also want to thank Andrei Serjantov, Joris Claessens and Dries Schellekens for their comments, questions and suggestions.

References

[Cha81]   David Chaum. Untraceable electronic mail, return addresses and digital pseudonyms. *Communications of the A.C.M.*, 24(2):84–88, 1981.
[Cot]   L. Cottrell. Mixmaster and remailer attacks. http://www.obscura.com/~loki/remailer/remailer-essay.html.
[Dan03]   George Danezis. Mix-networks with restricted routes. In *Privacy Enhacing Technologies*, LNCS, Dresden, Germany, April 2003.
[DP04]   Claudia Diaz and Bart Preneel. Taxonomy of mixes and dummy traffic. In *Accepted submission at I-NetSec04: 3rd Working Conference on Privacy and Anonymity in Networked and Distributed Systems*. Kluwer academic publishers, August 2004.

[DS03a]   George Danezis and Len Sassaman. Heartbeat traffic to counter (n-1) at-
            tacks. In *Proceedings of the Workshop on Privacy in the Electronic Society
            (WPES 2003)*, Washington, DC, USA, October 2003.
[DS03b]   Claudia Diaz and Andrei Serjantov. Generalising mixes. In *Privacy En-
            hacing Technologies*, LNCS, Dresden, Germany, April 2003.
[DSCP02]   Claudia Diaz, Stefaan Seys, Joris Claessens, and Bart Preneel. Towards
            measuring anonymity. In *Privacy Enhancing Technologies*, April 2002.
[DSD04]   Claudia Diaz, Len Sassaman, and Evelyne Dewitte. Comparison between
            two practical mix designs. Technical report, K.U.Leuven, 2004. Submitted
            to ESORICS 2004.
[Jer00]   Anja Jerichow. Generalisation and security improvement of mix-mediated
            anonymous communication. Ph.D. thesis, Technischen Universitat Dres-
            den, 2000.
[KEB98]   D. Kesdogan, J. Egner, and R. Buschkes. Stop-and-go-mixes providing
            probabilistic anonymity in an open system. In *Proceedings of the Interna-
            tional Information Hiding Workshop*, 1998.
[MC00]   Ulf Moeller and Lance Cottrell. *Mixmaster Protocol Version 3*, 2000.
            http://www.eskimo.com/~rowdenw/crypt/Mix/draft-moeller-v3-01.txt.
[PK00]   Andreas Pfitzmann and Marit Kohntopp. Anonymity, unobservability and
            pseudonymity — a proposal for terminology. In *Designing Privacy Enhanc-
            ing Technologies: Proceedings of the International Workshop on the Design
            Issues in Anonymity and Observability*, pages 1–9, July 2000.
[SD02]   Andrei Serjantov and George Danezis. Towards an information theoretic
            metric for anonymity. In *Privacy Enhacing Technologies*, LNCS, San Fran-
            cisco, CA, April 2002.
[SDS02]   Andrei Serjantov, Roger Dingledine, and Paul Syverson. From a trickle
            to a flood: Active attacks on several mix types. In F. Petitcolas, editor,
            Information Hiding Workshop, October 2002.
[SN03]   Andrei Serjantov and Richard E. Newman. On the anonymity of timed
            pool mixes. In *Workshop on Privacy and Anonymity in Networked and
            Distributed Sy stems (18th IFIP International Information Security Con-
            ference)*, Athens, Greece, May 2003.

The Hitting Set Attack on Anonymity Protocols

Dogan Kesdogan and Lexi Pimenidis

Aachen University of Technology,
Computer Science Department Informatik IV,
Ahornstr. 55, D-52074 Aachen, Germany
{kesdogan,lexi}@i4.informatik.rwth-aachen.de

Abstract. A passive attacker can compromise a generic anonymity protocol by applying the so called disclosure attack, i.e. a special traffic analysis attack. In this work we present a more efficient way to accomplish this goal, i.e. we need less observations by looking for unique minimal hitting sets. We call this the *hitting set attack* or just HS-attack.

In general, solving the minimal hitting set problem is NP-hard. Therefore, we use frequency analysis to enhance the applicability of our attack. It is possible to apply highly efficient backtracking search algorithms. We call this approach the *statistical hitting set attack* or SHS-attack.

However, the statistical hitting set attack is prone to wrong solutions with a given small probability. We use here duality checking algorithms to resolve this problem. We call this final exact attack the *HS*-attack*.

1 Introduction

Although anonymity and privacy is only a small part of what today is called computer or network security, it plays a vital role in data protection. There are a couple of issues where data encryption in public networks is not enough. Amongst those are important fields like free speech, elections, health care and social guidance systems. The simple fact of exchanging data packets with some of those entities might already be interesting to third parties, i.e. people would like to use these systems anonymously.

On the contrary most network protocols, and especially TCP/IP, are not designed for anonymous data transfer. Anyone along the route of the packet through a network can observe the origin and the destination of this packet even if the payload is encrypted. Therefore, Chaum et al. have proposed anonymity protocols that grant protection against this sort of eavesdropping in closed environments[1][Cha81, Cha88, CGKS95, CB95].

This paper focuses on an analysis of the strength of those protocols in an open system[2] like the Internet[GRS96, GT96, RR98, KEB98, KBS02]. In particular

---

[1] i. e. the number of the users is some known and not too large number n (e. g. $n \leq 1000$).

[2] i. e. the number of potential users is more than one million and usually not known exactly.

J. Fridrich (Ed.): IH 2004, LNCS 3200, pp. 326–339, 2004.

we investigate how long they can hide the user's communications from a passive attacker.

The first contribution of this paper is a new attack which also makes use of network traffic observations without interfering with the traffic of the network in any kind. By looking for hitting sets in the observations the new algorithm does the work faster, i.e. it needs less observations than any other attack known to us. We call the new attack the *hitting set attack* or **HS-attack**. However, it requires the solution of a NP-hard problem, i.e. the minimal hitting set problem.

We relax the strict approach of the minimal hitting set by using the most frequent candidates. We call this attack as the *statistical minimal hitting set attack* or **SHS-attack**. This attack does not rely upon solving NP-hard problems. It is also very easy scalable and can be applied in situations that were far beyond feasibility of the HS-attack.

But this advantage comes with a drawback: the risk of errors. The solutions found by the SHS-attack are approximations and thus object to possible errors. We present some error probability statistics of these and suggest strategies that can be applied to reduce the error to any arbitrarily measure.

Our third contribution is a method of refinement. We show how the approximation can be used to either show the correctness of itself or give a hint of how to look for more information in upcoming observations. Especially the work of Fredman and Khachiyan can be used to great advantage. We call this attack **HS*-attack**, since it is exact as the HS-attack and can use the statistical properties of the SHS-Attack, but requires more observations.

This paper is structured as follows: in the section 2 we discuss general information concerning anonymity techniques and related works. Thereafter we have laid down enough knowledge to start our work. After related works we derive and explain in section 4 the hitting-set attack in detail. Then, we present the statistical hitting set algorithm. There are details about it's implementation, optimizations and behavior. In section 6 we present the HS*-attack. Finally we conclude the paper in section 7.

2   Anonymity Techniques

As already mentioned in the introduction there are a number of anonymity techniques to prevent eavesdroppers from gaining information about a user's traffic. Since the content can be encrypted, our focus is on the traffic layer. Anyone that can read a packet can see the origin and the destination. Anonymity techniques strive to prevent this.

As an example: Alice wants to post her political opinion to a web forum where oppositional members exchange information. Unfortunately she lives in a country where the government is suspected to track down oppositional members. If she would just send the encrypted message, e.g. using HTTPS, her Internet Service Provider (ISP) could notice this action and save this to a record. This could lead to a point where Alice herself could get suspected because she has exchanged data with some entity.

To avoid this, Alice could use some service like JAP [BFK01]. For this she installs a proxy on her computer that encrypts all of her traffic and sends it to a JAP proxy (i.e. Mixes [Cha81]). Along with her there are several other, maybe several thousand, users doing likewise. The server decrypts those packets and forwards them on behalf of the users. Any returned data will be send to the users on the same way.

Thus, any primary evidence has now gone. What remains is that Alice sends out data to an anonymity server (e.g. Mixes) which itself does not provide any other service than untraceable packet forwarding. Because of this functionality a potential attacker is not able to link an incoming packet to an outgoing packet. Using this service, Alice is beyond any suspicion to have send any packets to the oppositional forum because any of the other users could have been done it, i.e. Alice and the other persons builds the so called *anonymity set*.

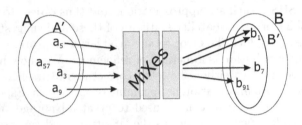

Fig. 1. Formal model of an anonymity set. In any anonymous communication (e.g. Mixes), a subset A' of all senders A sends a message to a subset B' of all recipients B.

2.1   The MIX Concept

MIXes collect a number of packets from distinct users (anonymity set) and process them so that no participant, except the MIX itself and the sender of the packet, can link an input packet to an output packet [Cha81]. Therefore, the *appearance* (i.e. the bit pattern) and the *order* of the incoming packets have to be changed within the MIX. The change of appearance is a cryptographic operation, which is combined with a management procedure and a universal agreement to achieve anonymity:

User Protocol: All generated data packets including address information are padded to equal length (agreement), combined with a secret random number RN, and encrypted with the public key of the MIX node (see also [PP90]). A sequence of MIXes is used to increase the reliability of the system.

MIX Protocol: A MIX collects a packets (called *batch*) from distinct users (identity verification), decrypts the packets with its private key, strips off the RNs, and outputs the packets in a different order (lexicographically sorted or randomly delayed). Furthermore, any incoming packet has to be compared with formerly received packets (management: store in a local database) in order to reject any duplicates. Every MIX (except the first) must include a functionality ensuring that each received packet is from a distinct user, because only the first MIX can decide whether or not the packets are from distinct senders.

Applying this protocol in closed environments where all subjects participate in all anonymity sets, the MIX method provides full security. The relation between the sender and the recipient is hidden from an omnipresent attacker as long as:

a) One honest MIX is in the line of the MIXes which the packet passes.
b) The $(a - 1)$ other senders do not all cooperate with the attacker.

[Pfi90] states that the MIX method provides information-theoretic deterministic anonymity based on complexity-theoretic secure cryptography.

2.2 Abstract Model

In this work we abstract from a specific type of anonymity service or implementation. Instead, we assume that a subset A' of all senders A sends a message to a subset B' of all recipients B, like shown in figure 1. Furthermore, in our model the adversary can easily determine anonymity sets, e.g. mixes assume that all network links are observable (see [Cha81]). However, this can be assumed also in a real world scenario if the attacker is able to observe messages to and from an anonymity service. We only assume the following properties of an anonymity system:

- In each anonymous communication, a subset A' of all senders A sends a message to a subset B' of all recipients B. That is, $A' \subseteq A$ and $B' \subseteq B$, as Figure 1 illustrates. In a particular system, the set of all senders A can be the same as the set of all recipients B.
- The size of the sender anonymity set[3] is $|A'| = a$, where $1 \leq a \ll |A|$. Note that a sender can even send multiple packets per batch.
- The size of the recipient anonymity set is $|B'| = b$, where $1 \leq b \ll |B|$ and $b \leq a$. That is, several senders can communicate with the same recipient.
- The anonymity system provides provides perfect untraceability between incoming and outgoing packets.

The typical values for $|A'|$, $|B'|$, $|A|$, and $|B|$ vary from implementation to implementation and with the environment in which they operate. In [BFK01] present an implementation in which $|A|$ is around $20,000$. They don't give typical values for $|A'|$, but we generally expect $|A'| < 100$.

To investigate the hitting set attack, we use the same formal model as suggested in [KAP02]. For the sake of simplicity we make certain assumptions. These assumptions are:

---

[3] Note that the above model can be easily adopted to other anonymity systems (e.g. pool-mixes) by determining the respective anonymity sets.

- In all observations $\mathcal{OBS} = \{B'_1, B'_2, \ldots\}$ Alice is a sender using the system to hide her m communication partners $\mathcal{B}_{Alice}$, i.e. $\forall B'_i \in \mathcal{OBS} : \mathcal{B}_{Alice} \cap B'_i \neq \emptyset$. This can be accomplished by restricting the attacker to observe only the anonymous communication of Alice. We will refer to the communication partners later on also as Alice's peers.
- Alice chooses a communication partner in each communication uniformly among her m partners $\mathcal{B}_{Alice}$, while the other senders choose their communication partners uniformly among all recipients B.

3   Related Works – Disclosure Attack

Disclosure attack is a traffic-analysis attack to identify all communication partners of a targeted user (Alice) [KAP02]. Since we follow here the same anonymity model disclosure attack has the same model properties, i.e. Alice uses the system to hide her communication partners $\mathcal{B}_{Alice}$ with $|\mathcal{B}_{Alice}| = m$ and the attacker knows the number of the peers, i.e. m.

A disclosure attack has a *learning phase* and an *excluding phase*.

Learning phase In this phase, the attacker's task is to find m mutually disjoint recipient sets – that is, each set has only one peer partner of Alice – by observing Alice's incoming and outgoing messages. We refer to these found sets as the *basis sets*.

Excluding phase The attacker's task in this phase is to observe new recipient sets until all Alice's nonpeer partners are excluded from the basis sets. Three possible outcomes exist:
- *No intersection.* Contrary to our assumption, since none of the peer communication partners in the basis sets appear in the recipient set.
- *Intersection only with one basis set.* The attacker knows that Alice's peer partner must be in the intersection (excluding act).
- *Intersection with more than one basis set.* The attacker cannot tell which intersection contains Alice's peer partner.

The disclosure attack is an NP-complete problem. The proof, detailed elsewhere [KAP03], is technical and involves showing that the learning phase of the disclosure attack is equivalent to the well-known NP-complete Clique problem.

An enhancement of the disclosure attack is suggested in [Dan03], the *statistical disclosure attack*. The attack follows the general structure of the disclosure attack as suggested in [KAP02], but makes use of statistical properties in the observations and identify the victim's peer partners without solving the NP-complete problem. However, this is not for free. The solution is only correct with a given probability.

4   The Hitting-Set Attack

To investigate the hitting set attack we restrict ourselves again to observe Alice and to identify all her hidden peer partners $\mathcal{B}_{Alice}$. As before we continue observing only the anonymity sets where Alice is involved as a sender. We do not use any other properties of the anonymity system, thus the complete system can be described formally as follows:

$$\forall B'_i \in \mathcal{OBS} \text{ and } B'_i \subset B \; \exists b \in \mathcal{B}_{Alice} \subset B : b \in B'_i$$

Obviously, having only the above abstract system definition we can not identify (or exclude) any recipient $b \in B$ as the peer partner (or as not the peer partner) of Alice. All recipients are a priori equally likely.

Suppose $\beta = \{b_1, b_2, \ldots b_m\} \subset B$ is the result of a successful attack, then informally the solution β has to be consistent with the system description, i.e. the following holds $\beta \cap B_i \neq \emptyset$ for all elements of $\mathcal{OBS}$. Suppose, two possible solutions $\beta = \mathcal{B}_{Alice}$ and $\beta' \neq \mathcal{B}_{Alice}$ are consistent with the anonymity system, i.e. $\forall B'_i : \beta \cap B'_i \neq \emptyset$ and $\beta' \cap B'_i \neq \emptyset$. There is no way for the attacker within the given system to pick the right solution. Clearly, it is not decidable wether β or β' is the true solution within the given model. Hence, to decide within the given system the following has to be met $\exists B'_j : \beta' \cap B'_j = \emptyset$. From this observations we suggest the following algorithm:

1. Since the attacker knows m, he can build all sets of cardinality m from the elements of B, we will call the collection of these sets of possible solutions as $\mathcal{S}_m$. Obviously, $\mathcal{B}_{Alice} \in \mathcal{S}_m$ because $\mathcal{S}_m$ contains all sets of size m. Note that $|\mathcal{S}_m| = \binom{n}{m}$.
2. The attacker excludes all sets in $\mathcal{S}_m$ that are not consistent with the observation, i.e. all sets in $\mathcal{S}_m$ that are disjunct with the observation.
3. If $|\mathcal{S}_m|$ becomes one, the remaining element has to be equivalent to $\mathcal{B}_{Alice}$ because all other sets of cardinality m proofed to be wrong.

Of course it is impossible for an attacker with space limitation to maintain a list of size $\binom{n}{m}$. For realistic numbers this would be about $\binom{20,000}{20} \approx 10^{68}$ elements. Although this number would decrease fast in the progress of the algorithm.

However, from the above problem description we can derive that the solution has to be a *unique minimum hitting set* of all observations in $\mathcal{OBS}$. First of all, the solution is not disjunct with any $B'_i \in \mathcal{OBS}$. So it is a hitting set. It is also unique, otherwise the algorithm would not have been stopped. And it is also minimal: if there would be some hitting set of a size smaller than m, all superior sets with cardinality m would be hitting sets, thus violating uniqueness. Consequently we define:

Definition 1 (Hitting Set) *Suppose $\mathcal{OBS}$ is a collection of sets. A hitting set for $\mathcal{OBS}$ is a set $H \subseteq \cup_{B'_i \in \mathcal{OBS}} B'_i$ such that $H \cap B'_i \neq \emptyset$ for each $B'_i \in \mathcal{OBS}$. A hitting set is minimal iff no proper subset is a hitting set.*

Garey and Johnson report that the hitting set problem is NP-complete. Notice, that the hitting set problem can be transformed to the vertex cover problem [GJ79].

5 Statistical Hitting Set Attack

Finding a unique minimal hitting set is NP-complete, but there is a helpful property that can be used, frequency analysis. Using frequencies we can apply some efficient though easy restrictions to the searching space. In fact Alice's peers appear more frequently in the recipient sets than the other hosts [Pim03]. Furthermore if an element is more frequent than others, it is more likely to be included in a hitting set. This fact can be exploited by a simple backtracking algorithm.

We restrict the search to those sets that are most likely to be a hitting set. This is done by counting the frequency of all elements in the observations. Those statistics are provided to backtracking algorithm. This algorithm will build a fixed number of hitting sets of size m. These sets are combinations of the elements with the highest frequency.

After checking some number of sets, the algorithm comes to decide whether the attacker has enough information. If only one out of those sets is valid, it is likely that it is the only one and thus equal to $\mathcal{B}_{Alice}$. If more than one sets have been found, the algorithm needs more observations and returns to the waiting status again (the same if no hitting set is found).

Applying the above strategy the search can be restricted to an arbitrarily small part of the complete searching space. However, this strategy is then of course not exact and may return a wrong result. In section 5.3 an analysis of failure probability depending on the number of tested sets is given.

5.1 Simulation of the Attack

In order to determine the properties of the attack we have written a simulation. Each simulation run was performed by generating observations until the stop criterion – only one valid combination is found – was given. The result was then validated for the number of observations needed and whether it was correct.

In fact, the code of the simulation could even be used to apply the attack, if real data is used as input data[4].

Inside the simulation the observations were generated using pseudo random numbers. The hosts in B are depicted by the numbers from 1 to n, and without loss of generality let $\mathcal{B}_{Alice} = \{1, 2, \ldots m\}$. Such any saved observation $B'_i \in \mathcal{OBS}$ consists of $a - 1$ numbers from the set B and one element from $\mathcal{B}_{Alice}$. The numbers are chosen from the given intervals uniformly with the help of a random number generator.

After a new recipient set has been build, the main algorithm is started that looks for the minimum hitting sets by backtracking. The searching space is restricted to some number of sets that can be chosen in accordance to available resources and desired error probability.

Since we are looking for hitting sets that are build out of the most frequent elements we need to compile a list of all hosts contained in the observations,

---

[4] We also wrote an implementation of the attack that can be deployed on real traffic.

sorted by frequency. We name this list $\mathcal{F} = \{F_1, F_2, \ldots\}$, with F_i having at least as many occurrences in the observations as F_j for $i < j$ and $|F_i| = m$.

The backtracking looks like this:

```
FUNCTION Backtracking(Chosen, Observations, m, F, counter)
# terminate after a given number of tests
if counter=0 then RETURN ∅
solutions = ∅
# backtracking recursion, if not chosen m elements
if |Chosen| < m then
    for each Fᵢ ∈ F do
        # add next element to chosen set
        solutions = solutions ∪
            Backtracking(Chosen∪Host, Observations, m, F−Host, counter)
else
    # generated set of size m, check validity
    solutions = solutions ∪ Check_Validity(Chosen,Observations)
    counter = counter - 1
RETURN solutions
```

The function is called with

Backtracking($\emptyset$,Observations,m, $\mathcal{F}$, counter)

and returns a set of valid hitting sets of size m. To determine whether or not a set is a hitting set ("*valid*"), a very simple routine is used. In case the set is not a hitting set an empty set is returned, otherwise the set is returned.

Additionally the amount of checked sets can be limited with the variable `counter`.

```
FUNCTION Check_Validity(Combination,Observations)
for each recipient_set ∈ Observations do
    if recipient_set ∩ Combination = ∅ then
        RETURN ∅
RETURN Combination
```

With this functionality the algorithm would already be ready for validation. Indeed there are still some possibilities to "adjust" the algorithm. Either the running time of the algorithm can be decreased or the probability of a wrong result. We discuss this in the next section.

5.2   Optimizations

There are a lot of parameters that can be used to improve the algorithm. The following list shows the most significant ones.

Interlace Since the backtracking in the basic form does not rely on any prior results, it may be considered unnecessary to start the backtracking algo- rithm on every new observation. Therefore, an attacker can collect a number of observations and then start the algorithm. Hence, the attack would be applied after a fixed number of observations, that can be specified by a step width.

This leads to a nearly linear improvement in speed. However, in average the number of observations would increase by the half of the step width.

Termination criterion To raise the probability of a correct result, the termination criterion can be changed. Instead of stopping at once if a unique set is found, the solution can be retained and further observations can be made. If no contradiction is found until then, the algorithm stops and returns the set.

Carry-over If there are more than one solution, it is quite likely that most of them will also be found at the next run of the backtracking. In this case following strategy can be applied: all found solutions are saved. The next time a backtracking should be started, all saved sets are checked for validity with the new observations. This can be done very fast. If at least two of those sets are still valid, the backtracking part is not needed to be started.

Our experience has shown that the gain is nearly independent of the number of saved sets. Therefore, it can be sufficient to save two sets.

Uniqueness The aim is to find a unique set. As soon as there is a second set (or even more) found during the course of the backtracking, it is clear that more observations will be needed and the backtracking can be stopped at once.

Since we have seen above that it is unnecessary to collect more than two solutions, we have another reason not to waste computing time by looking for more solutions per run.

As the success of the simulation depends heavily on the generated random numbers it had to be repeated several times until the mean values were acceptable.

Note that we run the simulation on a single personal computer with no special equipment. The speed of the computer is about 1 GHz and an average simulation run can be done in less than 10 seconds.

5.3   Validation

In our simulations we were interested in in the effect of n, m and a on the number of observations an attacker needs to succeed. To see the effect of changing, n, m, and a, we first chose typical values for these parameters, viz, $n = 20000$, $a = 50$ and $m = 20$. Then we ran simulations with different values for one of the parameters while keeping the other two parameters unchanged.

The average number of observations needed to compromise the system is shown in the next figures. To compare our result with the disclosure and the statistical disclosure attack we have added the respective results of the both attacks. The chosen error rate for both statistical attacks were 0.5%.

Figure 2 shows graphs of the number of required observations for all three algorithms, i.e. disclosure attack, statistical disclosure attack, and statistical

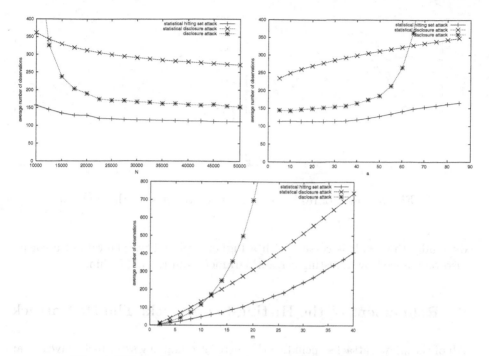

Fig. 2. Effect of n, a, and m on the number of observations

hitting set attack. Statistical disclosure attack and the statistical hitting set attack have nearly the same characteristic, i.e. for all values of n, b, and m the attack is still applicable (compare this with the exponential increase of the disclosure attack). The main difference between the statistical disclosure attack and the statistical hitting set attack is that the statistical hitting set attack needs less observations (see the figures).

Figures 3 shows two graphs of the number of tested sets per backtracking, i.e. the number of tested possible solutions. The possible solutions are built using all combinations of the most frequent items. Intuitively, one expects a better error probability and a definite reduction of required number of observations if the number of possible solutions increases from one thousand to one million. However, as shown in figure 3 for all values after $10,000$ of possible solutions it turned out to be not so critical even negligible for systems with practical dimensions, e.g. with $n = 20000$, $a = 50$, and $m = 20$.

Changing the termination criterion can additionally reduce the error probability. In some series additionally 10% of observations reduces the rate of error of 80%, while 15% more observations could drop the rate down for 95%. That would be as large as 0.025% on a normal error rate of 0.5%.

We conclude that the statistical hitting set attack can break an anonymity protocol with a smaller amount of observation than it was possible before. Ad-

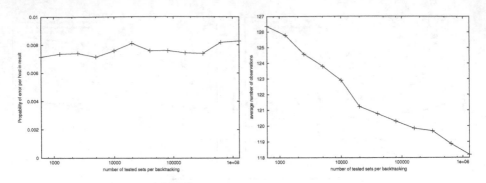

Fig. 3. Effect of tested sets on the correctness of the solution

ditionally the result is correct with a higher probability. The rate of error can also be reduced by adjusting certain parameters in the algorithm.

6   Refinement of the Hitting-Set Attack: The HS*-attack

All of the known attacks, including the introduced hitting set attack, have certain drawbacks:

The disclosure attack relies on solving a NP-complete problem. Furthermore it needs in average more observations than the HS and SHS-attack. But it is a deterministic attack, i.e. the result is always correct.

The statistical disclosure attack needs less observations than the disclosure attack but relies on a unified probability distribution of the elements in the recipient sets. The result of it can possibly be wrong.

The hitting set attack is a deterministic attack but is NP-complete. It needs less observations than the prior known attacks.

The statistical hitting set attack is not an exact attack, but it needs less number of observations than the statistical disclosure attack. In exchange it needs more computational power and memory.

Next we are interested in an algorithm with the efficiency of the SHS-attack, but whose result is not subject to some possible errors. A suggestion for this follows: running the SHS-attack on some observations an attacker gains a good approximation to the result. Is there a possibility to check whether the result is correct? The answer is yes. By using the algorithm of *Fredman and Khachiyan* we are able to solve the problem in $\mathcal{O}(n^{\mathcal{O}(\log n)})$, i.e. superpolynomial complexity. This algorithm solves a dual algorithm to the minimum hitting set problem, the problem of boolean duality.

We do not describe the algorithm of Fredman and Khachiyan here due to space limitations. The authors themselves give a detailed view in [FK96].

6.1   The Algorithm

Given the input of two boolean formulas the algorithm of Fredman and Khachiyan decides if the formulas are dual or not. If not then the algorithm returns a counterexample. The counterexample is equivalent to a second valid set of peer partners.

The counterexample is especially convenient and useful in this application: it is equivalent to a second set of hosts which is a valid guess for Alice's peer partners. In that case one has to go back to the stage of the algorithm that uses the hitting set attack in order to find a unique minimum hitting set. But the counterexample can be very useful right now: if saved in the carry-over memory, there is no more need to modify the first part of the algorithm since it runs until again there is only one valid solution left.

There is one difference to the original algorithm of Fredman and Khachiyan that has to be made: we are not interested in any sort of counterexample with less than m or more than m elements in it. But, this results in not a big change of the basic algorithm. In fact, there are just some parts of the searching tree left out, i.e. those that would create counterexamples with more than m elements. Other parts are just stepped over, as there are those that would return counterexamples with less than m elements.

```
FUNCTION Hitting_Set_Star_Attack(m,counter)
observations = ∅
solutions = ∅
repeat
    # start main loop of hitting set attack
    repeat
        observations = observations ∪ New_Observation()
        # more than one solution as a carry-over? check those first
        if | solutions | > 1 then
            solutions = { L ∈ solutions | Check_Validity(L) }
        # less than 2 solutions in carry-over: start backtracking
        if | solutions | ≤ 1 then
            solutions = Backtracking(∅,observations,m,counter)
        # carry on, until only one solution remains
    until | solutions | = 1
    # check result with algorithm of Fredman and Khachiyan
    solutions = Fredman_Khachiyan(observations,solutions,m)
# solution is correct if there was no counter example
until | solutions | = 1
return solution
```

Most of the above code should be self-explanatory. The set solutions is not only used to return the result of the backtracking, but is also the carry-over memory.

The function Fredman_Khachiyan is called with both boolean formulas, the observations and the solutions, and the number of Alice's peer partners m.

It will return either just the unchanged set `solutions` in case it was verified, or it will add the counterexample into the set.

6.2 Validation

The new hitting set algorithm (i.e. HS*-attack) is **always correct**, like in the deterministic HS and disclosure attack. Hence, it avoids the most severe problem of the statistical attacks.

On the other hand the new attack is now not efficient any more in the means of a polynomial time algorithm. Testing series have shown that the running time of the algorithm is within reasonable bounds for $m \leq 20$ and $a \leq 50$, if $n = 20,000$. Note that this is enough for todays systems, i.e. those that are called to be of *practical size* (see section 2.2).

Interesting enough that in the intervals of the parameter in which this algorithm is feasible to compute, the average number of observations needed to detect Alice's peers is not much higher than those needed by the hitting set attack. A conservative guess is that it needs in systems of *practical size* about 5% to 10% more observations.

7 Conclusions

In this work we have suggested new attacks on anonymity systems using the hitting set algorithm. The pure HS-attack needs less observations than any other attack known to us. However, it requires the solution of a NP-complete problem, i.e. exponential run time in the worst case.

The SHS-attack finds the most frequent recipients of the observation and checks them if they fulfill the minimal hitting set property (instead of checking all possible sets). This attack solves the problem in polynomial time complexity. However, it is not exact, even if we can reduce the error to any arbitrarily measure.

Our third contribution is the combination of the SHS and the HS attack, the HS*-attack. We first search for a good candidate of the solution of the minimal hitting set problem and check this by using the work of Fredman and Khachiyan. HS*-attack has superpolynomial run time in the worst case.

References

[BFK01]   Oliver Berthold, Hannes Federrath, and Stefan Köpsell. Web Mixes: A System for Anonymous and Unobservable Internet Access. In Hannes Federrath, editor, *Designing Privacy Enhancing Technologies, (PET2001)*, pages 115–129. Springer-Verlag LNCS 2009, May 2001.

[CB95]   D.A. Cooper and K.P. Birman. Preserving privacy in a network of mobile computers. In *1995 IEEE Symposium on Research in Security and Privacy*, pages 26 – 38. IEEE, 1995.

[CGKS95]   B. Chor, O. Goldreich, E. Kushilevitz, and M. Sudan. Private informa-
           tion retrieval. In *36th IEEE Conference on the Foundations of Computer
           Science*, pages 41 – 50. IEEE Computer Society Press, 1995.

[Cha81]   David L. Chaum. Untraceable Electronic Mail, Return Addresses, and
           Digital Pseudonyms. *Communications of the ACM*, 24(2):84 – 88, Feb
           1981.

[Cha88]   David L. Chaum. The Dining Cryptographers Problem: Unconditional
           Sender and Recipient Untraceability. *Journal of Cryptology*, (1):65 – 75,
           1988.

[Dan03]   George Danezis. Statistical disclosure attacks: Traffic confirmation in open
           environments. In Gritzalis, Vimercati, Samarati, and Katsikas, editors,
           Proceedings of Security and Privacy in the Age of Uncertainty, (SEC2003),
           pages 421–426, Athens, May 2003. IFIP TC11, Kluwer.

[FK96]   Michael L. Fredman and Leonid Khachiyan. On the Complexity of Du-
           alization of Monotone Disjunctive Normal Forms. *Journal of Algorithms*,
           (21):618 – 628, 1996. Article No. 0062.

[GJ79]   Michael R. Garey and David S. Johnson. *Computers and Intractability: A
           Guide to the Theory of NP-Completeness*. W. H. Freeman & Co., 1979.

[GRS96]   David M. Goldschlag, Michael G. Reed, and Paul F. Syverson. Hiding
           Routing Information. *Information Hiding*, pages 137 – 150, 1996. Springer-
           Verlag LNCS 1174.

[GT96]   Ceki Gülcü and Gene Tsudik. Mixing E-mail with Babel. In *Proceedings of
           the Network and Distributed Security Symposium - NDSS '96*, pages 2–16.
           IEEE, February 1996.

[KAP02]   Dogan Kesdogan, Dakshi Agrawal, and Stefan Penz. Limits of Anonymity
           in Open Environments. In *Information Hiding, 5th International Work-
           shop*. Springer Verlag, 2002.

[KAP03]   Dogan Kesdogan, Dakshi Agrawal, and Stefan Penz. Probabilistic Treat-
           ment of MIXes to Hamper Traffic Analysis. *IEEE Symposium on Security
           and Privacy*, 2003.

[KBS02]   Dogan Kesdogan, Mark Borning, and Michael Schmeink. Unobservable
           Surfing on the World Wide Web: Is Private Information Retrieval an Al-
           ternative to the Mix Based Approach? *Privacy Enhancing Technologies
           (PET 2002)*, Springer-Verlag (LNCS 2482):224 – 238, 2002.

[KEB98]   Dogan Kesdogan, J. Egner, and R. Büschkes. Stop-and-Go-Mixes Provid-
           ing Anonymity in an Open System. In D. Aucsmith, editor, *Information
           Hiding 98 - Second International Workshop*, pages 83 – 98. Springer Verlag,
           1998.

[Pfi90]   A. Pfitzmann. Dienstintegrierende Kommunikationsnetze mit teilnehmer-
           überprüfbarem Datenschutz. IFB 234, Springer-Verlag, Heidelberg 1990,
           1990. (in German).

[Pim03]   Lexi Pimenidis. Structure and Analysis of Chaumian Mixes. Nov 2003.
           Master Thesis at the RWTH Aachen, Germany.

[PP90]   B. Pfitzmann and A. Pfitzmann. How to break the direct rsa-
           implementation of mixes. pages 373 – 381. Eurocrypt '89, LNCS 434.
           Springer-Verlag, Berlin, 1990.

[RR98]   Michael K. Reiter and Aviel D. Rubin. Crowds: Anonymity for Web Trans-
           actions. *ACM Transactions on Information and System Security*, pages 66
           – 92, April 1998.

Information Hiding in Finite State Machine

Lin Yuan and Gang Qu

Department of Electrical and Computer Engineering
and Institute for Advanced Computer Studies
University of Maryland, College Park, MD 20742
{yuanl,gangqu@eng.umd.edu}

Abstract. In this paper, we consider how to hide information into finite state machine (FSM), one of the popular computation models. The key advantage of hiding information in FSM is that the hidden information becomes inexpensive to retrieve, yet still hard to remove or delete. This is due to the fact that verifying certain FSM properties is easy, but changing them requires efforts equivalent to redoing all the design and implementation stages after FSM synthesis.

We first observe that not all the FSM specifications (or transitions) are needed during the state minimization phase. We then develop a Boolean Satisfiability (SAT) based algorithm to discover, for a given minimized FSM, a maximal set of redundant specifications. Manipulating such redundancy enables us to hide information into the FSM without changing the given minimized FSM. Moreover, when the original FSM does not possess sufficient redundancy to accommodate the information to be embedded, we propose a state duplication technique to introduce additional redundancy. We analyze these methods in terms of correctness, capacity of hiding data, overhead, and robustness against possible attacks. We take sequential circuit design benchmarks, which adopt the FSM model, as the simulation testbed to demonstrate the strength of the proposed information hiding techniques.

1   Introduction

Finite state machine (FSM) is a powerful computation model. It consists of a finite set of states, a start state, an input alphabet, and a transition function that defines the next state based on the current state and input symbols. FSM may also have outputs associated with the transition. The outputs are functions of the current state and/or input symbols. Figure 1 is the standard state transition graph representation for an FSM with eight states. Each transition is represented by a weighted directed edge. For example, the edge from state 4 to state 1 labeled 0/1 corresponds to the fact that on input 0, there is a transition from state 4 to state 1 that produces an output 1.

FSM is the core of modern computability theory (for example, the Turing machine), formal languages and automata theory. It has also found numerous applications such as hardware verification and natural language processing. In this paper, we study the problem of how to hide information into an FSM.

J. Fridrich (Ed.): IH 2004, LNCS 3200, pp. 340–354, 2004.

Because FSM design and specification is normally the starting point for most of these applications, the information embedded in this early stage will be inherited throughout the implementation and hence will be robust.

Comparing to the existing information hiding or watermarking practice, FSM information hiding is different from traditional multimedia watermarking and shares a lot of similarity with the VLSI design intellectual property (IP) protection in the sense that the stego-FSM needs to be functionally equivalent to the original FSM. The constraint-based watermarking approach, state-of-the-art IP protection technique [7,14,15], embeds IP owner's digital signature into the design as additional design constraints such that the design will become rather unique. These embedded constraints can be revealed later for the proof of authorship. The correct functionality of the watermarked IP is guaranteed as none of the original design constraints will be altered.

The constraint-based watermarking technique is applicable to FSM information hiding, where the constraints are the transitions among the states. It is possible to add new edges in the state transition graph to hide information, but this will never be as easy as adding edges to a graph for the graph coloring problem [14] due to the following reasons. First, it is non-trivial to alter or add transitions while still maintain the FSM's functionality. Second, the watermarked FSM needs to be synthesized and the synthesis process (the FSM state minimization in particular) could remove the watermark. Finally, watermarking's impact to later development and implementation is hard to control and may be unacceptably high. For instance, the design overhead (in terms of performance degradation, increased area, power, and design cost) in VLSI IP watermarking is inevitable and the pseudo-randomness of the signature-based constraints makes these overhead unpredictable. Lach et al. [7,8,9] watermark FPGA by hiding information in unused LUTs. They experiment resource overhead from 0.005% to 33.86% and timing overhead from -25.93% to 11.95% for various techniques. Oliveira [11] proposes a technique to watermark sequential circuit designs by changing topology of FSMs. Their area and delay overhead can be negligible for large designs (due to the small size of the signature), but are as high as 2747% and 273%, respectively, for small designs.

In this paper, we challenge the fundamental assumption in constraint-based watermarking – "original design constraints cannot be touched in order to keep the correct functionality" – by manipulating 'redundant' original constraints to hide information. In the first approach, we introduce the concept of 'redundant' original constraints in FSM and propose a SAT based approach to identify the maximal set of redundant constraints in Section 2. In Section 3, we present our second approach, a state duplication technique, to create redundancy in the minimized FSM for information hiding. In Section 4, we empirically demonstrate the rich redundancy in the original FSM specification and show the state duplication technique's impact to the design quality on sequential circuit benchmarks. Section 5 concludes the paper.

2   Finding Redundant Specifications in FSM State Minimization

In constraint-based watermarking techniques, information is hidden in the additional constraints enforced by the designer. The original specifications of design is untouched in order to keep the correct functionality. However, we observe that not all the original specifications or constraints are necessary for achieving the design solution. We can manipulate some of the 'redundant' constraints to embed secret information. In this section, we will first show by a motivational example in FSM minimization the existence of redundant constraints. And then, in the framework of FSM state minimization, we formally define the problem of finding redundant constraints for information hiding. At last, we show that it can be converted to the problem of finding a truth assignment to a SAT formula with maximal number of 1s.

2.1   Motivational Example

Consider an incompletely specified finite state machine (FSM) with eight states in Figure 1. Each node in the graph represents one state. Each (directed) edge indicates a state transition and the attributes carried by the edge specify the input/output associated with the transition. For example, the edge from node 4 to node 6 with "1/0" means that on input "1", the system moves from state 4 to state 6 and outputs "0". An edge without ending state represent the case when the next state of that transition is a *don't care*.

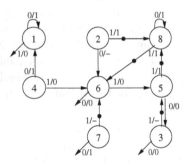
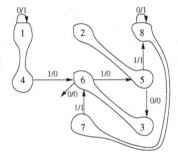

Fig. 1. State transition graph for the FSM.

Fig. 2. State transition graph for the minimized FSM. A = {1,4}, B = {2,5}, C = {3,6}, and D = {7,8}.

The state minimization problem seeks to find another FSM which (1) always gives the same output as the original FSM whenever it is specified, and (2) the number of states is minimized. The FSM in Figure 1 can be minimized to one with only four states, and there are two solutions: {{1, 4}, {2, 5}, {3, 6}, {7, 8}}, and $\{\{1,4,7\}, \{2,5\}, \{3,6\}, \{8\}\}$. The state transition graph for the first solution is shown in Figure 2. For example, if we start with state 5 in Figure 1, on input string "011", the output will be "0-1". In the minimized FSM in Figure 2, state 5 corresponds to state B, and if we start with this state, on the same input string "011", we have output "001" that differs from "0-1" only on the second bit which is not specified in the original FSM.

Surprisingly, if we keep all the output values and only five transitions (the edges with a dot) in Figure 1, the solution remains the same. In another word, this implies that these conditions are sufficient to obtain the above solution(s). The other transitions specified in the original FSM are *'redundant' constraints* in the sense that their absence (i.e., changing the next states of these transitions from *specific states* to *don't care states*) will have no impact on the final state minimization solutions.

We can leverage such redundant constraints to hide information in the FSM. Since the existence of any redundant constraint will not change the solution, we can embed one bit information on each redundant constraint by either specifying its next state as in the original FSM or replacing its next state by a don't care. Apparently, the length of the hidden information depends on the number of redundant constraints and the problem remains is whether we can find all the redundant constraints systematically.

2.2   Definitions and Problem Formulations

A finite state machine(FSM) is defined as a 6-tuple $\langle I, S, \delta, S_0, O, \lambda \rangle$ where:

- I is the input alphabet;
- S is the set of states;
- $\delta : S \times I \rightarrow S$ is the next-state function;
- $S_0 \subseteq S$ is the set of initial states;
- O is the output alphabet;
- $\lambda : S \times I \rightarrow O$ is the output function;

Finding an equivalent FSM with minimal number of states is generally referred as *state minimization* or *state reduction*(SR) problem. State minimization is an effective approach in logic synthesis to optimize sequential circuit design in terms of area and power. Our purpose is to identify and hide information in the redundant constraints of FSM such that the state minimization solution remains the same.

Given an FSM and a solution to the state minimization problem, we define a transition in the original FSM **redundant** if the given solution can still be obtained after we replace the nest state of this transition by a don't care (we call this the *removal* of this transition). A *maximal redundant set* (MRS) is a set of redundant transitions that can be removed without affecting the given state minimization solution, but removing one more transition will not preserve this solution.

Finding the MRS in FSM is non-trivial. First of all, the state minimization in incompletely specified FSM is NP-complete. The solution space grows exponentially large in the size of the FSM; removing a transition can make other transitions indispensable to achieve the same minimized FSM. Second, we can convert the problem of finding MRS to a MaxONEs SAT problem which is defined as: finding a SAT solution with the maximum number of variables assigned one. MaxONEs SAT is also NP-complete [2]. We will show this formulation in the following text.

2.3   Finding Maximal Redundant Set

Our approach takes the original and minimized FSM as input. By comparing them, it identifies all the possible redundant constraints in the original FSM. To extract the maximal set of them, it assigns a boolean variable to each of these constraints and generate a Boolean SAT formula. The variables assigned to be 1 in the formula will be redundant; the maximal number of "1" variables correspond to the MRS.

Figure 3 depicts the state transition table, another representation of FSM, for the same FSM given in Figure 1. Each table entry specifies the next state and the output given the current state (which row this entry is in) and the input (which column this entry is in). For each entry with a specific next state (i.e., not don't care), we introduce a Boolean variable x_i and stipulate that $x_i = 1$ means the entry is redundant. The clauses in the SAT formula are created as follows.

	In=0	In=1	In=0	In=1
1	1 (x_1)	-	1	0
2	6 (x_2)	8 (x_3)	-	1
3	-	5 (x_4)	0	-
4	1 (x_5)	6 (x_6)	1	0
5	3 (x_7)	8 (x_8)	0	1
6	-	5 (x_9)	0	0
7	-	6 (x_{10})	1	-
8	8 (x_{11})	6 (x_{12})	1	1
	Next State		Output	

Fig. 3. State Transition Table for the FSM.

First, we compute all the compatible sets of the given FSM. Recall that i) two states are *compatible* if they have the same output values whenever they are both specified and their next states are also compatible whenever they are both specified; and ii) a *compatible set* is a set of states that are compatible pairwise. The essence of the state minimization problem is to include all the states using the minimal number of compatible sets.

Next, we examine each pair of states that are not compatible according to the given state minimization solution to make sure that we include sufficient constraints in the FSM specification to distinguish them. If there exists some input value on which the two states output different values (e.g., states $s1$ and

$s2$ on input $i = 1$), then they are not compatible and no information on their next states is required. If, however, when the two states, for every input value, either have the same output value or at least one has a don't care as its output, then we need the information on their next states to distinguish them. Take states $s2$ and $s3$ for instance, the only way to distinguish them is to make both transitions x_3 and x_4 non-redundant, which can be done by including the expression $x_3'x_4'$ into the SAT formula.

A more complicated example is the pair of states $s2$ and $s8$. Their respective next states $s6$ and $s8$ are not compatible and we need the presence of both transitions x_2 and x_{11} or x_3 and x_{12} to distinguish them. This can be conveniently enforced by the following Boolean expression (in CNF format)

$$x_2'x_{11}' + x_3'x_{12}'$$
$$(DeMorgan) = ((x_2 + x_{11})(x_3 + x_{12}))'$$
$$(Distributive) = (x_2x_3 + x_2x_{12} + x_{11}x_3 + x_{11}x_{12})'$$
$$(DeMorgan) = (x_2' + x_3')(x_2' + x_{12}')(x_{11}' + x_3')(x_{11}' + x_{12}')$$

As a result, for the FSM in Figure 1 and its state minimization solution in Figure 2, we have the following SAT instance:

$$\mathcal{F} = x_3'x_4'x_{10}'(x_2' + x_3')(x_3' + x_{11}')(x_2' + x_{12}')(x_{11}' + x_{12}')x_8'$$

For variables that do not appear in this formula (such as x_1), we can safely assume that their corresponding transitions are redundant. Clearly, finding the MRS becomes equivalent to finding a solution to the corresponding SAT formula such that the number of variables assigned to be '1' is maximized. An exact algorithm is to formulate it as an integer linear programming(ILP) problem which has been discussed in [2]. Practically, one can also simply solve the SAT formula multiple times, each solution represents one MRS, and pick the one with the maximal 1s.

2.4   Analysis

Unlike the previous constraint based watermarking approaches, our information hiding technique conceals information in the original redundant constraints. We will now analyze this method in terms of correctness, information hiding capacity, overhead and robustness.

Correctness   In our algorithm, we identify the redundant constraints by comparing two states that are uncompatible in the minimized FSM; we keep all the necessary constraints to distinguish them. Therefore, in any state minimization solution, these two states must be in different compatible sets. On the other hand, if two states are reduced to one state in minimized FSM, they are also compatible in the original FSM, because no other constraints have been modified to distinct them. As a result, the same minimized FSM can still be achieved even with the removal of redundant constraints.

Information hiding capacity   For a pair of uncompatible states in minimized FSM, there is at most one pair of transition constraints under one input symbol needed in original FSM to separate them; the rest of transitions under other input symbols (if not *don't cares*) can be used to hide information. In a FSM with l input bits (i.e., 2^l symbols) at each state, a pair of uncompatible states can have up to 2^l of redundant constraints. Suppose there are k reduced states in minimized FSM corresponding to a compatible set of $n_1 \ldots n_k$ states in the original FSM, we can embed up to

$$2^l \cdot \sum_{1 \leq i < j \leq k} n_i n_j$$

bits of information in such FSM.

Overhead   Since no additional constraints are attached to original specification, the optimal solution will not be affected. As we have seen in the FSM minimization example, we can always achieve the same minimized solution even if we embed information by removing some of the redundant constraints.

Robustness   Information is embedded in the original redundant constraints, so there is no such way of "removing" them. On the other hand, the rest of constraints are necessary; removal of them will definitely affect the design solution. Similarly, in order to change or fake the watermark, the attacker has to know the original FSM transition graph. However, it is private to designers.

3   Creating Redundancy in Minimized FSM

The previous technique discovers a maximal set of redundant transitions with respect to a minimized FSM. Information can be hidden then by the way how we manipulate these redundant transitions. Therefore, its information hiding capacity is limited by the size of the maximal set of redundant transitions. In this section, we overcome this limitation by a state duplication technique which creates redundancy in the minimized FSM to facilitate information hiding.

3.1   An Illustrative Example

We first illustrate the idea of state duplication by the following example Figure 4(a) shows the state transition graph of a 2-input 2-output FSM with five states $\{S1,S2,S3,S4,S5\}$. The FSM has already been minimized. We reconstruct this FSM by introducing a new state $S6$ as shown in Figure 4(b). One can easily verify that these two STGs are functionally equivalent. In fact, state $S6$ is an equivalent state of $S1$. The 3-bit number next to each state is the code assigned to that state by a state encoding tool.

Considering the continued development from the two STGs in Figure 4 (a) and (b), we observe the following:

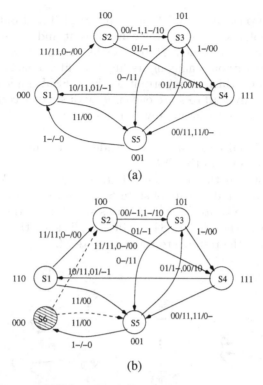

Fig. 4. A 5-state FSM and a functionally equivalent 6-state FSM.

- they result in functionally equivalent designs.
- the quality of the two designs in general has little difference.
- information can be hidden by the way we introduce state *S6*, namely, which state we want to duplicate, how we will duplicate it, and how we assign codes to the newly duplicated state.

The first observation guarantees the correctness and the second one reveals that design overhead due to watermarking or information hiding is limited. Finally, the last one implies the flexibility of this technique in hiding information. In the rest of this section, we formally discuss these issues.

3.2   State Duplication

We consider a minimized (and encoded) FSM with n states and an m-bit message. Our goal is to embed the message into the FSM. The proposed state duplication method consists of three steps 1) select a state for duplication. 2) duplicate the selected state. 3) encode the duplicated state. Information can be hidden in each of these three steps and they will be repeated until the entire message is embedded.

Recall that two states S and S' are equivalent if and only if on every possible input symbol, they produce the same output and move to the same state or equivalent states. Equivalent states can be collapsed to one single state to simplify the FSM without changing its functionality. This is the basis for FSM state minimization, which is important for later FSM implementation because fewer states normally lead to state encoding with smaller code size. An FSM is minimized if it does not contain any equivalent states. In the state duplication approach, we reverse the state minimization process by introducing equivalent states into the minimized FSM. This is guided by the message to be embedded and creates redundancy in the FSM.

Figure 5 illustrates the basic idea of state duplication. We see that a new state, S', is added as a duplicate of state S as follows: S' goes to the same next state under the same transition condition as state S; the transitions from other states to state S in the original STG will be split such that some of them still go to state S while the rests go to the new state S'.

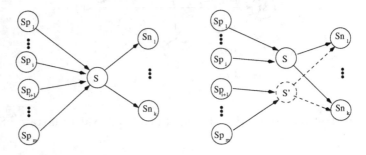

Fig. 5. A simple way to duplicate a state in an FSM.

Selection state for duplication   Technically, every state can be duplicated. If we restrict to deterministic FSMs, only states that are reachable from the starting state through different sequences of transitions can be considered as candidates for duplication. To see this, we assume that the FSM in Figure 4 (a) has state $S1$ as its starting state. Clearly state $S3$ is duplicable because there are two paths $S1 - S2 - S3$ and $S1 - S5 - S3$ to reach $S3$ from $S1$. State $S2$ can also be duplicated despite of the fact that it is only reachable from $S1$ directly. This is because the direct edge from $S1$ to $S2$ actually represents three transitions: moving to state $S2$ from $S1$ when the inputs are 00, 01, or 10. However, if this edge only carries the label "10/11", then state $S2$ cannot be duplicated.

This suggests us that we can simply sort all the candidate states by, for example, their codes and then select the one based on the message to be hidden. To limit the impact of state duplication to the performance of later development, we propose to consider only the states with the following properties if the candidate pool is rich: (1) states with more than one previous states, to simplify the duplication process; (2) states with large average Hamming distance (the Hamming distance between two states is the number of different bits they have in their codes) from all their previous states; (3) states with fewer next states. The last two properties in general will help us to find a better code for the duplicated state and/or the state being duplicated.

Duplicating the selected state   As we have described in Figure 5, the duplicated state S' needs to have the same next states as the original state S to maintain the functional correctness. However, the previous states of state S can go to either S or S'. This flexibility gives us the opportunity to hide information. For example, a simple watermark encoding scheme can be defined as: *for each transition from a previous state S_p of S to S, define its next state to be S to embed a bit 0 and choose its next state to be S' to embed a bit 1.*

Encoding the duplicated state   When the original FSM is encoded, we need to give the duplicated state a code too. Suppose that the FSM has n states and each state has a k-bit code, where $k \geq \lceil \log_2 n \rceil$. The newly introduced state can take any one from the $2^k - n$ unused codes as its code and this code selection can again embed information.

Finally, we mention that multiple states can be duplicated by repeating this process if the size of the message is large.

3.3   Analysis

We now analyze the proposed state duplication information hiding technique.

Correctness   Clearly, the stego-FSM has the same functionality as the original FSM because we only introduce states that are equivalent to existing states. Further development from the stego-FSM rather than the original FSM guarantees the functional correctness.

Information hiding capacity   Suppose that the original FSM has n states and is encoded with k bits, where $k \geq \lceil \log_2 n \rceil$. To select a state for duplication, we can hide $\lfloor \log_2 n \rfloor$ bits of information; to duplicate a selected state with p previous states, we can hide p bits of information; to assign the duplicated state a new k-bit code, we can hide $\lfloor \log_2(2^k - n) \rfloor$ bits of information. Let l be the number of input bits, then there are 2^l transitions from each state. The average number of previous states (count duplicates if there are multiple transition from the same previous state) a state has is 2^l. Furthermore, when minimal code length encoding is assumed, we have $k = \lceil \log_2 n \rceil$. The average number of bits being embedded in the final encoding step can be estimated as follows:

$$\sum_{n=2^{k-1}+1}^{2^k-1} \frac{1}{2^{k-1}} \lfloor \log_2(2^k - n) \rfloor = \frac{1}{2^{k-1}} \sum_{n=1}^{2^{k-1}-1} \lfloor \log_2 n \rfloor$$

$$\approx \frac{1}{2^{k-1}} \log_2(2^{k-1} - 1)!$$

$$\approx \frac{1}{2^{k-1}} \log_2(\sqrt{2\pi}(2^{k-1})^{2^{k-1}-\frac{1}{2}} \cdot e^{-2^{k-1}})$$

$$\approx k - 2$$

In sum, duplicating one state can hide approximately $(2k + 2^l - 2)$ bits of information, where $k = \lceil \log_2 n \rceil$ is the length of the (minimal length) encoding scheme and l is the number of input bits. This number will be multipled when we duplicate more than one state.

Overhead   The general goal of state minimization is to reduce the number of states such that the encoding length (or hardware implementation of the FSM) is minimized. From this point of view, assuming the minimal length encoding scheme is applied, we conclude that the state duplication technique will not introduce any overhead as long as we keep the number of duplicated states less than $2^{\lceil \log_2 n \rceil} - n$. The impact of duplicated states to other design and implementation objectives are hard to analyze before we have the final design. In next section, we consider a large set of sequential circuit design benchmark to demonstrate this impact in terms of area and power consumption.

Robustness   The robustness of state duplication watermarking approach relies on the fact that FSM design and synthesis occurs at the early stage of the underlying application. Given a synthesized FSM (after state minimization and state encoding), the possible attacks include: 1) Removing the hidden information by identifying and deleting duplicated states in the STG. 2) Tampering the watermark by duplicating additional states. In the first case, removing or changing duplicated states (and thus delete or alter the hidden information) will affect the synthesis solution and the following design implementation stages, which eventually result in re-sign. In the second case, the attacker can only infringe a small part of watermark, if possible (e.g., changing the previous states of duplicated states); most of the hidden information will remain intact. To tamper more hidden information, the attacker has to duplicate a large number of states, which is not always feasible and will cause serious design quality degradation.

Detectability   The easy identification of duplicated states provides an inexpensive mechanism for revealing the hidden information, which is in general referred as copy detection problem and considered as a problem harder than watermark embedding [13,15].

4   Experimental Results

In this section, we will first show how many redundant constraints for state minimization are there in each FSM benchmark. Next, for a minimized FSM, we demonstrate how much redundancy we can create to hide information via state duplication. With the knowledge of these redundant information, we evaluate the possible impact on FSM design by hiding additional information in these constraints. In experiment, we use the standard KISS format as representation of FSMs from MCNC benchmark suite [17]. The FSM minimization tool we use is *stamina* from the logic synthesis design package SIS [18]. And we use a power-driven state encoding algorithm *pow3* [3] to encode the FSM.

Table 1 reports the number of next-state transitions in the original FSMs that are 'redundant' for state minimization. We first extract the redundant state transitions and generate a SAT formula in the way as we explained in section 2. Solving the MaxONEs SAT via a ILP solver CPLEX [16], we find the maximal number of redundant transitions. The fourth column in the table lists the number of constraints in original FSM. The maximized redundant constraints and the redundancy ratio are given in the fifth and sixth columns. One can observe that 5 to 176 state transitions are redundant for state minimization in the FSMs, which accounts for 20% to 100% of the original constraints in the FSMs. Interestingly, in 5 of these 16 benchmarks, all of the original next-state transitions are redundant for state minimization. This is because either the original FSM is reduced to a single-state machine or every pair of incompatible states in the original FSM can be distinguished purely by the different output bits. This redundancy provides us with a large space to hide information in the transitions; on the other hand, it ensures us that there will be no design overhead caused by embedding additional information. In the last two columns in the table, we use a SAT solver *zchaff* [10] to solve the SAT formula multiple times and choose among random solutions the one with maximal number of ones. Reported data show, for some benchmarks, the redundancy ratio obtained are very close to the maximum one. This tells us that in the case where the SAT formulas are too large for ILP solvers, we can use a SAT solver to find a random solution and still extract a considerable amount of redundancy.

Table 1. Number of redundant next-state constraints for FSM state minimization.

benchmark	states	input bits	orig. constr.	max. redundant constr.	ratio	rand. redundant constr.	ratio
donfile	24	2	96	96	100%	96	100%
ex2	19	2	72	27	38%	15	21%
ex3	10	2	36	19	53%	10	28%
ex5	9	2	32	19	59%	9	28%
ex7	10	2	36	20	56%	14	39%
example	6	2	24	24	100%	24	100%
example2	7	2	28	28	100%	28	100%
lion9	9	2	25	12	48%	12	48%
modulo12	12	1	12	12	100%	12	100%
s27	6	4	96	88	92%	85	89%
s8	5	4	80	80	100%	80	100%
train11	11	2	25	5	20%	3	12%
opus	10	5	176	176	100%	176	100%
beecount	7	3	51	36	71%	34	67%
bbara	10	4	160	36	23%	33	21%
mark1	15	5	240	129	54%	128	53%

Table 2. Adding maximum number of redundant states and resulted design overhead

Circuit	regs.	states	**add. states**	orig. area	incr	orig. power	incr
lin2	3	5	**3**	43616	12%	280.4	10%
mex3	3	5	**3**	46400	12%	314	-2%
ex5	4	9	**7**	70528	29%	405.2	44%
lion9	4	9	**7**	38976	62%	178.3	93%
ex7	4	10	**6**	78416	1%	405.8	-4%
train11	4	11	**5**	47792	17%	212.3	-3%
mmark1	4	12	**4**	94656	8%	280.7	3%
dk512	4	15	**1**	79344	2%	430.1	-5%
s1	5	20	**12**	321088	-1%	1388.7	-8%
ex1	5	20	**12**	234784	25%	744.9	21%
dk16	5	27	**5**	282112	-2%	1547.3	3%
styr	5	30	**2**	407856	0%	1347.6	1%
s510	6	47	**17**	302064	19%	923.1	44%
planet	6	48	**16**	504832	2%	2042.1	11%
				Avg. incr.	13%	Avg. incr.	15%

Next, we demonstrate that we can create redundancy by adding redundant states in the state encoding stage when there are not enough redundant constraints to hide information. We also show that this come at the costs of design overhead. We run experiments on 14 MCNC benchmarks, some of which are state minimized. To measure the design quality change, we map these FSMs after state encoding to sequential circuits using the SIS library. We then compare the design quality before and after embedding information in terms of area and power. In Table 2 we first create maximum number of redundant states in each benchmark. For simplicity, we constrain the number of total states to be less than 2^k such that the encoding bits remain minimal. Column 4 lists the number states we added. After adding these states, the FSM can still be encoded using the same number of state bits and there are no space to add more states. In this case, the design overhead is considerable ranging from -2% to 62% in area and -8% to 93% in power. Note that, once a redundant state is added, we can hide information in encoding of the duplicate state, and the partition of its previous states transitions as well. In a STG, where each state has multiple previous state, this means a huge space for information hiding. Thus we consider reducing the number of redundant states added. This can greatly reduce the design overhead as shown in Table 3. In this Table, for each benchmark, we change the number of redundant states added and the way to partition its previous states. We selectively duplicate states in the way mentioned in section 3 and report the results with the least design overhead. The average area increase drops from 13% in Table 2 to 1.3% and interestingly, the average power increase reduces from 15% in Table 2 to -9.4%. This means instead of increasing, the circuits now consume less power with the redundant states in FSM. The main reason of this is because by adding redundant states, we change the topology the FSM while maintaining its functionality such that the state encoding on these FSMs could give a smaller total switching activity and this eventually leads to the dynamic power reduction in sequential circuits.

Table 3. Adding less redundant state and the reduced design overhead

Circuit	regs.	states	added states	area incr	power incr
example	3	5	3	2.1%	2.6%
ex3	3	5	3	8%	-10%
ex5	4	9	2	13.8%	-32.9%
lion9	4	9	2	16.7%	-7.1%
ex7	4	10	1	-10.7%	-29.1%
train11	4	11	1	2.9%	-19%
mark1	4	12	1	5.4%	12.9%
dk512	4	15	1	2.3%	-5.1%
s1	5	20	1	-2.3%	-12.9%
ex1	5	20	2	-8.9%	-13.6%
dk16	5	27	2	-9.7%	-13.3%
styr	5	30	2	3.3%	0.4%
s510	6	47	1	-6.3%	-6.9%
planet	6	48	1	1.8%	1.9%
Average increase				1.3%	-9.4%

5   Conclusions

We study the information hiding problem in the context of finite state machine. It is an important problem because of the numerous applications of FSM. Hiding information in FSM provides a unique feature that combines robustness and detectability. We analyze the redundancy naturally in the FSM specification and develop a state duplication based method to introduce additional redundancy for a minimized FSM. We then discuss how to leverage such redundancy to hide information. Simulation on benchmark sequential circuit design demonstrates the correctness and low-cost of the proposed methods.

References

1. A. Adelsbach, B. Pfitzmann, and A. Sadeghi. "Proving Ownership of Digital Content". *The 3rd International Information Hiding Workshop*, pp. 126-141, September 1999.
2. F. Aloul, A. Ramani, I. L. Markov, K. A. Sakallah, "Generic ILP versus 0-1 Specialized ILP", *IEEE/ACM International Conference on Computer Aided Design*, pp. 450–457, June 2002.

3. L. Benini and G. D. Micheli, "State Assignment for Low Power Dissipation," *IEEE Journal of Solid-State Circuits,* Vol.30, pp.258-268, March 1995.
4. S. Craver. "Zero Knowledge Watermark Detection". *The 3rd International Information Hiding Workshop,* pp. 102-115, September 1999.
5. F. Hartung and B. Girod. "Fast Public-Key Watermarking of Compressed Video". *IEEE International Conference on Image Processing,* pp. 528-531, October 1997.
6. A.B. Kahng, et al. "Watermarking Techniques for Intellectual Property Protection". *35th Design Automation Conference Proceedings,* pp. 776-781, 1998.
7. J. Lach, W.H. Mangione-Smith, and M. Potkonjak. "Fingerprinting Digital Circuits on Programmable Hardware". *The 2nd International Information Hiding Workshop,* pp. 16-31, April 1998.
8. J. Lach, W.H. Mangione-Smith, and M. Potkonjak. "Signature Hiding Techniques for FPGA Intellectual Property Protection", *IEEE/ACM International Conference on Computer Aided Design,* pp. 186-189, November 1998.
9. J. Lach, W.H. Mangione-Smith, and M. Potkonjak. "Robust FPGA Intellectual Property Protection Through Multiply Small Watermarks", *36th ACM/IEEE Design Automation Conference Proceedings,* pp. 831-836, June 1999.
10. M. W. Moskewicz, C. F. Madigan, Y. Zhao, L. Zhang and S. Malik, "Chaff: Engineering an Efficient SAT Solver", *The 38th ACM/IEEE Design Automation Conference,* pp. 530–535, June 2001
11. A.L. Oliveira. "Robust Techniques for Watermarking Sequential Circuit Designs", *36th ACM/IEEE Design Automation Conference Proceedings,* pp. 837-842, June 1999.
12. B. Pfitzmann. "Information Hiding Terminology", *The 1st International Information Hiding Workshop,* pp. 347-350, May 1996.
13. G. Qu. "Keyless Public Watermarking for Intellectual Property Authentication". *The 4th International Information Hiding Workshop,* pp. 96-111, April 2001.
14. G. Qu and M. Potkonjak. "Hiding Signatures in Graph Coloring Solutions". *The 3rd International Information Hiding Workshop,* pp. 391-408, September 1999.
15. G. Qu and M. Potkonjak, "Intellectual Property Protection in VLSI Designs: Theory and Practice", Kluwer Academic Publishers, January 2003.
16. ILOG Inc. "ILOG AMPL CPLEX System Version 8.0 Use Guide", 2002
17. Saeyang Yang, "Synthesis and Optimization Benchmarks User Guide", 2002, ftp://mcnc.mcnc.org.
18. E. Sentovich, et al., "SIS: A System for Sequential Circuit Synthesis," *Electronics Research Laboratory Memorandum, U.C.Berkeley,* No. UCB/ERL M92/41.

Covert Channels for Collusion in Online Computer Games

Steven J. Murdoch and Piotr Zieliński

University of Cambridge, Computer Laboratory,
15 JJ Thomson Avenue, Cambridge CB3 0FD, United Kingdom
http://www.cl.cam.ac.uk/users/{sjm217, pz215}/

Abstract. Collusion between partners in Contract Bridge is an oft-used example in cryptography papers and an interesting topic for the development of covert channels. In this paper, a different type of collusion is discussed, where the parties colluding are not part of one team, but instead are multiple independent players, acting together in order to achieve a result that none of them are capable of achieving by themselves. Potential advantages and defences against collusion are discussed. Techniques designed for low-probability-of-intercept spread spectrum radio and multilevel secure systems are also applied in developing covert channels suitable for use in games. An example is given where these techniques were successfully applied in practice, in order to win an online programming competition. Finally, suggestions for further work are explored, including exploiting similarities between competition design and the optimisation of voting systems.

1 Introduction

In many games, a player who is able to collude with other participants can gain a significant advantage. In this paper we explore how, in a tournament, a player may surreptitiously authenticate players who may be colluded with, what actions can be taken and what advantage this may gain him.

One of the games for which much research in collusion has been performed is Bridge. Here, systems for transmitting information between partners during the bidding stage are legal and can provide a great advantage to the team more adept in their usage. These schemes typically provide a means by which one player can encode information about his hand in the cards that he plays. His partner (who he is not allowed to communicate with through any other means) can then make a more precise contract.

One complication in Bridge is that while covert channels are permitted by the rules, if the partner of a player making a bid is asked what the meaning of a bid is, then he must answer truthfully [1, 2], so the information sent through the channel cannot be secret. However, the two members of a team do share a secret, e.g. if one player holds all the aces then he knows that his partner holds none, but the opposing team does not know this [3]. If this secret is used as a key, then it is legal for the recipient of the information to only tell what the bid

J. Fridrich (Ed.): IH 2004, LNCS 3200, pp. 355–369, 2004.
© Springer-Verlag Berlin Heidelberg 2004

means in isolation. He does not need to tell his opponent what the bid means when combined with the knowledge of the player's own hand.

In Bridge, the collusion is between two members of a team, where communication, other than through bidding, is not permitted, however, in Section 2 we discuss the different situation, where the colluding parties are considered to be independent players. Here, communication is simply unexpected, since in a competition it is normal for each player to try to optimise his own performance, so there would be no need for communication with other opponents. In this paper, we examine the situation where several independent players cannot win the competition acting by themselves, but one of them can win if they collude. If the value of the prize can somehow be divided up between the winner and colluders, this option is attractive for all parties.

In order for collusion to work, there must be some means of communicating. If collusion is not expected, then it may be the case that communication is easy, but the case where it is banned is both plausible and more interesting. In Section 3, we discuss how communication can be established, and in particular we show how covert channels can be used for authentication. A number of possibilities are presented and compared, including a scheme which draws on techniques used in low-probability-of-intercept spread spectrum radio to increase the confidence that authentication has been performed correctly.

In Section 4, an example of where these techniques were successfully applied is given. This was a online programming competition where contestants were required to write a program to play *Connect-4* against the other programs entered. We found that it was in fact impossible to guarantee a win in any individual game, however by developing a collusion based system it was possible to win the contest subject to reasonable assumptions about other contestants.

Finally, in Section 5, defences against such types of collusion are discussed. These include prevention, detection, and modifying the competition so that the benefits of collusion are reduced. One option considered is to use the similarities between elections and competitions so as to design better tournament structures.

2   Competition Structures

The type of competition dictates how effective collusion can be and also how it can best be used. In this section, we introduce two simple but popular tournament arrangements (league and knockout) and show how collusion can be exploited. In Section 4, these two arrangements are combined to form the hybrid structure that the techniques described in this paper were designed to win.

2.1   League Tournaments

In a typical league, each of the n players competes against every other player, resulting in $n(n-1)/2$ matches. The structure of a game is not important, only that there are two participants and it may lead to three outcomes: win, lose, or

Table 1. Summary of winners in matches between Fox, Chicken and Optimal players ("—" denotes a draw)

	Fox	Chicken	Optimal
Fox	—	Fox	—
Chicken	Fox	—	—
Optimal	—	—	—

draw. It is almost universal for a win to gain a player more points than a draw and a draw to gain the player more points than a loss.

Without loss of generality, we can assume that the game is *fair*, that is, neither of the players has an advantage. This is because any game can be made fair by playing it twice with the roles of the players exchanged the second time. Fairness implies that a perfect player must draw against itself, therefore, no winning strategy exists for the player. Since the opponent has no winning strategy either, the player must have a strategy that guarantees at least a draw.

In order to calculate a lower bound for the benefit of collusion, we assume the worst case scenario — that non-colluding, independent opponents are optimal, i.e. they will win a match where possible and draw otherwise. Similarly, we make conservative assumptions for colluding players, namely that they will never lose, but also will never win against independent players. If every player was optimal, then each will gain the same number of points. However, this assumes that every player plays as well as possible all of the time. Where some colluding players (*Chickens*) aim to draw against all players except that they lose to colluding players (*Foxes*), then Foxes will get more points than would otherwise be possible.

In a competition, let us assume there are x Optimal players and c Chickens colluding with f Foxes whom the Chickens want to win. A match between an Optimal player and a Chicken, or between two Chickens, will result in a draw since the Chicken will play to draw. However, a match between a Fox and a Chicken will result in a win for the Fox, since the Chicken will recognise that it is playing a Fox. A win will gain the winner p_w points, a draw p_d points, and a loss p_l points (as noted above, $p_w > p_d > p_l$). We assume each player will also compete against himself and draw. This is summarised in Table 1.

In this competition, each of the x Optimal players will get $p_d x + p_d c + p_d f$ points, each Chicken will get $p_d x + p_d c + p_l f$ points, and each Fox will get $p_d x + p_w c + p_d f$. It can then be seen that under these assumptions a colluding player will score higher in the competition than the Optimal player since $c \geq 1$.

2.2   Knockout Tournaments

For knockout tournaments, the impact of collusion is much less than for league tournaments. The result of a match must be a win for one player so as to decide who will continue to the next round. Typically this will require some kind of tie-breaking system, such as the penalty shootout in soccer.

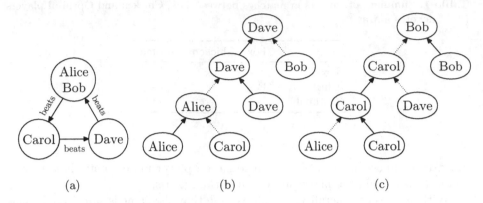

Fig. 1. Knockout tournament collusion example

The only way for a player to win in all arrangements of initial matches is if he can beat all other participants. Likewise if a player can beat all other players then he will win the competition regardless of the initial arrangement. However, it may be advantageous for a player to influence the arrangement of initial matches if there are cycles in the directed graph of game results, for example Figure 1(a). Here Alice and Bob are equivalent players, who both can beat Carol but will be beaten by Dave. Also Carol can beat Dave. In the scenario shown in Figure 1(b), if Alice plays as well as possible, then while Alice will win the first round she will be eliminated by Dave in the next round. Then Dave will eliminate Bob and go on to win the tournament. However, if Alice and Bob collude then the result can be as shown in Figure 1(c), allowing Bob to win. Alice can deliberately lose the first match and so Carol will go through. In the next round, Carol will eliminate Dave but in the final round Bob can beat Carol. This example shows that there are cases where, if a player is colluding with others in a knockout tournament, it may be in the best interest of the collusion group for one member to play less well than is possible.

Unlike the league tournament, it is clear that the result of a match between co-colluders does not contribute to the final result, if we assume that all players colluding with each other have equal abilities. However, in situations like those described above, it is useful for a colluder to lose against an opponent who possesses an ability that the colluders do not. We do not explore this further, and in the rest of this paper we concentrate on league-like tournaments.

3   Authentication Mechanisms

To manipulate a knockout tournament it is necessary for the abilities of the opponents to be known in advance, however, in a league all that is necessary is for colluding players perform normally against independent opponents, but selectively play poorly against other colluding players.

In order to identify a colluding player when the order of games is not known, there must be some form of authentication that happens before or during each game. This should be reliable and must identify the case where one player must lose before the result of the game is decided.

It may be the case that communication is easy, for example in a face-to-face game the players may recognise each other or be allowed to speak to each other. If the players are computer programs (the case which the rest of this paper will concentrate on), a standard program-to-program authentication can be accomplished.

However, there may be times when an overt channel is either not possible because of the constraints of the competition or not permitted by the competition rules. In these situations, a covert channel can be used. There are a variety of techniques developed for such communication channels, however, the majority of them are described in the literature for the analysis of multi-level secure computer systems (many of which are summarised in the "Light pink book" [4]), so while not directly relevant, they can be modified for use within games.

3.1   Timing

In the literature on multi-level secure systems, one frequent way to create a covert channel is for a program to signal to another by varying some kind of system-wide property. For example, this could be modifying the CPU load [5], hence changing scheduling patterns, or it could be modifying timing of acknowledgements of messages which may flow in only one way [6]. These techniques could be used directly, but there are also timing based covert channels that are specific to games.

One such channel would be to use the timing of moves to carry information by causing the sender to delay making a move and the recipient to measure this delay. Such schemes are easy to create and can have a relatively high bandwidth. However, if the transport mechanism is affected by latency and/or jitter, then this covert channel may be unreliable or even eliminated completely.

Where the latency is fixed, this can be easily cancelled out, but jitter is more problematic. If the jitter is sufficiently small, then it can be removed, at the cost of reducing bandwidth. However, the rules are likely to place an upper bound on the maximum time to make a move, and so fix the maximum possible delay. If the jitter is of similar magnitude to this limit, then the bandwidth of the channel will be very small. If the CPU time to make a move is limited by the competition rules rather than wall clock time (the amount of time to have passed in the real world), then the maximum delay can be fairly large, since in most operating systems the time that a program is paused is not counted towards the CPU time.

One form of jitter specific to a competition is if the time for a move to be sent is fixed to a value greater than the maximum allowable time for the delay. This may occur if the competition is to be shown live and the organisers wish to slow the competition to a speed that humans can watch. If this is done, then the move timing covert channel would be eliminated.

3.2 Choice of Equivalent Moves

The timing based mechanisms mentioned above are possibly unreliable in the presence of jitter. An alternative to this is to encode the authentication data in the moves themselves. In person-to-person games, this could be, for example, the way the pieces of a board game are held, or the place in which a card is put down in a card game (this is why there are complex physical arrangements in Bridge tournaments to prevent such communication). In contrast, for the case of an online competition the move will likely be expressed in an unambiguous form hence will allow no extra information to be carried in a side channel.

At a stage in the game, if there is more than one move which can be shown to not change the outcome of the game when compared to the best move, then this fact can be used to transmit information. One possible way for this to be achieved is by ordering the n equivalent moves. The order chosen can be arbitrary, but often there is an obvious solution, for example in the Connect-4 situation described in Section 4, ordering moves by column number would be sensible. In order to send $r \in \{1, \ldots, n\}$ then the rth move is chosen. After receiving a move from its opponent, a player can identify which move, out of the opponents possible moves, was chosen and hence identify r.

3.3 Analysis of Authentication Mechanisms

In order for a collusion strategy to succeed, a reliable covert channel must be established to allow a Chicken to identify when it is playing a Fox and thus should deliberately lose.

For the simple case where a Chicken needs to identify whether its opponent is a Fox or not (Section 2.1), the goal of the channel can be viewed as being able to transmit a single bit while the result of the game is still undetermined. While the required capacity of the channel is low, the reliability requirements are high, since a false positive will result in a Chicken losing to an independent opponent and so reduce the chance of the Fox winning.

Much research on bandwidth estimation of covert channels, for example [7], has concentrated on finding upper bounds for the data rate of the channels. These techniques can be used to design a coding system which approaches these upper bounds.

In the case where the timing information is used for authentication, it is possible that the communications channel will modify the meaning of the information being sent. However, where the move itself carries the information it is reasonable to expect that the signal will be received intact. For this reason a message sent using this covert channel will always be received correctly. This is in contrast to the timing channels, where interference from other processes on the machine could corrupt the signals.

However, this does not mean that the channel is noiseless, since the receiver cannot differentiate between the case where information is being sent, and the case where the moves carry no meaning (this is also the case for timing channels).

The moves of independent players are analogous to noise in communications theory. The situation is similar to low-probability-of-intercept spread-spectrum radio in that the "amplitude" of the signal cannot be any more than the noise (a particular move is either made or not, there is no concept of "magnitude").

In order to reliably transmit a single bit of information, a technique based on frequency-hopping can be used. For each move, the number sent is chosen according to a keyed generator. The receiver shares the key and so knows what move to expect from a colluding player. If, after a number of moves, the receiver has found that the opponent has made every move as expected, then it can assume that the opponent is colluding with it and act accordingly. The confidence level of the decision being correct can be increased by increasing the number of possibilities at each move or by increasing number of moves before a decision is made. While waiting longer before making a decision is preferable, if the player waits too long, then by the time a decision is made, it is no longer possible to change the game result.

3.4   Authentication Key

The goal of the generator is to distinguish itself from the "background noise" of other players. Where little or nothing is known about the game strategies of independent players, it is difficult to make any assertions about the characteristics of the noise. For this reason, it may be safe to assume that at each turn every move is equally likely — analogous to white noise. This assumption is particularly useful since it greatly simplifies the design of the generator, and allows a fast implementation so as to reduce CPU usage (which may be a factor in deciding a winner).

For spread-spectrum radio, typically a cryptographically secure pseudorandom number generator, such as a stream cipher, is used. In the case of spread-spectrum radio the transmission is effectively public but in a game the moves are typically only seen by the opponent. One threat in spread-spectrum radio is an adaptive adversary, whereas in a game the opponents may not be changed during the competition. When coupled with the fact that other opponents are probably not aware of the collusion strategy, it is reasonable to assume that cryptanalytic attacks are unlikely. Again, this assumption simplifies the design of the generator and so reduces processor time requirements.

The only goal of the generator is to appear different from a white noise source so a repeating constant could be used, such as always picking the first move. However, it is feasible that an opponent could accidentally pick the same strategy. A small change can be made where the move chosen depends on the stage in the game. For example r could simply be the result of a pseudorandom number generator (PRNG) seeded by a shared secret. This simple authentication system could also be used with the timing based covert channels. A linear congruential PRNG is very fast and simple, and with well chosen parameters [8, Section 3.2.1] meets all the requirements (assuming no cryptanalytic attacks).

4   Real World Example

The above techniques were developed for and used with the Cambridge University Computing Society (CUCS) Winter Competition [9]. This was a programming competition where entrants submitted one or more programs which played a variant of Connect-4. These programs then played against each other and a winner was decided.

4.1   Rules of the Game

As with normal Connect-4, the game is played on a 7 × 6 board. Each player takes turn to choose a column and places his token at the lowest free square. The first player to have four tokens in a row, either horizontally, vertically or at a 45° diagonal, wins the game. In the standard game, a player must place exactly one token at each turn, but in the variant used in the competition, the player also has the option to pass. This change was made so that standard Connect-4 strategies would not work and thus force entrants to come up with their own techniques. However, an unforeseen result of the modification to the rules was that the possibility of a guaranteed winning strategy was eliminated, regardless of whether the player makes the first move, since a move cannot be forced.

The competition was split into two stages, a league followed by a knockout tournament. The league proceeds by every entered program being played against every other entered program. Each match consisted of six games, with each player alternately starting first. The winner of the match was the player with the most number of wins and was awarded two points. If both players had an equal number of wins in the match, then each player is awarded one point.

The five programs with the highest scores in the league were selected for the knockout tournament. Firstly, the fourth and fifth programs were played in a match of six games as in the league. However, if this match was a draw, then the winning program would be the one with the least CPU usage, and if that was equal, then memory usage and finally code size were considered. Then, the remaining four programs were played in a standard knockout tournament, with each match following the rules for the fourth/fifth playoff, i.e. fourth/fifth vs. first, second vs. third, and finally the winners of the previous two matches.

4.2   Collusion Strategy Chosen

In this competition, overt communication was not permitted in order to prevent programs communicating with more able humans or more powerful computers. Also, the only information that a program received from its opponent was the move number, in ASCII, so there was no redundancy in the encoding. However, the rules did not explicitly prohibit collusion between opponents. For these reasons a covert channel was required for communication, but it would not break the rules. There were plans for the final stages of the competition to be run live so there was a possibility of jittering timing information, even unintentionally.

Table 2. Summary of winners in matches between Fox, Chicken, Rooster, Rabbit and Optimal players ("—" denotes a draw)

	Fox	Rooster	Chicken	Rabbit	Optimal
Fox	—	Fox	Fox	—	—
Rooster	Fox	—	Rooster	—	—
Chicken	Fox	Rooster	—	—	—
Rabbit	—	—	—	—	Optimal
Optimal	—	—	—	Optimal	—

Because of the advantages in reliability and simplicity of the *Choice of Move* covert channel described in Section 3.2, this was used for communication.

One refinement to the authentication method described in Section 3.4 was rather than having only two types of colluding player (the Fox and the Chicken, where a Fox always wins against a Chicken), three were used. The additional category, *Rooster* would beat a Chicken but would be beaten by a Fox (see Table 2). This was because collusion is ineffective in the knockout stage, so the only way to win was for all five participants to be our colluding players. This could be achieved by having five Foxes and the rest Chickens, but there remained the risk that another independent player would get into this stage (due to *Rabbits*, the category which will be introduced in Section 4.6). Since, by applying the strategy described in Section 4.3, our players will never lose, CPU usage would be the decider and so this should be optimised. Hand optimising a program is time consuming so it is preferable to minimise the number of programs that this needs to be done on. If only one of the five Foxes was optimised, then there is the risk that another will knock it out of the tournament before it has a chance to play the independent player. To mitigate this risk, two optimised Foxes were entered, along with four Roosters, so the optimised Foxes would be guaranteed to play any remaining independent players. Two Foxes were entered to reduce the impact of any programming errors. This reduced the number of points given to the Roosters and Fox slightly, but it was decided to be worthwhile.

4.3 Game Strategy

In order for collusion to be feasible, it was necessary to have a strategy which guaranteed a draw in every game. It was also desirable to design the strategy such that the all outcomes of the game remain possible for as long as feasible, so that the decision as to whether to lose or not can be delayed. Finally, so as to optimise the bandwidth of the covert channel, the number of possible moves at each turn should be maximised.

We developed a very efficient strategy which allowed a draw to be forced, regardless of who made the first move. This was in contrast to the non-pass version of Connect-4 where a strategy [10] exists which guarantees a win if used by the player who starts and almost never loses when if he plays second.

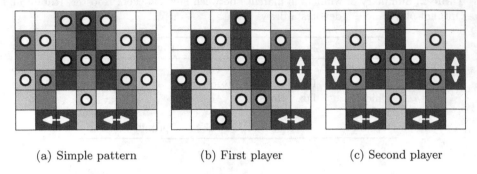

| (a) Simple pattern | (b) First player | (c) Second player |

Fig. 2. Possible board patterns used for the game strategy

Our strategy relies on finding a subset of the squares on the board, such that every winning line must pass through at least one of these, and preventing the opponent from occupying any of them. We achieve this by designing a pattern of non-overlapping rectangles on the board as shown in Figure 2(a).

If the opponent plays on the bottom square, then our player plays on the top square. Our player never plays on the bottom square. Therefore, the opponent can never occupy the top square.

If the opponent plays on one of the squares, then our player plays on the other. Therefore, the opponent can never occupy both squares.

If our player moves first, then it plays on this square, thereby preventing the opponent from occupying it.

Three possible patterns are shown in Figure 2. The different shades of grey have no semantic meaning; they are used only to differentiate the rectangles from each other. Since the rectangles do not overlap, the strategy forces our player to play on at most one square per move, thereby guaranteeing at least a draw.

4.4   Implementation

The competition allowed ten entries per person and three people entered from our research group. While the rules explicitly stated that it was permitted to implement an algorithm developed by someone else, using someone else's code was not allowed. For this reason each member of the group entered a program written independently in a different language.

As intended, no players lost other than times when it was designed to lose against another colluding player. While there was some risk that this (false positive) could have happened by accident, the design of the covert channel reduced this to an acceptable level. As shown in Figure 3, after ten moves (the point at which a decision was made) the number of possible move sequences ranged between 960 and 5760. Therefore, even if an opponent happened to choose an identical game strategy, the probability of a false positive was at least 1 in 960 (subject to previous assumptions). In contrast, the risk of a false negative (that one colluding player who should lose to its colluding opponent, fails to identify in time) can be reduced to the risk of programming error. This is because the covert channel used can be assumed to introduce no noise. Furthermore, for deterministic players, all possible games between colluding opponents can be exhaustively tested in a reasonable time, before entry to the competition.

4.5 Optimisation

The final stage of the competition would take CPU usage into account so there was a potential advantage to optimise the Foxes. Aside from standard code efficiency improvements, one domain specific optimisation was to remove all detection code from the Foxes. The simplification was feasible since it was not necessary for a Fox to identify that it is playing a colluding player, as the responsibility for the match result can be given to the losing player. To achieve this a player who has identified that it must lose continually passes until the game has ended. Additionally no evidence of collusion can then be found by inspecting the source code of the Foxes.

To ensure the game will result in a win for the Fox when the Chicken passes the game strategy must be changed slightly. Firstly, the Chicken must start losing sufficiently early in the game such that it is still possible to lose. Secondly, a different pattern must be used for the player starting first and the player starting second. This is because both players having the same pattern would result in them drawing the game by default after playing four passes before the authentication could be completed. Thirdly, more flexible patterns (Figure 2(b) and Figure 2(c)) give the players more equivalent moves, thereby increasing the reliability of the authentication procedure.

4.6 Rabbits

In the simple example of Optimal players and colluding players, it was seen that only one Chicken was necessary for the Fox to win, however, the situation is not so simple when not all independent players are Optimal. That additional worst-case category of players (so as to find a lower bound) encountered in practice is a *Rabbit*, which will play poorly, so lose to Optimal players, but draw with everyone else. From Table 2 it can be seen that an Optimal player will act as if it is colluding with any Rabbits in the tournament. Therefore the only way to win the tournament is to have greater number of Chickens than there are Rabbits, no matter how many Optimal players exist. While it was likely that several approximately Optimal players would be entered, it was hoped that there would be a small number of people who would enter a player that would play so badly that the chances of winning would be low.

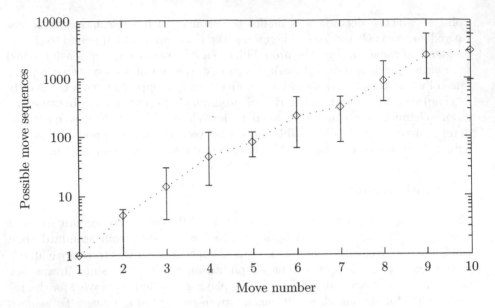

Fig. 3. Number of possible move sequences after a given number of moves. Three classes of colluding players were used so for each move number, the lower limit, mean and upper limit of the nine possible matches is plotted

4.7   Results

A summary of the final league table is shown in Table 3.

Since the algorithm used by the Fox, Rooster, and Chicken would only win in exceptional circumstances, the actual results for colluding players in the competition were very similar to the worst case scenario estimates. Some players appeared to play randomly, so when played against programs using a tree-searching algorithm the tree-searching algorithm won. This behaviour approximates the expected results from ideal Rabbits and Optimal players, so the random players are classed as Semi-Rabbits and the tree-searching players are classed as Semi-Optimal. However, as expected only six Semi-Rabbits were entered by other participants and 28 Chicken/Roosters were entered by our group, so we won the competition with a safe margin of 30 points.

5   Further Work

The above example dealt with the case where neither non-colluding participants nor the competition management expected collusion to be used. In the case where collusion is expected and not desired, there are interesting possibilities for preventing collusion from being effective.

Table 3. Summary of results at end of league stage. Players are ordered in descending order of points

No	Category	Won	Drew	Lost	Points
1	Fox	58	26	0	142
2	Fox	58	26	0	142
3	Rooster	51	29	4	131
4	Rooster	49	31	4	129
5	Rooster	49	31	4	129
			cut-off point		
6	Rooster	48	32	4	128
7	Semi-Optimal	16	67	0	99
⋮	⋮	⋮	⋮	⋮	⋮
13	Semi-Optimal	12	64	8	88
14	Chicken	3	69	12	75
⋮	⋮	⋮	⋮	⋮	⋮
37	Chicken	0	72	12	72
38	Semi-Rabbit	4	63	17	71
⋮	⋮	⋮	⋮	⋮	⋮
43	Semi-Rabbit	1	52	31	54

5.1   Collusion Resistant Competitions

In order to prevent collusion, the competition could be designed such that collusion provides no advantage. During discussion of the problem one observation made was that the problem of deciding a winner in the competition is similar to the problem of electing a candidate in an election. While there are some differences, for instance, that the number of candidates is identical to the number of voters, there are also many similarities.

One possibility investigated was of a game tournament similar to the Single Transferable Vote (STV) system. Here, every player plays every other player, in a similar fashion to a league tournament. However, the winner evaluation is more complex. At each stage, the normal league rules are applied and an ordering established, but then the players with the lowest score are eliminated, along with their contribution to all other players' scores. The process is repeated until no more players can be eliminated.

This system has the advantage that Chickens will be eliminated before Foxes, so the Chickens' scores can have no effect on the final result, however, they can control the order in which players are eliminated so it is not clear that this system is free from manipulation. Additionally, the number of "voters" is identical to the number of "candidates" so the final stage will likely result in more than one winner. This was confirmed by running the results of the above example competition through this algorithm. As expected, all the Chickens were eliminated but the final result included the Foxes and all the Semi-Optimal players. Since all these players will draw against each other, deciding a winner is difficult.

Not only should competitions be resistant to collusion but they should be fair and this is a very difficult quantity to measure. There are a variety of proofs which state, given certain assumptions, that it is not possible to design an *ideal* election. These include Arrow's theorem [11], Gibbard-Satterthwaite [12, 13] and Gärdenfors' extension [14]. These primarily deal with manipulation by voters, but there has been some work on manipulation by candidates, such as a general result in [15] and an analysis of the particular case where the election is made out of a series of pair-wise comparisons in [16]. These state that, given certain assumptions, non-dictatorial elections are manipulable by candidates deciding whether or not to participate in the election. This result is not directly applicable since it assumes that each candidate who votes will vote himself the highest, and the stronger version of the result also assumes that no candidates vote. However it may still be partially applicable. Whether these theories imply that an *ideal* competition is impossible depends on a formal definition of fairness and collusion resistance, which is outside the scope of this paper.

5.2   Detecting Collusion

In some games, it may not be desirable or possible to re-arrange the competition to make collusion infeasible. In these cases, the only alternative may be to detect collusion and eliminate players if caught. For example, an expert could examine the match results [17], and in a similar way that a Bridge expert would look for players being exceptionally lucky in a tournament, an expert suspecting collusion would look for players being exceptionally unlucky. The expert could also monitor the games in progress looking for an suspicious changes in apparent skill. If a player is aware of such monitoring, then countermeasures to both techniques could be taken.

6   Conclusion

In this paper, we show that collusion can offer significant advantages in tournaments which are based around leagues. We present a simple algorithm for acting on the basis of authentication information which will guarantee winning a competition, assuming only one team is using a collusion strategy and the standard of players is good. We also introduce a covert channel built using only redundancy in the moves of a game and show how this can be used to authenticate colluding players. We demonstrate these techniques being successfully applied in order to win a real world competition. Finally, options for resisting and detecting collusion are explored, including drawing parallels between the design of competitions and the design of elections.

7 Acknowledgements

Thanks are due to Phil Cowans, John Fremlin, Ian Jackson, Matt Johnson, Stephen Lewis, Andrei Serjantov, and Hanna Wallach for their helpful contributions, and to Microsoft for donating an X-Box as the prize for the competition. We also would like to thank the anonymous reviewers for their suggestions.

References

[1] American Contract Bridge League: Law 20. Review and Explanation of Calls. (1997) in Laws of Duplicate Contract Bridge (American Edition).

[2] American Contract Bridge League: Laws of Contract Bridge (Rubber Bridge Laws, American Edition). (1993)

[3] Winkler, P.: The advent of cryptology in the game of Bridge. Cryptologia **7** (1983) 327–332

[4] Gligor, V.D.: DoD NCSC-TG-030 A Guide to Understanding Covert Channel Analysis of Trusted Systems (Light-Pink Book). National Computer Security Center (1993)

[5] Huskamp, J.C.: Covert Communication Channels in Timesharing System. PhD thesis, University of California, Berkeley, California (1978) Technical Report UCB-CS-78-02.

[6] Kang, M.H., Moskowitz, I.S.: A pump for rapid, reliable, secure communication. In: 1st ACM Conf. on Computer and Communications Security, Fairfax, VA, Center for High Assurance Computer Systems (1993) 119–129

[7] Millen, J.K.: Finite-state noiseless covert channels. In: Proceedings of the Computer Security Foundations Workshop, Franconia, New Hampshire (1989) 81–85

[8] Knuth, D.E.: The Art of Computer Programming. Third edn. Volume 2, Seminumerical Algorithms. Addison-Wesley (1998)

[9] Cambridge University Computing Society: Winter programming competition (2002) http://www.cucs.ucam.org/competition.html.

[10] Allis, L.V.: A knowledge-based approach of connect-four. Master's thesis, Vrije Universiteit, Amsterdam, The Netherlands (1988) ftp://ftp.cs.vu.nl/pub/victor/connect4.ps.Z.

[11] Arrow, K.J.: Social Choice and Individual Values. Second edn. Yale Univ Press (1970)

[12] Satterthwaite, M.: Strategy-proofness and Arrow's condition: Existence and correspondence theorems for voting procedures and social welfare functions. Journal of Economic Theory **10** (1975) 187–217

[13] Gibbard, A.: Manipulation of voting schemes: a general result. Econometrica **41** (1973) 587–601

[14] Gärdenfors, P.: Manipulations of social choice functions. Journal of Economic Theory **13** (1976) 217–228

[15] Dutta, B., Jackson, M.O., Breton, M.L.: Strategic candidacy and voting procedures. Econometrica **69** (2001) 1013–1038

[16] Dutta, B., Jackson, M.O., Breton, M.L.: Voting by successive elimination and strategic candidacy. Journal of Economic Theory **103** (2002) 190–218

[17] Yan, J.: Security design in online games. In: 19th Annual Computer Security Applications Conference, Acteve (1993)

Author Index

Lecture Notes in Computer Science

For information about Vols. 1–3247

please contact your bookseller or Springer